HUMANISTIC VIEWPOINTS IN PSYCHOLOGY

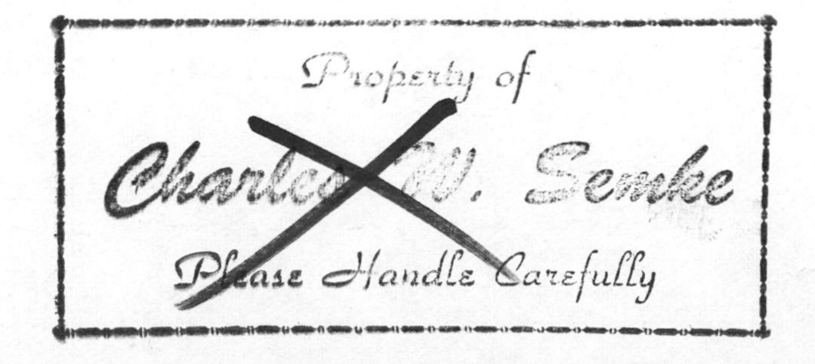

HUMANISTIC VIEWPOINTS IN PSYCHOLOGY

FRANK T. SEVERIN
Department of Psychology, Saint Louis University

A BOOK OF READINGS

McGraw-Hill Book Company
New York
St. Louis
San Francisco
Toronto
London
Sydney

HUMANISTIC VIEWPOINTS IN PSYCHOLOGY

Library of Congress Catalog Card Number: 65–17395

PREFACE

Man has considered himself the earth's master since his species was established. After teasing out nature's secrets with incredible patience and ingenuity from the subatomic structure of matter to the dynamics of galaxies; after analyzing the composition of stars all but infinitely distant; after creating a world of comfort never dreamed of in fairy tales, it is perhaps paradoxical that he is still asking, "Who am I?"

Such feelings of insecurity, uncomfortable to the layman, are a cause for deeper concern to the behavioral scientist. Many psychologists who ask themselves "What is man?" are less than satisfied with the human image their science has created. It seems too fragmentary, too rigid, too lacking in unity and individuality to reflect adequately the autonomy, spontaneity, and creativity of the real people with whom they deal. In particular, they believe that greater emphasis needs to be placed on the nonmechanical aspects of personality, and that conscious experience should be restored to a place of honor in psychology.

At the present time a new humanistic development is under way in psychology which aims to supplement existing theories along these lines. This volume attempts to bring together the viewpoints of its most articulate spokesmen. Excerpts from authors in other fields have been included when they seemed to advance the general theme. In making the selection, the editor had no clear guidelines to follow since the range and scope of this new movement has not fully crystallized. It can be justly said, however, that this set of readings represents his own concept of the emerging humanistic orientation.

These readings are addressed to students in introductory psychology, personality, educational psychology, social psychology, mental hygiene, philosophical psychology, and experimental psychology. In the absence of textbooks for courses in the rapidly developing field of humanistic psychology, it should also serve there as a convenient point of departure.

A credit line acknowledges both author and source on the page where each title appears. Only the most essential references and footnotes have been reprinted. References given in a table in the original text are cited as footnotes.

The editor's chief indebtedness is to the authors of the original publications who contributed most of the material in this book. He also wishes to express his gratitude to his colleagues, Theodore V. Purcell, who read the manuscript, and to Eugene O. Gerard and Richard C. Nickeson, for their helpful suggestions.

FRANK T. SEVERIN

CONTENTS

PART TWO

Science and the Study of Man

PART THREE

Psychology and Human Values

THE CONTRIBUTORS

Gordon W. Allport, Professor of Psychology, Harvard University

Carlton W. Berenda, Professor of Philosophy, University of Oklahoma

Gustav Bergmann, Professor of Philosophy and Psychology, State University of Iowa

P. W. Bridgman, formerly Professor of Physics, Harvard University

J. F. T. Bugental, Partner, Psychological Services Associates, Los Angeles, California

Charlotte Buhler, Clinical Psychologist in private practice and Assistant Clinical Professor of Psychiatry, School of Medicine, University of Southern California

Charles H. Bumstead, formerly Professor of Psychology, Knox College

Hadley Cantril, Social Psychologist, Chairman, Institute for International Social Research and Research Associate, Princeton University

Ernst Cassirer, formerly Professor of Philosophy, Columbia and Yale Universities

James C. Coleman, Associate Professor of Psychology and Director, Clinical School, University of California, Los Angeles

James B. Conant, former Chairman, Department of Chemistry and President Emeritus, Harvard University

Willis W. Harman, Professor of Electrical Engineering, Stanford University and Research Associate, International Foundation for Advanced Study, Menlo Park, California

D. O. Hebb, Professor of Psychology, McGill University

Werner Heisenberg, Professor of Theoretical Physics and Director, Max Planck Institute of Physics and Astrophysics, Munich, Germany

Frank J. Kobler, Professor of Psychology and Director of Clinical Training, Loyola University (Chicago, Ill.)

Joseph Wood Krutch, Author and Dramatic Critic, Tucson, Arizona, formerly Professor of English, Columbia University

Louis S. Levine, Professor of Psychology, San Francisco State College

Henry Margenau, Eugene Higgins Professor of Philosophy and Physics, Yale University

A. H. Maslow, Professor and Chairman of the Department of Psychology, Brandeis University

Floyd W. Matson, Lecturer in Speech, University of California, Berkeley, California

Rollo May, William Alanson White Institute of Psychiatry and Adjunct Professor of Clinical Psychology, New York University

David C. McClelland, Professor of Psychology and Chairman of the Department of Social Relations, Harvard University

Harold Grier McCurdy, Professor of Psychology, University of North Carolina

Clark Moustakas, Supervisor, Child and Adult Psychotherapy, Merrill Palmer Institute of Human Development and Family Life, Detroit, Michigan

Henry A. Murray, Professor of Psychology, Harvard University

Joseph Nuttin, Professor of Psychology, Institut de Psychologie, Louvain University

Robert Oppenheimer, Professor of Physics and Director, Institute for Advanced Studies, Princeton, N. J.

Carl R. Rogers, Resident Fellow, Western Behavioral Sciences Institute, La Jolla, California. Formerly Professor, Departments of Psychology and Psychiatry, University of Wisconsin

Edward Joseph Shoben, Jr., Professor of Education and Psychology, Teachers College, Columbia University

M. Brewster Smith, Professor of Psychology, University of California, Berkeley, California

Anthony Sutich, Clinical Psychologist in private practice and Editor, *Journal of Humanistic Psychology*

Pierre Teilhard de Chardin, formerly Professor of Geology, Catholic Institute of Paris, Director of the National Geologic Survey of China, and Director of the National Research Center of France

Maurice Kahn Temerlin, Director of Guidance Services, University of Oklahoma

G. H. Turner, Professor and Chairman, Department of Psychology, University of Western Ontario

Adrian L. Van Kaam, Associate Professor of Psychology, Duquesne University, Editor, *Review of Existential Psychology and Psychiatry*

Gerhardt von Bonin, Professor Emeritus of Anatomy, College of Medicine, University of Illinois

Edmund G. Williamson, Dean of Students and Professor of Psychology, University of Minnesota

J. O. Wisdom, Reader in Philosophy, London School of Economics and Political Science and Editor, *British Journal for the Philosophy of Science*

C. Gilbert Wrenn, Professor of Educational Psychology, Arizona State College, formerly, University of Minnesota

INTRODUCTION

Students in introductory psychology usually expect to study about people as they perceive them in their normal day-to-day contacts. As the course proceeds some students become puzzled by the topics covered. Sensation, perception, learning, drives, emotions, and other human activities are studied in great detail, but nowhere are they integrated into a picture resembling man. The "self" which everyone experiences as the focal point of reality seems to be fragmented into a number of processes. The existence of a real "I," while not denied, goes by default. It is better to avoid speaking of a "self" lest it be mistaken for a "little man inside." Even the treatment of personality is more concerned with traits and their assessment than with a theory that adequately accounts for such qualities as creativity, autonomy, meaning, flexibility, and a host of other non-mechanical aspects of behavior.

Instructors give various explanations to neutralize their students' negative feelings. They say, for example, that a first course in any science merely surveys the field and makes no pretense at being exhaustive. They admonish the student to remember that man is the most complex entity in nature, and that before a total synthesis can be attempted, millions of small facts about every aspect of behavior must be carefully verified and fitted together. Perhaps at some future date psychologists will be able to predict behavior accurately; for the present the well-adjusted student must learn to tolerate a certain amount of ambiguity. At any rate, if he wishes to make psychology his life work, he should be more concerned with the cultivation of scientific attitudes than with vague feelings of "interest in people."

Although such explanations are useful in the classroom, not all psychologists are equally convinced they resolve the difficulty. Within recent years a crescendo of voices has stressed the need of reexamining the basic assumptions of behaviorism and psychoanalysis—the two major forces in American psychology. Both have made significant contributions to the science of man: one by developing a rigorous objective methodology, and the other by suggesting a global theory of human dynamics. Neither is completely satisfactory. Behaviorism lightly dismisses mental activities as behavior conditioned by the verbal community [1] or ignores such activities as unknowable in any precise way even though life without conscious experience would lack all meaning. Orthodox psychoanalysis, while seeming to account for certain aspects of neurotic functioning, fails to do justice to normal personality. The exaggerated role of the id with its blind, self-centered obsession with bodily pleasure seems inappropriate to explain the detached, outer-directed striving of a well-adjusted person.

Humanistic psychology is a new movement sometimes referred to as a "third force" between behaviorism and psychoanalysis. It aims to introduce a new *orientation* to psychology rather than a new *psychology*. Through constructive criticism and research it hopes to bring psychology of every theoretical complexion into closer contact with our everyday perceptions of man. The *Articles of Association* of the American Association for Humanistic Psychology [2] define its role as follows:

> Humanistic psychology is primarily an orientation toward the whole of psychology rather than a dis-

[1] B. F. Skinner. "Behaviorism at fifty." *Science,* 1963, **140,** 951–958.
[2] From A. J. Sutich. *American association for humanistic psychology: Articles of association.* Palo Alto, California (mimeographed), August 28, 1963.

tinct area or school. It stands for respect for the worth of persons, respect for differences of approach, open-mindedness as to acceptable methods, and interest in exploration of new aspects of human behavior. As a "third force" in contemporary psychology it is concerned with topics having little place in existing theories and systems: e.g., love, creativity, self, growth, organism, basic need-gratification, self-actualization, higher values, being, becoming, spontaneity, play, humor, affection, naturalness, warmth, ego-transcendence, objectivity, autonomy, responsibility, meaning, fair-play, transcendental experience, peak experience, courage, and related concepts.

(This approach finds expression in the writings of such persons as Allport, Angyal, Asch, Buhler, Fromm, Goldstein, Horney, Maslow, Moustakas, Rogers, Wertheimer, and in certain of the writings of Jung, Adler, and the psychoanalytic ego-psychologists, existential and phenomenological psychologists.)

Three areas of major emphasis in humanistic psychology are represented in the divisions of the present volume. Part I deals with the development of a concept of human nature that will account for unity of personality, self-determination, and the primacy of self. Part II provides a critical reexamination of the assumptions basic to psychological methodology in an attempt to discover satisfactory techniques for dealing with immediate experience. Conscious processes are considered valid data for scientific investigation. Part III takes up the values and inner strivings related to creativity, self-actualization, and other characteristic human activities.

It should be noted from the outset that the authors of these readings do not speak with a single voice. Humanistic psychology is only now attaining its full development and some writers are more concerned with one aspect of the movement than with others. The name "humanistic psychology" may also be misleading. "Humanism" usually conjures up memories of the ancient classics or of literature in general. In this book it implies an attitude toward psychology that stresses the adjective rather than the noun in the *human* animal, approximately as defined by Joseph Wood Krutch in his "Meaning for 'Humanism':" [3]

> "Humanism" has been used to mean too many things to be a very satisfactory term. Nevertheless, and in the absence of a better word, I shall use it here to stand for the complex of attitudes which this discussion has undertaken to defend.
>
> In this sense a humanist is anyone who rejects the attempt to describe or account for man wholly on the basis of physics, chemistry, and animal behavior. He is anyone who believes that will, reason, and purpose are real and significant; that value and justice are aspects of a reality called good and evil and rest upon some foundation other than custom; that consciousness is so far from being a mere epiphenomenon that it is the most tremendous of actualities; that the unmeasurable may be significant; or, to sum it all up, that those human realities which sometimes seem to exist only in the human mind are the perceptions, rather than merely the creations, of that mind. He is, in other words, anyone who says that there are more things in heaven and earth than are dreamed of in the positivist philosophy.

[3] From *Human Nature and the Human Condition,* by Joseph Wood Krutch. © Copyright 1959 by Joseph Wood Krutch. Reprinted by permission of Random House, Inc.

"Unlike the primitives who gave a face to every moving thing, or the early Greeks who deified all the aspects and forces of nature, modern man is obsessed by the need to depersonalise (or impersonalise) all that he most admires. There are two reasons for this tendency. The first is *analysis,* that marvelous instrument of scientific research to which we owe all our advances but which, breaking down synthesis after synthesis, allows one soul after another to escape, leaving us confronted with a pile of dismantled machinery, and evanescent particles. The second reason lies in the discovery of the sidereal world, so vast that it seems to do away with all proportion between our being and the dimensions of the cosmos around us." (From Pierre Teilhard de Chardin, *The Phenomenon of Man,* Harper & Brothers, New York, 1959, pp. 257–258. Reprinted with permission of Mlle Jeanne Mortier, Paris and Harper & Row, New York.)

PART ONE

The Nature of Man

CHAPTER 1

The Whole Is Greater than the Part

As a matter of convenience, we sometimes think of personality as being made up of a large number of uniform traits and part-processes. But the central core of personality consists in its unity and uniqueness. The rich, inimitable personalities of living people are difficult to compare. In the abstract, individual portraits, no matter how different, can be reduced to a simple wavy line on a psychograph. But this approach, while not lacking in utility, fails to reflect the idiosyncratic nature of personality. Every individual can truthfully say, "There will never be another like me. My traits are personalized traits, woven into a design that cannot be duplicated." Human beings are not constructed of interchangeable parts like the diodes and capacitors of computers. It would be impossible, even in fantasy, to assemble a Lincoln or a Gandhi from standardized off-the-shelf traits for the whole patterns as well as the individual parts are unique and significant.

If the psychologist could ignore this troublesome aspect of reality, his task would be greatly simplified. The scientific methods he uses are geared to the discovery of uniformities in nature. Their primary goal is to analyze what is common to populations, not what is unique to individuals. The insistence upon human uniqueness to a point where one man's sociability is different from another's would seem to impose an unreasonably difficult burden on the psychologist and hence, he may be reluctant to accept such a starting point. Yet the fact remains that methods of study must be selected because they are appropriate to the subject matter, not because they are convenient. In the human personality, as elsewhere, nature did not follow the simplest plan. Astronomers encounter a similar problem in the study of galaxies.

Even when personality traits are considered as roughly uniform throughout the human species, personality assessment remains exceedingly difficult. A knowledge of any isolated part-process is less effective in understanding and predicting behavior than knowledge of the pattern in which it occurs. The trait of compulsiveness may drive one person to the heights of scholarship while his equally compulsive brother dissipates his energies in senseless ritual. Obviously the total pattern accounts for the distinction and therein lies its significance.

Human traits are like colored threads in a tapestry. Woven at random, the fabric will lack distinctive character. Combined in a meaningful way, the threads acquire definition as part of a pattern. A scientist wishing to study the tapestry, perhaps to understand its esthetic qualities, might begin by sorting the threads according to color in order to determine their length, number, and thickness. Such measurements would be useful for certain comparisons. But it is doubtful whether exclusive attention to these structural elements would contribute significantly to an understanding of the tapestry as a work of art.

While part-process methods and more global techniques have been separated for purposes of discussion, fortunately they are not mutually exclusive. Each adds something to the study of the individual, and each has its corresponding dangers. The attempt to assess personality on too broad a base, without sufficient emphasis upon basic elements, is likely to result in vague generalities. On the other hand, trait profiles do not add up to a person. Like snapshots of a man in action, they furnish some basis for speculation about behavior and psychic structure without revealing the constellation of motives.

Even in inanimate nature, nothing exists in isolation: each part is dependent upon every other part. According to one cosmic theory, the weight of objects on the earth's surface would be grossly affected by the annihilation of even a minute group of distant stars. If this is true even of the impersonal forces of gravitation and electrostatic attraction, the psychologist can scarcely be justified in ignoring personal forces such as intentional strivings related to creativity and self-fulfillment. That neat operational definitions of the "person-as-a-whole" are unrealistic, at least for the present, does not absolve one of the need to search for a satisfactory—if compromised—working definition. The aspects of personality he can study rigorously in the laboratory are not necessarily the most revealing, or the most germane to such a search. It would be extremely difficult to write a convincing description of man without adding other constructs to those found in the typical textbook in psychology.

In the words of A. H. Maslow, psychology should be bolder. Even if the part-process approach to personality were the only practical one at present, such a limitation would not be a virtue. In seeking to understand the nature of the part and the whole, and the nature of their interrelationships, cautiousness in science must not become timidity. Some insights based on intuition, and even some vagueness must be tolerated along the frontier of the unknown if new hypotheses are ever to arise.

Editor's Note

Bugental's description of the new humanistic developments in clinical psychology suggests a number of interesting questions. Is it futile for psychologists to attempt to study the individual as a whole? If conclusions derived from statistics are true only of people in groups and not of individuals, how does psychology differ from sociology? Man is more than the sum total of our empirical observations. What must be added to them to make him specifically human? *Is it necessary for the experimental psychologist and the clinician to answer this question differently? What aspects of the real "I" are "controlled out" in objective experimentation? Since every individual is unique, is it legitimate to regard human subjects in an experiment as interchangeable units?*

The relationship of physics to psychology to which Bugental refers is treated at greater length in Chapter 6.

1. Humanistic Psychology: A New Break-through *

J. F. T. Bugental
Psychological Service Associates
Los Angeles

I want to present the thesis that a major break-through is occurring at the present time in psychology. Like man's other major changes—the introduction of the steam engine, the decline of feudalism, the beginnings of the laboratory method in psychology—its presence and potentialities are difficult to recognize for those of us who are so deep in daily concerns. Yet, I am convinced that the parallels I cite are not vainglorious. I think we are on the verge of a new era in man's concern about man which may—if allowed to run its course—produce as profound changes in the human condition as those we have seen the physical

* From J. F. T. Bugental. Humanistic psychology: A new break-through. *Amer. Psychologist,* 1963, **18**, 563–567. Reprinted with permission of the author and publisher.

sciences bring about in the last century. The essence of this change is, I believe, the eroding away of some of the familiar parameters of psychological science and the concurrent emergence of a new appreciation for the fundamental inviolability of the human experience.

Psychology, as any social institution, is a constantly evolving set of assumptions, information, and speculations. As with any institution, it has its periods of stability and of rapid change. Sometimes the change may be clearly dated from a particular event, as with the rise of behaviorism after Watson's epochal book appeared. Sometimes the forces producing the change are more scattered, as in the rise of the mental testing wave. In either instance, hindsight reveals numerous stirrings before the change process became clearly apparent. This is certainly so at the present. Writings by many social scientists have prepared the way for what is now emerging (viz., James, Allport, Cantril, May, Maslow, Fromm, Rogers, and many others). What has brought this development to the fore now may be argued, but certainly some of the influences will include: the large number of psychologists now involved in the practice of psychotherapy, the failure of many promising approaches to produce a truly embracing and adequate theory of human personality from our existing orientations, the press of public interest in, and need for, psychological science and service. One may speculate also that just as when a single organism encounters a threat to its life maintenance, it evokes counter forces (e.g., antibodies), so this development may be part of an evolutionary response to the biology-threatening forces of nuclear destruction.

Psychological Parameters Undergoing Change

Let us examine eight parameters which have been traditionally accepted as given in psychology but which, I think, are being questioned increasingly as a result of the wave of change which is now occurring.

These eight parameters are:

1. The model of man as a composite of part functions
2. The model of a science taken over from physics
3. The model of a practitioner taken over from medicine
4. The pattern of a compartmentalized, subdivided graduate school faculty and curriculum as the appropriate agency for preparing students for psychological careers
5. The criterion of statistical frequency as a demonstration of truth or reality
6. The illusion that research precedes practice
7. The myth of the "clinical team"
8. The fallacy that diagnosis is basic to treatment

What I want to do now is to examine each of these models with a view to recognizing what changes may be occurring in them.

1. The Model of Man as a Composite of Part Functions

What has been said above already indicates my view that this fundamental conception of the nature of man is in the process of basic alteration. So long as we sought mental elements, in whatever form and given whatever sophistication of naming, we operated on the basis that the total human being could be sufficiently understood if only we had an inclusive catalogue of his parts. This is at root inevitably a structuralistic conception. Today we are more and more recognizing that we need a process conception of the human being. So basic do I feel this difference to be that I would propose that in the coming years we will increasingly recognize that the study of the part functions of human behavior is indeed a different science than is tl study of the whole human being. We are familiar with making this sort of division between psychology and physiology. It seems to me that part functions of what we have traditionally thought of as psychology—that is, such segments as habits, test scores, single percepts, learned items—differ more from the functioning of the total person than does the reflex arc from memory for nonsense syllables.

I propose that the defining concept of man basic to the new humanistic movement in psychology is that *man is the process that supersedes the sum of his part functions.*

2. The Model of a Science Taken Over from Physics

So long as we accepted the model of man as a composite of his part functions then it was appropriate for us to seek for the ultimate units of behavior. Such attempts followed the two main lines of the search for mental elements under Titchner or for the simple stimulus-response bond under the behaviorists, or on the other side the seeking for basic instincts or primary cathexes under the orthodox psychoanalytic banner. Physics has demonstrated tremendous versatility in increasing our knowledge of the physical world by analytic methods. But physics has built its record because of the fundamental interchangeability of the units which it studied. A true psychology of human beings is a psychology of noninterchangeable units. The past 50 years have seen a tremendous accumulation of data about people treated as interchangeable units. And yet it is clearly the case that only where we are concerned with masses of persons do these data yield useful results. This may seem a harsh judgment, but I think it is an accurate one. If psychology is the study of the whole human being, and this I believe is its primary mission, then results which are only true of people in groups are not truly psychological but more sociological. Just as psychology is emerging as distinct from the study of part functions, so it is distinguishing itself from the study of group phenomena.

Before leaving these comments on a model of a science taken over from physics, it would be worthwhile noting that physics itself has found that it must move beyond logical positivism and the mechanistic causality which long were its guideposts. Attention to process and to the experimenter's interconnection with the experiment are beginning to be recognized as essential to the further development of pure physics. How much more pertinent are they to psychology!

3. The Model of a Practitioner Taken Over from Medicine

The medical model for the practitioner has a long history which dates back, of course, to the shaman, the medicine man, and the occult priest. Psychological practitioners have taken it for granted that they must function in a similar fashion. This is increasingly being found to be a false assumption. Indeed many practitioners of psychotherapy find that such a pattern is all too readily accepted by patients and used as a resistance to taking responsibility in their own lives. A new concept of the practitioner is emerging to which it is difficult yet to give an adequate name. Lowell Kelly (1961) has suggested the term "consultants in living" which has much to commend it, though it does seem somewhat pretentious. Certainly the point is that we cannot follow a pattern of esoterically diagnosing our patients' difficulties and writing prescriptions in Latin and an illegible scrawl, which the patient dutifully carries to the pharmacist for compounding and then takes with complete ignorance of the preparation or its intended effects. We are recognizing more and more that essential to the psychotherapeutic course is the patient's own responsible involvement in the change process.

4. The Pattern of a Compartmentalized, Subdivided Graduate School Faculty and Curriculum as the Appropriate Agency for Preparing Students for Psychological Careers

Something of the ferment within psychology has been represented in the typical graduate school faculty. Especially in our larger schools, there has been a pattern of subdivision of the department into various specialties. Sometimes these reach rather extreme numbers of subpsychologies. The result has been a fragmented approach to our field which has created much confusion and threat for graduate students. I wish I could report that I see as many signs of healthful change in this area as in some of the others upon which I report; nevertheless, there are stirrings which indicate a recognition that our pattern of many specialties—clinical, counseling, industrial, child—is proving more self-defeating than implementing. My own feeling is that we must move toward recognizing three basic subdivisions of psychology: that concerned with part functions, that concerned with group functions, and that concerned with the total person as the unit. Quite probably for each of these there will need to be a research and teaching phase and a practitioner phase. All three are increasingly being employed in the solution of practical problems, and the number of practitioners in all three is sure to grow tremendously in the coming years. Much of the resentment of our experimental brothers toward the practitioners is apt gradually to fade away as more and more of the experimentalists themselves are drawn into consulting functions. Tryon (1963) has written his prediction that the academic ivory tower is a thing of the past and that the experimentalists soon will be deeply involved in practitioner roles. This will certainly have a profound effect on our graduate school educational philosophies.

5. The Criterion of Statistical Frequency as a Demonstration of Truth

In the abstract, the criterion of statistical frequency seems to be an excellent one. Certainly those things that happen regularly and uniformly seem to be self-evident samples of the nature of reality. However, in actual practice this is not borne out. Despite increasing elaboration of statistical methodologies, despite greater and greater refinement of laboratory procedure, the product of years of conscientious effort has not been such as to warrant confidence that we will eventually arrive at a genuine understanding of human behavior by this route. And this is not surprising when we look back to the model on which these efforts are founded. The effort to find the basic subperson unit of behavior has been vain. The total person is the basic unit. Only as we find ways to understand the behaving person can we understand his behavior. It is manifestly impossible with present techniques to control all factors involved in any behavioral sequence in which the human normally engages. Nor is this simply a matter of developing more and more tests and using larger and larger computers. Our definition of the human being as the process that supersedes the sum of its factors indicates that there is still a nonmeasurable aspect. There is still the person himself. It is not a matter of more time being needed; it is a matter of recognizing that we are following an unprofitable course.

Another way of conceptualizing the problem may throw light on it: This is to recognize that our traditional scientific approach as represented in so many journal articles, dissertations, and master's theses, has been founded on a finite universe conception. That is to say, implicitly it is postulated that the universe is a closed system in which there is a fixed quantum of potential knowledge. Today science generally—whether physical, biological, or social—is coming to recognize that knowledge is infinite even as the universe is infinite. Once we could study any isolated correlation between two psychological variables with the hope that eventually that correlation would link up with other such isolated studies and some embracing systematization would emerge inductively. We must recognize today that this is not so. Within a universe of infinite variability we can go on infinitely collecting isolated items of data, of correlations and variation, and no link-up will necessarily emerge. Investigators who have repeated experiments conducted by other investigators have not uniformly been able to replicate their findings, because of the infinite variety of variables, because of the infiniteness of potential knowledge.

6. The Illusion That Research Precedes Practice

We have long had the popular myth that the scientist develops knowledge and the engineer applies it. For this we could substitute that the researcher develops knowledge and the practitioner applies it. This has not been so in psychology, and it has never been so in physics and engineering either. More than one authority in the physical sciences has recognized that physics has received more contributions from engineering than it has given to engineering. Similarly, in clinical psychology, we have made more contributions to the body of psychological knowledge from the practitioner's end than have been received by the practitioner from the research investigators. One need hardly elaborate this point beyond citing the work of Freud as an overriding example. Perhaps one additional highly important instance is the reintroduction of humanism into psychology. This reintroduction—which is the revitalizing, indeed the saving event of this period in the history of psychology—is in large part due to the contribution of clinical practice. More particularly it is in great part due to the experience of psychologists who have been engaged in the practice of psychotherapy. The names of the leaders in the field who are in the forefront of this development are the names of people who have had intensive immersion in the work of psychotherapy: Carl Rogers, Abraham Maslow, Rollo May, Erich Fromm, and so on.

Again we can point to the influence of the model of the finite universe in which knowledge can be accumulated at random and eventually integrated and made available for the practitioner. Since we have disavowed this model, since we recognize that it is not veridical with the universe, then we must recognize that we need the practitioners' contributions to highlight those areas of greatest significance socially. We need the practitioners' testing of findings for pertinence and applicability; we need the practitioners' contribution of proposing questions for research inquiry.

7. The Myth of the Clinical Team

Let me make clear at the outset that I do know that in some settings the clinical team has proven a very useful and productive concept, but I am equally convinced that in most settings it is not, that in many instances it has been a disguise for the domination of the team by one or another of the professionals. Similarly, many times it has resulted in the subordination of the potential contributions of the two professionals not in the dominant role. But most importantly, the clinical team is founded again on the segmentalist view of human beings. The three-headed monster of the clinical team is not able, by its very nature, to meet the patient in genuine interpersonal encounter. The clinical team may be an excellent device to gather information about people, chiefly information which treats people as representatives of various classes or groupings of society. It may be a useful administrative tool to make case assignments or dispositions, but it is not a therapeutically useful tool. I am convinced that psychotherapy, which is truly depth psychotherapy, requires an authentic encounter between two human beings and that the divided responsibility, and relationships which the clinical team presupposes militate against such an authentic encounter.

One may also note that the clinical team is of questionable social viability. Today when the number of persons needing treatment so far exceeds the number of practitioners to meet this demand, the multiplication of persons working with any one patient is of dubious utility. Some work now being done on the use of lay persons capable of genuine interpersonal relationships suggests that there may be better ways of meeting this problem. Work such as that of Margaret Rioch at the National Institute of Mental Health, in training mature women to serve as counselors without requiring them to go through the usual professional curriculum, illustrates this possibility. True, these people need supervision and help, but they have demonstrated that they can make a genuine contribution. Again, some studies reported informally by Fillmore Sanford are pertinent. He told of sending a research team into a community and asking at random of the citizens, "To whom would you talk if you had an important personal problem?" In this manner they were able to triangulate and locate a small group of mature human people who, in a native and unschooled way, could give meaningful help to their fellows. If these people then are given help from professional sources and not contaminated in what they can do, they can meet human need also. Finally, some work (Tannenbaum & Bugental, 1963) may be mentioned in which we are investigating the possibility of using paired people involved in a sensitivity training experience to intensify the "product" of that experience. Our results are most encouraging, though most preliminary, at this time.

8. The Fallacy That Diagnosis Is Basic to Treatment

We have traditionally thought that we could only help the person when we had accumulated a great deal of information about that person. At one time we made elaborate diagnostic studies of each applicant for psychotherapy. Today we know that the accumulation of diagnostic information for most people contributes little to the actual therapeutic work, when that therapeutic work is of an outpatient, interview type. Diagnostic information is inevitably part-function information, while psychotherapy that is most effective is whole-person, relationship centered. Diagnostic information is knowledge *about* the patient, the most effective psychotherapy requires knowledge *of* the patient. This difference is more than a play on words. Knowledge about a patient treats that patient as an object, or a thing to be studied and manipulated. Knowledge of the patient recognizes the patient's essential humanity and individuality. It involves a knowing and relating, a being with, as opposed to a manipulating. Diagnostic information is useful when the need is to treat people as objects, as representatives of classes, rather than as individuals. For administrative functions, it often is essential. For research purposes it may be crucial, but for the psychotherapeutic purpose itself, diagnosis is not important once the grosser disturbances have been ruled out.

Conclusion

I have tried to give one view of a tremendously exciting development in our field of psychology. If I see it correctly, we are leaving the stage of preoccupation with part functions and getting back to what psychology seemed to most of us to mean when we first entered the field. We are returning to what psychology still seems to mean to the average, intelligent layman, that is, the functioning and experience of a whole human being.

Psychology has been going through an adolescence. This is an analogy we have often made. As an adolescent, psychology has little valued what its parents could give, while it has modeled itself on the glamorous outsider, physics. Now I hope that psychology has matured and at last is coming into its adulthood. As with most adolescents reaching maturity, it begins to look back at the old folks with some appreciation. (Was it Mark Twain who said that at 14 he didn't realize someone could be as stupid as his father and still live, while at 21 he was amazed at how much the old man had learned in 7 years?) Perhaps this can be so with psychology, and psychology can turn again to its parents, the humanities and philosophy, and from these take new strength to meet the challenges of our day.

Two great human traditions are converging, and from their convergence we may expect a tremendous outpouring of new awareness about ourselves in our world. One such tradition is that of science; the other is the humanities. It is as though we are suddenly made heirs to a tremendous storehouse of data which has been but little utilized scientifically before, or—to use a different analogy—as though a whole new hemisphere of our globe had been discovered by some new Columbus. Certainly much exploration and development must be done, but at last we are reaching its shores.

Editor's Note

When a Sir Isaac Newton of the future gains insight into the phenomenon of mental inertia, a special law may be necessary to explain the inner resistance to self-criticism. For two millenniums the mandate of ancient philosophy, "know thyself," has been repeated endlessly without notable results. Any critical evaluation of basic principles carries with it the threat of having to recatalog one's whole mental library. Since this is a task of staggering proportions, comfortable reasons can usually be found to ignore or even to attack the gadfly who points out inconsistencies.

In this respect the corporate body of a profession does not differ dramatically from its constituent members. Constant reassessment of basic assumptions is as painful to the group as to the individual, even when reassessment is recognized as an essential condition of progress.

In reading Maslow's constructive criticism of some shortcomings of psychology, the student may wish to refer to an introductory textbook. Does its approach to the study of man meet with your original and your present expectations? Are any important areas of human living omitted that should be covered? Attempt to formulate the author's unstated philosophy of human nature. How does it compare with your own?

2. A Philosophy of Psychology: The Need for a Mature Science of Human Nature *

A. H. Maslow
Brandeis University

I want to begin my remarks with a credo, a personal statement, which admittedly sounds presumptuous, but is nonetheless necessary.

I believe that psychologists occupy the most centrally important position in the world today. I say this

* From A. H. Maslow. A philosophy of psychology: The need for a mature science of human nature. *Main currents in modern thought,* 1957, **13,** 27–32. Reprinted with permission of the author and publisher.

because all the important problems of mankind—war and peace, exploitation and brotherhood, hatred and love, sickness and health, misunderstanding and understanding, happiness and unhappiness—will yield only to a better understanding of human nature, and to this psychology alone wholly applies itself. Therefore I believe that medicine and physics, law and government, education, economics, engineering, business and industry, are only tools though admittedly powerful. They are means but not ends; the end is human betterment.

The ultimate end to which they should all be bent, then, is human fulfillment, growth and happiness. But these tools produce such good and desirable results only when rightly used by good men. Wrongly and ignorantly used by evil men, they produce nothing but disaster. The wrong, the evil, lie in the men, not in the tools, and the only way to heal the sickness which displays itself as evil is to create good men by understanding the causes of the sickness and seeking the cures. Discovery of the nature of human good and evil, that is, of psychological health and psychological disease, is the job for which the psychologist tries to qualify himself.

Therefore I feel myself, as a psychologist, to be important as well as fortunate in being engaged in such a profession. Psychologists must be considered fortunate for several reasons. They deal with the most fascinating material in the world—human beings. They are, in a sense, their own studies, their own scientific work, and so can work out even their own personal problems more efficiently. But still more important, everything that one man may discover through psychological research will be magnified a million times. For the more we learn about human nature, the more we automatically discover about all the other sciences, as well as law, history, philosophy, religion and industry, since these are all essentially human products. Basic to the study of law or education or economics or history should be an improved study of the human beings who have made the law and the history. Paul Valery has said it well: "When the mind is in question, everything is in question."

It must be quite clear by now that I speak out of a special conception of the vocation of the psychologist. It seems to me that psychology imposes definite rules and responsibilities upon its practitioners. The most pressing and urgent problems which face us today arise out of human weaknesses: sorrow, greed, exploitation, prejudice, contempt, cowardice, stupidity, jealousy and selfishness. We know, however, that these are diseases which are intrinsically curable. Psychoanalysis, for example, is one process of deep therapy that can handle these problems if it has enough time and skill.

Death in another shooting war, or a tense, neurotic, anxious existence in an extended cold war will inevitably result if human beings continue to misunderstand themselves and each other. If we improve human nature we improve all, for we remove the principal causes of world disorder. But human improvement depends upon an understanding of human nature, and the simple and unavoidable fact is that we just don't know enough about people. It is for this reason that the world needs the insights that psychology can with time produce. More than bombs or new religions or diplomats or factories, more than physical health and the new drugs to win it, we need an improved human nature.

It is for these reasons that I feel a sense of historical urgency, as well as an increased awareness of the responsibility of the psychologist. This is a responsibility to the human race, and it should give the psychologist a sense of mission and a weight of duty beyond those of other scientists.

An important point I want to emphasize, however, is that my definition of psychologist is broad but specific. I mean to include not just professors of psychology but rather all those—and only those—who are interested in developing a truer, clearer, more empirical conception of human nature. This would exclude many professors of psychology and many psychiatrists, but would include some sociologists, anthropologists, educators, philosophers, theologians, publicists, linguists, business men, and so on.

There is one more qualification. Since psychology is in its infancy as a science, and so pitifully little is known by comparison with what we need to know, a good psychologist should be a humble man. Feeling his responsibility, he should be very conscious of how much he ought to know, and how little he actually does know. Unfortunately, too many psychologists are not humble, but are, rather, swollen with little knowledge. There is, in fact, no greater danger than an arrogant psychologist or psychiatrist.

With this preamble, I am going to cite below a number of "musts" which I feel are essential if psychology is to mature as a science and accept its full responsibilities.

I

Psychology should be more humanistic, that is, more concerned with the problems of humanity, and less with the problems of the guild.

The sad thing is that most students come into psychology with humanistic interests. They want to find out about people; they want to understand love, hate, hope, fear, ecstasy, happiness, the meaning of living. But what is so often done for these high hopes and yearnings? Most graduate, and even undergraduate, training turns away from these subjects, which are called fuzzy, unscientific, tender-minded, mystical. (I couldn't find the word "love" indexed in any of the psychology books on my shelves, even the ones on marriage.) Instead the student is offered dry bones, techniques, precision, and huge mountains of facts which have little relation to the interests which brought him into psychology. Even worse, they try, often successfully, to make the student *ashamed* of his interests as somehow unscientific. Thus the fine impulses of youth are often lost, and with them, the creativeness, the daring, the boldness, the unorthodoxy, the sense of high mission, the humanistic dedication. Cynicism closes in, and the student settles down to being a member of the guild, with all its prejudices and orthodoxies. I am horrified to report that most graduate students in psychology speak guardedly of the Ph.D. as the "union card," and tend to regard their dissertation research not as a privilege or an opportunity but as an unpleasant chore that must be done in order to get a job.

What cultivated man in his right mind would read a doctoral dissertation, or an elementary textbook of psychology? The psychology books, approved by technical psychologists, which I could recommend to this audience are few. The only ones which would help you to understand man better are inexact and unscientific, coming more from the psychotherapeutic tradition than from the scientific psychologist. For instance, I recommend that you read Freud and the neo-Freudians, but I doubt that Freud could get a Ph.D. in psychology today, nor would any of his writings be acceptable as a doctoral dissertation. Only a few months ago, in a standard journal of psychology, a presidential address compared Freud with phrenology. And this for the greatest psychologist who has ever lived—at least from the point of view of non-members of the guild.

In exchange for Freud, Adler, Jung, Fromm and Horney, we are offered beautifully executed, precise, elegant experiments which, in at least half the cases, have nothing to do with enduring human problems, and which are written primarily for other members of the guild. It is all so reminiscent of the lady at the zoo who asked the keeper whether the hippopotamus was male or female. "Madam," he replied, "it seems to me that would be of interest only to another hippopotamus."

Psychologists are, or should be, an arm of the human race. They have obligations and responsibilities to everyone now living, and to the future. But they are not fulfilling them as they should.

II

Psychology should turn more frequently to the study of philosophy, of science, of aesthetics, and especially of ethics and values. The fact that psychology has officially cut itself off from philosophy means no more than that it has given up good philosophies for bad ones. Every man has a philosophy, albeit uncriticized, unconscious and uncorrected. If it is to be made more realistic, more useful and more fruitful, its possessor must work consciously to improve it.

A philosophy of psychology, in the sense in which I am using the term, includes the study of values. A philosophy of science should inquire into the meaning and purpose of science: how does it enrich us? It should also include a philosophy of aesthetics, of creativeness, of the highest and deepest experiences of which a human being is capable—what I call the peak-experiences. This is a way of avoiding shallowness, and of setting a suitably high level of aspiration.

Too many psychologists have sought their philosophy in the physical science concepts of the 19th century, apparently merely because these sciences were successful. But psychology is in its infancy as a science, and must work out its own philosophy and its own methodology, suitable to its own nature, problems and goals.

I do not mean to intimate by the foregoing that professors of philosophy are any better or worse than psychologists or physicists or chemists. There are as many sterile areas in philosophy as in any other field. Yet in philosophy there are also many points of penetration and advancement in human thought. Unless psychologists acquaint themselves with the heights of philosophical thought, they tend to remain arrogant rather than humble, trivial rather than profound, repetitious rather than creative.

Many psychologists are content to work with but a portion of the human being, indeed making a virtue out of such limitation. They forget that ultimately their task is to give us a unified, empirically based concept of the whole human being, i.e., a philosophy of human nature. This takes courage, and demands a willingness to step away from the narrow platform of certainty. Such certainty is of necessity narrow, for the reason, mentioned before, that our knowledge is insufficient to allow us to be sure of anything but small bits of the complex human problem.

Everyone, even the year-old child, has a conception of human nature, for it is impossible to live without a theory of how people will behave. Every psychologist, however positivistic and anti-theoretical he may claim to be, nevertheless has a full-blown philosophy of human nature hidden away within him. It is as if he guided himself by a half-known map, which he disavows and denies, and which is therefore immune to intrusion and correction by newly acquired knowledge. This unconscious map or theory guides his reactions far more than does his laboriously acquired experimental knowledge.

The issue is thus not over whether or not to have a philosophy of psychology, but whether to have one that is conscious or unconscious.

Another truth we can learn from philosophy is that we must have a map if we are not to waste time. It may sound sensible to say that as knowledge is based on facts, if we accumulate facts of all kinds, merely making sure that they are valid, we will slowly nibble away at the unknown. There is really no need for theories. But we now know that most facts—perhaps *all*—are expressions of a theory. Anthropologists, and particularly linguists, have proven that even naming an object "a chair," or "a man," is an expression of a world outlook which must be taken into consideration if the statement is to be understood correctly.

This is by no means a plea against detailed work. Every clash of issues eventually works itself down to small crucial experiments, which of course must be done as well and as carefully as possible, for ultimately the experimenter is the Supreme Court before which all theories are tested.

But because we know so little for certain about human beings, intuition, experience, wisdom and insight all become extremely important. Even a stupid man can understand an idea which is sufficiently embodied in facts, but when there are few related facts only the innately perceptive man can know. Philosophies of human nature have been expounded by theologians, poets, dramatists, artists, statesmen, industrialists and many others. We should respect these theories almost as much as those of the psychologist, and use them as frameworks for criticism, for suggested experiments. The triumph of science is that it can take the innate wisdom of the great intuitors, correct it, test it, winnow it, and come out with more certain and reliable knowledge. When, after years of theorizing, debate and experiment, scientists arrive at the same conclusions that Rousseau or Shakespeare did, it is not actually the same. Then it was a theory; now it is new knowledge. And I remind you that we need a principle by which to select the correct one from among the various contradictory theories which have been offered. Who is to check them but the scientist, and on what basis if not that of empirical research?

We must pay special attention to the synoptic thinkers, the producers of theories of the whole man in his whole world. It is easy enough to develop a sound theory of the learning of nonsense syllables, or of rats running in mazes, or of the conditioning of the dog's salivary reflex. To integrate these miniature theories into the whole fabric of psychology is another matter. To relate them to love and hate, to growing and regressing, to happiness and pain, to courage and anxiety, exposes the weakness of nibbling away at the edges of reality, instead of making reconnaissance flights over the whole of it.

III

American psychology should be bolder, more creative; it should try to discover, not only to be cautious and careful in avoiding mistakes.

Why is it that there has never been a great, creative American psychologist? Our best men have been excellent scholars, systematizers and experimenters, but not great discoverers. All the great breakthroughs have come from Europe: all the brands of psychoanalysis, Freud, Adler, Jung, Rank, Fromm, Horney; all the Gestalt psychologists, Wertheimer, Koffka, Kohler, Lewin; the Rorschach test, Goldstein's organismic psychology. Even behaviorism, so specifically American, began with Pavlov.

I have been told that something very similar is true for the other sciences. In atomic physics, for example, Einstein, Bohr, Fermi and Szilard were all Europeans.

Why is American science so essentially conventional, so hostile to creativeness, to innovation, to unorthodoxy, to new ideas? Why are American psychologists characteristically appliers of other people's ideas? Why do they despise and attack the innovator for years, and then at last, when his idea has become more accustomed, seize upon it, make it conventional, and work it out in hundreds of experiments? As Picasso said, "First you invent something, and then they make it pretty."

I remember how saddened and irritated I was by an official report of a major committee of the American Psychological Association on the future of psychological science. The recommendations were principally methodological: how to be cautious, how to check, how to discover mistakes, how to validate, how to be accurate and precise. Hardly a word was mentioned about the need for creativeness, for new ideas, breaking out of the rut, taking a chance, encouraging uncertainty and exploration. It was all so much like the road maps given out at a gas station, that tell us how to make our way from known place to place. Not a word is given about the no-man's land where there are no street signs and paved roads; not a word about the pioneering and trail-breaking that are necessary before the maps can be made.

The fear seems to be that once we admit creativeness we may involve ourselves with all sorts of poets, artists, musicians and other questionable people who don't have a Ph.D. in psychology and are therefore clearly social climbers without any right or qualification to know anything about human nature.

IV

Psychology should be more problem-centered, and less absorbed with means or methods.

In Chapter 2 of my book, *Motivation and Personality,* I have considered this problem at length, and so will merely cite the general point: If you are primarily interested in doing what you can about important questions, then techniques become secondary. For example, if you propose to tackle the question, "What is love?" you will stick with the problem even though you are forced to improvise. In the early stages of exploration, you will have to be content with inexactness and uncertainty. If you demand exactness, elegance, and reliability, such a problem is unworkable, because the techniques now available are of little help. Those who insist on precision from the beginning therefore can never begin. All they can do is come in on the later stages of development of the problem.

Therefore, if science is identified with exactness, with quantifications, with precisely defined variables over which there is good control, all the first stages of work with any problem, when hunches, naturalistic observations, speculations and theories reign supreme, must be repudiated as "unscientific." Put even more bluntly, to define science primarily as method makes of it a senseless game or ritual. What is it a method *for*? If pertinence, goal and value are understressed, and the exclusive aim is validity and reliability, it is much like making the boast, "I don't know or care what I'm doing, but see how accurately I'm doing it."

The situation in American psychology, in which most researchers concentrate on doing well what they can, rather than seeking out what needs to be done, is largely due, I believe, to this mistaken notion of science.

V

Psychology ought to become more positive and less negative. It should have higher ceilings, and not be afraid of the loftier possibilities of the human being.

One major shortcoming of research psychology, and psychiatry as well, is its pessimistic, negative and limited conception of the full height to which the human being can attain. Partly because of this preconception, it has so far revealed many of man's shortcomings, weaknesses and ills, but few of his virtues, potentialities or higher aspirations. In the book to which I have referred I have made a number of positive suggestions for needed research.

This is not a call for optimism. Rather it is a demand for realism in the best sense of the word. It is ridiculous to identify realism with darkness, misery, pathology and breakdown, as so many contemporary novelists have done. Happiness is as real as unhappiness; gratification is as real as frustration; love is as real as hostility.

However, I want to stress the most important single example of this mistake, namely, the contrast between our knowledge of psychological sickness and our wholly inadequate attention to psychological health. I can understand this discrepancy, because my own efforts to study healthy people have taught me how difficult a task it is, ringed about with philosophical reefs of all sorts, particularly in the area of the theory of values. In addition, there are cultural, methodological and clinical problems. Yet it clearly calls for doing. We must know what men are like at their best; not only what they are, but also what they can become. The byproducts of such knowledge are incalculably important. My belief is that such a health-psychology will inevitably transform our deepest conceptions of human nature. It will wean us away from our almost universal habit of regarding normality as a special case of the abnormal, and teach us that instead the abnormal is a special case of the normal, and that psychological illness is primarily a struggle toward health.

Another aspect of this same mistaken preoccupation with the negative is the amount of time that has been spent on the defensive processes, on self-protectiveness, on safety and security, and on homeostatic processes. The easy implication is that life is a process of avoiding pain and of fighting unhappiness. But there is another set of motivations, the positive ones. A human being also tends to grow stronger, wiser, healthier, to actualize his potentialities, to be curious, to wonder, to be interested, to philosophize, to be creative, to enjoy. He does not only adjust; he also rebels.

It is perfectly true that we shrink within ourselves when something threatens. We try to avoid pain, and there is much pain in life for most people. Yet if life were simply and only an avoidance of pain, why would we not all cut our throats and thereby avoid pain forever? Clearly life has more to offer, and we should study this "something more."

VI

If all this is so, therapy should be taken out of the office and spread to many other areas of life. Furthermore, it should not only be more broadly used, but also more ambitiously defined to include the growth-fostering techniques.

Some of the more elementary psychotherapeutic techniques can be taught in simplified form to teachers, parents, ministers, doctors, and other laymen. Support, reassurance, acceptance, love, respect—all of these are therapeutic. We know also that many of the good life experiences are themselves therapeutic, such as the good marriage, good education, success at a job, friends, the ability to help others, creative work, and so on. All of these are basic medicine which should be studied carefully, and knowledge so gained should be widely taught.

In any case, the conception of therapy as the elimination of symptoms and illnesses is too limited. We must learn to think of it more as a technique for fostering general growth, for encouraging self-actualization. This means that many other techniques not now included under the head of psychotherapy will be shown to belong there. The meaning of therapy should be expanded to include all the growth-fostering techniques, particularly educational ones, and most particularly creative education in art, in play, and in all forms of expression that encourage creativeness, spontaneity, courage and integration.

VII

Psychology should study the depths of human nature as well as the surface behavior, the unconscious as well as the conscious.

I am aware that this may sound fantastic, yet the truth is that academic experimental psychology does not study the depths as it should, being preoccupied with what can be seen, touched or heard. The greatest single psychological discovery ever made was the discovery of unconscious motivations, yet the unconscious is still out of bounds for many research psychologists. Until recently, its study has been mostly the task of psychoanalysts, psychotherapists and psychiatrists.

The consequence, judging from the standard texts in general psychology, is a kind of half-psychology, in which human nature is presented, so to speak, "from middle C upward." This is like defining an iceberg as only that portion which can be seen above the waterline. The result is an "official" psychology which deals with rationality but not with irrationality, with the cognitive far more than with the conative and emotional, with adjustment to external reality far more than to internal reality, with the verbal, mathematical, logical and physical far more than with the archaic, the proverbial, the symbolic, the illogical, the fluid, the intuitive, the poetic—all that the psychoanalysts call "primary process."

Not only do our depths make trouble for us; this is also where our joys come from. If we go about the world not knowing what goes on inside ourselves, unaware of what we are searching for, unconscious of the forces which largely determine our behavior, we are blind to the sources both of our ills and of our pleasures. This lack of understanding means a lack of control over our own fate.

VIII

Academic psychology is too exclusively Western. It needs to draw on Eastern sources as well. It turns too much to the objective, the public, the outer, the behavioral, and should learn more about the subjective, the private, the inner, the meditative. Introspection, thrown out as a technique, should be brought back into psychological research.

American psychology is particularly behavioristic, concentrating on overt actions. This originates in a praiseworthy, though naive, effort to be "scientific." Of course it is the hope and goal of scientists to demonstrate, to prove, and to repeat the experiment in another laboratory. Yet we must face the hard fact that this is an ultimate rather than an immediate goal. By confining ourselves to the observation of external behavior, we overlook all sorts of human activities which do not show themselves externally in a simple form.

Behaviorism originated in a sensible reaction against anthropomorphizing animal psychology, but the pendulum has swung too far, and instead it has rodentomorphized human psychology, studying the person as if he were just a complicated white rat. It is indeed a mistake to attribute human motives to laboratory animals, but is it a mistake to attribute human motives to humans?

I should like to bring back introspection for another

reason. We are discovering more and more, as we study personality in the depths rather than at the surface, that the deeper we penetrate the more universality we find. At men's deepest levels they seem to be more alike than different. Therefore, if the individual can touch these depths within himself, usually with the aid of a therapist, he discovers not only himself, but also the whole human spirit. The non-academic psychologists of the East have always known this; we in the West must learn it too.

IX

Psychologists should study the end experiences as well as the means to ends—the pragmatic, the useful, and the purposive.

What does man live for? What makes living worthwhile? What experiences in life justify the pains of existence? We know that we reach the heights of living in moments of creation, of insight, of delight, of love-sex experience, of aesthetic experience, of mystical experience—the "peak experiences." Were it not for these, life would make no sense.

We must remember, too, that end-experiences need not be only the peak-experiences of life. We gain milder rewards in simple zest of living, in having fun, in all the activities that are done for their own sake. A healthy organism enjoys just being. Our over-pragmatic psychology passes all this by.

X

Psychology should study the human being not just as passive clay, helplessly determined by outside forces. Man is, or should be, an active, autonomous, self-governing mover, chooser and center of his own life.

The so-called stimulus-response psychology has unintentionally created what might be called a Stimulus-Response man, passive, shaped, adjusting, learning. With him should be contrasted the creative, active man, who invents, makes decisions, accepts some stimuli and rejects others, who, in fact, creates his own stimuli. Posing this opposition may help in understanding why more and more psychologists are growing worried about the concept of "adjustment." Adjustment, whether to the culture, to other people, or to nature, essentially means being passive, letting oneself be shaped from the outside. It is trying to be what others want, instead of searching for one's real self. From this point of view, psychologists are increasingly beginning to criticize the conception of learning as a passive process.

XI

Intellectuals tend to become absorbed with abstractions, words and concepts, and to forget the original real experience which is the beginning of all science. In psychology, this is a particular danger.

My own remedy for this is two-fold: first, to turn to the general-semanticists, who devote themselves specifically to this problem; and second, to look to the artists, whose particular task it is to experience freshly, to see—and to help us see—the world as it really is, not screened through a web of concepts, verbalisms, abstractions, categories and theories.

XII

The lessons of Gestalt psychology and of organismic theory have not been fully integrated into psychology. The human being is an irreducible unit, at least as far as psychological research is concerned. Everything in him is related to everything else, in greater or lesser degree.

This has one important consequence. In his essential core, no human being is comparable with any other. Therefore his ideals for himself, his path of growth, must also be unique. His goal must arise out of his own nature, and not be chosen by comparison or competition with others. Each man's task is to become the best himself. Joe Doakes must not try to be like Abraham Lincoln or Thomas

Jefferson or any other model or hero. He must become the best Joe Doakes in the world. This he can do, and only this is necessary or possible. Here he has no competitors.

XIII

Psychologists should devote more time to the intensive study of the single unique person, to balance their preoccupation with the generalized man and with generalized and abstracted capacities.

There is one great difference between psychological studies and those of other sciences. All other sciences really study similarities, which means abstracting. One white rat is as good as another; one atom is like another; one chemical is like another. The differences are not significant. Psychology too must abstract, but it has the special task, which belongs to no other science except anthropology, of studying uniqueness.

XIV

Finally, as we begin to know more about legitimate wants and needs for personal growth and self-fulfillment, that is, for psychological health, then we should set ourselves the task of creating the health-fostering culture.

This is, to my mind, no more difficult a task in principle than the making of the A-Bomb. Naturally we don't know enough to do a good job right now. But part of the ultimate task would be the acquisition of necessary knowledge, and to this there could be, theoretically, no objections.

Such an enterprise, when begun, will be the proof that psychology has matured enough to be fruitful, not in individual terms alone, but in terms of social betterment as well.

Editor's Note

Gordon Allport has noted that all books on the psychology of personality are also books on the philosophy of person. The reason for this is obvious. No psychological theory is contained as such in the data gathered in the laboratory. Theories are constructs which must be worked out step by step in a speculative manner. In the process, the psychologist, whether he intends it or not, will be guided by his prescientific suppositions about human nature.

In reading the theories reviewed below, the student may wish to rank them according to how much liberty they allow the individual in becoming the kind of person he wishes to be.

3. The Person in Psychology *

Gordon W. Allport
Harvard University

Today people are asking more urgently than ever before, *What sort of creature is man*? Has he the potential for continued evolution and growth so that he may yet master the calamitous problems that face him—ideological schism, overpopulation, atomic disaster, and widespread disrespect of nation for nation and race for race?

Although the question is often addressed to philosophers and theologians, to historians and poets, the inquirer turns with special hope to the biological, psychological, and social sciences. For in an age of science he wants to hear what these relevant studies have to say.

So far as psychology is concerned, there is less agreement than we could wish for. Like other scientists and like philosophers, psychologists offer different sorts of answers—often only bare hints of answers, half-hidden in a

* From G. W. Allport, *Pattern and growth in personality.* Copyright 1937, © 1961, Holt, Rinehart and Winston, Inc., New York. Reprinted by permission of author and publisher.

network of unexpressed assumptions. Our task is to make some of the leading psychological answers explicit.

Positivist Formulations

We use the term *positivist* to stand for the traditional main stream of psychological science as it has existed in Western lands since the time of Locke and Comte. It is the empirical, experimental, chiefly associationist, and increasingly quantitative tradition known to all.

Perhaps the simplest way to characterize the positivist view of man is to say that he is regarded as a *reactive* being. What he does is determined by outer forces or by inner drives. Like traditional natural science, positive psychology sees movement as caused and determined by pressures. Man is like inanimate objects (including machines) and like elementary organisms.

The positivist view of man is seldom explicitly stated. Psychologists are too busy studying this reaction or that, in men or rats, to draw final implications from their work. They merely assume, in line with their procedures, that the human person is a purely reactive being. Even a cursory view of the psychologist's vocabulary shows that terms such as *reflex, reaction, response, retention* are far more common—perhaps a hundred times more common—than terms with *pro* prefixes, such as *proactive, programing, propriate, proceeding, promise*. Terms commencing with *re* connote againness, passivity, being pushed or maneuvered. Terms with *pro* suggest futurity, intention, forward thrust. Psychology for the most part looks at man not in terms of *pro*action but of *re*action.

Positivism does not pretend to be synoptic in its view of man. Its assignment is to find small facts under controlled conditions. The "fact" is bound to be small, since reliability can, as a rule, be obtained only when one deals with a limited fragment of behavior. Totalities of behavior are so inexact that the positivist turns away from them. Fragmentation yields firmer results. Therefore attention is devoted to the partial, the physical, the quasi-mechanical, the regular, the logical, because these aspects can be controlled. Attention is correspondingly withdrawn from the symbolic, the illogical, the uncoded, the configural because they cannot be reliably controlled.

Thus positivism teaches us how to be cautious and conservative, how to check and validate, how to be accurate and precise. Much of the detailed general information that goes into the psychology of personality, as we have seen throughout this volume [reference not pertinent here], is gathered by following the canons of experimental research. This procedure appeals to us because it offers the best means for verifying our discoveries. The price we pay is limiting our curiosity to only a portion of a human being. We suppress interest in the total pattern.

Since positivism seeks nomothetic generalizations about behavior it is likely to regard curiosity about the internal order of mind-in-particular as subjective and "unscientific." It somehow seems more scientific to send a platoon of white rats through a maze than to occupy oneself with the complex organization of a concrete personality. It is more respectable to pursue averages and probabilities for populations than to study the life-style of one person. Such preference is not hard to explain in a culture that is technological and machine-centered.

> It is interesting to recall that the founders of modern experimental psychology—Wundt, James, and Titchener—acknowledged the individual person as central in their definitions of psychology. The first wrote: *It [psychology] investigates the total content of experience in its relations to the subject.* The second: *Psychology is the science of finite individual minds.* The third: *Psychology is the study of experience considered as dependent on some person.* Yet none of these eminent authors developed his account of mental life to accord with his definition. All were preoccupied with the uniform aspects of mind. The

tradition in which they worked prevented them from following their own definitions consistently to the end. Like their successors, they stripped the person of all his troublesome particularity, and for the most part sought a science of averages.

The only real difficulty with the positivist formulation is that it does not know (or rarely knows) that it is a prisoner of a specific philosophical outlook, also of a specific period of culture, and of a narrow definition of "science." Positivism seldom defends its deterministic, quasi-mechanical view of the human person; it merely takes it for granted. Its metaphysics is unexamined, and, as the philosopher Whitehead once said, "No science can be more secure than the unconscious metaphysics which it tacitly presupposes."

It is certainly unfair to blame the positivist outlook in psychological and social science for the present plight of mankind, although many critics do so. Positivism is more a reflection than a cause of the fragmentation of personality in the modern world. The worst that can be said is that by keeping itself "method-centered" rather than "problem-centered" positivism has brought forth an array of "itty bitty" facts at the expense of a coherent view of the human person as a whole. In fairness, however, we should thank positivism for the wholesome safeguards it places on undisciplined speculation, and for many useful, if disconnected findings.

Psychoanalytic Formulations

Much has been written concerning the psychoanalytic image of man. Indeed, the image is so well known that only the briefest comment is needed here to supplement our [earlier] discussion. . . .

In some respects the picture is like that of positivism. Man is a quasi-mechanical reactor, goaded by three tyrannical forces: the environment, the id, and the superego. Man adjusts as well as he can within this triangle of forces. His vaunted rationality is of little account. Since he is full of defenses and prone to rationalize, his search for final truth is doomed to failure. If perchance he claims to find truth in religion, this discovery is dubbed an illusion and charged up to his neurosis.

There is a deep pessimism in orthodox psychoanalytic doctrine (Freudian style). Man is so heavily dominated by unconscious id forces that he never fully escapes the ferocity and passion in his nature. Sublimation is the best we can hope for. There is no genuine transformation of motives.

Grim as the picture is, no theory of modern man can safely overlook its elements of truth. How can we hope to see man whole unless we include the dark side of his nature? Many present-day psychoanalysts, however, feel that the image overweights the role of unconscious and libidinal forces in personality. Neo-Freudian "ego-psychology" has broadened the perspective, and would agree in many respects with the schools of thought we shall next consider.

Personalistic Formulations

There are several versions of personalistic thought.[1] They all agree that the individual person as a patterned entity must serve as the center of gravity for psychology. The intention of personalism is to rewrite the science of mental life entirely around this focus.

[1] The most detailed system is found in the writings of the German psychologist William Stern. See *General psychology from the personalistic standpoint* (Transl. by H. D. Spoerl: New York: Macmillan, 1938); also G. W. Allport, The personalistic psychology of William Stern, *Charact. & Pers.*, 1937, **5**, 231–246. The American philosophical school of personalism is exemplified in E. S. Brightman, *Introduction to philosophy* (New York: Holt, Rinehart and Winston, 1925); also in P. A. Bertocci, Psychological self, ego, and personality, *Psychol. Rev.*, 1945, **52**, 91–99. For a critical discussion see G. W. Allport, The psychological nature of personality. In *Personality and social encounters*, Chap. 2. A Thomistic version of personalism is M. B. Arnold and J. A. Gasson (Eds.), *The human person* (New York: Ronald, 1954). An eclectic textbook approach is that of G. Murphy, *Introduction to psychology* (New York: Harper, 1951). [Footnote renumbered.]

Why should such thoroughgoing reconstruction be demanded by the personalists? The reasons they advance are too numerous to be given in full. A brief hint of some of the arguments must suffice.

> Without the coordinating concept of *person* (or some equivalent, such as *self* or *ego*), it is impossible to account for the interaction of psychological processes. Memory affects perception, desire influences meaning, meaning determines action, and action shapes memory; and so on indefinitely. This constant interpenetration takes place within some *boundary*, and the boundary is the person. The flow occurs for some purpose, and the purpose can be stated only in terms of service to the person.
>
> The organization of thought or behavior can have no significance unless viewed as taking place within a definite framework. Psychological states do not organize themselves or lead independent existences. Their arrangement merely constitutes part of a larger arrangement—the personal life.
>
> Such concepts as *function, adaptation, use* have no significance without reference to the person. If an adjustment takes place it must be an adjustment *of* something, *to* something, *for* something. Again, the person is central.
>
> All the evidence—introspective and otherwise—that forces psychology to take account of the *self* is here relevant. The very elusiveness of the self—James says that to grasp it fully in consciousness is like trying to step on one's own shadow—proves that it is the ground of all experience. Although seldom salient itself, it provides the platform for all other experience.
>
> We cannot talk about strata of personality or of propriate, as distinguished from peripheral, states without implying that a superior totality includes both.
>
> A creative person is presupposed in the creeds he creates. Even a scientist of the positivist persuasion

intentionally limits his interest, designs his experiments, interprets the results. No sense could be made of this sequence without the assumption that the scientist himself is a prior creative unity.

Such are some of the philosophical arguments whereby personalistic psychologists (and self-psychologists) state their case for the reconstruction of psychology. They gladly consign to impersonal (natural and biological) sciences the task of exploring a certain range of problems. But they insist that psychology, whose task it is to treat the whole of behavior, cannot discharge its duty without relating the states and processes it studies to the person who is their originator, carrier, and regulator. There can be no adjustment without someone to adjust, no organization without an organizer, no perception without a perceiver, no memory without self-continuity, no learning without a change in the person, no valuing without someone possessed of desires and capacity to evaluate. Psychology must take seriously James's dictum that every mental operation occurs in a "personal form," and must take it more seriously than James himself did.

It is not uncommon in textbooks on general psychology to find wedged into the last chapter a separate and rather abrupt treatment of personality, as if to reward the reader who has waded through piles of abstractions concerning the generalized human mind. Personalistic psychology would reverse the procedure. The person would form the *point of departure*.

Stern's handling of space perception illustrates the point. Traditional psychology speaks of "visual space" or "auditory space" and treats these as wholly separate. Such a procedure, Stern argues, is misleading, a mere laboratory abstraction. There is only one space: *my* space. Tones and objects and touches are all related to *me*.

An impersonal psychology could not possibly account for the fact that my seatmate in a plane is distant from me while the friend toward whom I am riding (although still a thousand miles away) is already near to me. The essence of space, psychologically considered, is its personal relevance. Events are distant when they lack such relevance; near, when they possess it.

Time, too, is a personal, not chronological matter. A segment of life that is ten years behind me may be far nearer to me subjectively than a period two years ago; or some act I performed yesterday may today appear incomprehensible to me, a totally foreign element in my past.

Subjectively, space and time blend. We anchor experiences as here-and-now or as far-and-then. This personal blend is very unlike the psychologist's normal abstractions in classifying separately space perception (for separate modalities) and time perception.

To sum up, the personalistic point of view is based partly on philosophical argument and partly on appeal to immediate experience (phenomenology). It is in essence a rebellion against positivist science that tends to regard the individual as a bothersome incident. Different lines of personalism would answer somewhat differently the question, What sort of a creature is man? But they all agree that the final answer will disclose a creative unity, a purposive, growing individual—and not a dismembered reactor as pictured by positivism. The secret of man will not be found in a reductive analysis of his *being*, but only by tracing coherently the course of his *becoming*.

Existentialist Formulations

Existentialism, like personalism, has no single answer to our question concerning the nature of the human person. Indeed, in this movement we can find answers that in some respects are diametrically opposed to one another.

One existentialist tells us that "man is a useless passion"; another, that "man is a being who exists in relation to God." Existentialism is theistic and atheistic, despairing and hopeful, empirical and mystical—all depending on the devotee.

Yet certain features are common. One is the conviction that positive science alone cannot discover the nature of man as a being-in-the-world. Each special science is too narrow. None is synoptic. And the methods of positive science tend to rule out the most appropriate tool for research: phenomenology. It is not enough to know how man reacts: we must know how he feels, how he sees his world, what time and space are to *him* (not to the physicist), why he lives, what he fears, for what he would willingly die. Such questions of *existence* must be put to man directly, and not to an outside observer.

Common also is a passion not to be fooled about man's nature. If the Victorian image of man was perhaps too pretty, the Freudian image may be too grim. But grim or pretty, *all* knowledge about man must be faced. The findings of biology, psychology, anthropology are important, but so, too, are the findings of history, art, philosophy. We seek to know man in his entirety. Life demands that we know the worst and make the best of it.

It is probably true to say that all forms of existentialism hope to establish a new kind of psychology—a psychology of mankind. The pivot of such a psychology will lie in the perennial themes and crises of human life. Mere stimulus-response sequences, drives, habits, repetitions tend to miss the catastrophic coloring of life. Psychology should be more urgently human than it is.

What are some of the perennial themes and crises? A person is born in a condition of dependency; he is ordinarily nurtured in love and develops a measure of basic trust. Gradually there comes the poignant sense of selfhood and solitariness which he never can lose; he relates himself to life through his interests, and seeks always to enhance the value-experiences he has along the way; he falls in love, mates, nurtures his offspring; he suffers basic anxieties (fear of death, feelings of guilt, and a horror of meaninglessness); he seeks always the "why" of existence; he dies alone. Since psychology as a science has not oriented itself to these central themes it has not yet dealt fully with man's existence.

There are too many varieties of existentialism to be considered author by author. Many writers—Kierkegaard, Heidegger, Jasper, Sartre, Berdyaev, Marcel, Binswanger, Frankl, Tillich, and others—have made important contributions. But we shall confine our attention to certain questions that pertain to the movement as a whole.

IS EXISTENTIALISM IDIOGRAPHIC OR NOMOTHETIC? Each person is busy building his own peculiar constellation of ego-world relationships. His motives are his own, taking always the form of "personal projects." His inheritance is unique; his experienced environment is unique; all his ego-world relationships are unique. Existence ultimately resides nowhere except in the individual's point of view. Certainly no counselor or therapist can succeed unless he can understand the patient's dilemma from the patient's standpoint. A million mortals will experience their ego-world quandaries in a million ways.

Thus, at bottom the existentialist approach to man is urgently idiographic. As yet, however, it offers no special methods for representing the unique structure of persons. Phenomenology, of course, is the approved method, but it is difficult to specify just how it can be used for a proper configural comprehension. Fiction and drama (Camus, Sartre) and case studies (Minkowski, Binswanger) are employed. But the movement has not yet evolved genuinely novel methods for the representation of individuality.

WHAT IS MAN'S PRINCIPAL GOAL? All existentialist writers agree that existence is essentially a *restlessness*. But is it a blind, disconnected, and useless restlessness? Only a few "beatnik" existentialists say that it is. Most writers find a more stable project at the core of life. Formulations differ, but all agree that there is an anxious outreach, a compelling hunger in existence that goes beyond animal drives and sheer reactivity. The neurologist Goldstein, we recall, insists that only sick people in mental hospitals are reduced totally to the biological pressures of sex, thirst, hunger for food, oxygen, sleep, and so on. The rest of mankind, he observes, engage in activities beyond these basic drives. These activities amount to a striving for *self-actualization*. Other authors formulate the core motive differently, but all agree that the quasi-mechanical view of motivation is insufficient to the dynamics of human life.

Perhaps the commonest terms employed by existentialists are *anxiety, dread, alienation*. Man finds himself "thrown" into an incomprehensible world. He can scarcely avoid an undercurrent of fear with eddies of sharp panic. He lives in a whirlpool of instability, aloneness, suffering, and is haunted by the ultimate specter of death and nothingness. He would like to escape from the burden of anxiety, but he would also like to know its meaning. Meaninglessness is more of a torture than is anxiety, for if there is a clear purpose in life, then anxiety and dread can be borne. It was Nietzsche who said that he who has a Why to live surmounts almost any How.

Man, then, is not a homeostatic creature. He does not seek equilibrium within himself and with the environment. His restlessness is systemic, and too deep-rooted to be drugged by temporary satisfactions. He seeks a more solid formula for living, something that will enable him to surmount alienation and suffering. There is something bloodless about homeostasis; it favors laziness and belies our specifically human capacity to outstrip ourselves.

Fortunately we have the capacity to make commitments and to take risks. We can, if we wish, gamble our life on the value of some "personal project," even though we cannot prove its worth or be assured of its success. Our faith in a project may be only half sure, but that does not mean that we need to be halfhearted. To be able to make a life-wager is man's crowning ability. Members of the French or the Norwegian underground resistance movement in Hitler's Europe felt that they had little chance of success. But the goal was something worth living for, and worth dying for. Suffering and dread are surmounted if we have an ideal of this magnitude.

> When people are asked if they have projects for which they would willingly die, most of them reply in the affirmative. They may specify the welfare of their children, or their commitment to the cause of peace, or their religious faith. The whys may differ, but they are present in most lives.
>
> Even people who are discouraged and depressed can often be led to a freshening of their purposes by asking them the blunt question, "Why don't you commit suicide?" In answering this question the patient reveals his half-forgotten values and commitments. In them lies a firm foundation for therapy and recovery.

And so one answer to our question concerning the nature of the human person is that he is a creature bent on enhancing the value-attributes of his experience. Every day each of us is building many self-world relationships. Some of these become more and more meaningful, more propriate, more urgent. They are what make life worth while.

Some writers, Freud among them, feel that man's restlessness leads him to desire ultimate peace through annihilation. Religions of the Orient incline to this view, as expressed by the anonymous Japanese poet:

> Loathing both seas of life and death
> How deeply I long
> For the upland of Nirvana
> Untouched by the tides of change.

In theistic terms, Western religions echo the thought. St. Augustine wrote, "My heart is restless until it finds its rest in Thee, O God."

Short of this ultimate goal, and centering on the present course of life, many writers emphasize the indelible creativity of man, as does Buber:

> Every person born into this world represents something new, something that never existed before, something original and unique. It is the duty of every person to know . . . that there has never been anyone like him in the world, for if there had been someone like him, there would have been no need for him to be in the world. Every single man is a new thing in the world and is called upon to fulfill his particularity in this world.[2]

Here the emphasis turns to man's responsibility. It is not enough for man to question life concerning its meaning and purpose. More important are the questions life puts to each man: What creative acts will you perform? What responsibility will you assume for your existence now that you have it? Which of the world's needs (not your needs) will you fulfill?

This aspect of existentialist thinking goes beyond the goal of "self-actualization." For it asks in effect which of your many potentialities will you choose to actualize? To actualize all of them would be trivial self-indulgence. One must transcend himself, take an outside look at his abilities and desires within a context of meaning that is objective, even cosmic. From this point of view the capacity for self-transcendence and responsibility becomes the truly significant core of human nature.

To sum up, there is a tendency among existentialist writers to seek for one basic intentional theme in human life. A fairly wide range of proposals is the result—and yet

[2] Reprinted by permission of the publisher, Horizon Press, Inc., New York, from "Hasidism and Modern Man" by Martin Buber. Copyright, 1958. [Footnote renumbered.]

the varied proposals seem for the most part to be complementary and concordant, not in actual opposition. Man is inherently restless and anxious, desiring both security and freedom. He strives to counter his condition of alienation by seeking a meaning for existence which will cover the tragic trio of suffering, guilt, death. By making commitments he finds that life can become worth living. Along the way he enhances his own value experiences. If necessary he will sacrifice his life in order that some primary value can continue to be served. He is capable of taking responsibility, of answering by his deeds the questions life puts to him. In this way he rises above his own organic and spiritual urgencies, and achieves true self-transcendence. Although different writers place emphasis on different parts of this formula, the picture is consistent.

Editor's Note

In any area of scholarship new developments which may seem to spring from nowhere can usually be traced to the intellectual climate created by a few individuals. Among the writers who have done most to prepare the way for humanistic psychology are Gordon W. Allport and Henry A. Murray. The following selection from Murray's Explorations in Personality, *published in 1938, would need little revision to introduce a modern textbook in humanistic psychology.*

4. Explorations in Personality *

Henry A. Murray
Harvard University

Man is to-day's great problem. What can we know about him and how can it be said in words that have clear meaning? What propels him? With what environmental

* From *Explorations in Personality*, (pp. 3–5), edited by Henry A. Murray. Copyright 1938 by Oxford University Press, Inc. Reprinted by permission.

objects and institutions does he interact and how? What occurrences in his body are most influentially involved? What mutually dependent processes participate in his differentiation and development? What courses of events determine his pleasures and displeasures? And, finally, by what means can he be intentionally transformed? These are antique questions, to be sure, which in all ages have invited interest, but to-day they more insistently demand solution and more men are set for the endeavour. There is greater zest and greater promise of fulfilment.

The point of view adopted in this book is that personalities constitute the subject matter of psychology, the life history of a single man being a unit with which this discipline has to deal. It is not possible to study all human beings or all experiences of one human being. The best that can be done is to select representative or specially significant events for analysis and interpretation. Some psychologists may prefer to limit themselves to the study of one kind of episode. For instance, they may study the responses of a great number of individuals to a specific situation. They may attempt to discover what changes in the situation bring about important changes in response. But, since every response is partially determined by the after-effects of previous experiences, the psychologist will never fully understand an episode if he abstracts it from ontogeny, the developmental history of the individual. Even philogeny, or racial history, may have to be considered. The prevailing custom in psychology is to study one function or one aspect of an episode at a time—perception, emotion, intellection or behaviour—and this is as it must be. The circumscription of attention is dictated by the need for detailed information. But the psychologist who does this should recognize that he is observing merely a part of an operating totality, and that this totality, in turn, is but a small temporal segment of a personality. Psychology must construct a scheme of concepts for portraying the entire course of individual development, and thus provide a framework into which any single episode—natural or experimental—may be fitted.

The branch of psychology which principally concerns itself with the study of human lives and the factors that influence their course, which investigates individual differences and types of personality, may be termed 'personology' instead of 'the psychology of personality,' a clumsy and tautological expression.

Personology, then, is the science of men, taken as gross units, and by definition it encompasses 'psychoanalysis' (Freud), 'analytical psychology' (Jung), 'individual psychology' (Adler) and other terms which stand for methods of inquiry or doctrines rather than realms of knowledge.

In its intentions our endeavour was excessively ambitious. For we purposed nothing less than (1) to construct methodically a *theory* of personality; (2) to devise *techniques* for getting at some of the more important attributes of personality; and (3) by a study of the lives of many individuals to discover basic *facts* of personality. Our guiding thought was that personality is a temporal whole and to understand a part of it one must have a sense, though vague, of the totality. It was for this that we attempted comprehensiveness, despite the danger that in trying to grasp everything we might be left with nothing worth the having.

We judged the time had come when systematic, full length studies of individuals could be made to bring results. And more than this, indeed, it seemed a necessary thing to do. For if the constituent processes of personality are mutally dependent, then one must know a lot to comprehend a little, and to know a lot that may be used for understanding, good methods must be systematically employed. In our attempt to envisage and portray the general course of a person's life, we selected for analysis certain happenings along the way and, using these as points, made free drawings of the connecting paths. We judged that the spaces without definition would attract attention and it would become more evident than it has been in what quarters detailed research might yield important facts. For without some notion of the whole there can be no assurance that the processes selected for intensive study are significant constituents.

Actually, the scheme of concepts we employed was not exhaustive; one reason being the inability of the mind to hold so many novel generalities in readiness. The amount of space and time and the number of examiners available put a limit to the number of experimental subjects and the number of techniques that could be used. Thus, in the end, our practices and theories were not as comprehensive as we thought they could and should be.

Since in the execution of our plan we went from theory down to fact, then back to theory and down to fact again, the book may be regarded either as a scheme of elementary formulations conceived of to explain the ways of different individuals, or as an assemblage of biographic data organized according to a certain frame of reference.

CHAPTER 2

Living or Being Lived

Writers of psychology textbooks usually assume that human behavior is determined. In spite of an overpowering illusion of freedom, they imply that man is incapable of choosing between alternative courses of action. In the language of Freud, he "is being lived." Forces over which he has no control completely dominate everything he does. An extremely interesting reason is given for this assumption. Human acts must be the product of inexorable natural laws similar to those controlling the behavior of atoms; if it were not so, a rigorous science of man could not exist. If man were able to exert even a minimal influence over events in his life, accurate prediction of behavior would be impossible even in theory. Psychology as a science must have for its subject man who is as "lawful" as inanimate objects.

The contrasting viewpoint of humanistic psychology is one that most positivists would approve in other circumstances. Science must begin with reality. Its constructs and methods of investigation should be dictated, not by predetermined official policy, but by the nature of the objects under investigation. To assume that man is incapable of self-determination and then to control out as irrelevant all contrary evidence, as most positivists appear to do, can lead to only one conclusion regardless of the merits of the case.

One test of any assumption is to see where it leads if it is accepted as true. On this score determinism raises an insuperable difficulty for the scientist. How is research work possible unless the experimenter can choose to do whatever the situation calls for? Decisions about research design, the variables to be controlled, and other precautions are too important to be entrusted to irrelevant impulses or the blind effects of previous conditioning to which determinists must attribute even their own behavior. Intelligence would be of little utility to the scientist without the power of execution. Knowing what to do is not enough: he must also be able to do it, and he must be able to choose consciously and intelligently what to do.

How society as we know it could exist in a world of fully determined human beings is difficult to imagine. A scaled-down version would resemble the community life of an ant hill where each individual performs his preassigned task, not because he understands the master plan or has any choice in the matter, but because he is driven by impulse. Coleman [1] observes that while most animals come equipped with "built-in" adjustive mechanisms, man has few if any instinctive patterns. He must rely upon superior intelligence and reason in adapting his behavior to the demands of the moment. His unique mental gifts create a unique problem—that of choice and self-direction. Even in a Utopia like *Walden II*, some voluntary decisions based on the weighing of evidence would be necessary to regulate the behavior of other residents.

The concept of positive law is meaningful only if man exerts some measure of control over his actions. Personal responsibility is the correlate of freedom of choice. No man may choose to grow tall, nor is he held accountable for the consequences of his growth; but because he can choose to avoid deliberate injury to others, he is expected to do so.

The psychologist who accepts determinism as a methodological assumption in the laboratory necessarily lives according to an opposite set of assumptions in practical, everyday affairs. At least, he gives no indication of going through a meaningless ritual in deciding whether to

[1] J. C. Coleman. *Personality dynamics and effective behavior.* Chicago: Scott, Foresman, 1960. P. 6.

buy a house, to ask for a raise, or to get married. As a therapist he seems far more concerned about the illusion of unfreedom rather than freedom. The compulsive patient who comes for treatment complains of being a helpless spectator of his own behavior. From time to time he is seized by an irresistible impulse to carry out certain irrational actions regardless of his own wishes in the matter. It is precisely because he "is being lived" that he considers himself ill.

Mailloux [2] finds no cause for concern about self-determined behavior. Anyone choosing one course of action rather than another because it seems appropriate is likely to behave more "lawfully" than if he is coerced by needs, drives, and other nonrational motives. Only if he is free is he *capable* of acting reasonably.

[2] J. Mailloux. Psychic determinism and personality. *Canad. J. Psychol.*, 1955, **9**, 133–143.

Editor's Note

Some of the conclusions psychologists reach have but little relevance to everyday living. The "self concept" of few people is profoundly influenced by the relative superiority of one method of rote learning over another. Not so with the answer to the question, "Am I capable of making deliberate choices, or is freedom an illusion?" One's attitude toward personal responsibility, ego-development, and society in general hinges on his reply. Perhaps this query should be addressed to the philosopher from the beginning, but sooner or later every psychologist is forced to take a stand on it.

5. Conflicting Views of Man's Basic Nature *

James C. Coleman
University of California

Active or Reactive

In his everyday life man has always operated on the assumption that he is free to make decisions and choose his own course of action, at least within certain limits. Yet many philosophers, theologians, and scientists have raised the question of whether this freedom of action is *real* or merely *illusory*—whether man is in fact an active and responsible agent with "free will" or a puppet whose behavior is determined by forces beyond his control.

Determinism in philosophy, religion, and science

Various kinds and degrees of determinism have been argued since ancient times. The great dramatic tragedies of Aeschylus and Sophocles, for example, are pervaded by the ancient Greek belief that man, for all his nobility, is in the last analysis a pawn of fate. There is an inevitability in his action, an end from which he cannot escape. This fatalism is clearly illustrated in the well-known legend of Oedipus,

* From J. C. Coleman. *Personality dynamics and effective behavior.* Chicago: Scott, Foresman, 1960. Pp. 32–35. Reprinted with permission of the author and publisher.

who in trying to avoid fulfilling the oracle's prophecy that he would kill his father and marry his mother turned headlong into fate's trap and unwittingly did as was prophesied. The Calvinist doctrine of predestination, which holds that at the time of his birth every individual has already been elected to salvation or condemned to damnation, is a more modern example of religious or philosophic determinism.

Modern science is also concerned with the problem of determinism. In the field of atomic physics, some investigators have concluded that the inner workings of atoms obey simple and exact laws, and they reason that if we could make measurements with infinite accuracy, we could predict the future in every conceivable detail. Others feel that there is a certain amount of indeterminism, or "freedom," in the inner workings of atoms which makes it possible to predict only within certain degrees of probability and hence makes strict determinism untenable.

In the field of psychology, modern determinists have taken their lead from the seventeenth-century English philosopher John Locke, who concluded that the human mind at birth is a *tabula rasa,* or blank tablet, on which learning and experience write their script, giving the mind its content and structure. This view of man as an essentially passive, reactive organism is exemplified by the behaviorist school of psychology. In its most extreme form behaviorism has regarded the individual as a sort of mental robot, the helpless pawn of whatever influences happen to shape him. Thus, the very concepts of self-determination and freedom of choice are illusory; consciousness itself is regarded as only a by-product of "real" events—neurological processes—and thus is assumed to have no power to influence behavior.

Although behaviorists today do not necessarily hold to a strict determinism, American psychologists have by and large favored the view of man as a reactive organism. For evidence they have pointed to the diverse customs and habits of peoples throughout the world, all shaped by cultural conditioning. They have emphasized the experimental findings that the beliefs and values of people can be manipulated by society through punishment and reward and that suggestion and imitation are important forces shaping man's values and opinions. Particular emphasis has been given to the importance of early conditioning as the basis on which subsequent conditioned reactions are built. Recent findings on the effects of subliminal stimulation—or "hidden advertising"—in eliciting desires and action have seemed to lend some further support to a deterministic view of human behavior.

Man viewed as active and purposive

There is, however, another important school of psychological thought that looks upon man as a purposive and striving creature, continuously engaged in the meaningful activities of choosing, judging, and organizing. While acknowledging that human behavior is influenced by the individual's culture, this school of thought emphasizes that a personal factor also operates—that there is a subjective side of culture. Thus the effect of external stimuli on individual behavior is always partially determined by the way the individual views his group, by his ability to accept some ideas and reject others, by his tendency to behave in ways which are consistent with his concept of himself, and by his ability to objectify his experience and to be critical of his own values—to be self-aware and to strive for self-enhancement and self-growth.

This viewpoint, of course, is more consistent with our subjective experience of having freedom to evaluate and choose than is the behaviorist view of man as a purely reactive organism. The American clergyman Harry Emerson Fosdick [1] sees the issue as a question of response as opposed to reaction:

[1] H. E. Fosdick. *On being a real person.* New York: Harper & Row, 1943. P. 7. Quotation reprinted with permission.

> Things act under the influence of stimuli; they may even be said to *react* to stimuli, but persons can *respond*. Reaction is mechanical, while response is personal, and the endeavors of materialists to reduce the latter to the former are unconvincing because in actual experience the two are so radically different. Billiard balls react; persons can do more. A sneeze is a reaction, but the triumphant answers which some personalities make to life's difficult situations cannot be convincingly subsumed under such a category. Socrates' reply to his judges was not a sneeze, but a response.

The view of man as having a large potential for freedom also ties in with our approach to government—the democratic conviction that the average man, given access to the "facts," can evaluate public issues with some degree of objectivity and rationality rather than as a robot conditioned to think and behave in certain ways. We assume that the freedom granted by democracy to the individual to make decisions is not just an illusion. The view of man as free and active is likewise basic to our philosophy of education, with its emphasis upon developing young adults capable of rational problem solving, creativity, and critical evaluation and with its premise that the more information the individual has at his disposal, the more likely he is to choose and behave wisely.

An eminent American psychologist, Gordon Allport,[2] points up the need for psychology and the other behavioral sciences to come to grips with the problem of man's apparent freedom for self-direction:

> One may look through a hundred successive American books in psychology and find no mention of "will" or "fredom." It is customary for the psy-

[2] G. W. Allport. *Becoming: Basic considerations for a philosophy of personality*. New Haven, Conn.: Yale, 1955. Pp. 82–83, 100, 101. Reprinted with permission of the author and publisher.

> chologist, as for other scientists, to proceed within the framework of strict determinism, and to build barriers between himself and common sense lest common sense infect psychology with its belief in freedom. For the same reason barriers are erected against theology. But to our discomfort recent events have raised the issue all over again. Existentialism insists on freedom; much of the psychotherapy now in vogue presupposes it; psychology's new concern with values is at bottom a concern with choices, and therefore revives the problem of freedom. (Pp. 82–83.)

Allport (p. 100) later goes on to discuss the question of free will versus determinism as it relates to the problems of democracy:

> Up to now the "behavioral sciences," including psychology, have not provided us with a picture of man capable of creating or living in a democracy. These sciences in large part have imitated the billiard ball model of physics, now of course outmoded. They have delivered into our hands a psychology of an "empty organism," pushed by drives and molded by environmental circumstances. What is small and partial, what is external and mechanical, what is early, what is peripheral and opportunistic—have received the chief attention of psychological system builders. But the theory of democracy requires also that man possess a measure of rationality, a portion of freedom, a generic conscience, [personal] ideals, and unique value. We cannot defend the ballot box or liberal education, nor advocate free discussion and democratic institutions, unless man has the potential capacity to profit therefrom. . . .
>
> Curiously enough, many of the ardent adherents to the "empty organism" theory of human nature are among the most zealous fighters for democracy. No paradox is more striking than that of the scientist who as citizen makes one set of psychological

> assumptions and in his laboratory and writings makes opposite assumptions respecting the nature of man.

Allport is not advocating, of course, that our democratic ideals should dictate our scientific findings. Rather, he is pointing out that psychologists, in their efforts to be rigorously scientific, have often tended to concern themselves with relatively peripheral and fragmentary phenomena that happen to be amenable to objective and controlled scientific investigation. The result has been to focus scientific attention on those aspects of behavior which can be explained in terms of conditioned responses. This, in turn, has produced a deterministic view of man and tended to obscure the fact that, in real life, people do not seem to function entirely as reactive organisms. Much of human behavior, certainly, *is* determined by conditioning: our opinions, values, and ways of behaving all reflect the experiences we have had and thus the culture in which we live. But this does not seem to tell the whole story. Man is also creative and purposeful.

In maintaining that man is active as well as reactive, we are once again talking about the way man's inner nature tends to work under "normal" conditions—conditions that allow the individual adequate freedom to develop and use his inner potentialities. According to this viewpoint, an autocratic culture which seeks to indoctrinate its members with a uniform value orientation and political viewpoint may be regarded as a "pathological" condition under which man's inner tendencies toward self-direction are considerably thwarted. That such efforts have never been wholly or lastingly successful may be evidence that they are counter to an inborn characteristic of the human energy system—to evaluate rather than just to react mechanically.

Fortunately, modern psychology is gradually developing the scientific tools for tackling the complex problems of values, "free will," and purpose. The results of this broadened research are gradually leading to the emergence of a more realistic picture of man as "endowed with a sufficient margin of reason, autonomy, and choice to profit from living in a free society" (Allport, 1955, p. 101).

Editor's Note

The existence of unconscious motivation which can influence behavior without being recognized as the outgrowth of ulterior purposes seems too well established to need further comment. A curious paradox arises, however, when we ask ourselves how a person can act freely without fully understanding his motives.

Nuttin shows that the unconscious source of an impulse to act presents no special problem as long as it does not absorb the person's attention to the point of making him act automatically without considering alternative solutions. What is important in decision making is the "felt-value" of the motive and the way it influences behavior, not where it comes from. In extreme cases an unconscious motive may rob an act of freedom; at other times it merely causes something to appear unusually attractive or repulsive.

6. The Unconscious and Freedom *

Joseph Nuttin
University of Louvain

Having presented the doctrine of the unconscious and shown the influence it has had on the psychological view of man, it remains for us to consider our central problem: to what extent is the influence of unconscious factors on conduct compatible with a belief in *the freedom of human acts*?

1. Post-hypnotic Suggestion

To begin with, let us consider the hypnotic phenomena, from the consideration of which Freud's ideas

* From *Psychoanalysis and Personality* by Joseph Nuttin, Copyright 1953, © 1962, Sheed & Ward Inc., New York.

concerning the influence of the unconscious on conduct began.

Acts performed during hypnosis are not particularly relevant to our problem; for these acts do not form part of normal behaviour. But it is known that a hypnotized person, *after* coming out of a trance—and therefore back *into a normal state of consciousness*—may perform acts ordered during the trance, and do this without knowing that he is obeying an order.

These are cases of post-hypnotic suggestion, a phenomenon studied particularly at the school in Nancy. Here is how the director, Dr. Bernheim, describes it:

> The patient heard what I said to him while he was in the trance, but he remembers nothing about it, not even that I spoke to him. The suggested idea comes back into his mind when he wakes up; having forgotten where it came from, he believes it to be original. Facts of this kind have been proved by Bertrand, General Noiset, Dr. Liébault and Charles Richet. I have tried them out successfully again and again and am convinced that the people concerned are telling the truth.
>
> At eleven o'clock I suggested to C. that at one o'clock in the afternoon he would be seized by an irresistible desire to go all the way up Stanislas Street and back again, twice. At one o'clock I saw him come out into the street, walk from one end to the other, and then come back again, stopping in front of the shop-windows as though he was just taking a stroll.[1]

The phenomenon can be taken as established. It has been studied experimentally and checked both for its length and for its effectiveness. An order given during hypnosis may not only be obeyed immediately after the person con-

[1] Cf. Bernheim, *De la suggestion* (2nd ed., Paris, Doin, 1888), pp. 45 and 47.

cerned has wakened up; it may remain efficacious for many days and even for weeks afterwards.

For what concerns us, it must be assumed that the given order stays in existence *unconsciously* in the individual. Imagination of the act and the need to perform it rise into consciousness at a set moment, *but the source of the image and the need remains unconscious.* The act is performed as though it were a spontaneous achievement of the person himself.

It seems doubtful whether such an act, arising from the unconscious, can be called free, and, if this is so, whether any form of unconscious influence on action is compatible with freedom of behaviour.

The first important fact to realize when faced with this question is that *suggestions made during hypnosis are not invariably carried out.* Some authors have asserted the contrary and said that post-hypnotic suggestion is accomplished necessarily and invariably.

Thus Liébault, and after him Beaunis, declares, "One characteristic of actions performed a long time after the suggestion has been made is that the urge to do them seems to the individual to come from his own initiative; whereas in reality he goes towards his object under the influence of a decision which he has been made to take with the fatality of a falling stone, not as a result of that controlled and intentional effort which is the source of all our reasonable actions." "In short," adds Beaunis, "he thinks himself free but he is not free. This is a 'direct hit' at the argument for free will which is drawn from our *feeling* of freedom." [2]

If this were so, post-hypnotic phenomena would provide an illustration of Spinoza's maxim. For Spinoza, our consciousness of freedom is simply ignorance of the causes that make us act.

It seems quite certain that in *abnormal* cases such

[2] Cf. J. Morand, *Hypnotisme et Suggestion* (Paris, 1889), pp. 322–323. [Footnotes have been renumbered.]

as hysteria and abulia, post-hypnotic suggestion produces its effect quite automatically, despite the occasional feeling of spontaneity and freedom. Beaunis himself stipulates one condition, to ensure the accomplishment of suggestion: the individual must have been frequently hypnotized by the same person. But this, as is well known, means a weakening in the force of resistance.

And it is quite certain that in some cases the individual fights hard against performing the act, when it goes against strong tendencies. Thus Bernheim admits, as Charcot has also admitted:

> The effect of post-hypnotic suggestion is not absolutely a matter of fate; some people fight against it. . . . Here are a few examples. . . . To young G. I suggest that when he wakes up he must stand on the table. When he wakes up he looks at the table but he does not get up on to it. The desire to do so is no doubt there but respect for the people present gives him the strength to overcome the desire.[3]

Another case quoted by Bernheim brings out very clearly the inner conflict that can take place in the individual:

> One day I told one of my hypnotized patients, a girl, to kiss one of the men on duty when she woke up. As soon as she woke up she went up to him and took hold of his hand; then she hesitated and looked round, seeming embarrassed by the attention that was being paid to her. She remained like this for a few moments, with an anxious look on her face, obviously experiencing the acutest distress. When she was questioned, she finally confessed that she wanted to kiss Mr. X but that she could never bring herself to behave so improperly.[4]

[3] Cf. Bernheim, *De la suggestion*, pp. 52–53.
[4] This case is quoted from Dr. J . S. Morand, *Hypnotisme et Suggestion* (Paris, Garnier, 1889), p. 320.

2. The Unconscious Source of Normal Needs

There are then three main points established by the study of post-hypnotic phenomena. First, the individual *experiences a conscious inclination* to perform an action. Second, this inclination emanates in actual fact from *psychic contents which are not conscious* (for example, from an order given previously), and the act which is performed rises from these unconscious contents. Third, the individual may, or may not, give way to his inclination.

The crucial point is this, that the inclination—and consequently the behaviour—*has an unconscious source,* i.e. derives from an *unconscious* order.

Now an analysis of human behavior soon reveals that it is not at all unusual for an inclination to arise or start from the unconscious layers of the personality. Most of our tendencies and natural needs—hunger, thirst, sex—have their source in unconscious biological states of the organism. From these dynamisms a single thing emerges into consciousness: at a fixed moment, and in pursuance of the satisfaction of a need, we feel drawn or driven to perform an act whose image rises up in our mind. The source or basis of this desire is not immediately given to consciousness. Or, again, we may be mistaken about the source of our desires. What we take to be our real motives for being attracted towards a certain object may merely be pretexts for justifying our behaviour. The real source of a tendency can often only be discovered by scientific research into its antecedents and the factors which brought it into existence.

From this comparison with the process of normal need it should be clear that in both cases the problem of the unconscious is the same. Nevertheless there is an interesting difference between the two processes. In post-hypnotic suggestion it is a forgotten *psychic content*—the command or order received—which is the unconscious source of the image and need which rise up in the individual; whereas in natural needs the inclination emanates fundamentally from *physiological states* of the organism itself. Neither, however, is in itself *directly or fundamentally conscious*. Notice, finally, that the problem is the same both for Freud's dynamic unconscious and for post-hypnotic suggestion. In both cases unconscious psychic contents are the starting-point for images and inclinations which rise up into consciousness. And, as we have shown, it was in post-hypnotic phenomena that Freud found the prototype of his active unconscious.

3. Freedom and Tendencies Rising from the Unconscious

We have now to inquire whether facts such as these can be reconciled with activity that can properly be called free. But what exactly is the process known as a free act?

The fact that we are impelled by a certain need—which has its own *source*—towards such and such a form of behaviour, does not mean that the act is not free. It is not so much the *source* of the need, conscious or unconscious, that interests us, as the *felt need itself* and *the way it influences* behaviour.

When behaving freely, in fact, the individual takes up an attitude towards the different elements of "value"—the motives—which are *actually being lived* in the given situation, i.e. are being experienced. The "attractive power" or value of each motive depends on the power of the *aspirations and impulses which are being experienced at the moment*. The ultimate source of these aspirations and impulses does not come into it, either into any scrutiny of the motives or into the attitude which the individual may adopt towards them. In other words, *it is to the extent that they are actually "felt" that the "motives" are to be considered as forces influencing freedom of action*. Ignorance of their source does not alter the case at all.

Whether the act is free or determined will therefore depend on the way the dynamic factors which the individual experiences within himself release the activity. The act will *not* be free when the "motives" or motive forces cause a reaction which is like a link in a chain, materially determined by natural processes. On the other hand there *will be* a free act when the individual *faces motives as value-elements which he recognizes intellectually without being completely absorbed by them;* for in this case, in an act of full self-possession he transcends the impression or the attraction experienced *hic et nunc* and consents to motives to which *he himself gives a value, according to the concrete system of values which makes up his own personality.*

From this it should be clear, then, that because a certain act arises from an unconscious dynamic source, this does not raise any *special problem* as regards its freedom. As with all other acts, the freedom or necessity depends on whether the dynamism behind the act has developed and acted on the volitional level. This depends on whether the individual *transcends* the actual impression he experiences or is simply "affected" by it. The question whether this volitional level of activity exists in man, whether there is a certain element of freedom—i.e., volition—involved in human conduct, does not arise here. It is a question for philosophical psychology, and outside the scope of this treatise. Here it is sufficient to have shown that no *new* problem is raised by the fact that certain tendencies *derive from the unconscious.*

As we have said, there seem to be a great number of acts, arising out of unconscious tendencies or suggestions, which are *not* performed *automatically.* It can even happen that a person *fails to* perform the act he has been told to perform because of a tendency to respect propriety or the conventions. Occasionally, again, a compromise will be reached and the patient will simply shake hands with someone he has been told to kiss. In some cases, however, it really does seem as though certain acts—especially those performed as a result of post-hypnotic suggestion—can actually be performed just like so many *automatic reactions.* This is particularly true of certain hysterical and abulic cases which have been interestingly described by Janet.

Janet maintains that for some patients the performance of a voluntary act demands considerably more effort than the act of obeying a post-hypnotic suggestion. He maintains, for instance, that a woman patient suffering from abulia and lacking the willpower to perform a certain act which she had been asked to do, performed the same act without any effort as the result of an unconscious suggestion. After hypnotizing this patient Janet said to her: "When I knock on the table, take this hat and hang it on a peg." He goes on.

> I woke her up. A little later I called her, as though I wanted her to do something for me. "Would you mind taking this hat? It is getting in my way while I am writing. Hang it up on the peg, will you?" "Of course I will," she replied. She tried to get up, shook herself and stretched out her arms, but her movements were uncoordinated, so she sat down; then she stood up again. This went on for twenty minutes. Then I knocked on the table. Immediately she got up, took hold of the hat, hung it up, and went and sat down again. The action had been done by suggestion in a moment; she had not been able to do it by an effort of will in twenty minutes.[5]

In cases of this kind the suggestion seems to act rather like a force of impulse and lead directly to the action without any interference from the individual concerned.

This kind of unconscious behaviour does not present any *special* problems either: such examples can be classed with ordinary automatic actions.

[5] Cf. Pierre Janet, *Médications Psychologiques* (Paris, Alcan, 1925), I, p. 226. Quotation reprinted with permission of George Allen & Unwin, Ltd., London, Copyright holder of the English edition.

The conclusion seems to be that as regards this question everything depends on the psychic equilibrium of the person concerned. When he has no will at all—i.e., when the psychic powers do not appear at the volitional level—the dynamism roused by an unconscious order is released automatically or impulsively in behaviour. But when the individual is normally balanced and has the normal psychic powers, *the tendency roused by suggestion does not have any different effect on behaviour from that of any of man's other tendencies which arise either from biochemical or physiological factors or ultimately, even, from cosmic forces.*

Editor's Note

Personality development as a form of learning is a product of self-activity. Other persons in the individual's life space may create conditions favorable or unfavorable to learning, but he alone can fashion the image and expression of the innermost self we call personality. In the process of making significant choices, he either transforms himself into the kind of person he plans to be or prepares the way for less conscious patterns of behavior. Either alternative implies some psychological responsibility for what he is now and what, by dint of personal effort, he may still become.

7. On Choice and Responsibility in a Humanistic Psychotherapy *

Maurice Kahn Temerlin
University of Oklahoma

In clinical practice most psychotherapists use the concept of free choice and personal responsibility; unless the patient is psychotic and institutionalized, he is expected to make his own choices and decisions and to be responsible for his overt behavior. Even Freud (1949), although

* From M. K. Temerlin. On choice and responsibility in a humanistic psychotherapy. *J. humanistic psychol.*, 1963, **3**(1), 35–48. Reprinted with permission of author and publisher.

a strict determinist *in theory*, spoke of therapeutic practice as an attempt "to give the patient's ego *freedom* to choose one way or the other." (Italics his.) Thus Freud implicitly used the concept of personal responsibility because one is held accountable for the consequences of his choices. In spite of this use of the concept of personal responsibility in therapeutic practice, scientific theories of personality and of psychotherapy are based upon psychological determinism.

Psychoanalytic theory, for example, is strictly deterministic in the sense that behavior is assumed to be lawful and caused. Specific acts and experiences, as well as behavior in general, are assumed to be related causally to antecedent conditions. The view of man which emerges from the theory is essentially mechanistic, for he is seen as a creature who always responds to the present and the future in terms of historical determinants, propelled inexorably by a multiplicity of drives, motives, and impulses from within, in conjunction with the harsh demands of reality from without. Human experience and behavior are compromises, effects of competing and complexly interrelated causes. This picture of man, however, approaches the scientific ideal because behavior is caused and ultimately predictable to the extent that all the determinants and their relative magnitudes can be known. In such a system there is no freedom, no spontaneity, no novelty, and no emergent uniqueness, except as epiphenomena—that is, as effects of highly infrequent arrangements of determinants.

Consider, for example, Knight's (1946) classic article on freedom and determinism. In exploring the paradox between the common human experience of freedom to choose and the concept of psychic determinism, Knight begins by considering determinism and free will to be mutually exclusive. He then seems unable to abandon the conceptual methodology of the physical sciences or to adapt such methods to capture the meaning and often ambivalent nature of phenomenological data, and he concludes wholeheartedly in favor of determinism as the exclusive principle governing human behavior. The freedom to make choices experienced by the human being, says Knight, "has nothing whatever to do with free will as a principle governing human behavior but is a subjective experience which is itself causally determined." This conclusion, that the experience of freedom to choose is a causally determined illusion, has found a nearly unanimous acceptance among psychoanalysts and is the dominant notion among all psychotherapists trained in the behavioristic or positivistic tradition (Knight, 1946; Wheelis, 1956). Yet, this position is incompatible with the data, the methods, and the goals of a humanistic psychotherapy. It is inconsistent with the data of such a psychotherapy because most people verbalize the experience of free choice, at least in many contexts; it is incompatible with the methods of a humanistic psychotherapy, for psychotherapeutic practice implicitly assumes that the patient is or can become the active agent in selecting and controlling—i.e., in "choosing"—his own overt behavior; and it is inconsistent with the goals of such a psychotherapy for these are often defined as freedom to choose and to select and to control one's own behavior efficaciously, in terms of its consequences.

The purpose of this paper, then, is to examine experience as verbalized in a humanistic psychotherapy without an a priori commitment either to determinism or to free will; to ascertain the extent to which determinism and free will are concepts descriptive of experience as verbalized in psychotherapy; and to note the conditions under which the experience of determinism and choice occurs for different kinds of people, without regard to whether or not such experiences are, in fact, free or determined. When this phenomenological study of free will and determinism in psychotherapy is completed, three concepts crucial to psychotherapy—free association, transference, and self-hatred—are discussed in terms of choice and personal responsibility. First, however, it is necessary to define a humanistic psychotherapy.

Humanistic psychotherapy is the kind of psychotherapy exemplified in the writings of Maslow, May, Rogers, Fromm, Whitaker and Malone, Colm, and many other. Although there are differences in the therapeutic theories of these writers, their conceptions have a common tendency to de-emphasize such medical analogies as symptom reduction, cure, or "adjustment." Rather, the primary aim of such a therapy is to help the individual become the best possible version of himself as a human being, as defined essentially by his own values, aspirations, and limitations. The concern is with increasing individuality, with being one's self, and the frame of reference is neither normative nor statistical, for the average man seems neither content, whole, productive, nor at peace with himself. Instead, the goals are defined as what a particular man might become under optimum conditions for him.

The implicit value judgments in such a psychotherapy are that, ideally, man "should" be free to organize and to control his own behavior; that man "should" be at peace with himself and, if possible, with his fellow man; that he "should" enjoy life; that his pleasure and satisfaction are better than suffering; that his individuality is a basic given; and that his selfhood, individuality, and autonomy are better than human standardization and mechanization.

Such a psychotherapy is phenomenologically oriented, for it accepts as basic data the immediate experience of the patient, with only a passing glance at the congruence of the experience with external events. It considers experience itself real in the sense of having effects upon behavior, whether or not the experience is congruent with external reality. And finally it values the capacity for experience and attempts to increase the person's tolerance for experience.

Given this framework, to view the feeling of freedom to choose as a causally determined illusion is to impose upon the data an assumption which, however necessary in the physical sciences, is simply not descriptive of the majority of experience reported in psychotherapy. Neither patient nor therapist, for example, feels himself to be inescapably bound by deterministic forces beyond his wish or control; if such were the case there would be no point to therapuetic effort. Determinism thus contributes nothing to the understanding of the experience of freedom qua experience; it simply labels it an illusion. Nor does a strict determinism recognize that the experience of choice is often followed by changes in behavior, and that what Knight seems to depreciate as the "illusion of choice" may be one of the most important experiences in psychotherapy in the sense of preceding significant changes in overt behavior. It is also possible that a strict adherence to determinism on the part of the therapist may set an a priori limit to the progress of the client by prejudging and thus depreciating his capacity to organize, control, and select his own behavior.

If the therapist accepts the possibility of free choice and personal responsibility—at least in some contexts—he remains consistent with the data of experience as expressed in therapy as well as with the exigencies of most therapeutic practice. Theoretical commitments notwithstanding, few, if any, therapists act in practice as if an absolute determinism applied. Determinism views the patient as the helpless victim of fate past, present, or future, while an effective psychotherapist programmatically emphasizes the patient's potentialities for organizing and controlling his own behavior in the present and in the future, *regardless of the past.* Indeed, freedom and responsibility in a humanistic therapy may be considered a programmatic assumption in direct analogy to the programmatic assumption of determinism by science. A psychotherapy based exclusively upon determinism runs the risk of entrapping both therapist and patient in a search for causes which were operating in the patient's past, and it is quite possible that overemphasizing past determinants may have two antitherapeutic consequences: first, it may subvert psychotherapy from a dynamic emotional experience in the present to a passive intellectual consideration of the past; second, by overemphasizing causes operant in the past, it may do violence to the patient's capacities for organizing and controlling his own behavior in the present (Mazer, 1960).

There is little doubt that determinism is useful in science. Without it there would be limited predictability, and without predictability there could be no control. Indeed, there are areas in psychotherapy in which determinism is a useful idea for the same reason. Freud, for example, was led by determinism to consider interpersonal accidents, slips of the tongue, and the symbolism of dreams as motivated (determined) and thus meaningful through causal explanation. The argument here is not with determinism as a programmatic assumption of science, but with a total commitment to determinism on the part of the therapist. For, unlike scientific goals, the goals of a humanistic psychotherapy are neither predictability nor control. In fact, the more successful psychotherapy is, the less predictable the individual becomes, because his rigidity is reduced and his spontaneity and creativity are increased. Similarly, the more successful a psychotherapy oriented toward humanistic change, the more independent of external and environmental control the individual becomes (Maslow, 1961). Also, the therapist who is totally committed to determinism may fail to note conditions under which the experience of choice occurs, and changes in behavior which follow this experience. And he may also fail to see the subtle manipulations of responsibility which occur in much human interaction, particularly in the therapeutic hour.

Personal Responsibility as Subjective Experience

Personal responsibility, as a subjective experience rather than as a legal or moral concept, refers to a state of consciousness in which the individual holds himself accountable for his own actions. Usually, the behavior for which a person holds himself responsible is experienced by him as an expression of himself and his own wishes; he sees himself as the active agent in his own behavior. As contrasted to determinism, which is experienced as a compulsion to behave in a particular way, the experience of personal responsibility means that, in the past, the individual felt himself free to do what he now holds himself responsible for. Conversely, whenever the individual experiences his behavior as a causally determined consequence of forces beyond his personal wish or control, he usually does not consider himself responsible. Thus, the relationship between personal responsibility and the experience of free choice is intimate: without a prior feeling of freedom to choose between alternatives, the individual does not view himself as responsible.

A sense of personal responsibility, then, seems to follow the experience of free choice. The sequence raises the question: What experiences precede a feeling of free choice? At the experiential level, choice depends upon an experience of self, or of personal identity. To choose implies an identity, a sense of self or "I," *a person* who chooses in terms of his own thoughts or wishes. Choice requires a chooser. In a fundamental way, the very existence of the self in experience is affirmed by its choices. Diagnostically speaking, a man is usually defined either by his choices or by the techniques he uses to avoid making choices. For example, the man who chooses to hoard his surplus money rather than to spend it, to marry a career woman rather than a housewife, to study law rather than engineering, to stay in bed on Sunday morning rather than to go to church, is defined quite differently from his neighbor who chooses the opposite course of action. To consider the extreme case, the man who lacks the experience of being able to choose, as in psychosis, has lost a large part of his potentiality for selfhood. The point is that the experience of choice requires a sense of self; reciprocally, the exercise of choice is an affirmation of selfhood. "Man is never more human than at the moment of decision," as Tillich put it.

Choice which is not an expression of the self's own values and wishes, for example "choice" forced upon the individual by external circumstances, is really not choice, since it is not experienced as a free preference of the self. It may, in such case, be a decision or a "forced choice," but it is not followed by the experience of personal responsibility. The individual usually avoids responsibility for his behavior in these contexts by such maneuvers as: "I had to do it; I could not help making that choice or behaving that way." "I was only trying to do the right thing." "Everyone else was doing it." Or, "They made me do it."

The Anxieties of Responsibility

Freedom to choose is the immediate precursor of responsibility, for interpersonal life holds one accountable for what he chooses, not, ordinarily, for what he is forced to do. Thus, to avoid responsibility one in effect says: "I had no choice." For patients who do not have a clear and stable sense of self, or who suffer from what Eriksen calls identity-diffusion, freedom to choose produces anxiety because such people cannot select alternative patterns of behavior in terms of personal preferences. For example, when a person with an unstable or diffuse sense of self is faced with making a decision, he usually asks, "What should I do?" If the friend, parent, or therapist now answers: "Why don't you do what you want to do?" The reply usually is: "But I don't know what I want."

The identity of the patient deeply involved in psychotherapy is always in a state of flux, and observations of his search for identity illustrate well the anxieties associated with choice making. Each time the client makes a fundamental choice, there is the possibility of his self-affirmation, his growth, and his development; yet, on each occasion there is also the possibility that the consequences of his choices will define him in a negative way. Thus anxiety is engendered because anxiety is the experience of the possibility of real or phenomenological self-destruction (May, Angel, and Ellenberger, 1958). This anxiety, characteristic of the experience of most people, is far greater when the individual with an unstable sense of self becomes involved in making personal choices, for he anticipates that a negative definition of himself will be reflected in his choices. Indeed, he may even feel that responsibility for his behavior might actually destroy him, phenomenologically. Two examples are these: "If they really knew what I was like (by knowing my personal choices), they would despise me." Or, "If I were to do what *I really* want to do, what would they think of me?"

It is for these reasons that the most common defenses against anxiety in this culture are behaviors which reduce one's choices and personal responsibilities. As examples, consider such behaviors as: living in compulsive adherence to an externalized morality; blind conformity; intellectualistically considering all possibilities, but expressing no personal preference; an uncritical deference to authority; passivity; and the like.

From this phenomenological point of view, the patterns of defense in Freudian theory may be seen as techniques of avoiding the anxieties of choice and personal responsibility. If an individual through repression, for example, is unaware of his wishes, he is not in his own eyes responsible for the consequences of "choices" made in conformity with those wishes. For example, it is not uncommon to observe a repressed woman who is sexually provocative or even promiscuous without awareness, choice, or responsibility ("I simply can't understand why I went to bed with him—I certainly didn't want to"). Similarly, if one through projection experiences his own wishes as those of another, he is not in his eyes responsible, for he did not choose the course of his action ("It was his fault, not mine"). If one, with the aid of rationalization, intellectualistically considers all possible alternatives, or if he obsessively doubts everything, he is not held responsible, for he has no *personal* preference. Or, to take a final example, if one is defensively passive, he need not experience the anxieties of choice because others, or fate, or time will make his decisions for him.

At a level descriptive of naïve experiences, defenses do not protect against unconscious content as such, but against the personal ownership of certain experiences. To consider defenses as a means of avoiding responsibility in this way is consistent with the verbal production of many patients, particularly obsessionals or borderline psychotics, who verbalize the content of awareness while they simultaneously avoid responsibility for what is said. An obsessive young man, attempting to free associate for the first time, illustrated this process by saying: "Thoughts just went through the mind, but they were not my thoughts—should I say them anyway?" Any defense, regardless of its explicit verbal content, seems based upon an implicit reference to personal responsibility which rarely is made explicit in a deterministic system. Even in the case of repression, the most basic and least verbal ego defense, there is presupposed an implicit experience of personal responsibility as the motive for repression. There is no need to repress, or to avoid in any way, experiences which do not define, reflect, or affect the self. Repression is not an abstract force, but a decision: "I refuse to think about it!"

In sum, Freudian defenses against anxiety may be seen as attempts to defend the self by reducing the number of personal choices; for, since choices define the self, a threatened self may hide by expressing no choices. This means that in a humanistic psychotherapy oriented toward the wholeness of the personality the responsibility-avoiding function of defense needs to be thoroughly analyzed, for when defenses reduce responsibility and anxiety, the person pays a high price: a reduction of selfhood. The avoidance of responsibility reduces selfhood because the experience of personal responsibility affirms the very existence of the self. Without responsibility there is no self in the sense of an integrated and autonomous identity which can experience itself as having effects. Conversely, whenever the individual cannot experience choice and responsibility, he feels himself to be (and probably will act as) a robot or automaton whose behavior is causally determined not by himself, but by situational exigencies. A pawn of fate has neither responsibility, anxiety, nor selfhood.

Determinism and Choice as Descriptive of Experience

Whereas logically the concepts of determinism and free choice are mutually exclusive, it is possible in psychotherapeutic practice to observe that these concepts are in varying degrees descriptive of the characteristic experience of different kinds of people. Specifically, these concepts have a differential descriptive applicability to the characteristic experience of psychotics, neurotics, and persons completing successful psychotherapy or, by extension, well-functioning human beings.

The psychotic rarely may be observed to speak as if he experiences free choice. Determinism far more accurately describes his experience, for he usually speaks of his own behavior as if he felt it was caused by persons or forces beyond his own wish or control. These determinants to which the psychotic refers the responsibility for his behavior may be either internal or external, but in either case they represent forces described by him as determinants over which he exercises no personal control. For example, if asked why he behaved in a particular way, the psychotic will usually indicate, explicitly or implicitly, that other people or forces compelled him to behave as he did; rarely, if ever, will he say, "I behaved that way because I wanted to!" Even when the psychotic explains his behavior by reference to inner motives, he refers to his motives as if they were "foreign bodies" inside himself, but not aspects of himself as an identity. In this way he avoids responsibility by referring to internal determinants, and not his own choices. The classic example is the statement, "Something inside me, I don't know what, makes me act the way I do." The "something," of course, may refer to voices, hallucinative situations, evil, a delusional identification, or an introjected but not integrated parental image—to any internal variable, in short, except choice.

It is as if the same factors which made the individual psychotic in the first place also obliterated his choice-making abilities, or vice versa. This reduction of the capacity to experience choice and to make decisions exists phenomenologically whether the etiological factors in functional psychosis are conceptualized as massive anxiety (Arieti, 1955), a chaotic non-entity and a morass of false selves (Laing, 1960), or the result of a double-bind situation (Bateson *et al.*, 1956). In either case it seems typical of the psychotic that he avoids the experience of choice; with a highly fragmented selfhood, the responsibilities of personal choice are probably unendurable.

As the antithesis of psychotic, the well-functioning, whole, or psychologically healthy man—for example, the self-actualizing persons studied by Maslow (1954)—typically experiences his own behavior largely as a reflection of his own wishes. These people consciously make decisions and experience doing what they want to do. Of course, even with such well-functioning people, the experience of choice has certain existential limits such as the sequential categories of time, mortality, or the nature of physical reality, in which contexts determinism is felt. It seems that the sense of identity or selfhood of such people is sufficiently whole and clear to allow them to make choices and decisions in terms of personal preferences, and to allow them to perceive clearly the contexts of life in which it would be delusional to feel free choice.

For the above reasons it would seem that determinism is more adequately descriptive of the psychotic's experience than of the healthy man's; on the other hand, the concept of free choice more adequately describes the experience of the healthy man, for such persons tend to experience themselves as the active agents in choosing and selecting their own behavior, except, of course, when reality limits the experience of personal choice. At these times, determinism is experienced. Neurotics fall between these two extremes, with the most disorganized neurotics being those "borderline" persons who, to a great extent, experience their own behavior as a causally determined consequence of externalized determinants.

At the level of phenomenology it is, therefore, tempting to generalize that the experience of free choice is closely associated with the degree of wholeness or integration of the personality. The psychologically whole or healthy man and the psychotic seem to occupy opposite poles of a continuum, with the neurotic in the center, in terms of the extent to which free choice is experienced consistently. Verification of these observations would indicate that a central problem of psychopathology is the inability to make personal decisions and choices. Whether they accept a theoretical determinism or not, it is likely that, in the absence of such verification, most therapists already act in practice as if each sensible personal choice made by the neurotic or psychotic, and the assumption of any responsibility, represented at least some movement in the direction of integration, wholeness, and psychological health. Conversely, it is probably true that most humanistic psychotherapists intuitively consider each personal decision or choice made for the patient by the therapist a technical error—a result of authoritarian or narcissistic defects in the personality of the therapist, because it reduces the patient's implicit choice-making potentialities.

Neurosis as a Problem of Responsibility

Since both neurotic and psychotic persons tend to experience determinism rather than choice, their perception of the conditions under which choice may be experienced becomes distorted. Neither the neurotic nor the psychotic can differentiate clearly between those contexts in which it is possible to experience choice and to assume responsibility and those in which a strict determinism characterizes experience and behavior.

It is tempting to reason that the essence of neurosis lies in an inability to distinguish between one's personal freedoms and deterministic limits, because it is easy to achieve clinical verification for this observation: Even the most insightful neurotic, however rational he may be at a verbal level, is, in the actual conduct of his life, unable to make a clear distinction between his choices and responsibilities and those aspects of his interpersonal life for which he has no responsibility and over which he can exert no personal control. A careful look at the most typical neurotic conflicts will show that, at a phenomenological level, they consist of attempts to change, by an exercise of will and choice, situations, usually in the past, which are governed by a strict determinism, while simultaneously ignoring those contexts of life, usually in the present or future, in which the experience of free choice is possible.

Several classic examples of such neurotic struggles are these: hating and depreciating the self "because" of parental rejection; living in the past and continuing to hate the parents "who made me this way"; revolting against sexual identity; brooding obsessively about death; attempting to control the thoughts or behaviors of other people; denying one's self in an attempt to be "good" in order to force or cajole a reward from a fate indifferent to individual behavior; being "bad" as an attempt to punish other people or to deny the tender, more humanistic aspects of the self; attempting to change the past or entertaining unrealistic aspirations of controlling the future; obsessively fearing floods, tornadoes, or other natural phenomena; refusing to take cognizance of the inherent uncertainties of life; defining the self exclusively in terms of "What will other people think?" or "How will I look to them?" Regardless of differences in content, all these neurotic struggles represent attempts to control aspects of existence for which one has no personal responsibility and over which he can exercise no choice or control. Yet, the neurotic typically spends his life preoccupied with these or equivalent problems while he simultaneously takes far less responsibility for the only aspect of life which is inherently under his own control, and which offers him the experience of free choice—namely, his own behavior in the present or future. This raises the question, why does the neurotic not accept with grace those things which he cannot change, and devote himself to changing those painful aspects of his life which can be changed, and, through experience, developing the wisdom to know the difference? The answer, in large part, must be that continuing to act in neurotic and maladaptive ways is less threatening than experiencing the anxieties of responsibility described in an earlier section of this paper. That is, to experience one's self—and only one's self—as the active agent in his own behavior imposes a burden of responsibility and loneliness which the neurotic finds overwhelming.

Free Association

The neurotic's inability to distinguish his deterministic limits from situations in which the experience of choice is possible is one reason for his inability to free associate at the beginning of psychotherapy. Freud first made the observation that no patient could free associate at the beginning of treatment, even though he was highly motivated to do so and knew that the success of his psychotherapy depended upon it. Since Freud, this observation has been made by many therapists, confirmed by experimental evidence, and related to the individual's tolerance for his own experience (Temerlin, 1956). The neurotic is unable to free associate at the beginning of therapy because he assumes that he is responsible for what he thinks, feels, and remembers. When he attempts free association he cannot distinguish his overt behavior, for which the law, society, and the pragmatic exigencies of life require him to be responsible, from his inner experience and the verbalization of it, for which he explicitly is not held responsible. Even though he is explicitly not held responsible for his experience or the verbalization of it in the hour, the patient assumes that he is responsible, as is evident in these samples of initial attempts to free associate: "What I think is too trivial (or embarrassing, confused, etc.) to say out loud." "I'm afraid of losing control of my thoughts." "I cannot speak of this; you might think I was foolish." "If I just let go and say everything, what might I do?" Or, consider the patient who can only associate after the explicit assertion, "You put these thoughts in my mind." In other words, there is no need to avoid free association by controlling one's thoughts and feelings unless one feels responsible for them, or for their consequences, if any.

Since the neurotic considers himself responsible for his inner life, he cannot free associate even though, from the therapist's point of view, he need take no responsibility whatsoever for his experience. Experience is internal and private, and the capacity for experiencing is innately given as a part of being human; furthermore, and of particular importance, the free expression of experience has positive therapeutic value. Yet, it is typical of the neurotic to view himself as implicitly responsible for his experience while assuming far less responsibility for his behavior. Indeed, as stated earlier, the neurotic frequently experiences his behavior as being "caused" by external circumstances, his parent's behavior, or situational exigencies.

Free association is possible only after the person has tested and integrated the knowledge that he is not responsible for his experience or for his verbalization of it in the therapeutic hour; i.e., only after he discovers that, in relation to his therapist, he may relax his defenses (which means to cease anticipating personal responsibility). In a sense, free association is possible only when one surrenders to a determinism which permits thoughts, feelings, and memories to flow freely and uncritically into awareness and verbalization; i.e., when one is not responsible. Once the person has reached this point, he can begin to separate his inner experience, for which he is not responsible, and his overt behavior, for which he is responsible, and recognize that he, as a person, intervenes between experience and overt behavior and that he may select which ideas he will act upon and which he will not. This is a critical point in the therapeutic process, for, as a practical matter, one must organize and control—be responsible for—his overt behavior for effective interpersonal living. But he need not control his private thoughts and feelings or, indeed, accept any responsibility for his experience without paying a price in wasted energy and increased defensiveness. When the person in therapy can make these distinctions, he then may learn to choose between alternative courses of action by considering both his personal wishes and the consequences in reality of his overt actions. Thus is ego developed, both in Freud's sense of the capacity to organize the inner world in terms of outer realities, and in the existential sense of selfhood—for, as was stated earlier, the self is affirmed by its choices.

Transference

Transference is often an attempt to reduce personal responsibilities when one is faced with the anxieties and uncertainties of therapy. Whether positive or negative, transference involves an implicit shift of responsibility from the person in therapy to the therapist. By defining the therapist as an omniscient and omnipotent parent figure, and himself as a child, the patient shifts responsibility with the gambit, "You are so strong and so wise, while I am weak, childish, and helpless." This attitude almost always is followed by the implicit communication, "Therefore, tell me what to do, or do it for me." Or, to take another example of the implicit shift of responsibility involved in transference, the attitude of "You are wonderful, and I love you" is usually a mask for the feeling, "Since I love you, I need not expose myself further, make decisions, be independent, or stand on my own two feet, because you will take care of me." Conversely, the negative transference usually has its origin in an implicit "It's all your fault," which literally reduces personal responsibility by locating the causes for the patient's behavior in the therapist.

A common attitude of some patients is that "You don't love me" or "Nobody loves me." These attitudes in the transference may have a similar function, for they contain the implicit meaning of "What I do (or do not do) is done *because* you don't love me." Thus, transference represents a shift from the experience of choice and the assumption of responsibility to a deterministic position in which one experiences his behavior as "caused" by the personality or behavior of the therapist. Hundreds of articles have described the patient's passive, dependent, or manipulative behavior in psychotherapy; the general agreement is that such behaviors represent an attempt to escape from the anxieties of choice and responsibility, for if one is passive, dependent, or manipulative, the probability is increased that the therapist or some significant other person will take (or at least share) the responsibility for the patient's crucial decisions. Determinism may be a trap, but it can be reassuring when one is faced with the uncertainties of decision, choice, and responsibility. Yet, for the therapist to be "jockeyed" into assuming such responsibility is a tremendous mistake, for it reinforces the infantile pattern and retards progress in the direction of the patient's taking an ever-increasing amount of responsibility for himself.

A humanistic psychotherapy, devoted to the emergent selfhood of the person, may profit from interaction in which therapist and patient mutually recognize these shifts in responsibility. The therapist, through a careful delineation of his own ego boundaries, must avoid taking the implied responsibility for the patient and instead should dramatize the patient's alternatives, so that he may increase his capacity to make his own decisions and choices. Although this may well produce anxiety, the individual in psychotherapy probably cannot grow without the exercise of his choice-making capacity; the ego cannot be strengthened without decision and choice. As a matter of fact, unless the patient has made the basic choice that he wants psychotherapy and has decided to devote all his resources to the therapeutic effort, personal change is limited. Probably the greatest difficulty in the therapy of the psychotic stems from the fact that his self is so diffuse and fragmented that he cannot make this basic choice.

In therapy, personality can be developed with the exercise of choice and the experience of responsibility because these experiences permit the individual to observe the consequences of his choices. That is, the patient can profit from his failures and mistakes, as well as from his successes, if in his eyes he was responsible for the behavior which was a "mistake." But one can glean only suspicion from one's mistakes when they "were all your fault." The ego is strengthened, not by a submission to determinism or by slaving before its two "harsh masters," but through the exercise of choice and through observations of the effects in reality of its own choices and decisions.

Self-hatred

The tendency of the neurotic to deprecate or even to hate himself is intimately related to his inability to distinguish his freedoms, choices, and responsibilities from the areas of his life which are governed by a strict determinism. The neurotic's self-hatred persists long after he has left the family context in which it originated. The functional value of persistent self-hatred may be understood by noting the reduction of responsibility which accompanies it. By sustaining negative attitudes toward himself, the neurotic implicitly says, "I am no good; I hate myself—*therefore,* do not expect me to achieve, to be productive, to be independent, or to behave in a mature or responsible fashion." In other words, a negatively valued identity may persist as a defense against personal responsibility in the present. With many neurotics in psychotherapy, self-hatred can best be resolved by the repeated confrontation that, as a practical matter, he *now* has a functional responsibility for his own self-hatred. That is to say, when the neurotic can see that at present he behaves in a manner which makes it difficult for him to like himself, he then can reduce his self-hatred by choosing to behave in ways which permit him to like himself, the specific actions, of course, being defined by his own values. In this sense, the self-hatred of the neurotic adult can be conceptualized as a kind of implicit, self-perpetuated "choice." Once he is able to accept a larger measure of responsibility for his own behavior, i.e., to accent himself as the active agent in his own behavior, the neurotic is free to behave in a manner which permits him to like himself in the present, his traumatic past notwithstanding. If the neurotic's feelings about himself can be experienced by him as a part of *his* organization of his *perceptual* world, rather than as a determined (and thus inevitable) consequence of the rejection by parents or others, responsible behavior, with an increased positive regard for the self, is possible. On the other hand, as long as the patient attempts to place the responsibility for his self-hatred (or his neurosis in general) on anyone else—his past, his parents, or his therapist—therapeutic change is reduced. In a similar vein, whenever the responsibility for one's self-hatred, or self-esteem, for that matter, rests exclusively upon external criteria—prestige, success, wealth, status, physical attractiveness, or the lack of any of these factors—the adult individual is in a trap: his definition of himself in such case is determined by factors external to him and largely beyond his control. In a sense, he then has an identity alienated from himself as subject, for his "self-as-object" is defined in terms of these externalized criteria and becomes reified (Schachtel, 1961).

It no doubt is true that the self-hatred of the neurotic originated in a difficult and traumatic childhood which is related causally to his current character structure. As a programmatic matter in a humanistic therapy, however, the past is past, and he currently is responsible for changing; he cannot realistically expect the therapist to take responsibility for his behavior or, in a sense, for his personal change. Therapeutic experience is only an opportunity, an opportunity best realized by the abandonment of a strictly deterministic experience and the assumption by the patient of responsibility for his behavior and the exercise of choice over it. It is quite likely that many of the therapeutic benefits so often attributed to the therapist's acceptance and love actually have occurred because the therapist has recognized and repeatedly demonstrated the choice-making and responsibility-assuming potentialities of the client; and by so doing the therapist has affirmed a selfhood which, in his neurosis, the client could not himself recognize or accept. Indeed, such an affirmation of the patient's selfhood may be the real meaning of therapeutic love.

Summary

Humanistic psychotherapy was considered a unique opportunity for a phenomenological study because human experience is verbalized more freely, accurately, and intimately in this kind of psychotherapy than in any other interpersonal situation. An attempt was made to examine experience as expressed in therapy without an a priori commitment either to determinism or to free will, to see the extent to which these concepts accurately described the characteristic experience of different kinds of people. It was observed that determinism more accurately described the experience of the neurotic and the psychotic, and that free will more adequately described the experience of the healthy man. Neurosis was considered an inability to differentiate freedoms and deterministic limits, and free association, transference, and neurotic self-hatred were discussed in terms of the concept of free choice and personal responsibility.

CHAPTER 3

The Unique Animal

In calling attention to several distinct breaks in the course of animal evolution, Erich Fromm [1] observes that, "Self-awareness, reason and imagination disrupt the 'harmony' which characterizes animal existence. Their emergence has made man into an anomaly, into the freak of the universe. He is part of nature, subject to her physical laws and unable to change them, yet he transcends the rest of nature."

Such unequivocal acceptance of the uniqueness of man is relatively rare in psychological literature. More frequently man's superiority to animals is considered a matter of degree rather than of kind. Two converging trends in the science of behavior reinforce this viewpoint. First, the assumption of continuity in evolution leads many scientists to suppose that every ability to be found in a higher form of life must necessarily be found in those below it on the phylogenetic scale. This topic is discussed in the selection by Teilhard de Chardin. Secondly, the widely held doctrine of reductionism maintains that all complex phenomena must be explained by analyzing them into their most elementary components. Thinking, learning, and other conscious activities thus become functions of the nervous system and, since the same general types of structures are present in the brains of all vertebrates, there seems to be no reason to consider man's psychic endowments unique.

Three distinctly human characteristics, concept

[1] E. Fromm. *The sane society.* New York: Holt, Rinehart and Winston, 1955. P. 23.

formation, the use of conceptual language, and cultural progress, should serve to test any presumed qualitative superiority of man over animals. The empirical evidence for the first is somewhat ambiguous. Studies in animal reasoning frequently do not discriminate between true concept formation and other types of learning. Field's experiment with white rats is typical of the investigations that seem to confirm the existence of humanoid ideas.[2] When his animals were trained to recognize one kind of triangle they responded positively to triangles of different types, even to some not used in the training period. Since the only common element in the figures appeared to be triangularity, he concluded that his white rats had successfully abstracted a geometrical principle.

It should be noted, however, that a conclusion like this does not spring ready-made from laboratory observations but is a logical construct of the observer. The evidence on which it is based can be interpreted in a different way. Animal insight appears to involve sensory perception of concrete relationships between objects rather than concept formation in the human sense of grasping *abstract meaning* or *general principles*. A white rat in a Skinner box moves about at random until it accidentally stumbles on the correct solution. Success reinforces this general approach until the amount of random activity is reduced to the vanishing point. Such learning is based on the association of concrete perceptual elements in a *gestalt* rather than the testing of hypotheses or application of a theoretical principle. There is no denying animal abstraction in the sense of isolating and associating concrete sensory impressions such as visual forms. Through generalization of stimuli, they are even able to recognize similar forms, but there is no need to suppose that they understand the geometry of triangularity. Their learning attitude might be

[2] P. E. Fields. Studies in concept formation: I. The development of the concept of triangularity by the white rat. *Comp. Psychol. Monog.*, 1932, **9** (2), 1–70.

described as concrete rather than abstract.[3] Concept formation, by contrast, is not predominantly perceptual. After reviewing a large number of studies on animal intelligence, Moore [4] concludes that, ". . . when we attempt to measure their power of abstract thought and their ability to see and form general principles in the logical order, we obtain zero scores, for such abilities are simply not present."

In the same way that animals can be conditioned to visual or tactual stimuli, they can be trained to recognize definite sounds. A dog knows his name and may carry out simple commands without necessarily understanding the content of spoken language. Most species of animals possess some stereotype method of communicating perceptual information, but none uses language as a vehicle for expressing humanoid thoughts by word or gesture. A bee which by its waggle dance informs other workers of the source of nectar has nothing to say about the frayed condition of its wings or the foibles of the queen. Chimpanzees can modulate sounds well enough to be understood, yet in spite of attempts to train them to speak under the same conditions as a human child, little success has been reported.[5, 6]

It seems reasonable to suppose that animals with sufficient intelligence to understand geometrical principles would have, within the space of several million years, invented a conceptual language, or at least have made some attempt to apply their knowledge in a meaningful way to everyday living. On the contrary, most social relations among animals remain on an instinctual level. Not even

[3] H. B. English and Eva C. English. *A comprehensive dictionary of psychological and psychoanalytical terms.* New York: Longmans, 1958. P. 106.

[4] T. V. Moore, Human and animal intelligence. In H. S. Jennings et al., *Scientific aspects of the race problem.* New York: Longmans, 1941. Pp. 93–158.

[5] W. N. Kellog and Luella A. Kellog. *The ape and the child.* New York: McGraw-Hill, 1933.

[6] K. J. Hayes and Catherine Hayes. The intellectual development of a home-raised chimpanzee. *Proc. Amer. philosophical Soc.*, 1951, **95**, 105–109.

among the apes is there to be found any cultural development approaching that of even the most primitive tribe of human beings.[7] The common perception of man's uniqueness has not been disproved by the findings of science.

Editor's Note

According to Teilhard de Chardin's account of creation as it continues to take place before our eyes, the gradual unfolding of life involves an internal as well as an external aspect, and evolution is primarily concerned with psychic development. This steady ascent of consciousness could scarcely continue indefinitely without transforming itself in depth, somewhat as a gradual rise in temperature causes water to be transformed into steam. With its sudden appearance in man self-consciousness endows him with the capacity to reflect about himself and about his knowledge as objects to be known. From this point onward he can no longer be understood in terms of the animals below him in the scale of life, but only in terms of this unique function.

8. The Birth of Thought *

Pierre Teilhard de Chardin

Preliminary Remark: The Human Paradox

From a purely positivist point of view man is the most mysterious and disconcerting of all the objects met with by science. In fact we may as well admit that science has not yet found a place for him in its representations of the universe. Physics has succeeded in provisionally circumscribing the world of the atom. Biology has been able

[7] R. M. Yerkes. *The great apes: A study of anthropoid life.* New Haven, Conn.: Yale, 1929.

* Abridged from Pierre Teilhard de Chardin, *The Phenomenon of Man,* (Translated by Bernard Wall), Harper & Brothers, New York, 1959, pp. 163–169. Reprinted with permission of Mlle Jeanne Mortier, Paris and Harper & Row, New York.

to impose some sort of order on the constructions of life. Supported both by physics and biology, anthropology in its turn docs its best to explain the structure of the human body and some of its physiological mechanisms. But when all these features are put together, the portrait manifestly falls short of the reality. Man, as science is able to reconstruct him today, is an animal like the others—so little separable anatomically from the anthropoids that the modern classifications made by zoologists return to the position of Linnaeus and include him with them in the same superfamily, the hominidae. Yet, to judge by the biological results of his advent, is he not in reality something altogether different?

Morphologically the leap was extremely slight, yet it was the concomitant of an incredible commotion among the spheres of life—there lies the whole human paradox; and there, in the same breath, is the evidence that science, in its present-day reconstructions of the world, neglects an essential factor or, rather, an entire dimension of the universe.

In conformity with the general hypothesis which throughout this book has been leading us towards a coherent and expressive interpretation of the earth as it appears today, I want to show now, in this part devoted to thought, that, to give man his *natural* position in the world of experience, it is necessary and sufficient to consider the *within* as well as the *without* of things. This method has already enabled us to appreciate the grandeur and the direction of the movement of life; and this method will serve once again to reconcile in our eyes the insignificance and the supreme importance of the phenomenon of man in an order that harmoniously re-descends on life and matter.

Between the last strata of the Pliocene age, in which man is absent, and the next, in which the geologist is dumbfounded to find the first chipped flints, what has happened? And what is the true measure of this leap?

It is our task to divine and to measure the answers

to these questions before we follow step by step the march of mankind right down to the decisive stage in which it is involved today.

The Threshold of Reflection

The Threshold of the Element: the Hominisation of the Individual

A. NATURE. Biologists are not yet agreed on whether or not there is a direction (still less a definite axis) of evolution; nor is there any greater agreement among psychologists, and for a connected reason, as to whether the human psychism differs specifically (by 'nature') from that of man's predecessors or not. As a matter of fact the majority of 'scientists' would tend to contest the validity of such a breach of continuity. So much has been said, and is still said, about the intelligence of animals.

If we wish to settle this question of the 'superiority' of man over the animals (and it is every bit as necessary to settle it for the sake of the ethics of life as well as for pure knowledge) I can only see one way of doing so—to brush resolutely aside all those secondary and equivocal manifestations of inner activity in human behavior, making straight for the central phenomenon, *reflection*.

From our experimental point of view, reflection is, as the word indicates, the power acquired by a consciousness to turn in upon itself, to take possession of itself *as of an object* endowed with its own particular consistence and value: no longer merely to know, but to know oneself; no longer merely to know, but to know that one knows.

Now the consequences of such a transformation are immense, visible as clearly in nature as any of the facts recorded by physics or astronomy. The being who is the object of his own reflection, in consequence of that very doubling back upon himself, becomes in a flash able to raise himself into a new sphere. In reality, another world is born. Abstraction, logic, reasoned choice and inventions, mathematics, art, calculation of space and time, anxieties and dreams of love—all these activities of *inner life* are nothing else than the effervescence of the newly-formed centre as it explodes onto itself.

This said, I have a question to ask. If, as follows from the foregoing, it is the fact of being 'reflective' which constitutes the strictly 'intelligent' being, can we seriously doubt that intelligence is the evolutionary lot proper to man and to man *only*? If not, can we, under the influence of some false modesty, hesitate to admit that man's possession of it constitutes a radical advance on all forms of life that have gone before him? Admittedly the animal knows. *But it cannot know that it knows:* that is quite certain. If it could, it would long ago have multiplied its inventions and developed a system of internal constructions that could not have escaped our observation. In consequence it is denied access to a whole domain of reality in which we can move freely. We are separated by a chasm—or a threshold—which it cannot cross. Because we are reflective we are not only different but quite other. It is not a matter of change of degree, but of a change of nature, resulting from a change of state.

So we find ourselves confronted with exactly what we expected at the end of the chapter we called *Demeter*. [Reference not pertinent here.] Life, being an ascent of consciousness, could not continue to advance indefinitely along its line without transforming itself in depth. It had, we said, like all growing magnitudes in the world, to become different so as to remain itself. And at the same moment we find the whole curve of biogenesis reappearing summed up and clarified in this singular point.

B. THEORETICAL MECHANISM. All along, naturalists and philosophers have held opinions of the utmost divergence concerning the 'psychical' make-up of animals. For the early Schoolmen instinct was a sort of sub-intelligence, homogeneous and fixed, marking one of the ontological and logical stages by which being grades downwards from pure spirit to pure materiality. For the Cartesian only thought existed; so the animal, devoid of any *within,* was a mere automaton. For most modern biologists, as I have said already, there is no sharp line to be drawn between instinct and thought, neither being very much more than a sort of luminous halo enveloping the play—the only essential thing—of the determinisms of matter.

In each of these varying opinions there is an element of truth, which becomes immediately apparent at the same time as the cause of error when, following the point of view put forward in these pages, we make up our minds to recognise (1) that instinct, far from being an epiphenomenon, translates through its different expressions the very phenomenon of life, and (2) that it consequently represents a *variable* dimension.

What exactly happens if we look at nature from this angle?

Firstly we realise better in our minds the fact and the reason for the *diversity* of animal behaviour. From the moment we regard evolution as primarily psychical transformation, we see there is not *one* instinct in nature, but a multitude of forms of instincts each corresponding to a particular solution of the problem of life. The 'psychical' make-up of an insect is not and cannot be that of a vertebrate; nor can the instinct of a squirrel be that of a cat or an elephant: this in virtue of the position of each on the tree of life.

By the fact itself, in this variety, we begin to see legitimately a relief stand out and a gradation formed. If instinct is a variable dimension, *the* instincts will not only be different; they will create, beneath their complexity, a growing system. They will form as a whole a kind of fan-like structure in which the higher terms on each nervure are recognised each time by a greater range of choice and depending on a better defined centre of co-ordination and consciousness. And that is the very thing we see. The 'psychical' make-up of a dog, despite all that may be said to the contrary, is positively superior to that of a mole or a fish.[1]

This being said, and I am merely presenting in a different light what has already been revealed in our study of life, the upholders of the spiritual explanation have no need to be disconcerted when they see, or are obliged to see, in the higher animals (particularly in the great apes) ways and reactions which strangely recall those of which they make use to define the nature and presence in man of 'a reasoning soul.' If the story of life is no more than a movement of consciousness veiled by morphology, it is inevitable that, towards the summit of the series, in the proximity of man, the 'psychical' make-ups seem to reach the *borders of intelligence*. And that is exactly what happens.

Hence light is thrown on the 'human paradox' itself. We are disturbed to notice how little 'anthropos' differs anatomically from the other anthropoids, despite his incontestable mental pre-eminence in certain respects—so disturbed that we feel almost ready to abandon the attempt to distinguish them, at least towards their point of origin. But is not this extraordinary resemblance precisely what had to be?

When water is heated to boiling point under normal pressure, and one goes on heating it, the first thing that follows—without change of temperature—is a tumultuous expansion of freed and vaporised molecules. Or, taking a series of sections from the base towards the summit of a cone, their area decreases constantly; then suddenly, with another infinitesimal displacement, the surface vanishes

[1] From this point of view it could be said that every form of instinct tends in its own way to become 'intelligence'; but it is only in the human line that (for extrinsic or intrinsic reasons) the operation has been successful all the way. Having reached the stage of reflection, man would thus represent a single one of the innumerable modalities of consciousness tried out by life in the animal world. In all those other psychological worlds it is very difficult for us to enter, not only because in them knowledge is more confused, but because they work differently from ours.

leaving us with a *point*. Thus by these remote comparisons we are able to imagine the mechanism involved in the critical threshold of reflection.

By the end of the Tertiary era, the psychical temperature in the cellular world had been rising for more than 500 million years. From branch to branch, from layer to layer, we have seen how nervous systems followed *pari passu* the process of increased complication and concentration. Finally, with the primates, an instrument was fashioned so remarkably supple and rich that the step immediately following could not take place without the whole animal psychism being as it were recast and consolidated on itself. Now this movement did not stop, for there was nothing in the structure of the organism to prevent it advancing. When the anthropoid, so to speak, had been brought 'mentally' to boiling point some further calories were added. Or, when the anthropoid had almost reached the summit of the cone, a final effort took place along the axis. No more was needed for the whole inner equilibrium to be upset. What was previously only a centred surface became a centre. By a tiny 'tangential' increase, the 'radial' was turned back on itself and so to speak took an infinite leap forward. Outwardly, almost nothing in the organs had changed. But in depth, a great revolution had taken place: consciousness was now leaping and boiling in a space of super-sensory relationships and representations; and simultaneously consciousness was capable of perceiving itself in the concentrated simplicity of its faculties. And all this happened for the first time.

Those who adopt the spiritual explanation are right when they defend so vehemently a certain transcendence of man over the rest of nature. But neither are the materialists wrong when they maintain that man is just one further term in a series of animal forms. Here, as in so many cases, the two antithetical kinds of evidences are resolved in a movement—provided that, however, in this movement the essential part is allowed to the highly natural phenomenon of the 'change of state.' From the cell to the thinking animal, as from the atom to the cell, a single process (a psychical kindling or concentration) goes on without interruption and always in the same direction. But by virtue of this permanence in the operation, it is inevitable from the point of view of physics that certain leaps suddenly transform the subject of the operation.

Editor's Note

Although paleontological evidence points to a qualitative difference between the human and animal ways of knowing things, one further point needs to be clarified. Studies in conditioning prove conclusively that animals frequently react to one thing as though it were a sign of another. In the selection which follows, Cassirer clearly differentiates between signs and symbols and shows how the latter add a new dimension to cognitive experience.

9. From Animal Reactions to Human Responses *

Ernst Cassirer

By our definition of man as an *animal symbolicum* we have arrived at our first point of departure for further investigations. But it now becomes imperative that we develop this definition somewhat in order to give it greater precision. That symbolic thought and symbolic behavior are among the most characteristic features of human life, and that the whole progress of human culture is based on these conditions, is undeniable. But are we entitled to consider them as the special endowment of man to the exclusion of all other organic beings? Is not symbolism a

* Abridged from E. Cassirer. From animal reactions to human responses. In *An essay on man.* New Haven, Conn.: Yale, 1944. Pp. 27–41. Reprinted with permission.

principle which we may trace back to a much deeper source, and which has a much broader range of applicability? If we answer this question in the negative we must, as it seems, confess our ignorance concerning many fundamental questions which have perennially occupied the center of attention in the philosophy of human culture. The question of the *origin* of language, of art, of religion becomes unanswerable, and we are left with human culture as a given fact which remains in a sense isolated and, therefore, unintelligible.

It is understandable that scientists have always refused to accept such a solution. They have made great efforts to connect the fact of symbolism with other well-known and more elementary facts. The problem has been felt to be of paramount importance, but unfortunately it has very rarely been approached with an entirely open mind. From the first it has been obscured and confused by other questions which belong to a quite different realm of discourse. Instead of giving us an unbiased description and analysis of the phenomena themselves the discussion of this problem has been converted into a metaphysical dispute. It has become the bone of contention between the different metaphysical systems: between idealism and materialism, spiritualism and naturalism. For all these systems the question of symbolism has become a crucial problem, on which the future shape of science and metaphysics has seemed to hinge.

With this aspect of the problem we are not concerned here, having set for ourselves a much more modest and concrete task. We shall attempt to describe the symbolic attitude of man in a more accurate manner in order to be able to contradistinguish it from other modes of symbolic behavior found throughout the animal kingdom. That animals do not always react to stimuli in a direct way, that they are capable of an indirect reaction, is evidently beyond question. The well-known experiments of Pavlov provide us with a rich body of empirical evidence concerning the so-called representative stimuli. In the case of the anthropoid apes a very interesting experimental study by Wolfe has shown the effectiveness of "token rewards." The animals learned to respond to tokens as substitute for food rewards in the same way in which they responded to food itself. According to Wolfe the results of varied and protracted training experiments have demonstrated that symbolic processes occur in the behavior of anthropoid apes. Robert M. Yerkes, who describes these experiments in his latest book, draws from them an important general conclusion.

> That they [symbolic processes] are relatively rare and difficult to observe is evident. One may fairly continue to question their existence, but I suspect that they presently will be identified as antecedents of human symbolic processes. Thus we leave this subject at a most exciting stage of development, when discoveries of moment seem imminent.[1]

It would be premature to make any predictions with regard to the future development of this problem. The field must be left open for future investigations. The interpreta- of the experimental facts, on the other hand, always depends on certain fundamental concepts which have to be clarified before the empirical material can bear its fruit. Modern psychology and psychobiology take this fact into account. It seems to me highly significant that nowadays it is not the philosophers but the empirical observers and investigators who appear to be taking the leading roles in solving this problem. The latter tell us that after all the problem is not merely an empirical one but to a great degree a logical one. Georg Révész has recently published a series of articles in which he starts off with the proposition that the warmly debated question of so-called *animal language*

[1] Robert M. Yerkes, *Chimpanzees, A Laboratory Colony,* (New Haven, Yale University Press, 1943), p. 189. Footnotes have been renumbered.

cannot be solved on the basis of mere facts of animal psychology. Everyone who examines the different psychological theses and theories with an unbiased and critical mind must come at last to the conclusion that the problem cannot be cleared up by simply referring to forms of animal communication and to certain animal accomplishments which are gained by drill and training. All such accomplishments admit of the most contradictory interpretations. Hence it is necessary, first of all, to find a correct logical starting point, one which can lead us to a natural and sound interpretation of the empirical facts. This starting point is the *definition of speech* (*die Begriffsbestimmung der Sprache*). But instead of giving a ready-made definition of speech, it would be better perhaps to proceed along tentative lines. Speech is not a simple and uniform phenomenon. It consists of different elements which, both biologically and systematically, are not on the same level. We must try to find the order and interrelationships of the constituent elements; we must, as it were, distinguish the various geological strata of speech. The first and most fundamental stratum is evidently the language of the emotions. A great portion of all human utterance still belongs to this stratum. But there is a form of speech that shows us quite a different type. Here the word is by no means a mere interjection; it is not an involuntary expression of feeling, but a part of a sentence which has a definite syntactical and logical structure. It is true that even in highly developed, in theoretical language the connection with the first element is not entirely broken off. Scarcely a sentence can be found—except perhaps the pure formal sentences of mathematics—without a certain affective or emotional tinge. Analogies and parallels to emotional language may be found in abundance in the animal world. As regards chimpanzees Wolfgang Koehler states that they achieve a considerable degree of expression by means of gesture. Rage, terror, despair, grief, pleading, desire, playfulness, and pleasure are readily expressed in this manner. Nevertheless one element, which is characteristic of and indispensable to all human language, is missing: we find no signs which have an objective reference or meaning. "It may be taken as positively proved," says Koehler,

> that their gamut of *phonetics* is entirely "subjective," and can only express emotions, never designate or describe objects. But they have so many phonetic elements which are also common to human languages, that their lack of articulate speech cannot be ascribed to *secondary* (glosso-labial) limitations. Their gestures too, of face and body like their expression in sound, never designate or "describe" objects (Bühler).[2]

Here we touch upon the crucial point in our whole problem. The difference between *propositional language* and *emotional language* is the real landmark between the human and the animal world. All the theories and observations concerning animal language are wide of the mark if they fail to recognize this fundamental difference. In all the literature of the subject there does not seem to be a single conclusive proof of the fact that any animal ever made the decisive step from subjective to objective, from affective to propositional language. Koehler insists emphatically that speech is definitely beyond the powers of anthropoid apes. He maintains that the lack of this invaluable technical aid and the great limitation of those very important components of thought, the so-called images, constitute the causes which prevent animals from ever achieving even the least beginnings of cultural development. The same conclusion has been reached by Révész. Speech, he asserts, is an anthropological concept which accordingly should be entirely discarded from the study of

[2] Wolfgang Koehler, "Zur Psychologie des Schimpansen," *Psychologische Forschung,* **1** (1921), 27. Cf. the English ed., *The Mentality of Apes,* (New York, Humanities Press, 1951), App. p. 317. Quotation reprinted with permission of the Humanities Press.

animal psychology. If we proceed from a clear and precise definition of speech, all the other forms of utterances, which we also find in animals, are automatically eliminated. Yerkes, who has studied the problem with special interest, speaks in a more positive tone. He is convinced that even with respect to language and symbolism there exists a close relationship between man and the anthropoid apes. "This suggests," he writes, "that we may have happened upon an early phylogenetic stage in the evolution of symbolic process. There is abundant evidence that various other types of sign process than the symbolic are of frequent occurrence and function effectively in the chimpanzee." [3] Yet all this remains definitely prelinguistic. Even in the judgment of Yerkes all these functional expressions are exceedingly rudimentary, simple, and of limited usefulness by comparison with human cognitive processes.[4] The genetic question is not to be confused here with the analytical and phenomenological question. The logical analysis of human speech always leads us to an element of prime importance which has no parallel in the animal world. The general theory of evolution in no sense stands in the way of the acknowledgment of this fact. Even in the field of the phenomena of organic nature we have learned that evolution does not exclude a sort of original creation. The fact of sudden mutation and of emergent evolution has to be admitted. Modern biology no longer speaks of evolution in terms of earlier Darwinism; nor does it explain the causes of evolution in the same way. We may readily admit that the anthropoid apes, in the development of certain symbolic processes, have made a significant forward step. But again we must insist that they did not reach the threshold of the human world. They entered, as it were, a blind alley.

For the sake of a clear statement of the problem we must carefully distinguish between *signs* and *symbols.*

[3] Yerkes and Nissen, "Pre-linguistic Sign Behavior in Chimpanzee," *Science,* LXXXIX, 587.

[4] Yerkes, *Chimpanzees,* p. 189.

That we find rather complex systems of signs and signals in animal behavior seems to be an ascertained fact. We may even say that some animals, especially domesticated animals, are extremely susceptible to signs.[5] A dog will react to the slightest changes in the behavior of his master; he will even distinguish the expressions of a human face or the modulations of a human voice.[6] But it is a far cry from these phenomena to an understanding of symbolic and human speech. The famous experiments of Pavlov prove only that animals can easily be trained to react not merely to direct stimuli but to all sorts of mediate or representative stimuli. A bell, for example, may become a "sign for dinner," and an animal may be trained not to touch its food when this sign is absent. But from this we learn only

[5] This susceptibility has, for instance, been proved in the famous case of "clever Hans" which a few decades ago created something of a sensation among psychobiologists. Clever Hans was a horse which appeared to possess an astounding intelligence. He could even master rather complicated arithmetical problems, extract cube roots, and so on, stamping on the ground as many times as the solution of the problem required. A special committee of psychologists and other scientists was called on to investigate the case. It soon became clear that the animal reacted to certain involuntary movements of its owner. When the owner was absent or did not understand the question, the horse could not answer it.

[6] To illustrate this point I should like to mention another very revealing example. The psychobiologist, Dr. Pfungst, who had developed some new and interesting methods for the study of animal behavior, once told me that he had received a letter from a major about a curious problem. The major had a dog which accompanied him on his walks. Whenever the master got ready to go out the animal showed signs of great joy and excitement. But one day the major decided to try a little experiment. Pretending to go out, he put on his hat, took his cane, and made the customary preparations—without, however, any intention of going for a walk. To his great surprise the dog was not in the least deceived; he remained quietly in his corner. After a brief period of observation Dr. Pfungst was able to solve the mystery. In the major's room there was a desk with a drawer which contained some valuable and important documents. The major had formed the habit of rattling this drawer before leaving the house in order to make sure that it was safely locked. He did not do so the day he did not intend to go out. But for the dog this had become a signal, a necessary element of the walk situation. Without this signal the dog did not react.

that the experimenter, in this case, has succeeded in changing the food-situation of the animal. He has complicated this situation by voluntarily introducing into it a new element. All the phenomena which are commonly described as conditioned reflexes are not merely very far from but even opposed to the essential character of human symbolic thought. Symbols—in the proper sense of this term—cannot be reduced to mere signals. Signals and symbols belong to two different universes of discourse: a signal is a part of the physical world of being; a symbol is a part of the human world of meaning. Signals are "operators"; symbols are "designators." [7] Signals, even when understood and used as such, have nevertheless a sort of physical or substantial being; symbols have only a functional value.

Bearing this distinction in mind, we can find an approach to one of the most controverted problems. The question of the *intelligence of animals* has always been one of the greatest puzzles of anthropological philosophy. Tremendous efforts, both of thought and observation, have been expended on answers to this question. But the ambiguity and vagueness of the very term "intelligence" has always stood in the way of a clear solution. How can we hope to answer a question whose import we do not understand? Metaphysicians and scientists, naturalists and theologians have used the word intelligence in varying and contradictory senses. Some psychologists and psychobiologists have flatly refused to speak of the intelligence of animals. In all animal behavior they saw only the play of a certain automatism. This thesis had behind it the authority of Descartes; yet it has been reasserted in modern psychology. "The animal," says E. L. Thorndike in his work on animal intelligence, "does not think one is like the other, nor does it, as is so often said, mistake one for the other. It does not think *about* it at all; it just thinks *it* . . . The

[7] For the distinction between operators and designators see Charles Morris, "The Foundation of the Theory of Signs," *Encyclopedia of the Unified Sciences* (1938).

idea that animals react to a particular and absolutely defined and realized sense-impression, and that a similar reaction to a sense-impression which varies from the first proves an association by similarity, is a myth." [8] Later and more exact observations led to a different conclusion. In the case of the higher animals it became clear that they were able to solve rather difficult problems and that these solutions were not brought about in a merely mechanical way, by trial and error. As Koehler points out, the most striking difference exists between a mere chance solution and a genuine solution, so that the one can easily be distinguished from the other. That at least some of the reactions of the higher animals are not merely a product of chance but guided by insight appears to be incontestable. If by intelligence we understand either adjustment to the immediate environment or adaptive modification of environment, we must certainly ascribe to animals a comparatively highly developed intelligence. It must also be conceded that not all animal actions are governed by the presence of an immediate stimulus. The animal is capable of all sorts of detours in its reactions. It may learn not only to use implements but even to invent tools for its purposes. Hence some psychobiologists do not hesitate to speak of a creative or constructive imagination in animals. But neither this intelligence nor this imagination is of the specifically human type. In short, we may say that the animal possesses a practical imagination and intelligence whereas man alone has developed a new form: a *symbolic imagination and intelligence*.

Moreover, in the mental development of the individual mind the transition from one form to the other—from a merely practical attitude to a symbolic attitude—is evident. But here this step is the final result of a slow and continuous process. By the usual methods of psychological observation it is not easy to distinguish the individ-

[8] Edward L. Thorndike, *Animal Intelligence* (New York, Macmillan, 1911), pp. 119ff.

ual stages of this complicated process. There is, however, another way to obtain full insight into the general character and paramount importance of this transition. Nature itself has here, so to speak, made an experiment capable of throwing unexpected light upon the point in question. We have the classical cases of Laura Bridgman and Helen Keller, two blind deaf-mute children, who by means of special methods learned to speak. Although both cases are well known and have often been treated in psychological literature, I must nevertheless remind the reader of them once more because they contain perhaps the best illustration of the general problem with which we are here concerned. Mrs. Sullivan, the teacher of Helen Keller, has recorded the exact date on which the child really began to understand the meaning and function of human language. I quote her own words:

> I must write you a line this morning because something very important has happened. Helen has taken the second great step in her education. She has learned that *everything has a name, and that the manual alphabet is the key to everything she wants to know.*
>
> . . . This morning, while she was washing, she wanted to know the name for "water." When she wants to know the name of anything, she points to it and pats my hand. I spelled "w-a-t-e-r" and thought no more about it until after breakfast. . . . [Later on] we went out to the pump house, and I made Helen hold her mug under the spout while I pumped. As the cold water gushed forth, filling the mug, I spelled "w-a-t-e-r" in Helen's free hand. The word coming so close upon the sensation of cold water rushing over her hand seemed to startle her. She dropped the mug and stood as one transfixed. A new light came into her face. She spelled "water" several times. Then she dropped on the ground and asked for its name and pointed to the pump and the trellis and suddenly turning round she asked for my name.

> I spelled "teacher." All the way back to the house she was highly excited, and learned the name of every object she touched, so that in a few hours she had added thirty new words to her vocabulary. The next morning she got up like a radiant fairy. She has flitted from object to object, asking the name of everything and kissing me for very gladness. . . . Everything must have a name now. Wherever we go, she asks eagerly for the names of things she has not learned at home. She is anxious for her friends to spell, and eager to teach the letters to everyone she meets. She drops the signs and pantomime she used before, as soon as she has words to supply their place, and the acquirement of a new word affords her the liveliest pleasure. And we notice that her face grows more expressive each day.[9]

The decisive step leading from the use of signs and pantomime to the use of words, that is, of symbols, could scarcely be described in a more striking manner. What was the child's real discovery at this moment? Helen Keller had previously learned to combine a certain thing or event with a certain sign of the manual alphabet. A fixed association had been established between these things and certain tactile impressions. But a series of such associations, even if they are repeated and amplified, still does not imply an understanding of what human speech is and means. In order to arrive at such an understanding the child had to make a new and much more significant discovery. It had to understand that *everything has a name*—that the symbolic function is not restricted to particular cases but is a principle of *universal* applicability which encompasses the whole field of human thought. In the case of Helen Keller this discovery came as a sudden shock. She was a girl seven years of age who, with the exception of defects in the use

[9] See Helen Keller, *The Story of My Life* (Doubleday, Page & Co., 1902, 1903), Supplementary Account of Helen Keller's Life and Education, pp. 315ff.

of certain sense organs, was in an excellent state of health and possessed of a highly developed mind. By the neglect of her education she had been very much retarded. Then, suddenly, the crucial development takes place. It works like an intellectual revolution. The child begins to see the world in a new light. It has learned the use of words not merely as mechanical signs or signals but as an entirely new instrument of thought. A new horizon is open up, and henceforth the child will roam at will in this incomparably wider and freer area.

If the child has succeeded in grasping the meaning of human language, it does not matter in which particular material this meaning is accessible to it. As the case of Helen Keller proves, man can construct his symbolic world out of the poorest and scantiest materials. The thing of vital importance is not the individual bricks and stones but their general *function* as architectural form. In the realm of speech it is their general symbolic function which vivifies the material signs and "makes them speak." Without this vivifying principle the human world would indeed remain deaf and mute. With this principle, even the world of a deaf, dumb, and blind child can become incomparably broader and richer than the world of the most highly developed animal.

Universal applicability, owing to the fact that everything has a name, is one of the greatest prerogatives of human symbolism. But it is not the only one. There is still another characteristic of symbols which accompanies and complements this one, and forms its necessary correlate. A symbol is not only universal but extremely variable. I can express the same meaning in various languages; and even within the limits of a single language a certain thought or idea may be expressed in quite different terms. A sign or signal is related to the thing to which it refers in a fixed and unique way. Any one concrete and individual sign refers to a certain individual thing. In Pavlov's experiments the dogs could easily be trained to reach for food only upon being given special signs; they would not eat until they heard a particular sound which could be chosen at the discretion of the experimenter. But this bears no analogy, as it has often been interpreted, to human symbolism; on the contrary, it is in opposition to symbolism. A genuine human symbol is characterized not by its uniformity but by its versatility. It is not rigid or inflexible but mobile. It is true that the full *awareness* of this mobility seems to be a rather late achievement in man's intellectual and cultural development. In primitive mentality this awareness is very seldom attained. Here the symbol is still regarded as a property of the thing like other physical properties. In mythical thought the name of a god is an integral part of the nature of the god. If I do not call the god by his right name, then the spell or prayer becomes ineffective. The same holds good for symbolic actions. A religious rite, a sacrifice, must always be performed in the same invariable way and in the same order if it is to have its effect. Children are often greatly confused when they first learn that not every name of an object is a "proper name," that the same thing may have quite different names in different languages. They tend to think that a thing "is" what it is called. But this is only a first step. Every normal child will learn very soon that it can use various symbols to express the same wish or thought. For this variability and mobility there is apparently no parallel in the animal world.

Another important aspect of our general problem now emerges—the problem of the *dependence of relational thought upon symbolic thought*. Without a complex system of symbols relational thought cannot arise at all, much less reach its full development. It would not be correct to say that the mere *awareness* of relations presupposes an intellectual act, an act of logical or abstract thought. Such an awareness is necessary even in elementary acts of perception. The sensationalist theories used to describe perception as a mosaic of simple sense data. Thinkers of this persuasion constantly overlooked the fact that sensation itself is by no means a mere aggregate or bundle of isolated impressions. Modern Gestalt psychology has corrected this view. It has shown that the very simplest perceptual processes imply fundamental structural elements, certain patterns or configurations. This principle holds both for the human and the animal world. Even in comparatively low stages of animal life the presence of these structural elements—especially of spatial and optical structures—has been experimentally proved. The mere awareness of relations cannot, therefore, be regarded as a specific feature of human consciousness. We do find, however, in man a special type of relational thought which has no parallel in the animal world. In man an ability to isolate relations—to consider them in their abstract meaning—has developed. In order to grasp this meaning man is no longer dependent upon concrete sense data, upon visual, auditory, tactile, kinesthetic data. He considers these relations "in themselves"—*αὐτὸ καθ' αὑτό*, as Plato said. Geometry is the classic example of this turning point in man's intellectual life. Even in elementary geometry we are not bound to the apprehension of concrete individual figures. We are not concerned with physical things or perceptual objects, for we are studying universal spatial relations for whose expression we have an adequate symbolism. Without the preliminary step of human language such an achievement would not be possible. In all the tests which have been made of the processes of abstraction or generalization in animals, this point has become evident. Koehler succeeded in showing the ability of chimpanzees to respond to the *relation* between two or more objects instead of to a particular object. Confronted by two food-containing boxes, the chimpanzee by reason of previous general training would constantly choose the larger—even though the particular object selected might in a previous experiment have been rejected as the smaller of the pair. Similar capacity to respond to the nearer object, the brighter, the bluer, rather than to a particular box was demonstrated. Koehler's results were confirmed and extended by later experiments. It could be shown that the higher animals are capable of what has been called the "isolation of perceptual factors." They have the potentiality for singling out a particular perceptual quality of the experimental situation and reacting accordingly. In this sense animals are able to abstract color from size and shape or shape from size and color. In some experiments made by Mrs. Kohts a chimpanzee was able to select from a collection of objects varying extremely in visual qualities those which had some one quality in common; it could, for instance, pick out all objects of a given color and place them in a receiving box. These examples seem to prove that the higher animals are capable of that process which Hume in his theory of knowledge terms making a *"distinction of reason."* But all the experimenters engaged in these investigations have also emphasized the rarity, the rudimentariness, and the imperfection of these processes. Even after they have learned to single out a particular quality and to reach toward this, animals are liable to all sorts of curious mistakes. If there are certain traces of a *distinctio rationis* in the animal world, they are, as it were, nipped in the bud. They cannot develop because they do not possess that invaluable and indeed indispensable aid of human speech, of a system of symbols.

The first thinker to have clear insight into this problem was Herder. He spoke as a philosopher of humanity who wished to pose the question in entirely "human" terms. Rejecting the metaphysical or theological thesis of a supernatural or divine origin of language, Herder begins with a critical revision of the question itself. Speech is not an object, a physical thing for which we may seek a natural or a supernatural cause. It is a process, a general function of the human mind. Psychologically we cannot describe this process in the terminology which was used by all the psychological schools of the eighteenth century. According to Herder speech is not an artificial creation of reason, nor is it to be accounted for by a special mechanism of associations. In his own attempt to set forth the nature of language Herder lays the whole stress upon what he calls *"reflection."* Reflection or reflective thought is the ability of man to single out from the whole undiscriminated mass of the stream of floating sensuous phenomena certain fixed elements in order to isolate them and to concentrate attention upon them.

> Man evinces reflection when the power of his soul acts so freely that it can segregate from the whole ocean of sensation surging through all his senses *one* wave, as it were; and that it can stay this wave, draw attention to it, and be aware of this attention. He evinces reflection when from the whole wavering dream of images rushing through his senses he can collect himself into a moment of waking, dwell on *one* image spontaneously, observe it clearly and more quietly, and abstract characteristics showing him that *this* and no other is the object. Thus he evinces reflection when he can not only perceive all the qualities vividly or clearly but when he can *recognize* one or several of them as distinctive qualities. . . . Now by what means did this recognition come about? Through a characteristic which he had to abstract, and which, as an element of consciousness, presented itself clearly. Well then, let us exclaim: Eureka! This initial character of consciousness was the language of the soul. With this, human language is created.[10]

This has more the appearance of a poetical portrait than of a logical analysis of human speech. Herder's theory of the origin of language remained entirely speculative. It did not proceed from a general theory of knowledge, nor from an observation of empirical facts. It was based on his ideal of humanity and on his profound intuition of the

[10] Herder, *Über den Ursprung der Sprache* (1727), "Werke," ed. Suphan, V, 34f.

character and development of human culture. Nevertheless it contains logical and psychological elements of the most valuable sort. All the processes of generalization or abstraction in animals that have been investigated and described with accuracy clearly lack the distinctive mark emphasized by Herder. Later on, however, Herder's view found a rather unexpected clarification and confirmation from a quite different quarter. Recent research in the field of the *psychopathology of language* has led to the conclusion that the loss, or severe impairment, of speech caused by brain injury is never an isolated phenomenon. Such a defect alters the whole character of human behavior. Patients suffering from aphasia or other kindred diseases have not only lost the use of words but have undergone corresponding changes in personality. Such changes are scarcely observable in their outward behavior, for here they tend to act in a perfectly normal manner. They can perform the tasks of everyday life; some of them even develop considerable skill in all tests of this sort. But they are at a complete loss as soon as the solution of the problem requires any specific theoretical or reflective activity. They are no longer able to think in general concepts or categories. Having lost their grip on universals, they stick to the immediate facts, to concrete situations. Such patients are unable to perform any task which can be executed only by means of a comprehension of the abstract. All this is highly significant, for it shows us to what degree that type of thought which Herder called reflective is dependent on symbolic thought. Without symbolism the life of man would be like that of the prisoners in the cave of Plato's famous simile. Man's life would be confined within the limits of his biological needs and his practical interests; it could find no access to the "ideal world" which is opened to him from different sides by religion, art, philosophy, science.

Editor's Note

Psychologists find that a complex process can usually be studied with greater rigor by concentrating upon the simpler elements, especially those that can be isolated in the laboratory. While this approach has obvious advantages, it also exacts a price. Some important aspects of the problem are neglected, and the many partial solutions may be difficult to integrate into a meaningful pattern.

So it is with learning. A prodigious amount of information has been painstakingly collected from animal studies, while many questions concerning human insight still go unanswered. Before a truly comprehensive theory can be formulated, a corresponding amount of effort must be devoted to understanding those aspects of learning which are uniquely human.

10. Contemporary Learning Theory and Human Learning *

Frank J. Kobler
Loyola University

The importance of learning and the closely allied psychology of motivation in contemporary psychology can be gauged by Boring's statement in the second edition of his classic *History of Experimental Psychology* that these topics now have the right to stand as companion topics in experimental psychology with sensation and perception.

Learning is gradually taking the center of the stage in American psychology. It is the factor through which we can hope to come to an understanding of nongenetic, nonmaturational changes in man. It is the area in psychology through which we can hope to understand that aspect of man that offers the greatest and currently the only prospect of working realistically with him.

* Abridged from Frank J. Kobler, "Contemporary Learning Theory and Human Learning," in Magda B. Arnold and John A. Gasson, S. J., *The Human Person*, Ronald Press, New York, 1954, Chapter 11. Reprinted with permission of author and publisher.

The importance of learning in relation to the understanding of man can readily be gauged by a consideration of the following questions: "How is the human personality formed?" "What leads to its malformation, as for example in the appearance of a neurosis?" "How are ideas acquired?" "How are habits formed?" "The attitudes and opinions of men—how are they crystallized?" "How are walking, talking, reading, thinking, good manners, and feeling acquired and perfected?"

The influence and importance of learning in American psychology can likewise be gauged from the marked increase in learning articles published in the professional journals, and particularly in the *Journal of Experimental Psychology,* as well as from an examination of the roster of presidents of the American Psychological Association, many if not most of whom in the past two decades have had a great interest in learning and learning theory. Learning theory is likewise of major importance for the more general theory of psychology, and in the past ten years it has assumed an increasing importance for clinical psychology. Learning appears to hold the key to the future solution of many complex problems in psychology.

The difficulty that arises as one reads the literature on learning theory is to find a theory that adequately encompasses the known facts, that synthesizes the various interpretations, and that offers a suitable experimental framework in which to attack the unsolved problems of human nature. The need is for a theory sufficiently broad to encompass all the kinds of learning found in man. The major criticism that can be leveled at contemporary learning theory is that, in segmentalizing human learning and in concentrating upon significant aspects of learning, it has neglected equally important aspects, or it has set up a system of parts that has made it impossible to entertain in the theory other more crucial elements of human personality. That this has been done in the interest of a justifiable scientific parsimony is known and is commendable. Such a restriction has made for intense scientific activity and for considerable progress. A simple monistic interpretation of the facts of learning is useful in the interests of rigor and clarity. It is particularly useful if it is not a closed system that precludes the erection of a sound psychology of learning. That the limits of such a systematic structure have been reached, that dissatisfaction with it is being expressed, particularly in the light of the crucially important new clinical interests and experiences that are coming to dominate American psychology, is evident on many sides in the attempts to reconstruct, to resynthesize the systems that have dominated the American scene in the past two decades.

It is useful to examine the current learning theories in the light of their historical development, in the light of their limitations and suggested inadequacies, and in relation to a substitute theory that proposes to function in the stream of psychological tradition, and yet proposes to offer a more satisfactory set of principles for an explanation of the perplexing problems posed by experience with the human person.

The systematic discussion of learning is a relatively new event in psychology, having its inception in the twentieth century. Learning theory in any formal sense is still more recent, having developed largely within the past two decades. The earlier concern with learning was largely experimental and methodological, finding its characteristic expression in the work on memory by Ebbinghaus, the work on the acquisition of skill by Bryan and Harter, and the work on problem solving in animals by Thorndike. Prior to these experimentalists and in line with the tradition in which they worked, learning was discussed under the topic of remembering, and particularly under the topic of association. For the associationists of the nineteenth century, learning was a process of acquiring sensory experiences called "ideas" from the sensory experiences called "sensations."

There is no question about the legitimacy of identifying contemporary learning theory with the associationistic tradition because the bulk of present-day learning theorists are avowed associationists of one type or another. The major exception to this are the field theorists whose tradition stems from Plato through Leibnitz and Kant to the modern *Gestalt* psychologists.

Aristotle in his brief essay on memory (Boring) outlined the basic principles of association which dominate learning theory today. For some obscure reason his specific doctrine languished, or was interpreted differently until it was refurbished in the seventeenth century and flowered in the nineteenth century, where in modified form it was regarded as the sole basis for all mental operations.

It was the mechanism, the dualism, and the artificial interactionism of Descartes that were instrumental in the inauguration of associationism as we see it expressed in learning theory today. His thought made possible the work of subsequent writers whose theories we have with us today. All modern learning theory stems from Descartes' theory of knowledge. It is the gap that he created between mind and body that must in some way be bridged in an adequate comprehensive theory.

Typical of the new psychology of learning which protested the oversimplification of the associationistic hypothesis were the new experimental approaches of such workers as Marbe on thought, Ach on determining tendencies, Binet on problem solving, Judd on transfer of training, and Fernald on memory.

From this historical development two major trends have emerged in learning theory. One trend is reflected in the several contemporary variations and revisions of the associationistic hypothesis which in greater or lesser degree have taken into account the criticisms that have been leveled in our own time. The other trend is reflected in the field theories that have proliferated by way of rebellion against the shortcomings of structuralism, behaviorism, and associationism. One writer (Hilgard) points out that the modern associationists prefer to emphasize the influence of the environment, to consider wholes according to their composition from constituent elements, to concentrate on response behavior rather than introspection. They have a preference for mechanical models and historically oriented causation. The field theorists, on the other hand, are nativists and consider wholes according to their unique pattern and organization. They gravitate toward perception and ideas (rather than responses) as materials to analyze, and as a consequence utilize introspection. Their models are dynamic and their emphasis is on contemporary causation. They account for the present by the present and not by the past. The differences and similarities between the associationistic and the field theories of learning can be illustrated by a consideration of the theories of Thorndike, Hull, Tolman, and Mowrer.

Thorndike defines his theory of connectionism as the "doctrine that all mental processes consist of the functioning of native and acquired connections between the situations and the responses." He is an associationist whose system is fundamentally but vaguely physiological, since he postulates a one-to-one connection in the neurons between the stimulus and the response. Learning for him is the end product of all one's experiences added together. Thorndike uses reflexes and instincts in addition to habits to explain learning. Basic to an understanding of Thorndike's theory of learning are his so-called laws of learning. These are of two types: the primary laws of effect, exercise and frequency; and the secondary laws such as belongingness, associative shifting, and set. The most fundamental of these laws in Thorndike's system is that of effect. He states it as follows: "a modifiable bond is strengthened or weakened as satisfiers or annoyers attend its exercise." This law of effect has become the basic issue around the acceptance or rejection of which theories of learning have been built (Postman). Thorndike may be called a psychological hedonist, since the pleasure-pain principle is essential to the functioning of his law of effect. For many years Thorndike thought that pleasure and pain or reward and punishment had similar effects on learning. During the third decade of this century, however, as the result of further experimentation, he modified his views to emphasize reward and to minimize punishment. He also discarded the law of exercise, for he discovered that practice is effective only in so far as it permits other factors to operate. It is these factors which really determine whether or not learning will occur. Connections are made stronger by being rewarded, not alone by being repeated.

A phenomenon called the spread of effect was discovered by Thorndike about 1933. This refers to the strengthening of connections adjacent to the one directly related to the reward. It works backwards and forwards in time, and diminishes gradually as it leaves the point of origin. This was an important experimental finding for connectionism because it supports the law of effect and this law's mechanical influence on connections. With it, there is no need of a symbol or an idea to account for learning. Later experimenters, however, have shown that principles of organization other than the spread of effect must operate to explain learning. Thorndike's learning theory excludes ideas or any element of consciousness. His is an automatic sort of behaviorism that has little or nothing to do with such human activities as meaning or understanding. This theory is adequate for the explanation of most of the learning processes of children, and it is in the field of educational psychology that it has had an enormous but not altogether favorable influence. It does not explain adult learning except on the most rudimentary levels.

Hull places his emphasis on logical behaviorism mathematically analyzed. His basic attempt is to reduce all learning of even the most complex type to simple rote learning. The fundamental laws of the latter are then sought in the hope that these will be applicable or importantly related to all learning. The basic principle in Hull's system is simply association reinforced by tension-reduction. Activity of the organism is brought about by a need for tension-reduction which stresses object goals. This reinforcement theory has been summed up in this way: to learn an organism must want something, notice something, do something, and get something (Miller and Dollard). Hull clearly emphasizes the external or the behavioral factors and he seeks to found this realistically on a physiological basis. He relates goals to the organism by way of gradients. In other words, the closer the activity to the goal, the more effective is the learning. This is simply a sophisticated re-statement of the law of contiguity. For Hull, goal attainment and tension reduction are similar to the classical reward or pleasure, and hence, we have a refined hedonism. Hull has devised a set of extremely complex postulates which he sets out to test and which revolve around a series of so-called intervening variables or factors within the organism that will effectively anchor the stimulus and the response.

Hull's theory of reinforcement through tension reduction is crucial in his system, and in the sense that it is a rigorously scientific statement of hedonism, it has a relation to what is true in learning. However, Hull uses it as a single principle to explain all learning, even that of the most complex type. There is no experimental evidence to support such a claim and common sense disavows it. Some learning takes place because of contiguity; more learning—or more exactly, more performance—takes place as a result of need reduction. However, learning is also something perceptual and cognitive that occurs at several levels of organization and that must be mediated by several principles of organization. The experiments on latent learning, for example, which are related to these ideas, tend to undermine the entire complicated and elaborate system devised by Hull.

Tolman's sign-significate theory of learning approximates more closely a system that incorporates a sufficient and adequate set of principles to explain the complexities of human learning. It appears that by a blend of nativism and behaviorism spiced with a touch of a slightly transmogrified unconsciousness we shall arrive at a palatable learning theory. There is an approach to this in the system of Tolman and the persuasiveness of this system demonstrates the relationship between eclecticism and common sense. Tolman's system combines associationism and field ideas. He uses purpose, objective observation, cognition, and intervening variables as essential ingredients in his system. Tolman maintains that organisms respond to a sign-gestalt, and not to stimuli. Learning for Tolman is not a process of conditioning, but one of setting up expectations and of inventing solutions which may eventuate in performance. Tolman, however, is not "mentalistic," since the ends that regulate behavior are "objectively determined." He thinks of behavior as molar rather than molecular, which reflects an emphasis on the observable rather than the physiological or the mentalistic. In this respect his system aims toward a science of psychology rather than a physiology or a philosophy.

One of the most challenging and interesting aspects of Tolman's learning theory is his development of the doctrine of intervening variables. It is here that he touches on cognition and on purpose and thereby gets closer to a workable system. A further challenging aspect of his system is the notion of sign-gestalt learning introduced as a substitute for the more usual response learning. The essence of this suggests that the organism learns meanings and not responses or movements. It goes away from the mechanical and toward a purposive explanation of learning. A large amount of experimental evidence on latent learning, on place learning, and on expectancy has been collected to support this point of view.

To explain how cognitive structure activates behavior without resorting to the principle of reinforcement or to the law of effect, Tolman has recourse to a special brand of motivation. In this system the learner acquires a knowledge of a means-end relationship largely through the influence of emphasis or interest. We learn those things to which we attend, which we emphasize, or in which we have an interest.

Tolman's system, as we have noted, has distinct advantages over other systems previously proposed. However, a theory based on the psychology of rats, no matter how sophisticated and adequate for rats, will suffer from certain limitations when applied to human beings. Tolman himself recognizes this in his rather sweeping explanations of clinical and cultural data on the basis of rat psychology. His writings here are a good illustration of a beautifully trained technician who is engagingly ingenuous in recognizing the limitations of his procedure but because of his apparent lack of expert knowledge in related areas of human behavior is in no position to do more than make delightfully irrelevant and humorously inapt remarks.

Writers who have tried to compare these systems of learning or who have tried to reconcile them or mediate between them have faced a difficult problem (Dashiell and McConnell). Too often, the various learning theorists attack different problems, or they attack the same problem at different levels. Hence, comparisons become difficult or impossible. Perhaps the most telling criticism that can be leveled is that all these systems are part systems. They explain a segment of the total learning process, and then tend to generalize from this to an explanation of all human learning. The importance of this can be illustrated indirectly when we compare the experimental evidence in those areas where the theorists have worked on comparable and crucial problems. For example, in the areas of latent learning, of continuity versus discontinuity in discrimination learning, and in place versus response learning, we find different results and different conclusions by different investigators on essentially similar problems. Some results favor one theory, others favor another theory, and some results could lend support to any theory.

One would hope that as a minimum an adequate learning theory would incorporate the processes experimentally established by the different theorists. It seems possible, also, that an entirely different theory will be necessary to explain human learning. However, it is more reasonable to suppose that learning is a matter of levels, and that the current learning theories have operated at the lowest possible levels in the interest of a parsimonious science. It seems improbable that there is only one learning process. If they have taught us anything, the *Gestalt* theorists have shown that there are learning processes qualitatively distinct from conditioning and trial-and-error learning.

Munn emphasizes that none of these theories gives a satisfactory account of how new responses are learned. If a response must occur before it can be reinforced or learned, how can it be learned when it is new? A new set of responses, such as a new learning theory, for instance, can only be accounted for in terms of perceptual and ideational processes aroused by a stimulus. The *Gestalt* psychologists solve this by suggesting that the stimuli arouse innately organized perceptual processes. This seems reasonable on a perceptual level and it could form a groundwork for ideational functioning. However, to explain such phenomena as insight and intention and hypotheses, we have to postulate a third order of events to which we may now address ourselves.

A very recent theory of learning that holds considerable promise because it appears to be working in the right direction of encompassing all the relevant aspects of human nature is the two-factor theory proposed by Mowrer. One reason why this theory is particularly challenging is that it begins to build a bridge between learning, personality, and the problems of clinical psychology. In this way it humanizes American learning theory that has been and is a rat psychology. Such a theory reflects the currently appearing limitations felt by an increasing number of observers in reinforcement and association theories generally. Mowrer's two-factor theory restricts the term "conditioning" to the learning of emotional or autonomically determined responses which are explicable by the principle of contiguity. He uses problem solving behavior to explain the learning by reinforcement mediated by the central nervous system. This abandonment of a single principle to explain learning is much more in accordance with the facts of human learning despite the violence that a multiple principle might do to the widely held principle of parsimony. In Mowrer's theory this departure from the principle of parsimony appears defensible to him because the two factors that are suggested are grounded in two distinct physiological systems—the skeletal muscular system and the viscero-vascular system. The acceptance of two basic learning processes, one problem solving and the other conditioning, is a much more tenable hypothesis regarding learning. Its greatest limitation is its failure to articulate these levels of learning organization, that is, the viscerogenic and the sensory perceptual processes, with insight or the activity of the ego.

Two major problems that confront the theorist unwilling to make such an extension are the factors of human conflict and the fact that the human animal works characteristically in terms of the future rather than in terms of the past. It is this reaching out into time, which is done with the characteristic mark of humans, namely, symbolic speech, that represents the greatest challenge to the contemporary truncated learning theories. It is in the concern with the psychology of ego involvement that we shall be able to come to grips with the role and importance of thought and volition in systematic learning theory.

In the area of mature, normal adult human relations we find evidence for the repudiation of the law of effect, of the principle of reinforcement, and of the doctrine of hedonism (Allport). For it appears that the distinguishing mark of mature adulthood is *renunciation.* It is this that exposes the limitations inherent in a one- or even a two-factor theory of human learning. To act symbolically—to act with the ego involved—is to go counter to the principles used to explain learning on the lower levels. When I feel obligated, when I act from sentiments of honor, when I sacrifice, when I succeed at being virtuous, I thereby do violence to all that is associationistic, hedonistic, and evolutionary in myself. In doing this I stand above conditioning, above trial and error or perceptual problem solving—and my ego demands a principle to explain that which is so peculiarly human, and often distinctly uncomfortable, in me. Learning and behavior are biological, hedonistic, *and ethical* (Mowrer and Kluckhohn).

It is important to recognize, in this connection, that while learning theory could be based on associationism (conditioning), hedonism (problem solving), and rational ego processes, the last is based upon and derived from the other two while simultaneously maintaining an essential distinction. The "functional autonomy" notion is an illustration of the possibility of this in the scientific context lending itself to experimental determination (Allport).

The problem of meaning and the notion of conscience, particularly the latter, are good illustrations of the need for a learning theory which recognizes these three levels. Since both conditioning and trial-and-error learning work mechanically, a third factor must be postulated to account for the complex nature of conscience. Conscience as an act or a habit of making moral judgments is essentially a product of learning and consequently requires integration into learning theory. In the evaluation of the conscience factor we see the limitations of the effect theory. The self-reward of conscience can easily overcome the most severe internal or external punishment, and the disapproval of conscience, as shown for example in guilt feelings, can torpedo the most objectively effective stratagem of rewards that can be devised by any therapist.

Learned behavior that is integrated at these higher or specifically human levels requires an essential harmony between the actions of the self or the ego and the conscience. To acquire such an integration of learning, a rational power is essential. The paramount function of this power operating in the interests of integration is to deal on an abstract or symbolic level with remote and present consequences and to organize them into an effective unity. The function of the ego is to deal with conscience, which is learned act or habit inclining to good, and of integrating this within the total personality.

Nonintegrative or neurotic behavior is learned behavior in which remote and present consequences have been inadequately integrated. It is what we have done and would that we had not, rather than what we would do but cannot permit ourselves to do, that is the core of the neurosis (Mowrer). It is this interplay between the ego and the conscience which can lead to adjustment or a failure in adjustment that illustrates the need for a third principle of learning. This principle is peculiarly human and therefore rational.

It is the neurotic individual, then, who illustrates all too clearly the need for including a third factor in an adequate learning theory. The conscious repudiation of conscience by the ego dissipates conscious guilt and substitutes for it the neurotic signals of anxiety and self-condemnation. The ego cannot deal effectively with these feelings because they have no "real" relation to the events that make for conscious guilt. When we have learned to have rational insight into this relationship, we have learned adjustment. When our conscience gives us pleasure rather than anxiety, we have learned to be in the best possible condition for lasting human happiness. This is directly contrary to the

Freudian notion which states that happiness is a function of properly liberating the instinctual and aggressive life from an "overlearned conscience." When we have learned to be no longer neurotically anxious or guilty about what we have done or about how we have repudiated our moral urgings (and not when we have "learned" to liberate our repressed impulses—this leads to neurosis and psychopathy), then we can think of ourselves as adjusted. Adjusted means distinguishing adequately between normal anxiety and guilt and the neurotic anxiety that disables the human organism. Conditioning and trial-and-error learning cannot do this for us. Only a third factor of rational insight permits the ultimate adjustment on the human level.

It seems clear from all this that a comprehensive learning theory must include the three factors of contiguity, reward, and freedom. It is the last—the feeling of obligation, of conscience, of oughtness that is crucial to uniquely human learning. Whether one learns to become a mature adult or a neurotic depends upon the set of habits, the set of attitudes, and the set of ideals that one has learned to integrate into a consistent or inconsistent pattern of personality. To ask the question of how one learns to behave in terms of "I ought" is to see the neglected crucial factors of learning theory. In the area of conscience, specifically as related to other characteristics of man, we require a factor of rationality to explain man's adjustment.

The importance of these statements about learning theory is minimal in present-day psychology unless they afford an opportunity for scientific or experimental verification. Unless these principles can be introduced into an experimental design that will make their objective verification possible, they will have little value for science, however useful and valid they may be in terms of common sense.

If experimentation is to concern itself with the crucial third or rational factor of systematic learning theory, it must perforce use human beings and not rats as subjects. Human beings learn by conditioning or association, and they learn by problem solving or reinforcement, but their peculiarly human learning is rational or ego-involved. To state this points the direction of research without specifying its details. There is no reason why some programmatic research on reasoning, on willing, and on conscience could not be systematically instituted along lines similar to that suggested by low-level theorists on rats, or on man's lower learning activities. Let us devise experimental situations that will not control out these elements in man that are most useful in understanding his unique human learning and adjustment.

CHAPTER 4

Minding the Body

"Mind" and "body," like most words in our ordinary vocabulary, seem exceeding simple. Everyone knows what a body is and everyone understands the meaning of mind, or so he imagines until he attempts to define them more accurately. Then he may discover latent implications of the terms, which he had not anticipated.

For many centuries the relationship between mind and body seemed to present no special problem. Aristotle, for example, thought of it in terms of compositionism. According to his formulation, man is a single integral substance, not two. Mind and body are part-principles essentially incomplete in themselves and designed by nature to complement each other. In a union immeasurably closer than that of oxygen and hydrogen, which do not lose their identity in producing water, they merge to form a living human being. Mind is characteristic of the part-principle that specifies that material elements become a man rather than something else. Had Aristotle been faced with the current tendency to identify thinking with brain activity, he probably would not have objected very strenuously. The brain, in his theory, is a human organ: not mere inanimate matter. Mind and body do not enjoy a separate existence in living persons.

The modern problem grew out of the way Descartes contrasted mind and body. Using the model of a horse and its rider, he pictured them as distinct entities completely separated from each other except for an elusive point of contact in the pineal gland. This cleared the way for him to treat the body as a machine-like structure, but only at the price of shattering the idea of a unity of personality. If, as Descartes believed, the mind remains locked up in the body out of contact with the senses, how can it be aware of outside objects as we experience them to be? It would have no windows opening out on the world. The influence of thought on somatic processes in hypnosis and psychosomatic illness is equally difficult for him to explain. Unless there is some possibility of interaction between mind and body, one cannot influence the other.

One way to cut through the gordian knot of dualism is to think of man as mind or body, but not both. The Irish philosopher, Berkeley, considered all material objects to be projections of the mind no more substantial than daydreams of the flickering images in a movie. A professor in the classroom labors under the illusion he is lecturing to students. In reality, the classroom does not exist outside his mind and the people in it are merely thoughts. The world of reality is too convincing to make this solution a popular one.

Current thinking favors monism of an opposite kind: body exists but not mind. Thought is the chemicoelectrical activity of billions of brain cells discharging in incredibly complex patterns throughout the cortex and brain stem. While this theory has the virtue of simplicity, it does not bring the problem much closer to a solution. There is a vast disparity between awareness of meaning and the discharge of electrical circuits regardless of their complexity. While neural events are obviously a correlate of thinking they do not offer a complete explanation. An analogous situation exists when a person calls his friend on the telephone. The voice and its meaning are carried by fluctuations in the line potential but such a restricted operational viewpoint does not throw much light on the real nature of the thought being communicated.

Perhaps some obstacles to a solution of the problem can be removed by analyzing the manner in which the concepts of body and mind are formed. In reflecting on the human organism and our own immediate experience, we discover that some processes are more closely related to the typical forces of nature than are others. Locomotion and digestion, for example, can be adequately explained in terms of physics, chemistry, and biology, whereas thinking and choosing cannot. These and similar observations serve as the basis for the notions of body and mind. The concepts can be further sharpened by emphasizing the contrast between them. Each is what the other is not, somewhat like the wave-particle description of light in wave mechanics. What we end with are logical constructs, not real entities. Neither singly nor together are mind and body a human being. Instead they are abstract representations of something existing quite differently in a real person. As a result, the problem becomes hopelessly complicated by artifacts of conceptualization which obscure the basic issues. There is no incompatibility of mind and body in people as we know them, only in our thinking about them.

Editor's Note

In the selection that follows, J. O. Wisdom reexamines the mind-body relationship from a novel point of view. Electromagnetism provides a model from nature of two observably distinct phenomena interacting almost as if they were one and the same thing. Although he thinks in terms of dualism, the model can be adapted to different theoretical orientations. Whether or not the reader finds his analogy of the mind-body relationship and electromagnetism convincing, it is likely to stimulate original thinking about a perennial problem in psychology.

11. A New Model for the Mind-Body Relationship *

J. O. Wisdom
The London School of Economics and Political Science

1. The Ontological Problem

Language analysts of the present century who have written about the mind-body relationship have confined themselves to epistemological problems, or rather to some of these. They have asked such questions as: how does one mind know about the existence and feelings of another mind from the behaviour of a body? I am not concerned with such questions here. Nor do I ask what is meant by statements about mind-body relationships. I am concerned solely with the old-fashioned ontological problem, which predominated in the philosophy of the past, particularly from Descartes onwards, but which has very rarely been discussed in recent times. My aim is to describe a model that shall express a very general relationship between minds and bodies.

* From J. O. Wisdom. A new model for the mind-body relationship. *Brit. J. Phil. Sci.*, 1952, **2**, 295–301. Reprinted with permission of the author and publisher.

Setting out from the assumption that a mind and a body are in some sense or other *two* things, the well-known theories about the possible relations between them can be divided into the following: (1) the mind acts on the body and the body acts on the mind (Interactionism or Interactionist Dualism); (2) occurrences in the mind are paralleled by occurrences in the body and *vice versa*, without Interaction (Parallelism or Parallelistic Dualism); (3) the mind is 'reducible to' the body (Epiphenomenalism or Materialistic Monism); (4) the body is 'reducible to' the mind (Idealism or Idealistic Monism); and (5) the mind and the body are 'reducible to' a third 'stuff' (Neutral Monism).

Parallelism arose because of the difficulties that beset Interactionism, and one of the main reasons for adopting monism lies in the difficulty of accepting either form of dualism. If interactionism could be rendered more acceptable, a great part of the reason for holding any of the other theories would disappear. Probably the chief difficulty is to understand, on the dualistic view that mind and body are 'irreducible', by what mechanism interaction between them could take place. To overcome this I wish to provide a model that shall exemplify 'irreducibility' together with interaction, and exemplify an appropriate kind of interaction.

2. The Nature of Unifying Theories

There is a common belief that two theories can be unified in only one way, namely by 'reducing' one to the other. This can undoubtedly happen. Thus the theory of light in the hands of Maxwell was 'reduced to' his electromagnetic theory. Here 'reduced to' means the same as 'deduced from.' It is this sense that is behind abortive attempts or wishes to 'reduce' biology to physics, and so on.

But there is another and even more important sense in which two theories, say t_1 and t_2, can be unified; and that is by means of a theory T, from which t_1 and t_2 can be separately deduced either as special cases or as approximations (these may shade into one another). There are important examples of unifying theories in this sense. Newton's theory of gravitation unified Galileo's laws of acceleration and Kepler's laws of planetary motion. Maxwell's electromagnetic theory unified the laws of Faraday and Ampère. Einstein's 1950 theory claimed to unify his gravitational theory of 1915 and electromagnetics. The important point here is that neither of the two theories, t_1 and t_2, can be deduced from the other: Kepler's laws cannot be deduced from Galileo's, nor can Galileo's from Kepler's.

The best example of unification for present purposes is afforded by electromagnetic theory. In certain conditions we may study fruitfully electrical phenomena or magnetic phenomena, without considering the other; and we can obtain laws about either that do not refer to the other. Thus the magnetic law, that the force between two poles is proportional to their strength and decreases with the square of the distance between them, makes no reference to electrical concepts. Likewise the electrical law, that the current flowing along a conductor is proportional to the potential difference between its ends, is independent of magnetic concepts. On the other hand, there are also relations between electricity and magnetism, the discovery of which was begun by Ampère and Faraday and completed by Maxwell. Ampère's law may be expressed in the form that a magnetic force induced by an electric current bears a quantitative relation to the flux of that current. Faraday's law asserts that, if a magnetic field is moved in space so that the lines of magnetic flux cut a conductor, then an electric current is set up in the conductor whose electromotive force is proportional to the rate of decrease with which the lines of flux cut the conductor. Though these laws would serve the present purpose it will be useful also to have them in general form, as given by Maxwell after he had inserted a factor unknown to Ampère or Faraday. All the relations between electricity and magnetism are contained in Maxwell's equations

$$\text{curl}\,\mathbf{H} = 4\pi\mathbf{c} + \kappa\dot{\boldsymbol{\epsilon}}, \quad \text{curl}\,\boldsymbol{\epsilon} = -\mu\dot{\mathbf{H}}$$
$$\text{div}\,\mathbf{H} = 0, \quad \text{div}\,\boldsymbol{\epsilon} = 4\pi\rho/\kappa$$

where the vectors $\mathbf{H}$, $\mathbf{c}$, $\boldsymbol{\epsilon}$ are respectively the magnetic force, the current (strictly, the current density), and the electromotive force, where the curl and divergence are mathematical operators, where ρ is the volume density of electrostatic charge, and where π, κ, μ are constants. By means of these equations, if we are given the current and electromotive force we can calculate the magnetic field induced, and if we are given the magnetic field we can calculate the electromotive force and thence the current. The mutual influence is thus very marked. In general there is no current without a magnetic field, and no magnetism that does not set up a current. Whether this is absolutely general is debatable, but not important for present purposes. *Conceivably* it is quite general, and that will suffice for the construction of a model. Yet despite this mutual dependence we can often work with either electricity or magnetism separately and consider changes in one without concerning ourselves with the other, as when we are dealing with the resistance in a conductor or with the force between two magnetic poles. Sometimes, of course, it is necessary to take account of changes in, say, electricity that induce a magnetic field that in turn modifies the electric current; but for some purposes this is not important.

We can now see that two theories, t_1 and t_2, say those of electricity and magnetism, need not lose their identity; they are not mutually deducible; the concepts of one are not 'reducible to' those of the other; for we cannot work even in principle with the concepts of one alone. What this means can be seen by contrasting it with the situation where one theory t is 'reduced to' another T. Maxwell found that light was a special form of electromagnetic wave. That is to say, the theory of light is not a different kind of theory from the theory of electromagnetic phenomena. Light is simply an electromagnetic wave with a special wave-length. Naturally we retain the concept of light, because we are particularly interested in electromagnetic waves with just the wave-length that we associate with light. Nonetheless, the theory of light does lose its independent identity—it is 'reducible to' the theory of electromagnetics. (Strictly, light is associated not with one wave-length but with a small group of them.)

Let us now sum up the relations between electricity and magnetism. The phenomena of the two spheres are mutually dependent in an important sense, namely they are existentially dependent on each other. Nonetheless they are also independent in the sense that they are 'irreducible,' for their concepts are 'irreducible.' Moreover, since we can work with electricity and electrical laws without reference to magnetism, and *vice versa,* whether this is only approximately true or whether it is true only in certain conditions, we can say that each sphere possesses a certain 'autonomy.'

3. A Dualistic Model

Whether or not electricity can exist without magnetism or magnetism without electricity is a question that does not concern us. The close linkage between the two suffices as an approximation to the model we require. Nor do we need the Maxwell unifying theory for our model. All we have to have are (1) laws connecting electrical phenomena with one another without reference to magnetism and laws connecting magnetic phenomena with one another without reference to electricity, and (2) a way of passing from electrical phenomena to magnetic, as given by Ampère's law, and a way of passing from magnetic phenomena to electrical, as given by Faraday's law. In this way we can have two spheres of phenomena, described by two sets of concepts and ordered by two theories, together with a bridging theory. The two spheres are existentially dependent, but to a certain approximation or in certain conditions they can function independently, i.e., they are autonomous, and the two sets of concepts and the two theories are 'irreducible.' We thus have a model that may be called 'dualistic.'

I here use this term expressly for any assemblage or model that can be described only by two sets of 'irreducible' concepts, where the two associated spheres of phenomena are existentially dependent but where despite mutual influence there is a certain autonomy pertaining to each. Whatever other associations the word 'dualism' may have for the historian of philosophy are here excluded from its meaning.

The point of the model is to show that the difficulty about the concept of interaction does not appear in the electromagnetic model of interaction.

We may now turn to the mind-body problem. The generality of the dualistic model is such as to enable us to treat a body and its mind in some sense or other as *two* things. More specifically it enables us to make bridging statements between the two spheres of mind and body, some of which express universal laws. Thus we can have: 'Whenever adrenalin is injected into the blood the associated mind feels on edge' and 'Whenever a mind is made angry the level of adrenalin in its associated bloodstream rises.' Here we have laws of two-way interaction, analogous to those of Ampère and Faraday. Again, on account of the autonomy in each sphere, we can have physiological laws, such as 'Kidney disease leads to increased blood pressure,' analogous to the law of potential difference in an electrical conductor; and we can have psychological laws, such as 'Retention of learned nonsense-syllables falls off in proportion to the logarithm of the time,' analogous to the law of force between two magnetic poles. But the local autonomy in either sphere holds approximately only so long as there is (1) no considerable effect upon the other sphere and (2) no considerable change in that sphere from any other source. We can have mutual induction phenomena. Thus 'A certain standard meal is digested in about four hours' would be true only in normal emotional conditions; if a person gets a bad fright his meal will not digest in that time or perhaps at all. Again 'Fear of failing in an examination makes a person work hard' might be subject to interference, and we might have 'His fear of failing led to duodenal ulcer, the pain of which prevented him from concentrating on his work.' Further, the model affords us the possibility of a certain kind of choice. If we wish to increase a magnetic field, we can do so either by adding more magnets or by passing an electric current, and if we wish to increase an electric current, we can do so either by introducing an additional current or by rotating a magnet. Similarly if we wish to increase the irritation a person feels at captious remarks we can do so either by making our conversation still more captious or by injecting adrenalin, and if we wish to alter the composition of a man's blood we can do so either by giving him an intravenous injection or by giving him frightening information. Put generally, we can bring about mental changes (or bodily ones) by either mental or bodily means, just as we can bring about magnetic changes (or electrical ones) by either magnetic or electrical means.

According to the model, in which magnetic phenomena cannot exist without electric phenomena and *vice versa*, mind and body have dominion status without right of secession. Thus while the model does not make a place for disembodied minds, neither does it give priority to bodies in the inventory of the fundamental furniture of the earth—though it does not provide for minds without bodies, neither does it provide for living bodies without minds.

The model does not even preclude direct action of one mind upon another mind; for, if a mind is analogous in the model to a magnetic field, one magnetic field can exert a direct effect upon another one.

It is obvious that the model differs markedly from the classical one, put forward by Geulincx, of two synchronising though mechanically unconnected clocks.[1]

4. Limitations of the Model

The dualistic model does not *prove* that there is interaction between mind and body. All it does is to draw attention to an unfamiliar fact, culled from electromagnetics, which displays the compatibility of 'irreducibility', existential dependence, and autonomy. This should dispel the mystery from mind-body interaction.

If anyone should object that this model dispels the mystery of mind-body interaction as little as it dispels that of electromagnetic interaction, that must be admitted; no attempt has been made to dispel any mystery there may be about electromagnetic interaction. If this is felt to be a mystery, then all that can be claimed is that the mind-body problem has been generalised by showing that it is not *sui generis*.

The model rules out parallelism without interaction but it does not rule out the possibility of some sort of parallelism between mental and bodily spheres. Whatever parallelism there may be, however, must be much less simple in

[1] It might appear that quantum mechanics would provide us with an equally good model; but this would be an error. It gives us the following important relations

$$E = h\nu,\ p = h/\lambda$$

where E, p are respectively energy and momentum, which characterise a particle, where ν, λ are respectively frequency and wavelength, which characterise a wave, and where h is a constant. These relations enable us to express quantum results wholly in terms of the concept of a particle or else wholly in terms of the concept of a wave —we can translate from one to the other at will. Now it might appear that we could express everything about a person wholly in terms of his body or else wholly in terms of his mind—that in fact all statements about a mind were translatable into statements about a body and *vice versa.* This would give us a language-analysis version of Neutral Monism. But it would not serve as a model for *interaction.* All the bridging statements and laws we wish to make connecting mind and body would have to remain unsaid.

nature than has been supposed by supporters of the traditional doctrine.

The use of the laws of Ampère, Faraday, and Maxwell may lead to disappointed hopes. It is not suggested that the bridging laws between mind and body, such as those I have used for illustration, possess anything like the great generality and definiteness of the electromagnetic laws. We may hope to attain very general and definite laws of this kind but we certainly have not yet succeeded in this. In particular, the bridging laws between mind and body are not, as Maxwell's are, statable in precise quantitative terms. It should not be overlooked, however, that many such laws are in fact quantitative, even though definite numbers cannot be given: thus courts of law commonly assume that degree of irresponsibility has a quantitative relation to the amount of alcohol consumed (though of course it is also related to other things as well, e.g. a person's individual constitution). These limitations are after all minor and do not affect the utility of the model.

It is most important to stress that, despite the model, the whole notion of mind-body interaction, consisting of 'irreducibility,' existential dependence, and local autonomy, may turn out to be untenable. All that the model is designed to do is to make it reasonable to make and take seriously certain kinds of hypotheses about minds and bodies.

Editor's Note

Within the past two decades several structures in the brain have been found to contribute in an important way to various types of behavior. The dramatic studies of Olds and Von Holst and Von Saint Paul (see Suggested Readings for Chapter 4) demonstrate the effectiveness of implanted electrodes in eliciting a wide variety of predictable responses. In case the student concludes from these experiments that scientists now understand fairly well how the mind functions, a moment's thought will convince him that while the frontier of mystery has been pushed back a few paces, the secret of consciousness remains as stubbornly entrenched as before. How does the discharge of neurons account for one's enjoyment of a sunset or the warm glow one experiences in the presence of a friend? All nerve impulses, regardless of their function, are produced by the movement of ions through the cell membrane coupled with the release of a traducer substance at the axon terminal. Why then should one impulse be associated with the movement of a muscle and another with the creative thinking of an Einstein? In spite of major advances in neurophysiology, the role of cortical neurons in thinking is still unknown.

12. Brain and Mind *

Gerhardt von Bonin
formerly College of Medicine
University of Illinois

Introduction

Brain and mind mean for many people brain anatomy and mind. It is, of course, true that the anatomical arrangement imposes certain enduring restrictions upon the ways in which the brain can work, but that leaves the way in which it actually works still largely undefined. Similarly, the mind is mainly known by its functions, but

* Abridged from G. von Bonin. Brain and mind. In S. Koch (Ed.), *Psychology: A study of a science.* Vol. 4. *Biologically oriented fields: Their place in psychology and in biological science.* New York: McGraw-Hill, 1962. Reprinted with permission of the author and publisher.

it, too, has certain restrictions imposed upon it by such things as character. In any event, it is probably correct to say that in the case of the brain, we think first of anatomy; in the case of the mind, we think first of its functions. But in either case, it is important not to lose sight of the other side.

Nerve Cells

We shall start with a short account of the workings of nerve cells. Many of the data concerning nerve cells are actually derived from peripheral nerves, frequently sensory nerves. These receive their impulses from organs which are exposed to long-lasting stimulations—long as compared with the duration of nervous impulses. Moreover, these stimuli are of very different strengths at different times. Also, in the central nervous system nerve cells are always found in great masses, so that the behavior of a single cell is not a true indicator of what happens in the brain when a stimulus goes through. With these things in mind, let us review briefly some of the main characteristics of nerve cells.

Modern electron-microscopic work has made it clear that there is a membrane around a nerve cell. What this membrane consists of is not so clear. It is seen as a thin line in the image, sometimes double, somewhat darker than the plasma inside the cell. Some of the Nissl bodies appear to lie immediately adjacent to the membrane, but that is certainly not the rule. Nissl bodies and mitochondria can easily be made out. Their detailed structure, although of great interest, does not concern us here.

There is the "all-or-nothing" law, which seems to govern the workings of nerve cells. At a given moment, the cell will either fire or not, but if it fires, it will do so with all the power it is at that moment capable of putting out. Strength of a stimulus is therefore not transmittable by graded impulses from a cell; the only way a cell can indicate the strength of a stimulus is by the rate of firing. The stronger the stimulus, the faster the firing of a given cell.

That the impulse is generated by the breakdown of the membrane is now pretty generally admitted. The breakdown leads to a depolarization which must occur within a fairly large region of the cell in order to lead to a propagated impulse. How large is "fairly large" is a moot point, and we do not know whether it is of the same absolute size in all cells or whether it is a certain percentage of the surface of the cell. A single impulse lasts at best about 1 msec. After firing, the nerve cell remains incapable of firing again for a few milliseconds, while it recover and builds up the membrane again. The time of recovery varies in different nerve cells; it may be as short as 1 or 2 msec—the cerebellar units are supposed to be able to fire 500 times per second—or may be 15 msec or longer.

That a nerve cell will not respond to one stimulus alone, but only when a "conditioning" stimulus has preceded the actual stimulus, is well known. It is generally stated that the whole of a synaptic field must get excited before the stimulus can break through.

The dendrites conduct with much lower velocity than the axon, or even the cell body, so that what takes milliseconds on a cell body may take hundredths of even tenths of seconds on a dendrite. Thus the time within which stimuli on a dendrite may sum up may be as much as 15 msec.

These characteristics are, of course, mainly important for the first neuron, where the rate of firing depends on the strength of the stimulus applied to the end organ. This can be detected easily enough in the peripheral nerve, and has been measured hundreds of times. Once the impulse is in the central nervous system, the rate of firing is determined partly by the rate in the peripheral organ, partly by interactions between the neurons making up the second order nucleus.

A point to keep in mind is that practically never do we find the firing of just one nerve cell as the initial condition for an impulse. For example, in the eye, an adequate stimulus consists of five to eight quanta transmitted to about five different rods. In the muscle, a proprioceptive stimulus activates a large number (about fifty) of muscle spindles simultaneously. Taste buds are generally found in large groups, and so on. Since the individual thresholds within each group of end organs vary somewhat, this is usually a way of answering to the intensity of a stimulus: the more cells become involved, the more intense a stimulus will have been. Whether stimuli from various cells will reenforce each other at the next station (nucleus) or whether, on the contrary, they will narrow down to fewer channels depends on circumstances which are still shrouded in mystery.

In addition to these impulses, there are inhibitory impulses in the nervous system, about which we will not concern ourselves here.

Character and Brain

What we mean by character probably comes nearest to the enduring pattern in the realm of the mind. We mean that the person is forgetful, neat, has an even or easily aroused temper, for example. These attributes appear to be inborn and to stay with the individual for the duration of life. In most important cases, we are absolutely unable to point to anything in the brain with which it might be correlated. In the case of musical gifts, people have pointed to a large development of the gyrus of Heschl (on the supratemporal plane) as an anatomical counterpart, but even here the evidence is not very convincing.

Consciousness

Most of our psychology concerns conscious processes. Can we make any intelligent remarks about consciousness? We are fairly sure that it does not reside in the cortex, for we (or a disease) can take parts of the cortex away without our becoming aware of it, a state for which Babinski coined the term *anosognosia,* meaning not being aware of one's disease. But clinical experience as well as animal experimentation have shown that consciousness appears to be connected somehow with the midbrain and the brain stem. Operations near the quadrigeminal bodies lead almost invariably to a loss of consciousness. Consciousness may be restored after manipulations in that region are over, or it may never come back—the patient may become a vegetable. This latter state of affairs, with good care of the patient, may last for years. Experimentally, it was shown in dogs that pressure on the brain stem can abolish consciousness, but not manipulations of the cortex.

This has recently been put on a much more understandable basis by Magoun and his co-workers, who practically discovered the reticular substance in the brain stem and showed its connections up and down the central nervous system. In particular, they showed the importance of this substance for the arousal reaction and for a proper functioning of the cortex.

The observations by Penfield, who was able to bring to recall in some persons—the number really does not matter—concrete incidents in their former life, does not really belong to the phenomena with which we are here concerned. These stimulations of the temporal lobe only change the contents of consciousness—not consciousness itself.

Introspective observations in themselves may not be very convincing, yet it may be pertinent to remark that the idea of the little man sitting somewhere in the brain and watching what goes on is easiest to explain on the assumption that *consciousness* does not reside in the cortex—only the *contents of consciousness.*

Another important aspect of the problem is that the processes underlying consciousness must go on fairly slowly as events are measured in neurophysiology. For consciousness involves planning ahead, and it involves a continuity which can only come from remembering what has gone before and realizing that what has been planned is what is executed now. Whether that is the way the reticular substance works we do not know, but it would be interesting to find out, and probably could be done with modern electrophysiological apparatus. Some cortical events, of course, would have to go equally slowly.

Brain and Mind

In a sense, there is really no intelligent question that one can ask about the relation of the two sciences of physiology and of psychology. The simile of the two viewpoints when observing the circle may still be valid. For a person outside the circle, it looks convex; for a person inside, it looks concave. That the two views are of the same thing simply has to be taken for granted. We cannot accept the causal theory. We simply have to admit that conscious processes and mental processes do not mean the same thing. Our viewpoint is better expressed by Bohr, who invoked the principle of complimentarity. Just as we need both the wave picture and corpuscular theory to explain the behavior of the electron, so we need both the physiological and psychological picture to explain the working of the brain. If we investigate the brain with the hope of finding the working of the mind, we have to apply all sorts of physical and chemical apparatus which disturb the process under investigation, until it has been disturbed so profoundly that the original process is lost sight of. "By the time you know everything about the atoms, the creature will be dead." More than a hundred years ago, Wordsworth said, "We murder to dissect." That somehow there must be a connection between the mind and the brain is clear, but what it is remains a mystery. Looking at sections is perhaps the least promising way to find out. The physiologist and the physiological psychologist appear to be in a much better position to advance our understanding.

It might be said, but again that leads to no more than generalities, that the mind models reality. To put it into slightly different words, the formal laws of the activity of the mind must be the same as the formal basis of nervous activity.

Sensorium Commune

The problem of the sensorium commune goes back to Aristotle, as everyone knows. Beyond saying that it is in the cortex, we probably cannot go. For in all higher activities the cortex appears to work as a whole. That the various parts may be involved with different intensity or in different patterns is probably true. The parietal lobe is probably the first part to be involved, situated as it is between the optic, the acoustic, and the somesthetic fields, but activity stretches to the frontal lobe and to the limbic region in a manner which we do not fully understand.

Von Weizsäcker and many others have emphasized that considering the two sides, sensory and motor, divorced from each other—in a sort of vacuum, as it were—is artificial and leads to a lack of understanding. They are actually intimately connected, and any sensory deficit will lead to a motor impairment and vice versa.

Motor Output

The main business of the brain has always been to do something rather than to contemplate serenely. Memory plays a paramount role in sensation and perception; in action, forecasting plays a similarly important role, which is frequently only imperfectly realized. Moreover, it is well known that with training, movements are performed with greater ease and probably actually with less expenditure of energy. This can only mean that the coordination of muscular activity has been improved. There is little doubt that we can learn to innervate our muscles properly, and also that this process is completely involuntary.

The next problem is: How does the brain steer the motor mechanisms, e.g., the muscles? For obviously something is first in the mind and then becomes an overt movement of some sort or other. Again, we must confess to our ignorance as to the exact way in which that happens. We know that always there is first an intention to do something, and then the actual execution follows. This was called by Liepmann the *Bewegungsentwurf* and has, in some form or other, survived till now. Where it is formed is a question that cannot be answered so easily. Liepmann's apraxia can be provoked by lesions in the parietal as well as in the frontal lobe, so we have probably to assume that the *Bewegungsentwurf* can be equally far strewn over the cortex. From these large areas, the impulses funnel down to those cortical areas from which the fibers to the deeper parts of the brain and spinal cord originate.

These fibers are grouped traditionally into pyramidal and extrapyramidal fibers. This distinction has of late been very much attacked and perhaps cannot be upheld. The arrangement of the extrapyramidal centers has recently been explained by Bucy in a number of diagrams to which the reader may be referred. All the extrapyramidal nuclei evidently funnel directly or indirectly into the reticular substance, and from there reach the spinal cord over a chain of short neurons, while the pyramidal fibers go directly from the cortex to the spinal cord. We do not know anything about the timing of these impulses. What we do know is that they all seem to arrive in good time to influence the muscles.

The prevailing ideas about the pyramidal system are extremely naïve. Coghill pointed out some years ago that the first function of the pyramidal system was to suppress the mass action which is the original mode of the working of the animal body. In a newt, for example, the whole body moves upon an impulse impinging upon any part of its surface. In man, only a very restricted group of muscles will respond to any stimulus. The young baby, when it wants to lift up its head or move its legs, will still move numerous muscles which have nothing to do with the movement in question. When the pyramidal tracts have developed, only small groups of muscles will become involved. The spasticity after a lesion of the pyramidal tract, the positive Babinski, are probably signs of primitive inhibitory function of the tract.

That the spinal cord alone is capable of a certain amount of coordination has been shown time and again. Goltz was probably the first to show that a spinal dog, when pinched at one hind foot or the tail, will make alternate movements with his hind legs. To some extent, this was confirmed later in man by von Monakow, who observed that patients with transverse lesions of the cord will, on peripheral stimulation, flex a leg and then, after a fairly long time (up to a minute), stretch it out again and flex the other leg and extend it again. Further repetitions of these movements have not been observed in man.

What the cortex does can better be circumscribed by such phrases as "The cortex wants to have the limb in such and such a position," rather than "The cortex wants the contraction of such and such muscles." The work of Gellhorn, who showed that cortical stimulation had different effects according to the proprioceptive inflow, points in the same direction.

With this in mind, we can perhaps say that the main purpose of the pyramidal tract is to send down to the cord a more or less general idea of what should happen, leaving the details to the apparatus that is in the cord itself. They send down, in other words, a command of the goal to be achieved, leaving the details of how to achieve it to the internuncials and the anterior horn cells. But this general information is not sufficient to assure a smooth execution of movements. We also need an extrapyramidal apparatus. Schaltenbrand and Hufschmidt have likened the activity of these centers to that of a brake and a spring, the pyramidal tract proper exercising the function of a motor. It does not do to spin this out too finely, but as a first approximation, so to speak, it is useful.

Cortex and spinal cord are coupled only loosely in the cat: four to five impulses have to come down the pyramidal tract before the final common pathway becomes activated. In the monkey it takes fewer impulses; according to Bernhard and others, it may even occur immediately. Moreover, the time is variable even in the same animal; with exercise it becomes shorter, so that it may go down from five to, say, two impulses in a matter of minutes.

The cortex is essentially a forecasting mechanism, forecasting primitively only for a short space of time, but gradually in phylogenesis lengthening that span until in man the problem of infinity has become almost threateningly persistent.

If this scheme is to work, we must have a system by which the higher center is informed of what has gone on in the lower one. The ideas of *Rückmeldung* were developed by von Holst. According to him, the higher center is informed of what has happened as the result of the impulses that went down to the lower center. Part of the apparatus of the muscle spindles is undoubtedly involved, but the fibers in the pyramidal system which run from the spinal cord up to the brain may also play a role here, as well as in numerous other systems. It cannot be our object to go into details here, but it has seemed appropriate to touch briefly on these ideas.

Speech

A few words should be said about speech, which occupies a unique place in the achievements of the human brain, for after all, it is only man who can use articulate speech to communicate and to impart information. Neurologically there are several peculiarities in the speech apparatus. While practically all other muscles of the body are steered by proprioception, the muscles of speech get their control from the spoken sounds—hence the congenitally deaf cannot speak properly, if at all. They are deaf-mute. In the second place, the uttering of intelligible speech demands a working together of larynx, pharynx, mouth, and lips, which can only be learned in the course of several years. Once established, it is fairly rigid; for example, it is extremely difficult to speak a foreign language without accent, since every language has its own peculiarities of pronunciation. This correlation of all the muscles cannot yet be explained neurologically.

The next question is whether we can point to certain areas in the brain which might be particularly involved in these activities. It used to be thought that Broca's and Wernicke's areas in the left frontal and the temporal lobes, respectively, were mainly involved. However, recent observations have cast serious doubts on this theory. It now appears as though aphasia can be produced by various lesions almost anywhere in the cortex, and it also was shown that Broca's area, at least, can sometimes be extirpated without causing aphasia.

Attention

One of the questions that may involve either motor performance or sensory input is that of the focusing of attention. Everybody knows that most people—Caesar was supposed to have been an exception—are able to concentrate on only one or, perhaps for a short time, two things at a time. They can listen to the ticking of the clock or they can concentrate on reading or writing, but they cannot do both at the same time—at least, not perfectly. It is true that Lashley stated during a conference in 1954 that he received sensory messages both from his right great toe and from Dr. Jasper simultaneously, but sooner or later one of the messages might have gotten dominance. Since Lashley does not say any more, it is possible that his great toe got the upper hand, so to speak!

Emotions

The fact that emotions have been located to some extent in the brain should be mentioned briefly. In 1937,

Papez was the first to develop a theory that large parts of what used to be considered olfactory brain really had to do with the emotional life of the individual. As somehow regulating the emotional life of the individual, he considered the cornu ammonis, the mamillary body, the anterior nucleus of the thalamus, and the medial aspect of the cerebral cortex, in particular its anterior part, area 24. This is certainly one of the circuits which may be involved. It should be noticed that it involves in the mamillary bodies a parasympathetic center. There probably is an orthosympathetic route, going from the septal region to the anterior part of the hypothalamus via the medial forebrain bundle, although less well worked out. Of course, we know very little in detail about the working of either system. It should be further mentioned that both nucleus amygdalae and the nucleus caudatus appear somehow to be connected with it, and that it has been said by the Montreal group that the former is facilitating, the latter inhibitory. But these things are still largely in the speculative stage. The Lange-James theory of emotion, with its primacy of the bodily states, is, in any event, no longer tenable.

Free Will

The problem of free will is extremely complicated. While it is fundamental to our civilization to assume that a man can do certain things or can abstain from doing them and that he is, therefore, responsible for his actions (our whole jurisprudence is built on this assumption), it is not at all sure how free he really is. Every man is born into the mental climate of his time, and it is generally possible to say how a certain person will act under certain circumstances, at least within certain limits.

Heisenberg's principle of indeterminacy has often been called in to explain the so-called "freedom of the will." Here, too, the indeterminacy is only relative. There may well be doubt whether, in nervous transmission, any processes are involved which are on the subatomic level. But that slight variations in the threshold of nerve cells do occur—variations which may make the difference between firing and not firing—can be admitted. If we realize that this happens in thousands or millions of cells, it is conceivable that impulses may be shunted on to different paths according to the exact state in which the cells are at the time when an impulse arrives there. In this somewhat loose sense, indeterminacy may be admitted, although this has little in common with the indeterminacy as formulated by Heisenberg. Thus, within limits, we are probably free but not completely lawless. Certain values are given us, and to these standards we have to adhere.

This brings us to the question of values. Köhler has tried to tie up the question of values with the facts of closure which had been determined by the gestalt school of psychology, of which he is now the leader. By *closure* is meant the tendency to augment figures which are defective to the status of whole figures, e.g., a circle out of which a segment of, say, 30° has been omitted will be seen, especially when tachistoscopically presented, as a whole circle. It is a far cry from here to the idea of value, but it cannot be denied that in both cases we have to do with something that *ought* to be rather than with something that *is*. In that sense, Köhler's rather ingenious explanation stands.

Summary

In summary, while the idea that the life of the mind and the life of the brain are correlated seems eminently reasonable and true, we cannot yet work it out in detail. We do not know exactly what the cortex does, how consciousness or, for that matter, the metric of the outside world arises, or how we move our bodies.

At the moment, we cannot do much more than point to the difficulties inherent in the questions we have raised. It might be said at the very end what perhaps should have been said in the beginning: To equate cortical events with conscious events is certainly quite unjustified. Many processes go on in the cortex of which we are not conscious. It should not be forgotten that the cortex develops properly only in the mammals, that the lower forms must guide their lives in some other way. It is most likely that the reticular substance is the oldest coordinating mechanism, and therefore probably the oldest seat of consciousness. How much the quadrigeminal bodies contribute is simply not known, but it seems clear that only by the working together of all these parts can the life of the human mind come about. To understand that completely will require many more years of study and research.

This article could only be a summary. It is hoped that the reader will be stimulated to look further into the literature and get a broader and deeper picture of this fascinating problem.

PART TWO

Science and the Study of Man

CHAPTER 5

The Human Dimensions of Science

The methods of science were invented for the sole purpose of minimizing bias, self-deception, and other subjective errors in the study of natural phenomena. Unsystematic observation is notoriously inaccurate where generalizations are concerned. For example, popular sayings based on casual experience can support both sides of a question. Shakespeare remarks that "absence makes the heart grow fonder," but another version of the same aphorism adds the phrase, "for somebody else." Only when a person is certain of his facts does theorizing become meaningful.

Any empirical investigation contains a double aspect: the collection of data by observation or measurement, and the interpretation of their meaning within the framework of the study in question. In other words, both perceptual and conceptual processes are involved and both must be capable of validation. Early Greek philosophers experienced some small success in the study of natural phenomena through the development of a system of logic to certify the correctness of a reasoning process. They discovered that valid relationships between the propositions of a syllogism can be reduced to rule, thus facilitating a check for accuracy. What they lacked was the perceptual counterpart of logic to authenticate their original observations. Without guidelines for controlling irrelevant factors and for guarding against self-deception in the collection of data, there was no way to determine whether first premises contained grist or chaff. Not until these were supplied in recent centuries did science become fully equipped to master the forces of nature.

Given this background, it is not surprising to find that many descriptions of science stress only its objectivity. Subjective and objective viewpoints are contrasted in a way that makes them appear entirely incompatible. David Hawkins [1] observes that, "What is lacking in the official accounts is a sense of the inwardness of science, of its creative impulses and its secret ambitions, of its rationalities and its irrationalities and its intellectual growth, of its pettiness and its greatness—in short, of the human character of science." Science is essentially a type of behavior, not a timeless, immutable Rock of Gibraltar existing in isolation from people. Human practitioners apply its principles in their own fallible way depending to some extent on private judgment in the process. Exaggerating the virtues of science can prove to be as embarrassing as criticism. Voltaire once said, "May God deliver me from my friends: I can take care of my enemies." The cause of any human undertaking is better served by calling attention to some of its limitations.

The articles in this chapter deal with several subjective aspects of applied science which are currently being discussed by scholars in various fields. Typical of the questions raised are the following: How does an hypothesis first arise? What types of subjective choices must be made? At what stage in the process is objective methodology first applied? What precisely is its purpose? How are the exact data of science related to primary experience? Is absolute objectivity possible even in theory? What role is played by the scientist's attitudes, beliefs, and readiness to be convinced by the outcome of an experiment? Is he unbiased? Are there beliefs that must be tested on nonscientific grounds? Do value judgments enter into the discussion of scientific and technical matters? Such questions probe the problematic areas currently demanding examination.

[1] D. Hawkins. The creativity of science. In H. Brown (Ed.), *Science and the creative spirit: Essays on humanistic aspects of science.* Toronto: University of Toronto Press, 1958. P. 131.

Editor's Note

One convenient way of dealing with abstractions is to treat them as actually existing things: "the average American," or "the cost-of-living index." Abstruse concepts seem more natural and satisfying when reclothed with some of the sensory qualities stripped away in the process of logical analysis. In the course of time, familiar personifications tend to acquire an imagined existence "out there," somewhat after the fashion of Plato's universals. Even "Science" may eventually be pictured, not as the personalized possession of each scientist in a form unique to him, but as an autonomous, homogeneous something occupying space outside. Yet scientific methodology, for all its impersonal austerity, was invented for the sole purpose of validating subjective *hypotheses. Viewed as a human attainment rather than an object, science is neither a mystic entity to be placed on a pedestal nor a bogeyman to be feared: science is people.*

13. Persons or Science? *

Carl R. Rogers
Western Behavioral Sciences Institute
La Jolla, California
formerly University of Wisconsin

A Changed View of Science

In the year which has elapsed since the foregoing material was written [reference not included here], I have from time to time discussed the issues with students, colleagues and friends. To some of them I am particularly indebted for ideas which have taken root in me. Gradually I have come to believe that the most basic error in the original formulation was in the description of science. I should like, in this section, to attempt to correct that error, and in the following section to reconcile the revised points of view.

* From C. R. Rogers. Persons or science? A philosophical question. *Amer. Psychologist*, 1955, **10**, 267–278. Reprinted with permission of the author and publisher.

The major shortcoming was, I believe, in viewing science as something "out there," something spelled with a capital S, a "body of knowledge" existing somewhere in space and time. In common with many psychologists I thought of science as a systematized and organized collection of tentatively verified facts, and saw the methodology of science as the socially approved means of accumulating this body of knowledge, and continuing its verification. It has seemed somewhat like a reservoir into which all and sundry may dip their buckets to obtain water—with a guarantee of 99% purity. When viewed in this external and impersonal fashion, it seems not unreasonable to see Science not only as discovering knowledge in lofty fashion, but as involving depersonalization, a tendency to manipulate, a denial of the basic freedom of choice which I have met experientially in therapy. I should like now to view the scientific approach from a different, and I hope, a more accurate perspective.

Science in Persons

Science exists only in people. Each scientific project has its creative inception, its process, and its tentative conclusion, in a person or persons. Knowledge—even scientific knowledge—is that which is subjectively acceptable. Scientific knowledge can be communicated only to those who are subjectively ready to receive its communication. The utilization of science also occurs only through people who are in pursuit of values which have meaning for them. These statements summarize very briefly something of the change in emphasis which I would like to make in my description of science. Let me follow through the various phases of science from this point of view.

The Creative Phase

Science has its inception in a particular person who is pursuing aims, values, purposes, which have personal and subjective meaning for him. As a part of this pursuit, he, in some area, "wants to find out." Consequently, if he is to be a good scientist, he immerses himself in the relevant experience, whether that be the physics laboratory, the world of plant or animal life, the hospital, the psychological laboratory or clinic, or whatever. This immersion is complete and subjective, similar to the immersion of the therapist in therapy, described previously. He senses the field in which he is interested, he lives it. He does more than "think" about it—he lets his organism take over and react to it, both on a knowing and on an unknowing level. He comes to sense more than he could possibly verbalize about his field, and reacts organismically in terms of relationships which are not present in his awareness.

Out of this complete subjective immersion comes a creative forming, a sense of direction, a vague formulation of relationships hitherto unrecognized. Whittled down, sharpened, formulated in clearer terms, this creative forming becomes a hypothesis—a statement of a tentative, personal, subjective faith. The scientist is saying, drawing upon all his known and unknown experience, that "I have a hunch that such and such a relationship exists, and the existence of this phenomenon has relevance to my personal values."

What I am describing is the initial phase of science, probably its most important phase, but one which American scientists, particularly psychologists, have been prone to minimize or ignore. It is not so much that it has been denied as that it has been quickly brushed off. Kenneth Spence has said that this aspect of science is "simply taken for granted." Like many experiences taken for granted, it also tends to be forgotten. It is indeed in the matrix of immediate personal, subjective experience that all science, and each individual scientific research, has its origin.

Checking with Reality

The scientist has then creatively achieved his hypothesis, his tentative faith. But does it check with reality? Experience has shown each one of us that it is very easy to deceive ourselves, to believe something which later experience shows is not so. How can I tell whether this tentative belief has some real relationship to observed facts? I can use, not one line of evidence only, but several. I can surround my observation of the facts with various precautions to make sure I am not deceiving myself. I can consult with others who have also been concerned with avoiding self-deception, and learn useful ways of catching myself in unwarranted beliefs, based on misinterpretation of observations. I can, in short, begin to use all the elaborate methodology which science has accumulated. I discover that stating my hypothesis in operational terms will avoid many blind alleys and false conclusions. I learn that control groups can help me to avoid drawing false inferences. I learn that correlations, and t tests and critical ratios and a whole array of statistical procedures can likewise aid me in drawing only reasonable inferences.

Thus scientific methodology is seen for what it truly is—a way of preventing me from deceiving myself in regard to my creatively formed subjective hunches which have developed out of the relationship between me and my material. It is in this context, and perhaps only in this context, that the vast structure of operationism, logical positivism, research design, tests of significance, etc. have their place. They exist, not for themselves, but as servants in the attempt to check the subjective feeling or hunch or hypothesis of a person with the objective fact.

And even throughout the use of such rigorous and impersonal methods, the important choices are all made subjectively by the scientist. To which of a number of hypotheses shall I devote time? What kind of control group is most suitable for avoiding self-deception in this particular research? How far shall I carry the statistical analysis? How much credence may I place in the findings? Each of these is necessarily a subjective personal judgment, emphasizing that the splendid structure of science rests basically upon its subjective use by persons. It is the best instrument we have yet been able to devise to check upon our organismic sensing of the universe.

The Findings

If, as scientist, I like the way I have gone about my investigation, if I have been open to all the evidence, if I have selected and used intelligently all the precautions against self-deception which I have been able to assimilate from others or to devise myself, then I will give my tentative belief to the findings which have emerged. I will regard them as a springboard for further investigation and further seeking.

It seems to me that in the best of science, the primary purpose is to provide a more satisfactory and dependable hypothesis, belief, faith, for the investigator himself. To the extent that the scientist is endeavoring to prove something to someone else—an error into which I have fallen more than once—then I believe he is using science to bolster a personal insecurity, and is keeping it from its truly creative role in the service of the person.

In regard to the findings of science, the subjective foundation is well shown in the fact that at times the scientist may refuse to believe his own findings. "The experiment showed thus and so, but I believe it is wrong," is a theme which every scientist has experienced at some time or other. Some very fruitful discoveries have grown out of the persistent *disbelief*, by a scientist, in his own findings and those of others. In the last analysis he may place more trust in his total organismic reactions than in the methods of science. There is no doubt that this can result in serious error as well as in scientific discoveries, but it indicates again the leading place of the subjective in the use of science.

Communication of Scientific Findings

Wading along a coral reef in the Caribbean this morning, I saw a large blue fish—I think. If you, quite independently, saw it too, then I feel more confident in my own observation. This is what is known as intersubjective verification, and it plays an important part in our understanding of science. If I take you (whether in conversation or in print or behaviorally) through the steps I have taken in an investigation, and it seems to you too that I have not deceived myself, and that I have indeed come across a new relationship which is relevant to my values, and that I am justified in having a tentative faith in this relationship, then we have the beginnings of Science with a capital S. It is at this point that we are likely to think we have created a body of scientific knowledge. Actually there is no such body of knowledge. There are only tentative beliefs, existing subjectively, in a number of different persons. If these beliefs are not tentative, then what exists is dogma, not science. If on the other hand, no one but the investigator believes the finding then this finding is either a personal and deviant matter, an instance of psychopathology, or else it is an unusual truth discovered by a genius, which as yet no one is subjectively ready to believe. This leads me to comment on the group which can put tentative faith in any given scientific finding.

Communication to Whom?

It is clear that scientific findings can be communicated only to those who have agreed to the same ground rules of investigation. The Australian bushman will be quite unimpressed with the findings of science regarding bacterial infection. He knows that illness truly is caused by evil spirits. It is only when he too agrees to scientific method as a good means of preventing self-deception, that he will be likely to accept its findings.

But even among those who have adopted the ground rules of science, tentative belief in the findings of a scientific research can only occur where there is a subjective readiness to believe. One could find many examples. Most psychologists are quite ready to believe evidence showing that the lecture system produces significant increments of learning, and quite unready to believe that the turn of an unseen card may be called through an ability labelled extrasensory perception. Yet the scientific evidence for the latter is considerably more impeccable than for the former. Likewise when the so-called "Iowa studies" first came out, indicating that intelligence might be considerably altered by environmental conditions, there was great disbelief among psychologists, and many attacks on the imperfect scientific methods used. The scientific evidence for this finding is not much better today than it was when the Iowa studies first appeared, but the subjective readiness of psychologists to believe such a finding has altered greatly. A historian of science has noted that empiricists, had they existed at the time, would have been the first to disbelieve the findings of Copernicus.

It appears then that whether I believe the scientific findings of others, or those from my own studies, depends in part on my readiness to put a tentative belief in such findings. One reason we are not particularly aware of this subjective fact is that in the physical sciences particularly, we have gradually adopted a very large area of experience in which we are ready to believe any finding which can be shown to rest upon the rules of the scientific game, properly played.

The Use of Science

But not only is the origin, process, and conclusion of science something which exists only in the subjective experience of persons—so also is its utilization. "Science" will never depersonalize, or manipulate, or control individuals. It is only persons who can and will do that. That is surely a most obvious and trite observation, yet a deep realization of it has had much meaning for me. It means that the use which will be made of scientific findings in the field of personality is and will be a matter of subjective personal choice—the same type of choice as a person makes in therapy. To the extent that he has defensively closed off areas of his experience from awareness, the person is more likely to make choices which are socially destructive. To the extent that he is open to all phases of his experience we may be sure that this person will be more likely to use the findings and methods of science (or any other tool or capacity) in a manner which is personally and socially constructive. There is, in actuality then, no threatening entity of "Science" which can in any way affect our destiny. There are only people. While many of them are indeed threatening and dangerous in their defensiveness, and modern scientific knowledge multiplies the social threat and danger, this is not the whole picture. There are two other significant facets. (1) There are many persons who are relatively open to their experience and hence likely to be socially constructive. (2) Both the subjective experience of psychotherapy and the scientific findings regarding it indicate that individuals are motivated to change, and may be helped to change, in the direction of greater openness to experience, and hence in the direction of behavior which is enhancing of self and society, rather than destructive.

To put it briefly, Science can never threaten us. Only persons can do that. And while individuals can be vastly destructive with the tools placed in their hands by scientific knowledge, this is only one side of the picture. We already have subjective and objective knowledge of the basic principles by which individuals may achieve the more constructive social behavior which is natural to their organismic process of becoming.

Editor's Note

A visitor from the planet Mars reading an elementary textbook might picture the scientist as a detached arbiter of ideas, unemotional as a computer, and eager to abandon his favorite theories at the first appearance of contradictory evidence. Further interaction with the species Homo sapiens would no doubt temper first impressions. Scientists, he would discover, are no more or less human than other scholars. In spite of every effort to be objective, some bias always remains in their professional thinking.

14. Science and Human Conduct *

James B. Conant
President Emeritus
Harvard University

Tonight I want to confine my attention to decisions affecting human conduct that seem to be fairly evenly balanced, where no deep-seated emotional reactions are involved—rational decisions, we may say. These may range from a determination to buy high-test gasoline rather than a cheaper grade, to the making up of one's mind to sign a petition to outlaw the atomic bomb. Or, if you are in a responsible position in the affairs of this highly industrialized world, you may have to vote yes or no on a proposed loan for the purpose of building a pilot plant to make a new product or a new machine.

There is a fairly common fallacy that if you are dealing with scientific and technical matters, judgment of values rarely, if ever, enters in. Facts speak for themselves in science, we are often told. Anyone who is familiar with the course of scientific research and development knows this is nonsense. What is true is that the area of debate is fairly definitely circumscribed. The proponent of a process

* Abridged from J. B. Conant. Science and human conduct. In *Modern science and modern man*. New York: Columbia, 1952. Pp. 65–70. Reprinted with permission of the author and publisher.

for making a new fabric, for example, is unlikely to quote either Plato or Aristotle on behalf of his proposal. Nor is he likely to appeal to the doctrines set forth in the Declaration of Independence or to the decisions of the Supreme Court. But that does not mean that what is proposed is not controversial. It means simply that the number of people qualified to take part in the controversy is highly limited. And this fact is one pregnant with trouble for our free society. Indeed, among the highly significant but dangerous results of the development of modern science is the fact that scientific experts now occupy a peculiarly exalted and isolated position. Of course, this is an age of experts of all types; one of the vital problems of education is to start a a trend of mind among our young people that will lead to a better understanding by one group of experts of what other groups of experts are doing. But I cannot take the time tonight to digress into this topic of general education.

The notion that a scientist is a cool, impartial, detached individual is, of course, absurd. The vehemence of conviction, the pride of authorship burn as fiercely among scientists as among any creative workers. Indeed, if they did not, there would be no advance in science. But this emotional attachment to one's own point of view is particularly insidious in science because it is so easy for the proponent of a project to clothe his convictions in technical language. Therefore it is necessary to explore ways and means of balancing the biases of experts whenever their opinions are of prime importance in the making of decisions.

First of all, a healthy skepticism is in order in listening to an expert, particularly an enthusiastic one. The next step is to try to find a person of equal technical competence but with an opposite emotional bias. If such a one is not at hand, some competent individual hitherto unconcerned with whatever project is in question should be asked to undertake the job of being "devil's advocate," as it were. He should be asked to devote himself to preparing the case for a reasoned opposition to what has been proposed. Such procedures for balancing the bias of technical men, particularly scientists turned inventors, have been worked out almost without plan in the successful industries of this nation. But similar methods of operating have not yet been evolved in other areas; they are absent in the United States Government. Yet here they are particularly needed, for, as I pointed out in my first lecture, the government has entered research and development on a very large scale indeed. It is inevitable that in any technological undertaking, conservatism must continually face enthusiasm. In so doing, emotions are aroused and personal fortunes become entangled with technological considerations.

There may be some who feel that my attitude towards science is defeatist, that instead of suggesting how the emotional reactions of scientists should be balanced when they are giving advice about future action, I should demand that scientists act like scientists and eliminate their prejudices. For example, a social scientist in answering affirmatively the question, "Can science save us?" has written as follows:

"Science, as a method, is a form of human behavior. It consists of asking clear, answerable questions in order to direct one's observations, which are made in a calm and unprejudiced manner and which are then reported as accurately as possible and in such a way as to answer the questions that were asked to begin with, after which any pertinent beliefs or assumptions that were held before the observations were made are revised in the light of observations made and answers obtained." All of which is a typical description of what is often called scientific behavior, but I venture to suggest it is not a description of the characteristic way the natural sciences have advanced; it is rather an account of the use of very limited working hypotheses not dissimilar to those employed in everyday life.

To illustrate what I mean by a limited working hypothesis, I shall have to revert for a moment to what I said in my first lecture about the development of modern science. I suggested that the activity we designate as scientific research is compounded of the empirical procedures by which man has improved the practical arts ever since the dawn of civilization, general speculative ideas, and mathematical or abstract reasoning. Science began to progress rapidly in the sixteenth and seventeenth centuries when people saw how to relate these three activities. When employed, the speculative ideas became working hypotheses on a grand scale; such conceptual schemes as "the earth is surrounded by a sea of air" could be tested by experiment only by being connected with actual manipulations by a series of limited working hypotheses. These are of the type "if I turn this stopcock, then such and such will happen." Only by a long chain of reasoning is the specific "if, then" proposition, which can be tested, related to the validity of the working hypothesis on a grand scale.

Editor's Note

Every scientific method begins with assumptions about the nature of the object under study, whether it be light, the electron, or man. Without some notion of what a thing is really like, objective techniques for observing it could not be developed. In psychology it is especially important to know what presuppositions have been made about the nature of man to avoid mistaking them for conclusions deduced from empirical evidence.

15. Assumptions in Psychology *

Adrian L. Van Kaam
Duquesne University

Important in the development of science is the realization that science is relatively subjective. It was physicists like Planck, Bohr, von Weizsaecker, and Heisenberg who made man aware of this. Especially the development of quantum physics made clear that the ideal of absolute objectivity and of an absolutely objective view of the universe was a dream never to be realized. Recent discoveries taught convincingly that every so-called scientific view of the world is extremely limited. Every scientist who approaches the universe selects necessarily one out of many viewpoints which could be taken. It is essential that the scientist does not look on man and the universe in all their dimensions but that he limits himself to a selected part of the universe. This selection is based on a choice and on assumptions which are relatively subjective.

Not only the physicists but other thinkers as well realized the relative subjectivity of science. Remarkable in this context is the so-called phenomenological way of thought. The phenomenologist studies man's primary experience. This experience is more comprehensive than the conceptual knowledge which man selects later from his original experience by means of analysis. This original ex-

* From A. L. Van Kaam. Assumptions in psychology. *J. indiv. Psychol.*, 1958, **14**, 22–28. Reprinted with permission of the author and publisher.

perience precedes clear conceptualization. It is the matrix of all partial concepts arbitrarily chosen by man. Man in his primary experience is still open to the universe. He is in contact with the fullness of reality in all its nuances. This experience is therefore essentially different from the scientific way of knowing. Man can only understand in a scientific way when he subjectively limits his original view. In order to be scientific he must adopt an attitude other than the open prescientific one. He has to change and to reduce that which was originally given in his primary experience. What are considered to be objects in science are not objects which are given as such, but which are viewed in a specific frame because man orients himself subjectively in a certain way toward reality. Naive experience does not know about the objects of science but knows people, houses, trees, birds and flowers, love, hate and anxiety.

When man determines subjectively that he will consider all these realities in a scientific way then he limits his experience of them by some subjectively created frame of reference. They are no longer what they were. So-called exact data are rather interpretations of man's primary experience. Scientific thinking forgoes primary experience instead of penetrating it. The scientific view of man and the universe is thus the result of a certain modification of the human attitude. The primary experience of the world is fenced in by science. Science modifies experience fundamentally. And it does this by means of a subjective choice by man.

The realization by contemporary physicists and phenomenologists that science is relatively subjective made man more aware of the fact that he always starts from certain assumptions in his scientific endeavors.

Denial of Assumptions

Psychology does not absorb easily these new realizations. Various psychologists try to escape the realization that assumptions are inevitable. Some of them profess that they consider all the views of all the schools of psychology as equally relative and that they themselves start without any assumption. But by declaring all these views to be relative the psychologist cannot escape having his own very definite view. The more this relativity of the different psychological viewpoints is stressed, the more forcefully the absolute character of one's own position in psychology reveals itself. Perhaps it could be called a superviewpoint, but nevertheless it remains a viewpoint. It offers no escape from a decisive, absolute choice of position in the understanding of man.

Others say that there are no assumptions because they cannot be proven by means of the scientific method. Even this effort to get rid of assumptions is in vain. For to declare that only these propositions of psychologists make sense which can be experimentally verified is one of the most sweeping assumptions one can think of because it contains a definite and irrevocable judgment concerning all possibilities of human knowledge and their relationship to what is knowable. There is no escape from assumptions in psychology. The psychologist of every school always makes an ultimate and absolute judgment about what is called the nature of man and about the way in which man can be understood. These assumptions of psychologists are not arrived at by psychological research. On the contrary, the assumptions of the psychologist are the point of departure for the kind of research that he will perform and for the evaluation of the results of this research.

Reasons for the Denial

It seems more difficult for the field of psychology than for other areas to assimilate the new realization that science is relatively subjective and always implies assumptions which cannot be arrived at by the scientific method itself.

The early psychologists were inclined to imitate

physics. This tradition still influences many psychologists today. But what they actually know about physics are probably the optimistic tenets of the early physicists. They seem less familiar with the realizations of such physicists as mentioned at the outset. They are therefore less sensitive to the relative subjectivity of science than some of their contemporaries are.

Early psychology had to free itself from the dominance of philosophy. It was understandable that the psychologist reacted against a domineering philosophy which at that time was rationalistic and abstract. An unfortunate consequence is that many psychologists now are inclined more than other intellectuals to underevaluate all publications which are of a more theoretical, philosophical or literary nature. This may result in a certain narrow-mindedness, an unawareness of what is transpiring on the contemporary intellectual scene. Because of this, certain psychologists may be less able to profit from the new realizations which are expressed in these other areas, concerning the nature of science.

Psychology was a relatively young science which had to prove itself. Science rightly claims a certain degree of objectivity and consistency in its methods and factual results, once the scientist has subjectively selected a small segment of reality as an object of research. It is easily understood again that the insecure psychologist of that day was inclined to over-stress his claims on objectivity. As a result of this historical condition certain psychologists today are more afraid than other scholars to admit in the light of the new realizations that assumptions are inescapable and that they are not provable by the scientific method itself.

The psychologist who believes that his assumptions and the interpretation of the outcomes of his research are absolutely objective may be inclined to construct his view of life on the basis of these findings. His science becomes his philosophy of life. This makes it more difficult for him to tolerate the realization that his scientism, as much as science itself, is finally built on assumptions which according to his feeling are not trustworthy because they are not based on results of the scientific method.

Another factor may be that certain scientists who are committed to a certain kind of minute research may have a more or less compulsive personality structure. Science in their lives may have the function of organizing reality in such a way that they feel sure that they can at least potentially measure, control and dominate the unknown. The realization that assumptions which are not experimentally demonstrable are at the base of their science could evoke anxiety. In this case the avoidance of this realization operates as a subtle defense.

Finally the character of experimental work does not lead directly to the realization of all the implications of experimental psychology. One even has to admit that as far as the psychologist is aware of these problems it is to his advantage to bar them from his awareness as long as he is engaged in experimental research. Paying attention to assumptions during the experimentation itself would make scientific work impossible. This attitude of abstraction from the assumptions involved during experimentation extends itself easily outside the laboratory and makes the experimenter blind to the very existence of the assumptions involved.

The education of the psychologist suffers necessarily from the imperfections which characterize psychology itself. From the very beginning the student may be inclined not to take seriously certain sources of knowledge of reality such as philosophy and literature which are common to other intellectuals in his culture. At the same time he does not have the preparation that would enable him to involve himself deeply in a modern science such as physics. So he misses also the realizations that are common to the modern physicist.

Awareness of Assumptions

In spite of all this one finds an increasing number of psychologists who become aware of the fact that their research necessarily takes its departure from relatively subjective assumptions. The reason is probably not that these psychologists are better acquainted with the latest results of quantum physics and the relativity of the scientific view that is one of the consequences of its recent development. Nor can it probably be explained by a deeper and more extensive knowledge of contemporary art, literature and philosophy.

How did these psychologists escape intellectual isolation? It seems that they are for the most part psychologists who are interested in the clinical area. This interest implies concern for the human person and especially for his experimental life. This genuine and lasting attention to the experience of man may lead to the realization that his relatively subjective experience is the source of all his endeavors even in science. And it is here that clinical psychology approaches the realizations of modern thinking and the perceptivity of contemporary existence. One of the results is that these psychologists tend to be more aware of assumptions and try to make them explicit.

We could in a somewhat inaccurate way draw a distinction between positivistic and phenomenological-existential psychologists. When we ask ourselves about their relative subjectivity, we may characterize this as follows. The subjectivity of the positivistic psychologist seems to be a more repressed and inaccessible, rigid and closed subjectivism. This means that he is inclined to see his relatively subjective assumptions as absolutely objective. He has a certain disdain for reflection on subjective assumptions, and even a certain fear of this reflection. This more or less repressed subjectivism tends to make him rigid and absolute regarding, for instance, the evaluation of his methods. He may, for instance, believe that quantifying methods are the only ones which are worthwhile. And because the relatively subjective basis for this belief is not open to his continual reflection he has no means to correct this attitude.

The subjectivity of the more phenomenological-existential psychologist seems to be more accessible, flexible and open. He is less inclined to believe that his assumptions are absolutely objective. He is more aware of what determines his scientific work. This prevents subjective influence from becoming too fixed and too rigid. It makes him more open to the subjective determinants which influence other people in psychology and other fields. He is inclined to reflect on his relatively subjective assumptions and to ask himself from time to time whether they are still tenable, whether they can be expanded or reconciled with the relatively subjective viewpoints of other men who study in one or another way the human person. He might even see the concept of science itself as a growing and changing concept. Dependent on relatively subjective assumptions, this concept takes on a different meaning and content in different periods of culture.

It is clear that such an open, flexible and accessible subjectivism could be promoted in students of psychology. One could require that they write down in every research paper what their basic assumptions are. While interpreting the results, they would have to indicate clearly what the interpretation would be in the light of their own assumptions and what, in the light of the assumptions of some other prominent schools of psychology.

Positivistic versus Phenomenological Assumptions

Finally one could ask, what are the assumptions of the positivistic psychologists and what are those of the phenomenologically existential ones? It would be impossible to elaborate on this extensively in this paper. It briefly comes down to this, that the more positivistic psychologist still adheres implicitly to the two assumptions of mechanism and determinism which were characteristic of early physics. Mechanism implies a wholly quantitative theory of atoms-without-qualities. This implicit assumption is more and more in contradiction with the facts discovered by the physicists. The same is true of the development in psychology. The implicit assumption that man can be understood by analyzing him into elements which are statistically the same is basically in contradiction with reality. In other words, the assumption of mechanism that all phenomena can be reduced to local change or to a change in position of intrinsically immutable particles is no longer tenable in view of the facts. But it still influences the scientific work of the positivistic psychologist. Another assumption of the early physicists, namely that of determinism, was that every situation of primordial particles at any given moment was determined by an inner law and by the situation at another moment. This assumption in its psychological form is still of great influence on the thinking of the positivistic psychologist. The physicists are far more cautious since the principle of uncertainty was formulated by Heisenberg. We call both tenets philosophical assumptions. We call them assumptions because they do not find support in strictly empirical theory. We call them philosophical because of the absoluteness with which they are held: they are applied by the positivistic mind to everything in man and in the universe.

The assumptions of phenomenological-existential psychologists are of as great a variety as those of the positivistic psychologists. The scope of our paper allows us only to refer to them negatively as the contrary of an absolute mechanism and an absolute determinism. They are the counterpart in psychology of the new assumptions of the quantum physicists and the existential philosophers. Becoming, creativity, growth, self-actualization are terms which more or less indicate in which direction these assumptions are developing.

16. Scientific Presuppositions *

Rollo May
William Alanson White Institute of Psychiatry and New York University

Another question that has perennially perplexed many of us in psychology has already been implied above [reference not pertinent here], and we now turn to it explicitly. What are the presuppositions which underlie our science and our practice? I do not say "scientific method" here; already a good deal of attention has been paid, and rightly, to the problem of methodology. But every method is based on certain presuppositions—assumptions about the nature of man, the nature of his experience, and so forth. These presuppositions are partially conditioned by our culture and by the particular point in history at which we stand. As far as I can see, this crucial area is almost always covered over in psychology: we tend to assume uncritically and implicitly that our particular method is true for all time. The statement that science has built-in self-corrective measures—which is partially true—cannot be taken as a reason for overlooking the fact that our particular science is culturally and historically conditioned and is thereby limited even in its self-corrective measures.

At this point, the existential insistence is that, because every psychology, every way of understanding man, is based upon certain presuppositions, the psychologist must continually analyze and clarify his own presuppositions. One's presuppositions always limit and constrict what one sees in a problem, experiment, or therapeutic situation; from this aspect of our human "finiteness" there is no escape. The naturalist perceives in man what fits his naturalistic spectacles; the positivist sees the aspects of experience that fit the logical forms of his propositions; and it is well known that different therapists of different schools will see in the same dream of a single patient the dynamics that fit the theory of their particular school. The old parable of the blind men and the elephant is writ large on the activities of men in the enlightened twentieth century as well as those of earlier, more "benighted" ages. Bertrand Russell puts the problem well with respect to physical science: "Physics is mathematical not because we know so much about the physical world but because we know so little; it is only its mathematical properties that we can discover."

No one, physicist, psychologist, or anyone else, can leap out of his historically conditioned skin. But the one way we can keep the presuppositions underlying our particular method from undue biasing effect is to know consciously what they are and so not to absolutize or dogmatize them. Thus we have at least a chance of refraining from forcing our subjects or patients upon our "procrustean couches" and lopping off, or refusing to see, what does not fit.

In Ludwig Binswanger's little book relating his conversations and correspondence with Freud, *Sigmund Freud: Reminiscences of a Friendship,*[1] there are some interesting interchanges illustrating this point. The friendship between Freud, the psychoanalyst, and Binswanger, a leading existential psychiatrist of Switzerland, was lifelong and tender, and it marks the only instance of Freud's continuing in friendship with someone who differed radically with him.

Shortly before Freud's eightieth birthday, Binswanger wrote an essay describing how Freud's theory had radically deepened clinical psychiatry, but he added that Freud's own existence as a person pointed beyond the deterministic presuppositions of his theory. "Now [with Freud's psychoanalytic contribution] man is no longer merely an animated organism, but a 'living being' who has

[1] From Ludwig Binswanger, *Sigmund Freud: Reminiscences of a Friendship,* Grune & Stratton, New York, 1957, p. 90. Reprinted with permission of the author and publisher.

origins in the finite life process of this earth, and who dies its life and lives its death; illness is no longer an externally or internally caused disturbance of the 'normal' course of a life on the way to its death." But Binswanger went on to point out that as a result of his interest in existential analysis, he believed that in Freud's theory man is not yet man in the full sense of the word:

> . . . for to be a man does not mean merely to be a creature begotten by living-dying life, cast into it and beaten about, and put in high spirits or low spirits by it; it means to be a being that looks its own and mankind's fate in the face, a being that is "steadfast," i.e., one taking its own stance, or one standing on its own feet. . . . The fact that our lives are determined by the forces of life, is only one side of the truth; the other is that we determine these forces as our fate. Only the two sides together can take in the full problem of sanity and insanity. Those who, like Freud, have forged their fates with the hammer—the work of art he has created in the medium of language is sufficient evidence of this—can dispute this fact least of all (*ibid.*).

Then, on the occasion of Freud's eightieth birthday, the Viennese Medical Society invited Binswanger, along with Thomas Mann, to deliver papers at the anniversary celebration. Freud himself did not attend, not being in good health and also, as he wrote Binswanger, not being fond of anniversary celebrations. ("They seem to be on the American model.") Binswanger spent two days with Freud in Vienna at the time of this birthday and remarked that in these conversations he was again impressed by how far Freud's own largeness and depth of humanity as a man surpassed his scientific theories.

In his paper at the celebration, Binswanger gave credit to Freud for having enlarged and deepened our insight into human nature more, perhaps, than anyone since

Aristotle. But he went on to point out that these insights wore "a theoretic-scientific garb that as a whole appeared to me too 'one-sided' and narrow." He held that Freud's great contribution was in the area of *homo natura,* man in relation to nature (*Umwelt*)—drives, instincts, and similar aspects of experience. And as a consequence, Binswanger believed that in Freud's theory there was only a shadowy, epiphenomenal understanding of man in relation to his fellow men (*Mitwelt*) and that the area of man in relation to himself (*Eigenwelt*) was omitted entirely.

Binswanger sent a copy of the paper to Freud and a week later received a letter from him containing the following sentences:

> As I read it I was delighted with your beautiful language, your erudition, the vastness of your horizon, your tactfulness in contradicting me. As is well known, one can put up with vast quantities of praise. . . . *Naturally, for all that you have failed to convince me.* I have always confined myself to the ground floor and basement of the edifice. You maintain that by changing one's point of view, one can also see the upper story, in which dwell such distinguished guests as religion, art, etc. . . . I have already found a place for religion, by putting it under the category of "the neurosis of mankind." But probably we are speaking at cross purposes, and our differences will be ironed out only after centuries. In cordial friendship, and with greetings to your charming wife, your Freud (*ibid.,* pp. 96 and 99).

Binswanger then adds in his book—and this is the central reason we quote the interchange—"As can be seen from the last sentence, Freud loked upon our differences as something to be surmounted by empirical investigation, not as something bearing upon the transcendental conceptions that underly all empirical research."

In my judgment, Binswanger's point is irrefutable. One can gather empirical data, let us say on religion and art, from now till doomsday, and one will never get any closer to understanding these activities if, to start with, his presuppositions shut out what the religious person is dedicated to and what the artist is trying to do. Deterministic presuppositions make it possible to understand everything about art except the creative act and the art itself; mechanistic naturalistic presuppositions may undercover many facts about religion, but, as in Freud's terms, religion will always turn out to be more or less a neurosis, and what the genuinely religious person is concerned with will never get into the picture at all.

The point we wish to make in this discussion is the necessity of analyzing the presuppositions one assumes and of making allowance for the sectors of reality—which may be large indeed—that one's particular approach necessarily leaves out. In my judgment, we in psychology have often truncated our understanding and distorted our perception by failure consciously to clarify these presuppositions.

I vividly recall how, back in my graduate days in psychology some twenty years ago, Freud's theories tended to be dismissed as "unscientific" because they did not fit the methods then in vogue in graduate schools of psychology. I maintained at the time that this missed the point: Freud had uncovered realms of human experience of tremendous importance, and if they did not fit our methods, so much the worse for our methods; the problem was to devise new ones. In actual fact, the methods did catch up—perhaps, one should add, with a vengeance, until, as Rogers has stated, Freudianism is now the dogma of American clinical psychology. Remembering my own graduate-school days, I am therefore inclined to smile when someone says that the concepts of existential psychology are "unscientific" because they do not fit the particular methods *now* in vogue.

It is certainly clear that the Freudian mechanisms invite the separation into discrete cause-and-effect formulations which fit the deterministic methodology dominant in American psychology. But what also needs to be seen is that this making of Freudianism into the dogma of psychology has been accomplished at the price of omitting essential and vitally important aspects of Freud's thought. There is at present a three-cornered liaison, in tendency and to some extent in actuality, between Freudianism, behaviorism in psychology, and positivism in philosophy. An example of the first side of the liaison is the great similarity between Hull's drive-reduction theory of learning and Freud's concept of pleasure, the goal of behavior, as consisting of the reduction of stimuli. An example of the second is the statement of the philosopher Herman Feigl in his address at a recent annual convention of the American Psychological Association, that Freud's specific mechanisms could be formulated and used scientifically, but such concepts as the "death instinct" could not be.

But the trouble there is that such concepts as the "death instinct" in Freud were precisely what saved him from the full mechanistic implications of his system; these concepts always point beyond the deterministic limitations of his theory. They are, in the best sense of the word, a mythology. Freud was never content to let go of this mythological dimension to his thinking despite his great effort at the same time to formulate psychology in terms of his nineteenth-century biological presuppositions. In my judgment, his mythology is fundamental to the greatness of his contribution and essential to his central discoveries, such as "the unconscious." It was likewise essential to his radical contribution to the new image of man, namely, man as pushed by demonic, tragic, and destructive forces. I have tried elsewhere to show that Freud's tragic concept of the Oedipus is much closer to the truth than our tendency to interpret the Oedipus complex in terms of discrete sexual and hostile relationships in the family. The formulation of the "death instinct" as a biological instinct makes no sense, of course, and in this sense is rightly rejected by American behaviorism and positivism. But as a psychological and spiritual statement of the tragic nature of man, the idea has very great importance indeed and transcends any purely biological or mechanistic interpretation.

Methodology always suffers from a cultural lag. Our problem is to open our vision to more of human experience, to develop and free our methods so that they will as far as possible do justice to the richness and breadth of man's experience. This can be done only by analysing the philosophical presuppositions. As Maslow pithily states in Chapter II [reference is not relevant here], "It is extremely important for psychologists that the existentialists may supply psychology with the underlying philosophy which it now lacks. At any rate, the basic philosophical problems will surely be opened up for discussion again, and perhaps psychologists will stop relying on pseudosolutions or on unconscious unexamined philosophies they picked up as children."

Editor's Note

In the study of nature, science is immensely successful in meeting the challenge, "How do I know I know?" No data are accepted as validating evidence unless based upon objective evidence, and nothing makes a person feel quite as certain of himself as being able to say, "I saw it with my own eyes," or "I measured it myself." Systematic procedures for controlling irrelevant factors and for providing for replication further reinforce the feeling of certitude.

Considered as a form of thinking, science does not differ dramatically from other disciplines. Reasoning is not the sole possession of any field. The scientist is unique in the way he obtains his data, not in the way he theorizes. Scholars in every area employ a similar strategy of problem solving whenever they do rigorous thinking.

17. Science and the Understanding of Behavior *

Louis S. Levine
San Francisco State College

The difficulties complicating man's effort to understand human behavior also are encountered whenever he tries to relate natural events to one another. His limited observational capacities, his inability to give accurate emphasis to all aspects of the problem before him, the influence of his emotions, and the difficulty of inferring meaning from his observations, all handicap him in his efforts to understand any aspect of his world. Through the years, man's awareness of these obstacles to knowledge has led to his developing methods for evaluating evidence and for systematically relating observations to one another, and procedures for testing assumptions about these relationships. These methods and procedures have contributed significantly to extending man's knowledge in all spheres, including the study of man himself, and while they will not be precisely the same for all problems, they have a common origin in what Dewey describes as the "scientific attitude":

> In short, the scientific attitude as here conceived is a quality that is manifested in any walk of life. What, then, is it? On its negative side, it is freedom from control by routine, prejudice, dogma, unexamined tradition, sheer self-interest. Positively, it is the will to inquire, to examine, to discriminate, to draw conclusions only on the basis of evidence, of taking pains to gather all available evidence. It is the intention to reach beliefs, and to test those that are entertained, on the basis of observed fact, recognizing also that facts are without meaning save as they point to ideas. It is, in turn, the experimental attitude which recognizes that while ideas are necessary to deal with facts, yet they are working hypotheses to be tested by the consequences they produce.[1]

Dewey's statement makes it clear that the possession of a scientific attitude is not limited to professional scientists. All men may share the scientist's desire to predict accurately the outcomes of specific situations or to modify conditions to achieve a particular result. But all men do not value the scientific attitude equally, and relatively few are skilled in the methods and techniques utilized in any one of the scientific disciplines.

However, these different methods and techniques are merely specific ways of applying the same principle. Regardless of the phenomena being considered the scientific acquisition of knowledge involves: (*a*) stating a research problem by asking a clear and answerable question; (*b*) formulating a hypothesis; (*c*) defining all terms and methods used; (*d*) collecting and analyzing the data; and (*e*) verifying the conclusion by repeating the study. Thus, all terms, procedures, and methods must be explicitly

[1] From John Dewey, Unity of science as a social problem, *International Encyclopedia of Unified Science*, Vol. I, No. 1–5. Copyright 1955 by the University of Chicago. Reprinted by permission. [Footnote renumbered.]

specified so that other investigators can corroborate or reject the findings. The body of knowledge arrived at by these five steps is what we know as science.

Science provides a means for evaluating the adequacy of beliefs concerning natural events and phenomena, but those pertaining to events or conditions outside the scope of objective human experience are scientifically untestable. The proposition that there is a life after death must be accepted or rejected on other than scientific grounds. Beliefs that cannot be communicated to others or cast in forms suitable for investigation also are outside the realm of science. The assertion that the poetry of Keats is superior to that of Shelley may be debated, but it cannot be evaluated scientifically until the definition of "superior" is agreed upon.

A person having a scientific attitude is willing to examine the evidence for his beliefs. Clinging to absolute convictions about natural events without considering the evidence is inconsistent with a scientific attitude, for science deals in tentative, not final, truths. In the kingdom of science, beliefs are always open to examination no matter how strongly held or imposingly supported.

Although the specific procedures employed by different sciences vary, they have in common the goal of accumulating and evaluating evidence. All sciences provide for careful observation, and many of the devices popularly associated with the scientist have been developed to extend the scope and power of his senses. The astronomer's telescope and the biologist's microscope enable the observer to see stars and cells that are invisible to the naked eye. In addition, the scientist deliberately and explicitly attempts to classify his observations. Such classification is helpful as he tries to understand how events and their antecedents and consequences are related. Classification also assists him in communicating his procedures and results to his colleagues, so that they can duplicate the investigation and verify his reported findings.

Editor's Note

At one time the brain was thought of as a complex switchboard, charged with the task of making appropriate connections between incoming and outgoing signals. Current neurophysiological models assign it a more active role, including some control over the things allowed to become conscious. In particular, the reticular formation is pictured as a brainstem secretary, monitoring all sensory information to determine which should be relayed to headquarters and which screened out. Without this assistance the brain would be overwhelmed with the logistics of finding places in consciousness for all the competing stimuli.

At the conceptual level scientific theories perform a similar secretarial service. The conditions surrounding and preceding any event are infinite, and no good purpose would be served by attempting to record them all. Some analogous screening device is needed to isolate relevant from irrelevant observations and, since nature does not supply it, creative imagination must. Selection is made in terms of mental constructs, exemplified by the atom, the electron, and magnetic lines of force which introduce order into the observations and, it is hoped, explain them. When a new phenomenon is discovered, one or another of these mental constructs can usually be revised to accommodate it into competing theories. For this reason the same objective data do not seem equally convincing to every scientist. Evidence which to one appears overwhelming may leave another quite unmoved.

18. The Need of Theory *

D. O. Hebb
McGill University

It has been suggested that physiology "cannot cast any vote" in the choice of psychological principles. Whether it should or not, it always has. It is now clear that Wert-

* From D. O. Hebb. The role of neurological ideas in psychology. *J. Pers.*, 1951, **20**, 39–55. Reprinted with permission of the author and publisher.

heimer and Köhler were on the right track about 1920 in their account of the afferent visual process, well in advance of the neurologist. Essentially, they were postulating an interaction among cells at the same level in transmission from the retina. If one will read for example Marshall and Talbot, one will find a very Gestalt-like account of activity in area seventeen of the cortex, based on physiological knowledge derived mostly after 1930. But despite the actual soundness of the Gestalt position, both psychologically and neurologically, it was vehemently rejected as mystical because it was "known" in 1920 that the nervous system does not act in that way.

Was such a vote (in this case, a wrong one) possible only in the neurologically deluded twenties? Not at all. Spence's brilliant treatment of insight and the sudden solution in discrimination learning had a profound effect on those "tough-minded" psychologists who were (and are) opposed to physiologizing. For them, to judge from the literature, the evidence of insight reported by Köhler and Krech was not so until Spence showed how it might be dealt with. But Spence's solution could be tough-minded (i.e., provide an intelligible mechanism of response) because the conception of physiological gradients was already familiar from embryological studies; familiarized in biology by Kappers and Child (it is credited to them by Lashley, who also used the idea theoretically), it was used as well in a frankly physiological sense by Pavlov and the Gestalt group. Spence had a physiological passport even while he denied physiologizing.

A final and extreme example of the present day: why do we not accept ESP as a psychological fact? Rhine has offered enough evidence to have convinced us on almost any other issue where one could make some guess as to the mechanics of the disputed process. Some of his evidence has been explained away, but as far as I can find out, not all of it. Until a complete rebuttal is provided or until we accept ESP, let us not talk about enlarging our notions of neurology to meet the psychological "facts" with no external criterion of what those facts are. We are still trying to find our way out of the magic wood of animism, where psychology began historically, and we cannot give up the talisman of a knowledge of material processes. Personally, I do not accept ESP for a moment, because it does not make sense. My external criteria, both of physics and of physiology, say that ESP is not a fact despite the behavioral evidence that has been reported. I cannot see what other basis my colleagues have for rejecting it; and if they are using my basis, they and I are allowing psychological evidence to be passed on by physical and physiological censors. Rhine may still turn out to be right, improbable as I think that is, and my own rejection of his views is—in the literal sense—prejudice.

The theory of behavior must ultimately be consistent with both behavioral and physiological evidence. Either discipline can blackball the idea that strays too far from existing knowledge, even conceivably the sound idea that it should not. If some ultra-genius, with divine revelation, suddenly turned up one day with a "true" and complete theory of behavior as it may ultimately be known some millennia from now, he might find it impossible even to get a hearing from psychologists for what would seem preposterously unreal notions. The situation would be like one in which Einstein on being admitted to the houseboat on the Styx tried to explain quantum mechanics to Archimedes and Euclid, these persons not having yet heard of the electron, of the way in which electromagnetic waves can exist in a nonexistent ether, or even of the theory of gravitation. We commonly think of a theory as right or wrong, true or untrue: but is there any possibility at all of having a true theory of behavior today? Newton was a genius because his theories could be accepted for 250 years or so, but they are not thought to be correct or adequate today. The best we can ask therefore is that a theory should be good, not correct.

And in psychology we must expect to have to work our way progressively through a series of ideas, of better and better theories. It is not by any means a condemnation of S-R theory to say that it is narrow or that there are facts which (we are now pretty sure) it cannot comprehend. The significant question is not whether Thorndike's account of animal learning was right, but whether it helped us to see better the problems involved and led to new analyses. In Hull's systematizing, in Tolman's ability to define purpose without philosophic teleology, in Lashley's analysis of animal perception, or Köhler's and Krech's experimental demonstrations of insight, the evidence is clear concerning the stimulating and clarifying value of stimulus-response theory and its erroneous (because incomplete) physiological foundation.

This point of view shows how to clear up a possible ambiguity in the discussion by MacLeod and Smith concerning the way in which a phenomenologist goes about his business. The suggestion is that the phenomenologist is one who puts aside bias (either of theory or of common sense) and simply observes what is before him. But MacLeod then adds that this is never entirely possible and speaks of observing with a "disciplined naïveté." The ambiguity comes in the possible interpretation that getting rid of theory completely would make for the clearest observation (or in the apparent contradiction of discipline and naïveté). From the point of view we have now arrived at, an answer is possible for this difficulty. It is not getting rid of theory entirely that is needed (otherwise the thing to do would be to get a backwoodsman, or someone else who had never heard of psychology, to observe in one's experiments), but to put theory in the background instead of the foreground where it blocks one's vision. The "discipline" is in a thorough knowledge of theory; the "naïveté" consists of trying to find other ways of looking at the world besides the one dictated by existing theory. Essentially, phenomenology means looking for new biases, not getting rid of bias.

I have spoken of the common observation that theory moves by short steps. This observation may be thought of as implying only a negative influence from earlier theory, as providing evidence simply of the inertia of human thought. But there must be more to the process than that. Einstein's formulation would not have been possible without the observations gathered under the influence of Newton's ideas. Earlier theories, then, are limiting for a very good reason. They are what one climbs on to get to the next stage—it is also a common observation that a stepladder is *very* narrow and limiting, when one is using it.

In other words, we must recognize the positive value even of "wrong" theories as guides to observation. If the phenomenologist could really divest himself of all his theoretical knowledge and tried then to record the facts of his own perception or of an animal's behavior, what would he choose to put down on paper? There are an infinite number of relationships and aspects of behavior, an infinitude of possible subdivisions of animal activity or of human thought. *Some* theoretical guide is necessary as a principle of selection.

What the phenomenologically minded individual has always recorded is what he sees that is related to, but inconsistent with, existing theory. It is in such a sense only that he avoids bias, and this of course is not really avoiding it. A better way of defining a phenomenologist might be to say that he is one of those who, at the extreme, do not like existing theories (and perhaps never will) but are interested in attacking them and finding evidence that is hard for theory to handle: an "agin-the-established-order" attitude, anti-theoretical but not a-theoretical, which historically has been an important source of new ideas and experiments.

A figure of speech used elsewhere may help to clear this up. There appears to be a left wing and a right wing in psychology, paralleling Left and Right in politics, and the activity of the Left cannot be understood if one does not see that the only continuity in its behavior is in being against the Right. In psychology the Right favors parsimony of explanatory ideas, a simple or mechanical account of behavior, and definiteness even at the cost of being narrow. The Left is prepared to postulate more freely and can better tolerate vagueness and a lack of system in its account of behavior. Thus Gestalt psychology, especially in its early years, could develop a theory of perception and a theory of thought that were not brought into any clear relationship with one another, and a theory of memory ("traces") that seemed downright inconsistent with the Gestalt account of perception. But the primary motivation was not to develop a theory; it was to demonstrate the shortcomings of stimulus-response theory, and the scientific benefits that accrued from this effort are obvious—just as obvious as the fact that such an attitude (which includes the phenomenologist's) is not possible without a theory to attack.

The Baconian Fallacy

The idea that one could observe more clearly if one could divest himself of all preceding theory, or that psychology would be better off without theory, is related to a widespread epistemological misconception concerning the scientific method. This notion goes back through J. S. Mill to Francis Bacon and can, for convenience here, be called the Baconian fallacy. It is in the first place the idea that scientific generalizations are arrived at by "induction," by counting noses, and from this derives the idea that scientific laws are empirical. It implies that there are a limited number of "facts," "events," or properties of any object or situation, so that the scientist can proceed by simply describing, even, if it is desirable, by recording *everything* that happens in conjunction with whatever phenomenon he is interested in. There is no useful purpose for creative imagination. Causes can be discovered simply by assiduity: list everything that preceded the to-be-explained event, on a thousand or ten thousand occasions if necessary, and if your lists are complete, the cause will be the one thing that is on every list. (In practice there are short cuts, and the lists may be remembered instead of written out.)

But anyone can see that there is something wrong here when the crude implications of the induction idea are followed up in this way. The next step is to abandon an interest in causes (especially hypothetical causes that can hardly get into one's lists) and at a high level of sophistication regard scientific law as a statement of probability only, and science as description. Theory is tautology and self-delusion.

To such views the following propositions may be opposed.

(A) Induction and counting cases are only methods of demonstration or of testing a generalization already arrived at (often on the basis of a single case).

(B) The typical scientific law is not a summary of observations and has nothing to do with probability but is a working postulate or mode of thought. If apparent contradictions of a useful law are observed, one promptly postulates something else to account for them instead of discarding the law.

(C) Of such modes of thought, the cause-and-effect one is still generally used though not a necessary way of thinking nor valuable in all situations.

(D) The scientist is characteristically concerned with his postulated entities more than with the phenomena they were inferred from (the chemist interested in atomic weights rather than in weights of actual materials, the physicist interested in neutrons and mesons rather than photographs of cloud chambers or even bombs). Science itself is characteristically an elaborate structure of imagined entities and events.

(E) Since there is an infinity of things that can be

recorded in any situation, a complete description is a meaningless conception along with a purely descriptive science. Constructs may be formally tautological and yet have the practical function of guiding observation.

These propositions may be clearer with a few examples. Newton's first law of motion has been a profoundly valuable theoretical tool, but it certainly was not an induction or summary description, for no such event as an object's continuing to move indefinitely with uniform speed in a straight line has ever been observed—not even once, nor an approximation thereto. To make the law a statement of probability is nonsense. One can assume that it is true, or that it is not true; and one can then go on to see what other assumptions must also be made and what deductions can be made from them. Experimental verification amounts to showing that the whole set is consistent with facts or leads to the discovery of new facts, also consistent.

The law of gravitation *is* a vast and impressive tautology: forces are mythical, and postulating a force of gravitation that is known only through the phenomena it is supposed to explain really adds nothing to the facts—not in this sense. But if we think of the construct of gravity as a statement of a new way of thinking, which made the tide, the orbit of the earth, and falling downstairs all examples of a single class of phenomena, one can see better the practical role of even a tautological construct. Reclassifying a group of facts does not add to the number of facts classified, but the reclassification is a significant fact itself. Logically, perhaps explanation reduces to ordering and classifying phenomena only, but it is impossible for man to think consistently in such terms.

The atom and the electron are just as much constructs as gravity, for no one has ever seen or handled either though it is now hard to realize that they are not facts (i.e., directly known phenomena). Their function too must be heuristic, as long as one is being utterly logical. It is perhaps a weakness of the human intellect that it must resort to such devices, but I think it is clear that thought is incorrigible in this respect. Thinking does not proceed according to formal logic, even in natural science or mathematics (Courant and Robbins, Conant, Hadamard) and attempting to act as if it did must be sterile.

If, as it seems, the scientist inveterately resorts to imagined things and properties of things to fill in the gaps as it were in natural phenomena, his problem is to imagine the right things, to choose the constructs that do increase order in perceived events (or make possible an orderly universe that is more imagined than perceived). Sometimes the clarifying effect of a newly postulated entity is so immediate and extensive that its value is obvious. It is a "discovery," at once accepted as "true." But often, because one is dealing with a number of postulates at once, so that the same effect might perhaps be achieved by changing some other postulate, the fruitfulness of the new conception is not clear at once, and often it is only an approximation to the fruitful one. At this stage in investigation the philosophically naïve scientist merely asks of his hunch, "Is it so?" and tries to test its reality in every way he can. He does not stay at the level of his original observations but applies any test he can think of. Such an idea of reality may be an innocent one, but it makes for scientific results. Perhaps we should describe the process of testing the value of a construct in other terms; but we cannot afford to omit it. In psychology the intervening variables, we know, are actually neural and physiological; the refusal to neurologize amounts to discarding a guide to the selection of one's constructs. It is refusing to look at data that might show that one's theory is wrong.

If only because of the frailty of man's intellect, we must theorize. In theorizing, we cannot afford to neglect any available information, so that theory must be consonant with knowledge of the nervous system although, if one wishes, one can choose terms that conceal the fact. Skinner is the one, of course, whose effective experimental work may make the strongest argument against such conclusions. But I believe that it is only Skinner's high personal level of ability, in despite of an erroneous epistemology, that has made these successes possible. Even he slips into the use of constructs occasionally (e.g., in the "reflex reserve"), and he may be much more dependent on earlier neurologizing than he thinks, as I have argued above of Spence and Tolman. If all theoretical systems of behavior were really forgotten, not even Skinner could continue with simple description.

CHAPTER 6

The Influence of Physics on Psychology

Physics has exerted a profound influence on the development of psychology. Because of its preeminence among the natural sciences, it has always served as a model to be emulated by others, but in the case of psychology there are additional reasons. As the youngest child in the family of philosophy, psychology experienced unusual difficulties in breaking the parental ties. Scholars in other fields were not convinced it deserved to be called a science and psychology itself was overly conscious of its philosophical parentage. One way to prove itself was to adopt the thorough-going rigor and objectivity of physics in its approach to the study of man—in itself a worthy ambition, but one which exposed it to the danger of imitating procedures and assumptions not appropriate to its own unique subject matter.

The physics current at the time psychology came into existence was based on the *Principia* of Sir Isaac Newton. Essentially it consisted of a mechanical interpretation of the universe derived from a set of definitions and axioms expressed in mathematical terms. To all appearances, classical physics was immutable and eternal. Not a single concept could be changed without destroying the whole structure, and wherever tested it seemed to be verified without shadow of a doubt. Optimism about a relatively simple explanation of nature kept pace with its brilliant success in accounting for gravity, the motion of planets, acoustics, hydrodynamics, and other phenomena. All that seemed necessary was to extend the principles of mechanics ever more widely to the other disciplines.

This attitude, carried over into philosophy by Auguste Comte, exerted a powerful influence on the theory of knowledge. He treated with contempt all knowledge not obtained by use of empirical methods and proposed a highly integrated superscience to explain every phenomenon in the simplest possible terms. The individual sciences were regrouped and placed in a hierarchy according to their complexity, with mathematics and mechanics providing the ultimate explanation of all things. It is not difficult to recognize in these beginnings the logical positivism which has provided the guiding principles for many scientists.

Psychologists busily engaged in the task of studying behavior have not been fully aware of changes taking place in the physics on which their science is modeled. Newton, for example, believed that his mechanics contained no assumptions not clearly necessitated by empirical data. Northrup comments that if this were true no modifications would ever be required since theory would then be as final and indubitable as the facts themselves. Einstein, Heisenberg, and other twentieth century physicists do not find this to be the case. Little by little they have been forced to the realization that a scientist arrives at his theory speculatively. As Northrup says,[1] "The deduction in his method runs not from facts to the assumptions of theory but from the assumed theory to facts and the experimental data."

For this reason physicists have become more cautious in pushing a successful scheme of interpretation to its ultimate conclusions. Newton's principles of mechanics which cannot be improved upon for explaining the behavior of much of our universe break down in limiting cases. Whenever the velocity of moving bodies becomes comparable to that of light, contradictions appear in the calculations. Neither can classical mechanics account for the phenomena of light or radiation of energy from black bodies. Other

[1] F. S. C. Northrup. Introduction. In Werner Heisenberg. *Physics and philosophy: The revolution in modern science*. New York: Harper & Row, 1958. P. 3.

closed theoretical systems—relativity and quantum mechanics—must be used. Like Newton's physics, they begin with definitions and axioms expressed mathematically, but there the similarity ceases. The assumptions on which they are based have little or nothing in common. Apparently each theory establishes points of contact with reality without providing an exhaustive explanation. A more vivid realization of this discovery might, perhaps, moderate the enthusiasm of some psychologists for reductionism and lessen the tendency to adhere rigidly to one theoretical position.

Another axiom of classical physics requires the experimenter to study nature without any reference to himself. Quantum mechanics necessitates a different assumption. The very act of observation introduces change in the object under investigation. In situations where this interference is not too minute to be neglected, the experimenter deals, not with concrete events, but with a whole population of possible events involving a probability function. In some psychological experimentation the behavior of human subjects is definitely altered by observation under controlled conditions, although it may be possible in the future to devise some analogous method to minimize this disruptive influence.

One vivid impression emerging from recent advances in physics is that science does not give a completely objective description of reality. Regardless of the method used, what is observed is not nature as such but nature interacting with our way of questioning it.

Editor's Note

Through discovery of the principle of indeterminacy in quantum mechanics, Werner Heisenberg became one of the leading architects of modern physics. What was not evident at the time was that the revolution he started in physics would profoundly influence the whole theory of science. Philosophical problems long considered dead issues were reopened with a new urgency. What is an object of scientific inquiry, and how do we know it? What, precisely, do theories tell us about nature? Is a scientist forced to think about his subject matter in terms that do not wholly correspond to reality?

In this selection Heisenberg traces the struggle of physics to free itself from the narrow, rigid outlook of the nineteenth century which stifled fresh approaches to the study of nature. His insight into the value of natural language should be of special interest to psychologists. Natural language, unlike precise scientific terminology, reflects an individual's immediate contact with the whole range of reality rather than with a limited, idealized aspect of it. In some ways natural language can be more useful in expanding knowledge than refined scientific terms can be.

19. The Role of Modern Physics in the Present Development of Human Thinking *

Werner Heisenberg
Max-Planck Institute for Physics and Astrophysics
Munich, Germany

In the meantime natural science proceeded to get a clearer and wider picture of the material world. In physics this picture was to be described by means of those concepts which we nowadays call the concepts of classical physics. The world consisted of things in space and time, the things consist of matter, and matter can produce and can be acted upon by forces. The events follow from the interplay between matter and forces; every event is the result and the cause of other events. At the same time the human attitude toward nature changed from a contemplative one to the pragmatic one. One was not so much interested in nature as it is; one rather asked what one could do with it. Therefore, natural science turned into technical science; every advancement of knowledge was connected with the question as to what practical use could be derived from it. This was true not only in physics; in chemistry and biology the attitude was essentially the same, and the success of the new methods in medicine or in agriculture contributed essentially to the propagation of the new tendencies.

In this way, finally, the nineteenth century developed an extremely rigid frame for natural science which formed not only science but also the general outlook of great masses of people. This frame was supported by the fundamental concepts of classical physics, space, time, matter and causality; the concept of reality applied to the things or events that we could perceive by our senses or that could be observed by means of the refined tools that technical science had provided. Matter was the primary reality. The progress of science was pictured as a crusade of conquest into the material world. Utility was the watchword of the time.

On the other hand, this frame was so narrow and rigid that it was difficult to find a place in it for many concepts of our language that had always belonged to its very substance, for instance, the concepts of mind, of the human soul or of life. Mind could be introduced into the general picture only as a kind of mirror of the material world; and when one studied the properties of this mirror in the science of psychology, the scientists were always tempted—if I may carry the comparison further—to pay more attention to its mechanical than to its optical properties. Even there one tried to apply the concepts of classical physics, primarily that of causality. In the same way life was to be explained as a physical and chemical process, governed by natural laws, completely determined by causality. Darwin's concept of evolution provided ample evidence for this interpretation. It was especially difficult to find in this framework room for those parts of reality that had been the object of the traditional religion and seemed now more or less only imaginary. Therefore, in those European countries in which one was wont to follow the ideas up to their extreme consequences, an open hostility of science toward religion developed, and even in the other countries there was an increasing tendency toward indifference toward such questions; only the ethical values of the Christian religion were excepted from this trend, at least for the time being. Confidence in the scientific method and in rational thinking replaced all other safeguards of the human mind.

Coming back now to the contributions of modern physics, one may say that the most important change brought about by its results consists in the dissolution of this rigid frame of concepts of the nineteenth century. Of course many attempts had been made before to get away from this rigid frame which seemed obviously too narrow for an understanding of the essential parts of reality. But it had not been possible to see what could be wrong with the fundamental concepts like matter, space, time and causality that had been so extremely successful in the history of science. Only experimental research itself, carried out with all the refined equipment that technical science could offer, and its mathematical interpretation, provided the basis for a critical analysis—or, one may say, enforced the critical analysis—of these concepts, and finally resulted in the dissolution of the rigid frame.

This dissolution took place in two distinct stages. The first was the discovery, through the theory of relativity, that even such fundamental concepts as space and time could be changed and in fact must be changed on account of new experience. This change did not concern the somewhat vague concepts of space and time in natural language; but it did concern their precise formulation in the scientific language of Newtonian mechanics, which had erroneously been accepted as final. The second stage was the discussion of the concept of matter enforced by the experimental results concerning the atomic structure. The idea of the reality of matter had probably been the strongest part in that rigid frame of concepts of the nineteenth century, and this idea had at least to be modified in connection with the new experience. Again the concepts so far as they belonged to the natural language remained untouched. There was no difficulty in speaking about matter or about facts or about reality when one had to describe the atomic experiments and their results. But the scientific extrapolation of these concepts into the smallest parts of matter could not be done in the simple way suggested by classical physics, though it had erroneously determined the general outlook on the problem of matter.

These new results had first of all to be considered as a serious warning against the somewhat forced application of scientific concepts in domains where they did not belong. The application of the concepts of classical physics, e.g., in chemistry, had been a mistake. Therefore, one will nowadays be less inclined to assume that the concepts of physics, even those of quantum theory, can certainly be applied everywhere in biology or other sciences. We will, on the contrary, try to keep the doors open for the entrance of new concepts even in those parts of science where the older concepts have been very useful for the understanding of the phenomena. Especially at those points where the application of the older concepts seems somewhat forced or appears not quite adequate to the problem we will try to avoid any rash conclusions.

Furthermore, one of the most important features of the development and the analysis of modern physics is the experience that the concepts of natural language, vaguely defined as they are, seem to be more stable in the expansion of knowledge than the precise terms of scientific language, derived as an idealization from only limited groups of phenomena. This is in fact not surprising since the concepts of natural language are formed by the immediate connection with reality; they represent reality. It is true that they are not very well defined and may therefore also undergo changes in the course of the centuries, just as reality itself did, but they never lose the immediate connection with reality. On the other hand, the scientific concepts are idealizations; they are derived from experience obtained by refined experimental tools, and are precisely defined through axioms and definitions. Only through these precise definitions is it possible to connect the concepts with a mathematical scheme and to derive mathematically the infinite variety of possible phenomena in this field. But through this process of idealization and precise definition the immediate connection with reality is lost. The concepts still correspond very closely to reality in that part of nature which had been the object of the research. But the correspondence may be lost in other parts containing other groups of phenomena.

Keeping in mind the intrinsic stability of the concepts of natural language in the process of scientific development, one sees that—after the experience of modern physics—our attitude toward concepts like mind or the human soul or life or God will be different from that of the nineteenth century, because these concepts belong to the natural language and have therefore immediate connection with reality. It is true that we will also realize that these concepts are not well defined in the scientific sense and that their application may lead to various contradictions, for the time being we may have to take the concepts, unanalyzed as they are; but still we know that they touch reality. It may be useful in this connection to remember that even in the most precise part of science, in mathematics, we cannot avoid using concepts that involve contradictions. For instance, it is well known that the concept of infinity leads to contradictions that have been analyzed, but it would be practically impossible to construct the main parts of mathematics without this concept.

The general trend of human thinking in the nineteenth century had been toward an increasing confidence in the scientific method and in precise rational terms, and had led to a general skepticism with regard to those concepts of natural language which do not fit into the closed frame of scientific thought—for instance, those of religion. Modern physics has in many ways increased this skepticism; but it has at the same time turned it against the overestimation of precise scientific concepts, against a too-optimistic view on progress in general, and finally against skepticism itself. The skepticism against precise scientific concepts does not mean that there should be a definite limitation for the application of rational thinking. On the contrary, one may say that the human ability to understand may be in a certain sense unlimited. But the existing scientific concepts cover always only a very limited part of reality, and the other part that has not yet been understood is infinite. Whenever we proceed from the known into the unknown we may hope to understand, but we may have to learn at the same time a new meaning of the word "understanding." We know that any understanding must be based finally upon the natural language because it is only there that we can be certain to touch reality, and hence we must be skeptical about any skepticism with regard to this natural language and its essential concepts. Therefore, we may use these concepts as they have been used at all times. In this way modern physics has perhaps opened the door to a wider outlook on the relation between the human mind and reality.

This modern science, then, penetrates in our time into other parts of the world where the cultural tradition has been entirely different from the European civilization. There the impact of this new activity in natural and technical science must make itself felt even more strongly than in Europe, since changes in the conditions of life that have taken two or three centuries in Europe will take place there within a few decades. One should expect that in many places this new activity must appear as a decline of the older culture, as a ruthless and barbarian attitude, that upsets the sensitive balance on which all human happiness rests. Such consequences cannot be avoided; they must be taken as one aspect of our time. But even there the openness of modern physics may help to some extent to reconcile the older traditions with the new trends of thought. For instance, the great scientific contribution in theoretical physics that has come from Japan since the last war may be an indication for a certain relationship between philosophical ideas in the tradition of the Far East and the philosophical substance of quantum theory. It may be easier to adapt oneself to the quantum-theoretical concept of reality when one has not gone through the naïve materialistic way of thinking that still prevailed in Europe in the first decades of this century.

Editor's Note

Two selections, one by an eminent American physicist, the other by a philosopher, indicate some ways in which the newer concepts of science can be applied to psychology. Both men imply that psychology needs to make certain that its climate of thinking is not influenced by physical concepts now outdated. The student may wish to construct his own checklist of critical areas where such an inquiry should begin.

20. Analogy in Science *

Robert Oppenheimer
Princeton University

But for all of that I would like to say something about what physics has to give back to common sense that it seemed to have lost from it, not because I am clear that these ideas are important tools in psychological research, but because it seems to me that the worst of all possible misunderstandings would be that psychology be influenced to model itself after a physics which is not there any more, which has been quite outdated.

We inherited, say at the beginning of this century, a notion of the physical world as a causal one, in which every event could be accounted for if we were ingenious, a world characterized by number, where everything interesting could be measured and quantified, a determinist world, a world in which there was no use or room for individuality, in which the object of study was simply there and how you studied it did not affect the object, it did not affect the kind of description you gave of it, a world in which objectifiability went far beyond merely our own agreement on what we meant by words and what we are talking about, in which objectification was meaningful irrespective of any attempt to study the system under con-

* From R. Oppenheimer. Analogy in science. *Amer. Psychologist*, 1956, **11**, 127–135. Reprinted with permission of the author and publisher.

sideration. It was just the given real object; there it was, and there was nothing for you to worry about of an epistemological character. This extremely rigid picture left out a great deal of common sense. I do not know whether these missing elements will prove helpful; but at least their return may widen the resources that one can bring to any science.

What are these ideas? In our natural, unschooled talk, and above all in unschooled talk about psychological problems, we have five or six things which we have got back into physics with complete rigor, with complete objectivity, in the sense that we understand one another, with a complete lack of ambiguity and with a perfectly phenomenal technical success. One of them is just this notion that the physical world is not completely determinate. There are predictions you can make about it but they are statistical; and any event has in it the nature of the surprise, of the miracle, of something that you could not figure out. Physics is predictive, but within limits; its world is ordered, but not completely causal.

Another of these ideas is the discovery of the limits on how much we can objectify without reference to what we are really talking about in an operational, practical sense. We can say the electron has a certain charge and we do not have to argue as to whether we are looking at it to say that; it always does. We cannot say it has a place or a motion. If we say that we imply something about what we ourselves—I do not mean as people but as physicists—are doing about it.

A third point is very closely related to this; it is the inseparability of what we are studying and the means that are used to study it, the organic connection of the object with the observer. Again, the observer is not in this case a human; but in psychology the observer sometimes is a human.

And then, as logical consequences of this, there is the idea of totality, or wholeness. Newtonian physics, classical science, was differential; anything that went on could be broken up into finer and finer elements and analyzed so. If one looks at an atomic phenomenon between the beginning and the end, the end will not be there; it will be a different phenomenon. Every pair of observations taking the form "we know this, we then predict that" is a global thing; it cannot be broken down.

Finally, every atomic event is individual. It is not, in its essentials, reproducible.

This is quite a pack of ideas that we always use: individuality, wholeness, the subtle relations of what is seen with how it is seen, the indeterminacy and the acausality of experience. And I would only say that if physics could take all these away for three centuries and then give them back in ten years, we may well say that all ideas that occur in common sense are fair as starting points, not guaranteed to work but perfectly valid as the material of the analogies with which we start.

The whole business of science does not lie in getting into realms which are unfamiliar in normal experience. There is an enormous work of analyzing, of recognizing similarities and analogies, of getting the feel of the landscape, an enormous qualitative sense of family relations, of taxonomy. It is not always tactful to try to quantify; it is not always clear that by measuring one has found something very much worth measuring. It is true that for the Babylonians it was worth measuring—noting—the first appearances of the moon because it had a practical value. Their predictions, their prophecies, and their magic would not work without it; and I know that many psychologists have the same kind of reason for wanting to measure. It is a real property of the real world that you are measuring, but it is not necessarily the best way to advance true understanding of what is going on; and I would make this very strong plea for pluralism with regard to methods that, in the necessarily early stages of sorting out an immensely vast experience, may be fruitful and may be helpful. They may be helpful not so much for attaining objectivity, nor for a quest for certitude which will never be quite completely attained. But there is a place for the use of naturalistic methods, the use of descriptive methods. I have been immensely impressed by the work of one man who visited us last year at the Institute, Jean Piaget. When you look at his work, his statistics really consist of one or two cases. It is just a start; and yet I think he has added greatly to our understanding. It is not that I am sure he is right, but he has given us something worthy of which to enquire whether it is right; and I make this plea not to treat too harshly those who tell you a story, having observed carefully without having established that they are sure that the story is the whole story and the general story.

It is of course in that light that I look at the immense discipline of practice, that with all its pitfalls, with all the danger that it leads to premature and incorrect solutions, does give an incredible amount of experience.

21. Is Clinical Psychology a Science? *

Carlton W. Berenda
University of Oklahoma

The rather hackneyed question raised in the above title is conceived within a broad framework and within a context of other questions and various accusations. There are some who have said or implied that psychology as a whole is not much of a science and that clinical psychology and the theories of personality dynamics and psychoanalysis are a combination of mere practical techniques and obscure or poetic speculations. Clinical work in psychology has been looked upon as an art rather than as a science:

* From C. W. Berenda. Is clinical psychology a science? *Amer. Psychologist,* 1957, **12,** 725–729. Reprinted with permission of the author and publisher.

one has a "feeling" for the work, or one does not, but there are no scientific rules or laws by which one can guide one's self in this area. Psychological tests and measurements are sometimes regarded as the really scientific part of this work, because some numbers or statistical figures are obtained; but the rest of the field is often dismissed as vague, intuitive, metaphysical meanderings and incantations, a survival of the *Malleus Maleficarum* of the Dark Ages.

Lurking behind the foregoing remarks are presumably some other presuppositions concerning the nature of a "real science"; and one may suppose that the guide and standard of such a science is modern physics—a collection of precise, quantitative, logico-deductive, verifiable natural laws.

The trouble with this standard often lies in a misconception on the part of those who uphold it; their insight into modern physics is frequently colored by implicit metaphysical concepts that date back to Copernicus, Galileo, Kepler, Descartes, and Newton. This misconception must apparently be deeply entrenched in our culture, since it has been explicitly recognized (in one form) even in a famous child's book: [1]

> Grown-ups love figures. When you tell them that you have made a new friend, they never ask you any questions about essential matters. They never say to you, "What does his voice sound like? What games does he love best? Does he collect butterflies?" Instead, they demand: "How old is he? How many brothers has he? How much does he weigh? How much money does his father make?" Only from these figures do they think they have learned anything about him. . . . But certainly, for us who understand life, figures are a matter of indifference.

[1] From A. de Saint-Exupery. *The little prince.* New York: Reynal & Hitchcock, 1943 (transl. by Katherine Woods). Quotation reprinted with permission of Harcourt, Brance & Co., New York, and William Heinemann, Ltd., London, (British Commonwealth ed. transl. by Lewis Galantiere.)

The roots of this sort of "number magic" can be traced back 2,500 years ago to Pythagoras, thence through Plato, and the mathematicians and astronomers, up to Copernicus. The conviction that ultimate reality is to be understood in terms of numbers, geometrical figures, and simple ratios and proportions stems from this ancient tradition and culminates in Galileo and Descartes. The real world becomes the quantitative world of mathematics; the "primary qualities" of the world are measurable: space, time, motion, and mass; while the merely "secondary qualities" are: colors, odors, tastes, sounds, etc.; and the "tertiary qualities" are: thoughts, wishes, emotions, moral and aesthetic value judgements, etc. The secondary and tertiary qualities are in the human mind that is somehow locked up in the brain and body. The human brain and body can be understood in terms of the primary qualities and are therefore properly a part of science, the study of ultimate (mathematical) reality; but the other qualities are in the soul of man and are to be left to the Church. Such are the conceptions more or less explicit in the views of Galileo and Descartes. And such is the Bifurcation of Nature that Descartes brought to fruition when he split the world into *res extensa* (the physical world of geometrical mathematics) and *res cogitans* (the human mind of sensations, feelings, wishes, ideas, etc.).

After Newton's success, there was gradually impressed upon men's thinking a world picture in which man was a small cog in a big cosmic machine that ran according to fixed and inevitable natural laws. The real, objective world was impersonal, mathematical, exact, and under strict causal law in all of its behavior. Similarly, the human body and its behavior were regarded as merely a more complicated machine. In the nineteenth century, statistical mechanics, electrodynamics, chemistry, and biological evolution under fixed natural laws were concepts added to this world picture; but, from a broader viewpoint, the general notion of man and the universe remained essentially the same. Watsonian behaviorism, early in the twentieth century, was the outcome of this world picture: Man, the electrochemical reflex machine.

Along with this world picture and theory of man, goes a methodological viewpoint: to understand this world, one must be like unto it—objective, impersonal, mathematical, precise. To discover, in detail, the natural laws of human behavior, one also must be committed to these procedures. The laws are there to be found; go thou and find them! Such is the way of the scientist and good psychologist.

It should be emphasized, at this point, that it is not the intention of the author to discard scientific method, and certainly not on the ground that its origins are to be found partly in the myth of number magic. To trace ideas historically to myths is not logically to refute them; it is simply to become more aware of the interesting fact that science, like religion, philosophy, and other such conceptual activities, are *human activities*, replete with implicit metaphysical commitments—that we live and think creatively by symbols and theories and that the established theories of today may be the "myths" of tomorrow. And in the specific world picture that we have just outlined, there is the further realization that man, as creative, imaginative, and emotional, has been read out of the world picture, to be conceptually explained away in terms (created by us!) of strict, objective, quantitative, causal mechanisms of our bodily behavior.

It has been the physical science of our century that has given its own revolutionary refutation to the foregoing world view. We are not referring so much to such ideas as Heisenberg's Indeterminacy Principle in Quantum Theory —the refutation of classical mechanical causality in atomic physics—but to something much more fundamental and far-reaching. Modern physics has broken with the old world view in two ways: (*a*) it questions the possibility of any imaginable pictures or models of the so-called real world of atoms, etc.; (*b*) it questions the nature and status of the so-called natural physical laws or equations.

Concerning Item *a*, modern quantum theory, as well as relativity theory, have passed far beyond the possibility of ordinary mechanical models to represent their basic equations or laws. Especially in quantum theory, who can claim to visualize the "wave-particles" as given in the equations for light (photons), electrons, protons, neutrons, etc.? It has now become apparent to the theoretical physicist that his science is no longer engaged in the business of providing a picture revealing the ultimate structure of reality. Rather his abstract mathematical equations are formulated (not "discovered") by the creative imagination of geniuses who are engaged in the human *attempt* to provide some logico-deductive system that most simply and consistently organizes some describable features of our observed world of *common experience* (*not* a world of colorless, mechanistic stuff).

And on Item *b*: the natural laws are no longer regarded as unique, unequivocal, absolutely true descriptions of some ultimate reality existing "objectively"; rather, a new view has come into being among the physicists. It has been found possible to provide *more than one* verified theory of a given subject matter: Dirac has given us one theory of the positron (an electron with positive charge), while Feynman has given us another. The basic equations of *both* men have been experimentally confirmed! This seems impossible, unless one gives up the preconception that physics is engaged in revealing the ultimate nature of some "real objective world" behind the world of phenomena or common experiences. Moreover, Feynman has proceeded to prove that his theory and Dirac's are "equivalent"—that is, one theory (a set of basic equations) can be "translated" into the other, *in toto*—much like German into English. In other words, more than one theory can be verified in the same area of inquiry, and either or both theories may be used interchangeably, as suits the convenience of the physicist.

The theories do not give us pictures or laws of an absolute reality, but (as John Dewey emphasized) are merely *intellectual tools or instruments created* by brilliant minds to deal more or less adequately with some selected aspects of observable phenomena. To quote two modern physicists: [2]

> How can we know that this world of ours is ultimately explorable? Is there a unique system of physical explanation? If there were, and the physicist were slowly learning it, his occupation would be that of a photographer who takes an enormous number of pictures in studying an object. If, however, there is no certainty about these questions, then his work is not photography; it is artistic creation. It seems that past experiences favor the latter alternative.

It is against the background of the previous remarks that we can seek to answer our leading question about clinical psychology as a science. A scientific system need not try to provide us with a *unique* theory of phenomena, nor need its abstract concepts be visualizable in terms of concrete or mechanistic imagery, nor need the theory be quantitative. More than one theory of personality or of therapy could be used by the clinician, and possibly the abstract terminology of various theories (all "verified") could be shown to be equivalent. Which of such theories the clinician uses may be a matter of personal preference, congenial to his own temperament. We can only seek to construct some self-consistent system of abstractions or concepts that, as simply as possible, logically organizes a given area of phenomena in the field of human behavior. More than one such system is possible.

The old bifurcation between science and art, between objective mechanical reality and subjective creative

[2] Lindsay, R., and Margenau, H., *Foundations of Physics*. New York, Wiley, 1936. p. 528. (Quotations from this reference are reproduced in this article with permission of John Wiley & Sons, Inc.)

symbolism is no longer as obvious as it once seemed. To be "objective" is also to have objectives! Even man as scientist is goal directed as well as goal creating or selecting—and *long range ideal* goals at that (e.g., the ideal objective of a science of man).

In a field as rich and varied as human behavior, it behooves us to become more thoroughly acquainted with our subject matter so that inspiration for formulating abstract concepts and for creative theorizing will be well-grounded in concrete experiences and so that "verification" of such theories can lose some of its present vagueness. A multiplicity of "competing" but equally simple verified theories is not in itself a scientific sin. And in the qualitatively rich area of clinical psychology, *different* abstract concepts and assumptions formulated into *various* verifiable theories are to be expected, and even encouraged. Science is a matter of *degree* of systematic logical organization of phenomena; clinical psychology is a science to a degree that will rise in proportion to such systematization; but the hope for such a rise must depend upon a freedom of creative thinking embedded in the warm and vital matrix of pervasive, sympathetic, and qualitative experiences in the clinical field.

CHAPTER 7

Operationalism

The most persistent challenge in any type of investigation is how to validate one's concepts. In past centuries, before the sciences enjoyed an existence independent of philosophy, scholars leaned heavily on deductive reasoning in explaining natural phenomena. Beginning with observations of a very general nature that could be verified by others, they then reasoned from premise to premise to a presumably necessary conclusion. An example of a "given" is the common perception of man as a social being capable of thinking, feeling, and problem solving who is at the same time restless, curious, and ambitious. From such empirical beginnings a concept of human nature and the ethical aspects of behavior can be deduced. Even today this method is the only available one for investigating some human problems which do not lend themselves to observation and measurement.

To some extent the same procedure is followed in objective experimentation. Constructs are not discovered fully formed in the original data, but must be painstakingly elaborated by inductive and deductive reasoning after the statistical calculations have been completed. Scientific methodology differs from philosophy, not in eliminating the need of logical thought processes that can be expressed in syllogisms, but in the need for more precise and accurate observation. Testing and retesting the original data increases the scientist's confidence that his conclusions are more than mere exercises in logic. Internal consistency is a minimum requirement of any explanation, but until it has been proved to conform to reality as well as to the rules for correct thinking, the explanation still remains an hypothesis.

Science is superior to philosophy in the study of natural phenomena to the extent that it can free itself from subjective factors. The complex system of controls, procedures, and instrumentation in objective studies attempts to eliminate errors due to bias and faulty perception in the collection of data. Similar precautions must be taken in the second and less objective phase of the investigation which consists in spelling out the implications of the data in hand. Some general guidelines can be established to minimize the possibility of error. The farther one's cognition is removed from sensory perception, the more difficult it is to verify. Hence scientific constructs should remain as close as possible to empirical observation. Thinking in terms of concrete objects and activities whenever possible provides a bridge between speculation and the world of fact. While it is true that the more abstract and generalized concepts have a wider range of application, they are for that reason more difficult to verify.

The method of operational analysis, familiar to every scientist, states this principle in summary form. Henry Margenau defines operationalism as ". . . an attitude that emphasizes the need of recourse whenever feasible to instrumental procedures where meanings are to be established." In a word, terms, constructs, and theories are identified as far as possible with the manipulations and calculations from which they are derived. One homely example is the chef's operational definition of crepes suzettes as a specific recipe in the cookbook.

Editor's Note

Although operationalism originated within the realms of physics, it has contributed in an important way to the development of psychology and still exerts considerable influence, in spite of the fact that few psychologists formally identify themselves with the movement. Tending to suppress the unverifiable assumptions of the early behaviorists, operationalism prepared the way for modern behavior theory.

22. Sense and Nonsense in Operationism *

Gustav Bergmann
State University of Iowa

The impact on psychology was tremendous. Again this is easily understood. Applied to psychological concepts, operationism becomes methodological behaviorism, that is, a behaviorism sobered and shorn of its metaphysics. Operationism can thus take credit for having facilitated the transition from Watsonianism to contemporary behavior theory. To be sure, there was also some nonsense, mostly misunderstandings owing to the philosophic naiveté of some psychologists. By now these misunderstandings have happily disappeared; at least they have been pointed out. The root of the trouble was that some psychologists in their enthusiasm mistook the operationist footnote for the whole of philosophy of science, if not for the whole of philosophy. So they thought, first, that operationism also provided rules for assuring the significance of concepts properly defined. There are, of course, no such rules. Second, while operations in the relevant sense are manipulations and nothing else, they saw operations everywhere. At the one extreme, the scientist's perceptions were decked out to be a species of operations; at the other, his verbal computational activities were as so-called symbolic operations herded into the same corral. This completely nonspecific use of "operation"

* Abridged from G. Bergmann. Sense and nonsense in operationism. *Sci. Monthly*, 1954, **79**, 210–214. Reprinted with permission of the author and publisher.

proved confusing. To give an extreme illustration, some refused, presumably on operationist principles, to "generalize" from one instance of an experiment to the next if the apparatus had in the meantime been moved to another corner of the room. Yet, there is no *a priori* rule to distinguish relevant from irrelevant variables. Nor is there any such thing as an exhaustive description. Generally, the operationist fashion provided some specious arguments to those who disliked all sorts of theorizing or, even, conceptualizing. But perhaps it was wholesome that psychology went through this phase.

Editor's Note

While in a very broad sense operationalism is little more than a modernized version of what scientists have always done to verify their ideas, a conviction exists in some circles that the operational principle has been overemphasized. Bridgman explicitly dissociates himself from the requirement that every definition must be formulated in operational terms. He conceives of operationalism as a general point of view rather than a dogma or philosophy of science. A scientist makes fewer mistakes if he habitually asks himself, "What did I do to arrive at this concept?" Nor does Bridgman consider operationalism the exclusive property of science. Even metaphysical definitions, like Newton's notion of absolute time, become clearer when subjected to a similar analysis.

23. Remarks on the Present State of Operationalism *

P. W. Bridgman

There would seem to be no reason why I am better fitted than anyone else to open this discussion. As I listened to the papers [reference not pertinent here] I felt that I have only a historical connection with this thing called

* From P. W. Bridgman. Remarks on the present state of operationalism. *Sci. Monthly*, 1954, **79**, 224–226. Reprinted with permission of the author and publisher.

"operationalism." In short, I feel that I have created a Frankenstein, which has certainly got away from me. I abhor the word *operationalism* or *operationism*, which seems to imply a dogma, or at least a thesis of some kind. The thing I have envisaged is too simple to be dignified by so pretentious a name; rather, it is an attitude or point of view generated by continued practice of operational analysis. So far as any dogma is involved here at all, it is merely the conviction that it is better, because it takes us further, to analyze into doings or happenings rather than into objects or entities.

What I conceive to be involved here may be a little clearer if the historical background is understood, and I hope you will pardon me if I interject some personal remarks. The date usually associated with this is 1927, the year of the publication of my book *The Logic of Modern Physics*, but preparation for this in my own thinking went back at least to 1914, when the task of giving two advanced courses in electrodynamics was suddenly thrust upon me. Included in these courses was material from the restricted theory of relativity. The underlying conceptual situation in this whole area seemed very obscure to me and caused me much intellectual distress, which I tried to alleviate as best I could. Another cause of distress was thc situation in dimensional analysis, which at that time was often so expounded as to raise doubt whether experimental work was really necessary at all. The dimensional situation proved comparatively simple, and I was able to think the situation through to my own satisfaction—an experience that perceptibly increased my intellectual morale. The analysis, which was essentially operational, although the word was not used, was published in 1922 (*Dimensional Analysis*, Yale Univ. Press). I think the word *operation* was first explicitly used in a discussion that I gave at the Boston meeting of the AAAS in 1923 at a symposium on relativity theory participated in by George Birkhoff, Harlow Shapley, and myself.

The Logic of Modern Physics was written during a half sabbatical in 1926 under a stringent time limit, for I knew that at the end of September my laboratory would reabsorb me. In view of this time limit, I had to map out the questions that to me appeared most pressing and to be satisfied with discussions of which I could say "at least this much must be true and be part of the final picture," and not attempt the more ambitious program of a complete analysis. In short, I was compelled to be satisfied with a "necessary" as opposed to a "sufficient" analysis. A great many interesting and important leads had to be left unexplored: for example, an analysis of what it is that makes an operation suitable for the formulation of a scientific concept; again, in what terms can operations be specified. It has, in fact, been a surprise to me that, since the publication of my book, so much of the concern of others has been with abstract methodological questions suggested by the endeavor to erect some sort of a philosophic system rather than with attempts to follow the more concrete and obvious leads.

Since writing the book, I have never again been able to devote as sustained attention to this field but have had to content myself with shorter excursions, resulting in a number of articles and a couple of thin books. But at the same time, with the continued practice of operational analysis, my ideas have been changing and growing and gaining in generality. If I were to start today to expound my attitude systematically, the order of presentation would be different. The general points of view would be presented earlier in the treatment, with, I think, avoidance of much confusion. It is often thought that there is a normative aspect to "operationalism," which is understood as the dogma that definitions *should* be formulated in terms of operations. As I see it, there is in the *general* point of view nothing normative whatever. An operational analysis is always possible, that is, an analysis into what was done or what happened. An operational analysis can be given of the most obscurely metaphysical definition, such as Newton's definition of absolute time as that which flows by itself uniformly and equably. What is more, any person can make an operational analysis, whether or not he accepts what he supposes to be the thesis of "operationalism," and whether or not he thinks he is wasting his time in so doing. So far as the "operationalist" is to be distinguished from the "nonoperationalist," it is in the conviction of the former that it is often profitable and clarifying to make an operational analysis, and also, I suspect, in his private feeling that often the "nonoperationalist" does not want to make an operational analysis through fear that it might result in a change in his attitude.

If one has consistently used operational analysis, I think one's general point of view comes to acquire a certain flavor and certain considerations come to be emphasized in his thinking; these I shall endeavor to characterize briefly. In the first place, one is impressed by the observation that operational analysis can always be pushed to the point where sharpness disappears. The "yes or no" signal of recent information theory, the "all or none" firing of a neurone of the physiologist, and so on, lose their sharpness when considered as processes occurring in time, and the operations of logic lose their sharpness when the analysis is pushed to the point of self-doubt. Again, one is impressed by the complexity of the verbal structure that mankind has erected through the ages. Here is an autonomous world in which a man can, and frequently does, live a more or less self-contained and independent existence. On the other hand, despite the complexity of the verbal world, the external world of objects and happenings is inconceivably more complex—so complex that all aspects of it can never be reproduced by any verbal structure. Even in physics this is not sufficiently appreciated, as is shown, for example, by the reification of energy. The totality of situations covered by various aspects of the energy concept is too complex to be reproduced by any simple verbal device. As a corollary of the continued interplay of the verbal and the "objective" worlds, I personally have come to feel the value of analyzing our operations as far as possible into their "instrumental" and "paper-and-pencil" components and think there is much here that is still unexplored. I think there is much to be done in nonscientific fields along these lines. For instance, I anticipate that many of the operations of philosophy will be found to be essentially verbal and incapable of being made to emerge into the instrumental world. I believe that revolutionary results will follow a full realization of the inescapability and immanence of the element of human enterprise.

Editor's Note

In the following article, which is a model of brevity and precision, Henry Margenau anticipates two questions which are likely to occur to the reader. What is an instrumental procedure? If operational definitions are necessary in scientific investigation, why are they insufficient for the purpose of developing theories?

24. On Interpretations and Misinterpretations of Operationalism *

Henry Margenau
Yale University

In introducing this symposium on "The present state of operationalism," I deem it proper to keep my remarks brief and general, leaving criticism and appraisal to the active participants.

Operationalism is an attitude that emphasizes the need of recourse, wherever feasible, to instrumental procedures when meanings are to be established. Bridgman

* From H. Margenau. On interpretations and misinterpretations of operationalism. *Sci. Monthly*, 1954, **79**, 209–210. Reprinted with permission of the author and publisher.

disavows its status as a philosophy, and wisely so, for as a general view it would be vulnerable on two counts. First, it cannot define the meaning of "instrumental procedure" in a manner that saves the view from being either trivial (which would be true if "instrumental" were construed to include symbolic, mental and paper-and-pencil operations) or too restrictive (if all operations are to be laboratory procedures). Second, it fails to impart meaning to substantive concepts—that is, concepts related to entities that are regarded as the carriers of operationally determinable qualities or quantities. To illustrate this latter point: it is possible to define, in terms of instrumental procedures, the charge, the mass, and the spin of an electron, but hardly the electron itself.

Yet every scientist feels the value of the operational approach. I shall try to indicate the reason for this by showing that operational definitions occupy a critical role in the methodology of science.

If, as is customary in much of traditional philosophy, we recognize within our cognitive experience two dominating poles, the *rational* (concepts, constructs, ideas, and so on) and the *immediate* (such as sensations, observations, and data), then there arises the problem of bridging the two. For it is clear that a concept is not identical with, or inductively derivable from, a set of percepts. The nonempirical requirements that render fertile and consistent the constructs of a given theory (in *The Nature of Physical Reality*, McGraw-Hill, 1950, I have called them "metaphysical requirements") can be stated without reference to actual observations; hence, they do not validate or reify the constructs they confine but establish them merely as an internally consistent set, a formal theory. The empirical requirement, the possibility of circuits of factual verification that mediate between observational data and constructs, confers validity, and such circuits are impossible without operational definitions—operational in terms of performed or imagined *laboratory procedures*.

This implies that operations are not the only means of defining scientific concepts; indeed, the analysis shows precisely why they alone are insufficient. A valid concept must belong to a satisfactory theory which obeys the metaphysical rules. This it cannot do unless it is susceptible to a formal definition that links it nonoperationally to other concepts or terms of the theory. But it must also be empirically verifiable, and this requires a linkage with observations via operational procedures. Thus, it is necessary, and a survey of scientific method shows this to be true, that every accepted scientific measurable quantity have at least two definitions, one formal and one instrumental. It is an interesting task to show how some sciences fail to become exact because they ignore this dual character of the definitory process. Omission of operational definitions leads to sterile speculation, to metaphysics in the sense of the detractors of that discipline; disregard of formal (or "constitutive") definitions leads to that blind empiricism which misses the power and the beauty of modern physical science.

Editor's Note

Operational analysis was introduced into science to purge it of all subjective elements. By restricting the content of concepts and theories to concrete operations which could be easily verified, the scientist seemed to free himself from bias and similar human failings. But second thoughts have been more sobering. Knowledge, in the last analysis, can never be as objective as things in the outside world. Knowledge is a personal possession, entirely dependent on self-activity both in its acquisition and use. Each individual should do everything in his power to insure the validity of what he knows. But, try as he may to objectify his ideas, they still remain an internal experience.

25. Humanization *

Floyd W. Matson
University of California

That old urge in all of us (which Sherrington remarked upon) to get away from the bogey of "subjective anthropomorphism" acquired perhaps its greatest reinforcement of recent decades through the method of "operational analysis" introduced by the mathematical physicist Percy W. Bridgman. In the perspective of operationalism, the meaning of a proposition is simply the particular set of "operations" required to implement or verify it. Bridgman's concept had the virtue of seeming to fulfill at a stroke the positivist yearning for absolute objectification—to get rid once and for all of that brooding omnipresence, the human observer, with his trembling fingers and contaminating biases. In the years following publication of *The Logic of Modern Physics* in 1928, numbers of scientific philosophers and scientific psychologists embraced Bridgman's method and proceeded to accord it the full degree of reverence to which Rollo May has given the name of methodolatry.

* From Floyd W. Matson, *The Broken Image: Man, Science, and Society*, George Braziller, New York, 1964, pp. 249–250. Reprinted with permission of the author and publisher.

But meanwhile a curious thing was happening. The author of operationalism had himself begun to reappraise and revise his concept in the light of momentous developments in his own fields of physics and mathematics—mainly those associated with Heisenberg's quantum principle and Gödel's logical theorem. And the conclusion to which Bridgman found himself more and more drawn was "the insight that we never get away from ourselves"—that the operations involved in any scientific performance, or for that matter any human act, are ultimately and irreducibly *individual.* There was, he concluded, simply no escaping the personal reference point, the stubborn particularity of the solitary knower doing his job. In time this heretical line of thought led Bridgman to an appreciation of "subjective anthropomorphism" so profound and unequivocal that he was compelled repeatedly to defend himself against the dread charge of solipsism—leveled at him in particular by his own erstwhile disciples, the operationalists. It might be said that Bridgman, having extracted meaning and relevance from the human subject through an ingenious feat of surgery, spent the balance of his career trying to put them back. In the process he became an outspoken advocate of the thesis of personal involvement—of the reality of participation and the importance of concern—in the behavior both of men in the street and of scientists in the tower.

This recognition that, in Polanyi's phrase, "knowledge is personal"—and most profoundly when it is knowledge of other persons—has been widely resisted on the assumption that it constitutes a confession of human frailty and therefore (as Hull considered it) a counsel of despair. And no doubt to those who are convinced that the stockpile of human knowledge increases in direct ratio to the distance between subject and object, the very notion of "personal knowledge" can have the appearance only of a blooming, buzzing confusion of logic. But it is instructive to be reminded, once more, of the singular fact that throughout threc centuries of scientific ascendancy the lingering suspicion that we cannot get away from ourselves—and even, perhaps, that we should not—has never been altogether silenced or suppressed. Phrased another way, this is the view which holds that to acknowledge the inner personal dimension in behavior, as well as in the *observation* of behavior, is not to confess a fatal defect but to identify a source of strength—a unique prerogative of the human condition which provides the sole basis for genuine communication between man and man, and hence for the understanding of other voices, other minds and other behaviors.

CHAPTER 8

Broadening Methodological Horizons

As David McClelland notes in one of the readings in this chapter, "Psychologists used to be interested in what goes on in people's heads." Until the present century it was unthinkable that psychology should be unconcerned about inner human experience. Thought, imagery, feeling, and choosing had been considered the most characteristic of all human activities: without them a physics or a physiology of man might be constructed, but not a psychology. The rise of behaviorism changed this outlook. In leading a revolt against the excesses of introspectionism, John Watson banished mental content from psychology. Henceforth, it was implied, the science of man would concern itself with externally observable aspects of behavior or "processes," explaining *how* psychological activities take place rather than *what* goes on in the mind.

Although Watson's original assumptions have been modified considerably in the development of modern behavior theory, many psychologists still doubt that mental content can be studied scientifically. Ideas are too varied, relative, and closed to external observation, they say, to make possible an empirical approach. McClelland responds that the only answer to this challenge is to prove that ideas can be studied fruitfully. Examples of successful experiments of this type are given here, but first an attempt is made to show on theoretical grounds why this is possible.

Any consideration of mental content is intimately bound up with a notion of consciousness. For decades consciousness has been thought of as an inner mirror held up to reality. If the ego wishes to know what is going on outside, it looks in the mirror, not through an open window. Perceptual knowledge is thus obtained through the intervening step of interpreting sensations. In pointing out the inadequacy of such a concept, Joseph Nuttin identifies consciousness with the direct, immediate experience of reality: the immersing of oneself in things. The perceived world is the real or behavioral world, not a reflection of it. If this were not the case, scientific data would not be objective because, like introspection, it would always be one step removed from reality. A subjective act of interpretation would necessarily intervene between sensory contact and perception.

If, then, consciousness is inseparably linked with experiencing the behavioral world, why is the method of introspection not more reliable? First of all, we must discriminate between two aspects of consciousness: primary consciousness, as we have described it, which brings us into immediate, *perceptual* contact with things around us, and reflective consciousness, or introspection. We are not here concerned with what Nuttin refers to as the vicarious presence of things in their absence through memory, thought, and imagery. Primary consciousness is concerned with ongoing factual experience which can be readily validated by repeating one's observations, comparing notes with other people, or making use of the elaborate methodology of science. It is in the process of reflective consciousness that a subject is more likely to go astray as he turns back on the content of immediate inner experience to evaluate, classify, or describe it in some way. His primary experience of *having* a thought or image, or *feeling* an emotion is not essentially different from the perception of an outside object. Like a pain in the back, the fact that it takes place within him does not destroy its usefulness as a datum of immediate observation which can be processed as objectively as any other.

Reflective analysis of a perception is another matter. McClelland judges the greatest weakness of Titchener's method to be his use of the same subjects first to supply the original observations and then to categorize them. In the terms of the foregoing discussion, introspectionism requires the subject to communicate both his primary and reflective consciousness. He reports not only the presence of a thought or image but processes it in some way according to the instructions he has received. The methodological breakthrough in research on the achievement motive [1] consists in confining the verbal report to facts of direct and immediate perception—the thoughts occurring to subjects when shown pictures projected on a screen. The subjects are not asked to comment on their written stories or to categorize the imagery. The experimenter merely collects raw perceptual data not unlike the kind of observations familiar in psychophysical studies requiring judgments about the weight of objects on the brightness of lights. By recording and processing the protocols objectively, the pitfalls of introspectionism are avoided. Nuttin and McClelland thus provide a rationale for psychological methods capable of studying "what goes on in people's heads." [2]

[1] For a brief description of the method of measuring the achievement motive, see D. C. McClelland. *The achieving society*. Princeton, N.J., Van Nostrand, 1961. Pp. 39–46.

[2] This discussion should be read together with the selections by Joseph Nuttin and David McClelland. Some of their concepts have been juxtaposed, and reinterpreted in a manner somewhat different than originally intended by the authors. The editor assumes full responsibility for any statement or interpretation not clearly contained in their articles.

26. Consciousness, Behavior, and Personality *

Joseph Nuttin
University of Louivan

The concept of consciousness still remains associated with one of the most traumatic experiences in the life history of scientific psychology, i.e., introspectionism. The wound has not yet healed; consciousness still means for many people a menace to behavioral science. It would not be justified, therefore, to run the risk of arousing emotional reactions by reintroducing the subject if there were no hope that a revocation and a restatement of the problem in the present situation might entail some therapeutic effect and eventually help psychology in its development to greater maturity. Maturity, in fact, means getting in contact with the real behavioral world and facing the problems arising there.

Consciousness, now, is just what brings man in contact with the behavioral world. Contrary to what is generally believed, it should not be considered as necessarily related to introspectionism and the study of so-called "states of consciousness."

Perception and the Representation Theory of Consciousness

Some trends in present-day psychology emphasize again the role of cognitive and perceptual functions in behavior. This may be an important step in the direction of a sound concept of behavior. I see a danger, however, in the fact that, frequently, theories of cognition and perception are still working with concepts adopted from introspectionist psychology. The perceptual world is currently conceived as a "representation" *in* the subject of the world outside

* From J. Nuttin. Consciousness, behavior, and personality. *Psychological Rev.,* 1955, **62,** 349–355. Reprinted with permission of the author and publisher.

him. Thus, this representation is a kind of duplicate of the outside world: a duplicate existing *in* the subject. In a recent symposium on cognitive theory and personality functioning contributors repeatedly expressed themselves in such terms of representation. "Cognitive theory," Scheerer argues, "assumes that the organism is in commerce with its environment through the medium of selective representation." Sweet claims that "via the mediate of sensory processes, representations of the environment are obtained." This perceptual representation is considered a "perceptual response present in the organism."

In the field of cognitive and perceptual processes, as in behavioral science in general, it appears to be necessary indeed to return to what have been called the "naturalistic" or primary facts. If not, psychology may lose contact with the specific phenomenon to be explained, i.e., man behaving in his world of concrete life situations. From the psychological or behavioral point of view, nothing corresponds less to reality than to conceive of perception as a representation *in* man of something which exists outside him. Perception is a *direct* contact with the outside world *itself*. No medium, no duplicate, no representation, is interposed between the subject and his world.

This deep-rooted representational theory stems from philosophical and physiological problems. The psychology of sensation, for instance, studies the physiological processes involved in perception. From that standpoint, perceptual responses are in fact "organismic states which the organism carries about in the nervous system and which *represent* the perceived object for me." Philosophy, on the other hand, raises the problem of a *reality* existing beyond the object of cognitive processes. The object perceived is considered only a representation or a duplicate of that unknown reality as it is supposed to exist in itself, independently of the behaving subject. From the behavioral or psychological viewpoint, however, there is no doubt that man perceives the things themselves, that is, the world itself. Perception does not give him a *representation* of the world, but a direct *presence* of the world itself.

The representational theory is responsible for introducing an erroneous concept of consciousness. Consciousness has been conceived as the enclosed world of inner representations in the subject. In fact, according to the representational theory, there is on the one hand the world of objective, observable things which transcends psychological activity; on the other hand, there is the psychological world of consciousness where the objective world is represented on an enclosed, inner stage. On this enclosed stage the inner representations of outside things are acting in a private and incommunicable play. Thus, representational theory is responsible for introducing a double stage in our world, and even a double world.

Consciousness: Exposure to the Outside World

As a matter of fact, the sciences of behavior are not directly interested in an incommunicable private world of consciousness. Psychology is right in turning to the observable world itself in which man really behaves. But turning to the objective, observable things does not mean denying consciousness. On the contrary, this world of objects, fellow men, and situations precisely *exists for us,* is *present* to us, by the very fact of man's "openness" or exposure to the outside things. This specific exposure constitutes consciousness.

Thus, the naturalistic fact to which behavioral sciences should return is that man, at any moment, *finds himself in a world* of things, fellow men, and meaningful situations. His behavior is nothing other than his commerce or dealing with this world of life situations. In other words, the primary fact to be taken into account in the conception and study of behavior is the fact that an outside world is *present to us.* This presence of an outside world consists in a *direct* contact with things and men outside ourselves. This means that man is not an enclosed structure in himself, but that he is essentially constituted as an "exposure" to an outside world. This concept of exposure and direct presence of the world to us is fundamental in this sense: it underlies the possibility of "meeting" people and things, and thus the possibility of *behavior* as a dealing with situations. Looking at something, speaking to an audience, attending a conference, going away or staying at home, feeling frustrated, etc. mean and imply being in the presence of an outside meaningful world.

This presence of the outside world to us is not to be conceived, of course, as a physical fact (physical neighborhood, for instance). A tree or a room may be situated in the same physical environment as we are, and nevertheless not deal with this environment as with their "world"; they do not manifest that a world is present to them or that they are living in a world. Their responses are limited to physical or chemical reactions to stimuli. Therefore, the presence of a meaningful world to us is a psychological or behavioral fact.

Consciousness in its primary sense means precisely this exposure of the organism to the world, or in other words the direct presence of a world to us. The very fact, for instance, that an audience is present to me, or exists for me, as a part of my world or situation at the moment I address them, derives primarily from the fact that I am conscious. Consciousness means exposure to the outside world, not enclosedness in the "inner self." Moreover, consciousness or the fact that man finds himself in the presence of an outside world is not to be considered as a "private" affair of inner life. On the contrary, it is an object of direct perception. Seeing a man speaking with other people or driving a car, I perceive the fact that streets, houses, and people are present to this man, that they exist for him, that he is aware of them, that his behaving organism is open to them, i.e., that he has consciousness.

In order to avoid any misunderstanding, it should be stressed that recognition of this primary fact of consciousness as exposure to the outside world does not contradict the theory of perception as a selective and constructive process. The concrete content of the behavioral world present to us is a selective construction of the functioning psychophysiological personality. But no specific content of a perceptual world could ever be built up if there were not this fundamental property and activity of the organism which is called consciousness. In other words, man's exposure to the world is not the result or the total sum of a series of concrete perceptual contents. On the contrary, selective and constructive perception can only be conceived as a continuous activity of specification of the outside world to which man finds himself exposed. This fundamental fact of exposure as such is what is meant by consciousness. Without the fundamental capacity of the organism to be open or exposed to an outside world, perceptual processes would be reduced to internal organismic changes. *Lack* of consciousness, therefore, means enclosedness in the realm of physical and biochemical interactions. Consciousness is psychophysiological activity underlying all psychological or behavioral processes, insofar as they are intrinsically directed toward objects. Even the so-called unconscious motivations and behavior patterns presuppose consciousness in this fundamental sense.

Psychological and physiological sciences, of course, have to investigate the processes involved in the subject's exposure to the world. But the scientific examination of these processes should not destroy the fundamental psychological fact that a world is present to us, or exists for us, and that man's behavior is meaningful dealing with this world. The purpose of scientific psychology is to explain and to account for this fact, not to replace it, for greater convenience, by underlying but different processes. In other words, the underlying processes discovered by scientific investigation should ultimately be related to that unique behavioral phenomenon to be explained. The concept of consciousness does not give a solution to any scientific problem about behavior, but it is necessary for an adequate conception of behavior itself, and for a realistic approach to behavior problems.

Thus, the introduction of the notion of consciousness does not mean going back to introspectionism. On the contrary, it simply means the recognition that the essential characteristic of behavior itself is its being related to a meaningful outside world with which the subject finds himself presented. We also should not forget that scientific research itself is a form of behavior, i.e., a form of dealing with the world we are living in. Communicating scientific results is another form of behavior. Both activities imply what we have called consciousness.

The Vicarious Presence of the World in Consciousness

Until now, we have considered consciousness as putting us in direct contact with the outside world and with the external behavioral facts. The problem of consciousness, however, becomes complicated by the fact that the world can be present to us in different ways. Man is able to find himself in the presence of an object or a situation which is not immediately presented to him from the outside. This is what I call the *vicarious presence* of an object. This possibility of vicarious presence of things to us, via images, concepts, and symbols, is a capital behavioral fact. It enlarges to an enormous extent the world in which man is living and, consequently, the possibilities of behavior. By this vicarious presence man's dealing with situations goes far beyond the limits of responding to actually present things. Man is, for instance, *thinking* about them; i.e., he is dealing with them in a cognitive way. Thinking and imagining are in fact nothing else than other ways of going along with the world and dealing with its situations. This inner, cognitive dealing with situations is intrinsically directed to, or projected toward, an outside world and it is, as a rule, preparatory or compensatory to effective external behavior. In some circumstances—as is the case, for instance, in science—thinking about things actually constitutes the effective form of behavior itself. In fact, man finds himself also in this very particular situation that the world is perceived as a problem to be solved, i.e., to be dealt with in a cognitive way.

Man's Presence to Himself

Man not only finds himself in the presence of an outside world; he may also be presented with himself. His own activities may become for himself the objects of his perception and cognition, as is the case in introspection. In this way man finds himself presented with his own activities, thoughts, and feelings about the world: he is reflecting on himself, on his activities, and on the content of his spontaneous or direct consciousness. This inner presence of man to himself and the reflection upon his own activities may be called *reflective consciousness* or consciousness raised to the second power.

Reflective consciousness is another way in which man escapes "enclosedness" in himself. By the very fact of being able to reflect on himself, man never finds himself completely enclosed in the actual phase of interacting with the environment. Reflecting on what he is and what he does, man "goes out" of himself, transcends the spatial and temporal determinations of the self by judging and evaluating himself and his activity.

At the same time, man's presence to himself enables him to look at himself and at the world from different points of view and to reshape at any time, to a certain extent, his own personality. It enables him to intervene, intentionally, in the course of his own development in order to restructure his relationships with the environment. This possibility seems to be implied in some phases of the therapeutic process.

Once more, this highest function of consciousness broadens man's world and the self in a considerable way. It frees him from enclosedness in his own subjectivity and enables him to look at things and at himself from an "objective" point of view. This possibility is the basis of such forms of behavior as science and intentional efforts of self-improvement. Thus, consciousness in its different functions frees man from enclosedness in his own organism, in the immediate physical world, and in his own subjectivity. While some degree of exposure to the world seems to be implied in all behavior, the higher functions of consciousness only manifest themselves in specific forms of human behavior (language, culture).

Consciousness and Behavioral Science

As a matter of fact, the vicarious presence of things and man's reflective consciousness of his own activity take place on the level of inner representation. These more complicated functions of consciousness, however, presuppose consciousness in its primary sense of direct presence of an outside world to man.

It is essential for the science of behavior not to separate representational consciousness from direct exposure to the world, as it is important not to separate the representational way of dealing with situations from effective behavior. The representational level of consciousness is not to be studied in itself, as opposed to real behavior, i.e., as a world of "existential" qualities of inner experience. Clinical psychology and projective techniques have shown how closely related these representations and images are with man's real behavior in the world he is living in. Therefore, the introspective data of reflective consciousness and the vicariously present world on the level of representation are to be studied in their functional relationship with behavior as a whole. Even for clinical psychology it is important to base its insights on a behavioral theory in which the representational and operational levels of behavior are functionally related.

On the other hand, the meaningful world itself as it is present to us by direct consciousness cannot be separated from behavior. In fact, the world of meaningful things and situations is a crystallization or condensation of behavioral patterns. A physical object or a part of the surrounding space becomes a desk, a phone, or an office insofar as a whole network of behavioral dealing, and possibilities of dealing, are involved in it. In this way, consciousness in the objective sense of "the world present to us" is crystallized behavior.

Moreover, man's conscious presence in the world is a *behavioral* presence. This means that, for the human personality, finding itself in the presence of a world implies and entails, necessarily, behavioral dealing with the world. In this sense, consciousness or exposure to the world is already *implicit behavior,* while behavior itself is externalized consciousness or *realized* presence to the world. In any case, instead of opposing consciousness and behavior, one should realize that no human realities are more inseparably united.

Consciousness, Personality, and Motivation

Finally, I have to indicate briefly the relationship between consciousness and the concept of personality. Psychologists as a rule conceive of personality as an internal organization of traits, attitudes, aptitudes, and behavioral consistencies. In fact, personality is such an internal organization; but the most essential characteristic of personality is lacking in such a definition. Personality is essentially a structure which goes beyond its internal organization. Its most characteristic feature consists in the fact that an outlook on and an exposure to the world is included in its own constitution. Personality is a way of being and behaving *in* a world that *exists for* the self. The outlook on a world or life situation is an essential constituent of personality itself. In this sense, the fundamental structure of personality is an "ego-world unity." Nothing could more profoundly mutilate the concept of personality than neglecting this aspect of exposure to the world which is an essential component of personality as such. This exposure, as I have said previously, is just what is meant here by consciousness. If, as Lewin says, it is true that the personality governing behavior is a part of the psychological field, it must not be forgotten that the psychological field itself, in the general sense of "living in a world," enters into the make-up of personality.

Personality conceived in this way as an ego-world structure provides us with a sound basis for a theory of human motivation. Motivation theory today tends, so to speak, to situate and localize needs in the organism itself. But from the behavioral point of view, needs are to be conceived as basic patterns of organism-environment or ego-world relationships which actually are required for organism or personality functioning. In fact, personality is made up of different types of such relationships, not only on the level of biochemical organism-environment interaction, but also on the level of cognitive and affective ego-world relationships. While the basic patterns of biochemical interaction—and thus the basic drives in this field—are performed in the physiological constitution of the organism, the cognitively elaborated ego-world relationships are more personal in origin and nature. Motivations on this level of behavior present themselves as an infinite variety of ego-world relationships in states of tension. Basic needs on this ego level are to be conceived as certain general and significant trends which eventually can be discovered in, and abstracted from, this variety of ways in which the individual tries to insert himself in his world. Such a general trend might be called "need for self-realization," as this "significance" is discovered in, or abstracted from, the innumerable concrete forms of man's behavioral dealing with the world of his fellow men and life situations.

The patterns of ego-world relationships which constitute the infantile personality will be different from the adult ego-world structure. The same significant trends, however, may be discovered in both. In that way, there may be infantile and adult forms of the same basic need, as there are infantile and adult patterns of ego-world relationships. There is no reason why the infantile form should be considered the *basic* one, and the adult pattern the derived or secondary need. Both are rather to be conceived as varieties of a basic type of ego-world relationship which the individual needs in order to maintain and develop the functional organism-environment and ego-world structure which constitute personality at a given stage of its development.

Summary and Conclusions

Psychologists who work in the fields of cognition and perception still frequently consider the perceived world as an internal representation of a real external world. This representational theory is strongly rooted in psychology, but it originates in a philosophical speculation which raises the question of a reality underlying the objects of cognition. From the viewpoint of the psychological study of behavior, the perceived world is by no means a representation *inside* of man (or inside consciousness) of some object whose real existence lies outside of him. The perceived world is the real world itself, and perception consists of direct contact with the environment. For this reason the notion of consciousness, as it has been developed within the framework of introspective psychology, is in need of revision. Consciousness does not refer primarily to an internal world made up of representations; it consists of a direct awareness and of an immediate *presence* of the world itself.

Consciousness therefore signifies, before all else, *exposure to the real behavioral world*, and not confinement in an internal world of representation. Consciousness establishes a man as a being who lives in the world, and thus consciousness is an essential aspect of behavior.

The world, however, can also be present to the behaving subject in a *vicarious* way, via representation. Moreover, man can be present to himself by reflective consciousness. These "higher" functions of consciousness also free man from specific forms of enclosedness.

As for the concept of personality, nothing is less in conformity with reality than to conceive of personality as a pure internal structure of traits, aptitudes, etc. Personality signifies a specific modality of existence and of activity which is characterized by the fact of involvement in a situation or in the world. The fundamental personality structure is therefore an ego-world unity, and not an internal organization of an ego. The psychological field itself, more basically, enters into the make-up of personality. Motivation also must be looked at in relation to the fact that man lives in a meaningful world. In fact, basic needs are general types of organism-environment and ego-world relationships which actually are required by the functioning of organism and personality.

The introduction of the notion of consciousness solves no concrete scientific problem regarding behavior, but it is necessary to appeal to the concept in order to formulate and to come to grips with the problems of behavior and of personality in a realistic fashion.

27. The Psychology of Mental Content Reconsidered *

David C. McClelland
Harvard University

Psychologists used to be interested in what went on in people's heads. In fact, for thousands of years this was practically all they were interested in. Psychologists from Aristotle to John Stuart Mill were concerned primarily with

* From D. C. McClelland. The psychology of mental content reconsidered. *Psychological Rev.*, 1955, **62**, 297–302. Reprinted with permission of the author and publisher.

This paper was delivered at the Fourteenth International Congress of Psychology in Montreal, June 9, 1954.

ideas and associations between ideas, but with the rise of modern scientific psychology we lost interest in ideas, by and large. The history of this development is well known, but let us review it for a moment. The psychology of mental content collapsed in the United States under the impact of two heavy blows. First, introspectionism seemed to run into a dead end. Titchener had argued manfully for a scientific study of the contents of mind, a kind of mental chemistry in which the basic elements would all be discovered and sorted out, but his laboratories simply failed to produce enough data to back up his theoretical position. It was not so much that his position was untenable. It was just that the data collected by the introspectionists did not seem to lead anywhere—to fruitful hypotheses, for example, which would serve to make theoretical sense out of the flux of mental events.

The second blow was even more devastating. It was, of course, the behavioristic revolution. Particularly in the United States, psychologists began to argue that conscious content could never form the basis of a science, whereas behavior could. J. B. Watson led the revolt in the name of scientific objectivity. After all, could you see or touch or feel or record with a machine a thought or a feeling? Now, a muscular contraction—an eye blink, a foot withdrawal, a right turn in a maze—that was something else again. That could be seen and touched and felt and often recorded entirely automatically by an impersonal, mechanical gadget. Here was the stuff of which a real science could be made!

Looking back with the perspective of 30 years we can begin to see why this movement was so appealing. In the first place, it did provide the kind of objectivity, methodologically speaking, that psychology had never had before and it could, therefore, lend real support to psychology's claim that it was a science. Secondly, it fit in with the traditional American pragmatic bias in favor of action rather than thought or feeling which were generally considered to be old-fashioned European concepts. After all, in the United States it is what a man does that counts, not what he says or thinks or feels. This tendency in American psychology is still so prevalent that to many of us prediction of behavior means *only* predicting gross motor behavior rather than predicting thoughts, conflicts, doubts, imaginings, feelings, etc. as reflected in verbal behavior. Thirdly, behaviorism tended to focus attention on problems which were of vital topical interest to a new country in which many of its citizens were attempting to adjust to new ways of life. In fact, adjustment or *learning* became the key concept. And this was natural in a country in which so many immigrants or their children had to give up traditional European ways of behaving for new American habit patterns. It was at this point that psychology became almost exclusively interested in "process variables," in how people went about doing things rather than in what they did. This was the time when Woodworth was stressing that we should rewrite psychology in terms of "ing" words—e.g., perceiving, emoting, thinking, learning, etc. No one was interested in *what* people thought, *what* they perceived, *what* they learned, etc. Instead we were to be concerned only with the laws which governed the *process* of perceiving, learning, etc.

Even personality and social psychology, which by definition are content oriented and which, therefore, should have resisted this trend, fell under the spell of this widespread movement. In personality psychology we were primarily interested in self-descriptive inventories in which the subject answered a lot of questions about his aches, pains, and anxieties. But, mind you, we did not look at his answers. We added them up to get a neuroticism score or dominance score or what not. We were not interested even here in *what* he said about himself, in *what* his ideas were. We were only interested in the extent to which his answer contributed to a total score which meant something else.

To be sure, an individual clinician sometimes went so far as to look at the actual answers a person had given on a personality inventory, but then, he was not a scientist! In social psychology, too, we managed to get along without much concern with content, although here, too, it was a little difficult. The problem was solved with the help of the attitude concept. An attitude is essentially what I have been calling a process variable. We are interested in *how* attitudes get set up, in how we can measure them, in their consistency, in their rigidity, their generality or specificity, etc.—all process variables. But we are not interested in *what* they are, particularly. Any old attitude will do for our purpose, just as in studying learning, any old task will do for our purpose—a maze, a bar to press, a list of nonsense syllables, or what not. So social psychologists chose as the attitudes to be investigated whatever happened to be of current interest at the moment—e.g., internationalism, feminism, pacifism, race prejudice, and so on. Few if any people thought it was even worth asking which attitudes were the "important" ones to use in describing a person or his culture. Many people probably would have wondered whether such questions really fell within the province of psychology at all.

It is against the background of this widespread social movement in psychology that we can see the beginnings of the projective testing movement as the source of a change in attitude which is finally beginning to be felt today, possibly in large part because of the success of projective tests. But certainly projective testing did not start as a conscious revolt against this interest in process. Quite the contrary. The Rorschach test, as one of the oldest of these new instruments, probably gained as wide acceptance as it did in the United States largely because it became primarily process-oriented. It became concerned with *how* people perceive and only secondarily with *what* they perceive. Quantitative indices could be computed according to how many responses were determined primarily by form, by color, by movement, and the like. Nevertheless, the good clinicians often found that the particular content of the association given by the patient was of value to them in understanding the person. And this has always been the case with a good clinician. He *has* to be interested in *what* his patient thinks as well as in how he thinks it. Even though his formal psychological training gives him very little assistance at this level, he knows that in order to handle this particular person he has to be interested in the patient's ideas. This, it seems to me, has been the great and continuing contribution of the clinic and the projective test in a time when psychological theorists have talked themselves out of being interested in content altogether. I am reminded here of a comment made to me once by one of my more cynical colleagues who claimed that no new ideas of importance ever appeared in the universities. Usually they appear outside first, and then are only gradually claimed by the universities. Certainly if we think for a minute of men like Descartes, Darwin, Freud, or Einstein, there would seem to be something in what he said. And this development seems to be a case in point. The projective testing movement grew up largely *outside* the conservative academic tradition and finally, because of its clinical success, has managed to dent the calm assurance with which many theoretical psychologists have discarded all problems of mental content.

But to continue with my story: The real change came with the development by Murray and his associates of the Thematic Apperception Test about 20 years ago. Now for the first time we had an instrument in which the primary concern was not form but content. The person interpreting a TAT record must ask such questions as: *What* motives activate this person? *What* conflicts plague him? *What* modes of defense does he adopt? *What* characteristics does the world have for him? No longer are we concerned primarily, as in the Rorschach, with *how* he approaches his task, although some have attempted to analyze the TAT in these terms. To help us in our analyses of such content, we have drawn heavily on psychoanalysis, the one system of content psychology which, isolated in the clinic, survived the mass attack of behaviorism in the laboratory. Murray in his original system of analysis for the TAT attempted to provide us with a much broader vocabulary for the analysis of content, but, by and large, in our analyses we draw upon relatively few general psychoanalytical concepts such as sex, aggression, parent-child relationships, and the like. This, to my way of thinking, is an impoverished set of concepts for dealing with mental content, but it is nonetheless the one real and vital one in the United States today.

What evidence is there that this tendency to concern oneself with mental content is of growing influence? In the first place, we must not underestimate the conservative resistance to the belief that such a psychology is possible. Even Freud's generalizations about the importance of certain basic conflicts such as those involved in the Oedipus complex are under constant attack. To some extent the attacks are motivated by the conviction that generalizations about content are really impossible. The argument runs that there are no general concepts which can serve to describe the human situation at *any* place or time in history. What about cultural relativism? After all, individuals differ widely in what they think and so do cultures. Some have an Oedipus complex and some do not. How can we generalize about anything except the process by which individuals arrive at their ideas? The ideas themselves are completely relative. One can perhaps be literary about them, but not scientific. This is the argument and there is no answer to it, except to prove that it can be done fruitfully. Many of us are convinced already, for example, that despite individual and cultural variations, it is a major scientific achievement to have focused attention on the framework of the mother-son relationship as of primary importance in the development of the individual, and to have worked out some of the taxonomy of this and the allied relationship with the father.

Meanwhile, there have been some new developments which would encourage us to believe that perhaps a psychology of content is possible. Take the research report on *The Authoritarian Personality,* for example. I would contend that the essential issues raised by this research are issues in the psychology of content. It represents to some extent a fusion of psychoanalytic structural concepts with certain concepts drawn from political ideology. Whether we like the fusion or not does not really matter too much. From the methodological point of view it represents an exciting step forward since its authors have drawn on political ideology as well as psychoanalysis to help explain the structure of personality. When our science has matured to the point where we can draw not only on political ideology, but on economic, religious, esthetic ideologies, and the like, then we will be on the way toward developing a really full-blown psychology of mental content.

Our own research on *The Achievement Motive* has contributed as much to these conclusions as anything else. We started with the relatively simple task of identifying those types of imagery in a TAT-type record which indicated the presence of a motive to achieve or succeed. After we were able to identify reliably this item of mental content, we were able to select individuals whosc thought processes contained a lot of such items and other individuals whose thought processes contained few such items. We were then faced with the question of how these people differed. Do they behave differently? Yes, they do. The ones with a lot of achievement imagery tend to learn faster, to perform better, to set different levels of aspiration, to have a better memory for incompleted tasks, to perceive the world in different terms, etc. Perhaps even more interesting was the question of how they got that way. How is it that some people tend to think more often in achievement terms? We were led back to the mother-son relationship and found that independence training seems to be associated with achievement motivation. That is, those mothers who encouraged their sons to develop independently, to learn their way around by themselves, seemed to have sons with higher achievement motives. But we pushed the question one step further back. How is it that some mothers favor independence training more than others? This raised the question of values, and values raised the question of religious ideology. Then we found that attitudes toward independence training were not randomly distributed through various population subgroups. Instead, Protestant and Jewish parents were much more likely to favor early independence training than were Catholic parents and this, in turn, seemed to fit into the belief systems and emphases of these three religions. And if this is so, we can begin to trace some of the details of the connection between Protestantism and the rise of capitalism as originally outlined by Max Weber and R. H. Tawney.

So our recent research has led us into the relationships between religious values, independence training, achievement motivation, and economic development. We think we are beginning to discover some connections among these phenomena which can be traced out with a fair degree of scientific confidence. But whether we succeed or not, the point I am trying to make is that by concentrating on one item of mental content, namely achievement imagery, we have opened up a whole new set of problems in social science that can be investigated by psychology.

Now let us pause a minute and try to reconsider what has happened. The "new look" in the study of mental content really involves neither introspection nor projective testing in their pure forms. Instead I prefer to call it "thought sampling," and to use the analogy of the "blood count" from the medical laboratory to explain what I have in mind. Just as we need a sample of blood to make a white cell count, we want a sample of thoughts or ideas to make our imagery counts. In general, we get these samples by asking the subject to write stories to certain cues, usually verbal or visual. Having gotten our thought sample, we have to learn to recognize certain types of imagery, just as the medical technician has to learn to recognize a white blood cell when he sees one. This involves a great deal of preliminary work so that we can define the characteristics of the imagery carefully and then train individuals to recognize what they are looking for. It does require training, but probably no more training than a medical technician needs to be able to distinguish one type of blood cell from another. That is, it does not involve high-level judgment, but is essentially a "pointing" operation which is a little, but not much, more difficult to make than pointing to an animal's right turn in a maze. Watson need not have feared for the objectivity of this kind of analysis. The record is permanent. The same person can look at it again and again, or several people can analyze it. It is quite possible to get a reliable and objective result.

If we put the "new look" in mental content in these general terms, it is immediately clear that we have a number of problems to solve. For example, there is the sampling problem. Under what conditions should we get our thought samples? What cues should we use? Should we get long samples or short samples? What about the subject's set? How does it influence content? Here it becomes obvious that traditional projective testing elicits only a very small segment of the possible types of mental content. To the extent that we stay within the limited framework of the traditional TAT cards, for example, we are bound to have a biased sample of what goes on in a man's mind.

An even more important problem has to do with the decision as to what categories for content analysis we use. This is the heart of the problem, since we will get theoretically meaningful results, or generalizations that hold for a wide variety of situations, only if we choose the right categories to begin with. How does one discover the right categories? The literature of social science is strewn with content analyses of everything from open-ended interviews to "soap operas"—analyses which are purely *ad hoc*—for the immediate practical purpose in hand. I am certainly not arguing for more of this industrious busy work. The categories must be meaningful; they must be related to theory; they must be trans-situational—i.e., applicable to more situations than the one to which they are first applied. It takes inspiration or luck or hard work or something to discover such a category, just as it did in biology to discover what was the most useful of many possible ways to classify blood cells. The only concrete suggestion I have as to how to proceed, which comes from our own experience, is to choose those categories which show significant shifts as a result of experimental operations. Whether this is an unnecessarily restrictive rule, I do not know. At any rate it certainly eliminates many possible categories, and it seems to be roughly the one which the chemists have used in setting up the classification of elements.

This brings us back to Titchener. Looking back with the perspective of history, we can now see that Titchener's structural psychology failed for two reasons. In the first place, the content categories he chose did not turn out to be fruitful. They were not related to experimental operations on the one hand or to other types of behavior on the other. For these or other reasons, they simply did not lead to theoretical development. Therefore they were the wrong categories. In the second place, and this is of major methodological importance, his students categorized their own data. The essence of introspection is that the same person serves both as a source of data and as a categorizer of them. This has an obvious weakness, a weakness which has been perpetuated in self-descriptive personality inventories. It is simply that the subject may have a very imperfect or incorrect idea of what categories his thoughts belong in. This may be because his categories are different from the ones we as scientists want to use or because he may really misperceive himself. The great contribution that both Freud and the projective testing movement made was that neither asked the subject to pass judgment on his thoughts as they appeared to him. Both simply asked for a sample of those thoughts and then left the categorization process to an outside observer. This was an important methodological advance, the significance of which I think we are only just beginning to appreciate.

If psychologists are to re-enter the field of mental content and start classifying it according to categories of genuine theoretical fruitfulness, I fear they will have to return to disciplines they have long neglected. In the twenties, in the heyday of behaviorism, we were proud that we knew nothing of religion, of art, of history, of economics, or politics (except in a personal, often naive way). We didn't need to know about these things if we were only interested in process variables. We could make our own choice of a task situation—for example, the rat in a maze—and what we found out there about how the rat learned the maze would apply equally well to *all* (including human) learning situations. We could afford to be ignorant of many things that man has thought about. But if the psychology of content develops as I think it will, we shall have to go back to getting a broad, general education. Certainly nothing in my training *as a psychologist* prepared me to handle problems in religious belief systems or economic development. Yet these are typical of the problems which I think will begin to arise increasingly often in the new psychology of content, and we simply cannot afford to be naive and pretend that research scholars in these fields have nothing to tell us.

If my analysis is correct, we are on the brink of an important new development in psychology. Because of methodological improvements, we are about to take up again some of the problems in mental content that formerly were considered to be an essential part of psychology. And it is my conviction that the projective testing movement is to be thanked for keeping an interest in content alive in an era when most theoretical psychologists were otherwise occupied, and for providing us with the methodological advance that enabled us to escape from the blind alley into which introspection had led us.

Editor's Note

Consciousness, or the awareness of oneself and the outside world, is sometimes contrasted with "public" events in a way suggesting they are mutually exclusive. An image experienced in the inner recesses of the mind is not as open to verification by others as is a flash of lightning or a falling star, yet it can be communicated in various ways. An oil painting or a graphic description illustrates how a private experience can become public. Without some ability to make people aware of our awareness, no communication would be possible, since all knowledge originates as a private conscious experience which can be expressed in some way.

28. Consciousness and the Conscious Self *

Harold Grier McCurdy
University of North Carolina

Our theme up to now has been the human being as a biological organism which we could observe from the outside, as an object in space. [Reference not relevant here.] By careful self-control it would be possible to hold rigidly to that point of view and include nothing in our description of the human being except spatial and kinetic properties. The preceding chapters have not been quite that behavioristic. They have now and then considered the human being as conscious of himself and his surroundings. In the present chapter human consciousness will be made the central theme.

Even if we were only interested in the prediction of bodily movements, we should be interested in consciousness and the conscious self, for, as the physicist Arthur Compton has underlined, a conscious human being can predict his

* Abridged from *The Personal World: An Introduction to the Study of Personality*, by Harold Grier McCurdy, © 1961, by Harcourt, Brace & World, Inc. and reprinted with their permission.

own behavior with far greater certainty than a physicist can predict the behavior of the objects of physical science. Or if we were primarily interested in the Unconscious as viewed by the psychoanalytically oriented, we should still be interested, because without some recognition of the fact of consciousness the very concept of the Unconscious would be impossible. Both historically and logically the study of consciousness precedes the study of the Unconscious. Entirely apart from such excuses as these, however, the topic of this chapter deserves a central place in a book on personality.

It is a curious twist in the history of psychology—and as a reviewer of a recent symposium on the mind-body problem has said in reference to Zener's paper on "The Significance of Experience of the Individual for the Science of Psychology," it is a tragic twist—that any apology should be needed for bringing consciousness into a psychological discussion. Yet we must realize how matters stand. Hilgard has stated it accurately: [1]

> Psychologists are by no means unanimous as to the place of private experience (consciousness) in a science of psychology. Some extremists believe that private experiences have no place in science; they believe that such experiences belong to the province of the artist or poet. But most psychologists hold that these private experiences are just as much a part of the real world as more observable activities, and they accept the *verbal report* of these experiences as data for science.

It is against this background that a discussion of consciousness must take place, and to avoid confusion it must be clearly stated that one who is serious about consciousness does not regard "private experiences" as somehow less ob-

[1] Ernest R. Hilgard, *Introduction to Psychology* (2nd ed.), Harcourt, Brace and World, Inc., New York, 1957, p. 4.

servable than "public experiences" and does not accept "verbal report" or any other index of conscious processes as a substitute for them. Skinner, who accepts the distinction between public and private events, is firm in rejecting the strategy of identifying verbal report with the event it reports.[2]

> The verbal report is a response to the private event and may be used as a source of information about it. A critical analysis of the validity of this practice is of the first importance. But we may avoid the dubious conclusion that, so far as science is concerned, the verbal report or some other discriminative response *is* the sensation.

I cannot state my own position better than by agreeing with Skinner here.

A word must be said about "public" and "private," however. A person may speak as confidently and truthfully of seeing the objects of a dream as of seeing his face in a mirror or the sun in the sky. All these are equally observable for him. So also are his feelings, his intentions, his decisions, though these cannot be classified as visible or even as "things." On the other hand, it is doubtful whether another person could ever take up exactly the first person's point of view with regard to *any* of these contents of consciousness. In that sense, all that anyone experiences is private to himself—the face in the mirror, the sun in the sky, as well as all the rest. But there is the marvelous fact of communication. By words, by gestures, by postures and facial expressions, by painting, by music, we manage to convey to others some awareness of our awareness and even, in a manner of speaking, give our private contents of consciousness to each other to handle and evaluate. The

[2] B. F. Skinner, *Science and Human Behavior,* Macmillan, New York, 1953, p. 282.

private thus becomes public; that is to say, it is shared by two or more persons. This communication gives us great pleasure and it is the indispensable foundation of those great public works, the sciences. But there would be no communication if there were nothing to communicate, and every communication originates in the content of someone's consciousness. Now, some of this communication takes the form of pointing. One can point at the sun in the sky or the face in the mirror, and others can follow the pointing finger and discover out there before them something corresponding to what was pointed at. Sometimes there is a little confusion, and one sees a bird instead of the sun or the frame of the mirror rather than the face in it; but, with persistence, we iron out these disagreements. Pointing, however, does not usually suffice for the objects of dreams, or for feelings, intentions, and decisions. The communication problem here is a trifle more difficult, but in principle it is the same problem. Perhaps it is not more difficult—a great deal depends on the state of consciousness of the communicators. To point out the sun to a person who cannot see at all is futile. Other approaches in that case are possible, to be sure; for instance, the sun's heat can be perceived by both the seeing and the blind. The face in the mirror would be a tougher problem. As for dreams and intentions and such, the problem is not really so grave if we happen to be dealing with someone who is conscious of dreams and intentions of his own; he can at least have a general knowledge of what is meant. But if he is a stranger to such contents of consciousness, the communication problem becomes very grave; in fact, as grave as that of sharing the face in the mirror with the blind man. We may then be driven to exclaim, in a burst of sympathy or exasperation, "Oh, I *wish* you knew!" In short, the problem of communication is basically a problem of common experience or the capacity for it.

How many of our disagreements in psychology stem

from the dissimilarity of our experience has never been fully explored, but it is a safe bet that most of them do. Take, for example, the matter of visualizing, i.e., the power of calling up a visual image of something formerly seen. Long ago Galton found, to his astonishment, that there were numerous scientists who did not have this power and who, moreover, were inclined to deny that anyone else did. "They had no more notion of its true nature than a colour-blind man, who has not discerned his defect, has of the nature of colour. They had a mental deficiency of which they were unaware, and naturally enough supposed that those who were normally endowed were romancing." Galton himself had the power, or it would have hardly occurred to him to start the investigation. Among modern psychologists the proportion who do not have visual imagery appears to be exceptionally high. Roe in a study of eminent research scientists in America asked biologists, physicists, psychologists, and anthropologists what sort of imagery they used in thinking out their research problems. Of the 9 experimental psychologists and 4 clinical, child, or social psychologists of her sample, only 2 professed to use any visual imagery in their work, and these were both experimentalists. Quite a number of them did profess to use *verbal* imagery, and this may have something to do with the stress on verbal report or verbalization which is so characteristic of psychological writings on thought and feeling these days. Roe's study, though based on small numbers, may furnish a clue to some of our debates about consciousness. Highly verbal or imageless psychologists may have trouble in realizing what the few with strong visual imagery mean when they refer to imagining something, and the small minority of visualizers may feel crushed under the verbalizing majority. However this may be, Roe found a significant difference between the psychologists and the anthropologists (social scientists) on the one hand and the biologists and physicists (natural scientists) on the other. This must mean that lack of visual imagery is not a prerequisite of *all* high-level scientific work, in spite of Galton's speculation that hard thinking may have reduced the visualizing capacity of the scientists he knew.

I have cited a dissimilarity of experience in a relatively private area of consciousness as a possible cause of scientific quarrels. It would be easy to cite many gross dissimilarities of a more public nature. I will mention only one, however, and this outside the field of psychology. When P. A. Čerenkov, the Russian physicist, first produced the luminescence now known as "Čerenkov radiation" by irradiating pure water with gamma rays, he was unable to convince many physicists who came to see the demonstration that the glow was really there. They were "highly sceptical and hinted at visual hallucinations"—for one thing, it had been an established principle that nothing moved faster than light and Čerenkov's claim appeared to violate this principle. But the skepticism must also have been partly due to nothing more profound than a visual sensitivity less acute than his. The fact of the matter is that certain particles *can* move faster than light *in certain media* (i.e., not *in vacuo*) and thus radiate light, a phenomenon which had not been recognized before Čerenkov did his experiment. Suppose, however, that Čerenkov's experiment—in the teeth of this skepticism—had not been repeated and expanded, as it has been; the charge of "hallucinations" might have stuck. If this kind of thing can happen in physics, it must surely happen in psychology. We have to beware of denying the reality of other persons' experiences solely because they fall outside our own range of perception and theory.

Editor's Note

Few topics in psychology have proved more resistant to scientific investigation than human motivation. If the "why" of a single act, such as the assassination of a President, can baffle a panel of experts, identification of the conscious forces that shape the whole life-pattern of every individual presents an even greater challenge. Some psychologists are of the opinion that science should not attempt to investigate the inner world of human intention where no outside observer is ever invited. Since what a person thinks or feels can never be known with certainty, psychology should concern itself with the more observable processes. The greatest shortcoming of studies based on this philosophy is their limited scope. Physiological drives and other organic factors which are relatively simple to study account for only part of man's behavior. Creativity and value orientation are difficult to integrate into a rigid need-drive theory. Freud's dynamic psychology offers an explanation of molar behavior, but his theory of motivation, based on clinical observation, fails to account for the self-actualizing tendencies of the normal person.

The work of Charlotte Buhler provides an example of how the above two approaches can be integrated. Beginning with her own clinical observations and all other information available to her, she hypothesized four basic life tendencies which actively influence the individual in his pursuit of self-fulfillment. Since her theory can be validated only by investigating people's actual motives, she has painstakingly tested several empirical methods of approach. The questionnaire described here illustrates how, with persistent effort, techniques can be developed to deal with problems involving mental content.

29. Some Empirical Approaches to the Study of Life's Basic Tendencies *

Charlotte Buhler
Clinical psychologist in private practice
and University of Southern California Medical School

One of the most decisive and most difficult problems in the study of the basic tendencies of human life is the question of how the innumerable concrete goals that we pursue in our daily living tie up with the ultimate overall tendencies of our lives.

This is, of course, the question which Freud asked and tackled ingeniously at a time when we all considered it impossible to even approach at all. And psycho-analysis has, in the half century of its existence, furthered an enormous wealth of material in answer to this question.

However, some of us felt it necessary to digress from the theoretical framework of psychoanalysis. The reason was that within it, it seemed impossible to explain certain phenomena of normal development satisfactorily. To these belong the primary nature of creativity, of a positive reality, of some of our value orientation.

As for myself, I have, in several publications, given my reasons for the necessity of this digression. I also showed how, from all the available relevant information, I derived four basic tendencies of life which I called: *need-satisfaction, self-limiting adaptation, creative expansion,* and *upholding of the internal order*. The overall end-goal I called *fulfillment* in preference to self-realization, because the concept of fulfillment allows for different possible types of satisfying closure experiences.

Very briefly, *need-satisfaction* comprises essentially

* From Charlotte Buhler. Some empirical approaches to the study of life's basic tendencies. In L. N. Solomon (Ed.), A symposium on human values. *J. humanistic Psychol.*, 1962, 2, 89–111. Reprinted with permission of the author and publisher.

the area covered by the psychoanalytic concept of discharge. It refers to more or less acute needs of any kind that call for satisfaction. *Self-limiting adaptation* is conceived of originating as a primary unconscious tendency in the infant. Its development on a secondary level as a conscious behavior takes place to the degree that hindrances and demands are experienced as negative realities.

Also *creative expansion* and *upholding of the internal order are* conceived of as originating in primary unconscious processes in the infant. Creative expansion begins in the newborn's experimental movements and becomes a matter of conscious goal-setting and planning of accomplishments from about two to three years on, when the child begins to build playfully with blocks and when he begins to feel like a person equipped with the power to *do* and to *decide* things.

The concept of *upholding of the internal order* refers first of all to the internal organization and integration of processes which again starts on an unconscious level. On the secondary conscious level, this order-making becomes related to principles and values which we might call matters of *conscience,* in which *self-assessment* plays a role. This also begins at about two to three years of age.

My thesis is that in every individual all of these tendencies are in operation at all times, but to individually varying degrees, and in individually varying patterns, consciously as well as sub- and unconsciously. All of these tendencies are necessary for life and survival. Everybody needs to satisfy his needs; everybody has to adapt; every individual needs to produce or create in the widest sense of planned accomplishments; everybody has to uphold a certain degree of internal order in terms of integrated and coordinated functioning, and in terms of consideration of principles of conscience.

However, different individuals seem from the beginning—and with this I refer to infant observations on activity degrees and other primary differences—more inclined to steer themselves in one or the other of these directions. Environmental influences and experiences of life may enhance or also modify these inclinations. Resulting are directional patterns in which more or less one-sided trends become sometimes temporarily, often lastingly predominant. Some people are primarily *need-satisfiers*. They are firstly set on *happiness* in the sense of comfort, pleasure, love. The person who is primarily adaptive, always appears strongly impressed by the human being's inadequacy in the face of the overwhelming power of circumstances and of the surrounding world. These people's feelings about human frailty induce them to curtail their own wishes in the interest of *security* often in submitting to a hopefully protective *authority* of one kind or another.

The primarily *expansively creative* individual is, on the contrary, confident of his strength, of his ability to *master* circumstances and to improve and change the world to suit man's needs.

The individual who is primarily concerned with the *upholding of his internal order* seems mostly determined by the need for inner *harmony* and *peace of mind*. These he hopes to attain in pursuing certain *beliefs* and *values*. By means of these pursuits he tries to establish his own *worth*.

Since all of these goals are fulfilling to all human beings to different degrees, everyone aspires to a certain amount of love, happiness and comfort; belonging, acceptance and security; mastery, expansion, creativity as well as feelings of worth and harmony in himself.

The best adjusted persons whose histories and personalities I was able to study, seem to strike a happy balance between these tendencies. Individuals who feel strongly about their self-realization and their selves were found to be primarily interested in their creativity and/or in their enjoyment of life. A. Maslow gives colorful examples of this type of person. Individuals who are more self-renunciating or self-dedicating tend to be adaptive and/or deeply concerned with their internal order, their peace of mind, their conscience.

The neurotic and psychotic individual shows extreme predominances of single trends or else irreconcilable conflicts.

One more word about the *developmental* sequence of these four basic tendencies. As we said, all four are at all times in operation within the person, although with an individual emphasis on one or the other. Besides the individual emphasis we also find a *developmental* predominance at different stages of life. We can observe the *sequence* of an initial predominance of need-satisfying tendencies in the infant, followed by predominantly adaptive trends in childhood, this again is followed by the predominance of creative expansion in adolescence and adulthood and this by an emphasis on self-assessment in the interest of internal order in the climacteric years. After this, many individuals regress to the need-satisfying tendencies of infancy or to childhood's self-limitation, which retirement imposes on them, while others seem able to keep up their creative expansion.

The *goals* pursued in these briefly outlined tendencies represent partly *factual,* partly *normative values,* to use Margenau's terms. Unfortunately, time forbids a discussion here of these two important aspects with respect to the four basic tendencies.

Instead, our main objective today is the presentation of attempts I made in the direction of *empirical* studies of the four basic tendencies.

The methodological question in the study of goals and values is as we all know, an extremely difficult one, in view of the fact that most conscious verbal responses represent only superficial or slated information. The most successful studies in this field like those of Kurt Lewin and his followers or like those using projective methods create situations in which *choices* occur that give *indirect information* rather than direct answers to questions.

However, in testing a hypothesis like that of the four basic tendencies, a verbal approach seems to me unavoidable and I do not yet quite see how it could be made a completely indirect one. The indirect approach which I tried, in asking for important *decisions* results in too sketchy types of data and it does not yield insight into the individual structure of the four basic tendencies.

I will now enumerate briefly the techniques which I tried and then dwell a little longer on my latest attempt which looks to me like the most hopeful one.

I tried (1) to obtain *biographical* and *autobiographical* data, comprehensive enough to interpret them in terms of conscious *self-determination.* These data I used in my German publication on the "Human Course of Life." They led me to the assumption of three phases of conscious self-determination in grown-up life. I called them the phases of *preliminary* and *definite* self-determination and the third the phase of *assessment of the results* of life.

In my opinion, these data helped to a degree to clarify the build-up of life in its developmental sequence. But they were unsatisfactory as far as unconscious tendencies are concerned and they apply primarily to people who live a sort of orderly life with same inner continuity.

(2) I tried a *Questionnaire about Goals.* In setting it up, I was helped by two experts in the construction of questionnaires—Hermann Harvey and Raymond Corsini. But as we anticipated, we got only rather superficial constructs in spite of much precaution in our questions.

(3) I studied my *psychotherapy records* with respect to information they would yield on goals of patients. This is naturally the most fruitful technique as far as *depth material* is concerned. However, since, in case records, statements about goals are incidental, conclusions about the structure of the basic tendencies would have to be partly based on conjecture.

There is the other limiting consideration regarding case records that here we deal with *neurotic individuals.*

We do not want to make the mistake of basing our assumptions about healthy people on case material exclusively. As Dr. Maslow showed in his studies of healthy personalities, their values look rather different than those of neurotics.

But, provided we do not lose sight of these limitations, psychotherapy records are still the most important source of depth material.

(4) So are *interviews* outside of psychotherapy situations important, provided they can be carried on by a clinician and for a sufficiently long time, so as to lead below surface information. They also should preferably be *structured* to the degree that the basic tendencies come into the fore. On his method I plan to work still further.

(5) Following Paul Lazarsfeld's suggestion, I devised a questionnaire on *decisions*. This yields very interesting information, although it has all the shortcomings of spontaneous material. However, I consider it worthwhile pursuing.

(6) The most promising in terms of systematic completeness and allowing for some degree of indirection is, however, a new questionnaire device which I conceived and tried only recently. It asks people to check off a list of suggested goals. The list of these was obtained in trying to envisage what the four basic tendencies would amount to in terms of *concrete objectives*. This, of course, involves some hypothesizing.

I will quote a few examples: a. have necessities of life, b. be accepted in contacts, c. be aggressive, go ahead, try things, d. have worthy beliefs, values.

There are 16 values and fulfillments representing each of the four tendencies, altogether 64. They appear on the form in intermingled order. The subject is asked to check each of these goals in choosing from five possible categories. These are called: "essential," "important," "desirable," "not my concern" and "rejected."

The 64 goals are all socially more or less acceptable. I did not see any usefulness in putting down unacceptable goals, at least not as long as I am working with more or less normal people who function in society, who would not admit to socially unacceptable goals and who might even become suspicious of the whole check-list if they were asked such questions. This could, of course, still be changed if it seemed advisable.

So far, the new check-list was given to only about a dozen people, but even with this very small sample certain most interesting trends become apparent:

1. With every one of the individuals one tendency is distinctly more emphasized than the three others.
2. Intense people call many things "essential," while more relaxed people call more things only "desirable."
3. In concentrating first on the extremes—the things which people call "essential" and the things they reject—I found definite patterns.
4. My small sample of healthy people agreed unanimously on two items: that "to give and receive love" was essential and also "to have worthy beliefs and values." To "have sex satisfaction" was considered either "important" or "desirable," in no case "essential."
5. Besides certain items which cluster, there are certain very individually characterizing items. For example, "to live a simple life" or "to be helpful, charitable" is considered essential only by one of the 12; "to find acknowledgment, praise" is violently rejected by only one out of 12 and so on.
6. The responses of this little sample seem to show the following pattern. There is a bulk of responses which appear indicative of a basically *constructive value system* of these persons. Each individual has, however, certain weak points.

> The weak points appeared in the form of *wishful thinking, self-deceptive* goals, goals suggesting tendencies to obtain *selfish gain,* and tendencies indicating *insecurity* and *anxiety.* This seemed to me a good picture of how essentially healthy people function.

These interpretations require naturally intimate clinically-oriented knowledge of the individuals. This appears to be of the essence, if one wants to obtain the full benefit from these or any questionnaires.

Summarizing I should like to say, that among a number of different methods I tried to obtain empirical material on basic tendencies of life, this last questionnaire method—asking for a reaction to suggested goals and fulfillments—appears to be the most promising. In conjunction with a clinically-oriented interview approach, I foresee in this questionnaire a useful new instrument for studying people's goal- and value orientation in terms of basic tendencies of life.

Progress Report on the Empirical Approach to the Study of Life's Basic Tendencies *

Since the preceding study was published in 1962, the questionnaire, now called *Life Goals Inventory,* has been developed to the point where it seems to be a usable instrument.

The original questionnaire has been enlarged from sixty-four to eighty-six questions, and factor analysis

* The following postscript was kindly prepared by the author for inclusion in this volume.

studies of two samples have been conducted by Andrew L. Comrey and Richard S. Coleman. Scoring procedures developed by William S. Coleman, which result in a profile of the individual's professed goals, appear in the jointly authored *Life Goals Inventory Manual* (1964). The goal profile graphically represents the distribution of choices among twelve factors arranged in groups corresponding to the four basic tendencies. The twelve factors are necessities of life; pleasure, love, and family; sex satisfaction; acceptance of limitations; submissiveness; avoidance of hardships; self-development; leadership, fame, and power; role in public life; moral values; social values; and having success.

Individual profiles indicating preferred versus less preferred or even rejected goals yield certain characteristic motivational patterns when subjected to analysis.

First, in comparing the profiles of relatively healthy individuals, we regularly find pronounced preferences expressed for "love and family," "moral values," and "social values." Depending upon the individual's potentials, there is strong or relatively strong belief in "self-development," adequate "acceptance of limitations," and an adequate belief in "having success." "Necessities of life" and "sex satisfaction" play a moderate to an important role.

The rest of the items, "submissiveness," "avoidance of hardships," "leadership," "role in public life," vary more widely in their distribution.

Second, in the healthy person's profile we do not find extreme scores. In fact, in cases of persons who live a rather contented, unimpassioned life all scores cluster around the middle score (fiftieth percentile).

Third, the neurotic person, by contrast, tends to exhibit jagged profile patterns with extreme scores on demands as well as on limitations. There may be excessive expectations regarding success, self-development, leadership, or sex. There may be complete denial of self-limitations or excessive self-limitations and submissiveness.

There may also be overemphasis on moral values or self-denial in terms of expecting very little satisfaction from life. Finally, there may be fear of sex expressed in very low scores.

Fourth, there are many incompatible scores in neurotic profiles. Extraordinary success may be hoped for without willingness to accept limitations or without interest in self-development. There may be profound submissiveness and yet the expectation of being a leader or disbelief in one's own success while aspiring to a role in public life.

We hope in the near future to have available typical profiles for each of these different structures. Two examples from our manual are reproduced below.

> LF 301, pseudonym *Bea,* is a 33 year old married woman, who is the mother of three and wife of a junior college instructor of English and Dramatics. She is a happy as well as an all-round very healthy person who feels that her marriage and family life are fulfilling to her and that her life is good. While she is not engaged in any career, she is interested in her husband's work and participates in many of his extra-curricular activities. Both are very socially inclined. Bea's husband is a very popular teacher and a man of many interests. The couple lead a very full and active life.
>
> Bea's profile indicates that her greatest concerns lie in the direction of her love and family life on the one hand and of moral and social values on the other. Her tendencies toward need-satisfaction are average, her interest in self-development is slightly above average, and while her interest in success and important roles in life is average, her self-limiting adaptation is slightly better than average.
>
> The two main signs of the neurotic personality, great variability of scores and low self-limiting adaptation, are not present.

BUHLER–COLEMAN
LIFE GOALS INVENTORY
Profile Analysis Sheet

Date March 1963 Name "Bea"

Age 33 Sex F File No. LF 301

Marr. Div. Si.

Need Satisfaction	RS.	10th percentile	25th percentile	50th percentile	75th percentile	90th percentile
A. Necessities of life, pleasure	21	12	17	20	23	27
B. Love and family	22	14	16	19	21	23
C. Sex satisfaction	18	12	16	19	23	26
Self-limiting Adaptation						
D. Accept limitations caution	23	12	17	21	25	30
E. Submissiveness	33	17	23	29	34	40
F. Avoidance of hardships	17	14	20	24	30	37
Creative Expansion						
G. Self-development	67	46	54	62	69	75
H. Leader, fame, power	31	18	24	29	35	41
I. Role in public life	13	8	11	13	16	19
Upholding the Internal Order						
J. Moral values	35	18	24	28	32	37
K. Social values	48	26	34	42	46	51
L. Having success	35	21	27	32	37	43

BUHLER–COLEMAN
LIFE GOALS INVENTORY
Profile Analysis Sheet

Date February 1963 Name "Burt"

Age 30 Sex M File No. M 219

Marr. Div. Si. X

	RS.	10th percentile	25th percentile	50th percentile	75th percentile	90th percentile
Need Satisfaction						
A. Necessities of life, pleasure	25	12	17	20	23	27
B. Love and family	21	14	16	19	21	23
C. Sex satisfaction	28	12	16	19	23	26
Self-limiting Adaptation						
D. Accept limitations caution	9	12	17	21	25	30
E. Submissiveness	24	17	23	29	34	40
F. Avoidance of hardships	35	14	20	24	30	37
Creative Expansion						
G. Self-development	76	46	54	62	69	75
H. Leader, fame, power	41	18	24	29	35	41
I. Role in public life	18	8	11	13	16	19
Upholding the Internal Order						
J. Moral values	29	18	24	29	32	37
K. Social values	37	26	34	42	46	51
L. Having success	46	21	27	32	37	43

LM 219, pseudonym *Burt*, is a 30 year old and single newspaper reporter and writer. He is a college graduate who is presently in psychotherapy with a psychologist.

His profile is characterized by the excessiveness of his demands with simultaneously low scores on what he is willing to give or to endure. He is not only excessive in his expectations for self-development, but also for leadership and fame as well as for success. He also makes high demands on sex satisfaction and fulfillment of other needs. His needs for love and family are high, but his social values are below average as is his willingness to accept limitations or to stand hardships. His emphasis on moral values is average.

The unseen analysis of Burt was confirmed by Dr. Albert Freeman. He described the young man as, "an ambitious writer who wants to be on top of the heap. He comes from a prominent family and makes great demands regarding status and income."

Our technique is still in its early stages of development. However, we hope that in conjunction with other test techniques as well as with depth interviews this method may yield a new type of insight into motivational processes.

References

Buhler, Charlotte. Theoretical observations about life's basic tendencies. *Amer. J. Psychother.*, 1959, **13,** 561–581.

Buhler, Charlotte. Goals of life and therapy. *Amer. J. Psychoanal.*, 1962, **22,** 153–175.

Buhler, Charlotte. Questionnaire on goals and fulfillments. *J. humanistic Psychol.*, 1963, **111,** 1.

Buhler, Charlotte & Coleman, W. *Life goal inventory manual* (private mimeographed edition). Los Angeles, 1964.

Editor's Note

A Berlin Wall of ideology divides the sciences and the humanities into different worlds in spite of many common goals and aspirations. To all appearances these disciplines are hopelessly at odds: one group wholly committed to objective methodology, and the other equally intent upon subjective experience. But looking beyond method to more ultimate objectives, some areas of agreement can be discovered. Both are motivated by an open-minded "scientific spirit of inquiry" which seeks an orderly explanation of natural phenomena.

A sizable passage could be opened if the wall were attacked from both sides. The humanist might resolve many of his problems by setting up specific hypotheses to be tested by every means at his disposal, while the psychologist might search for ways of validating conscious experience. If we put aside for the moment the assumption that nothing beyond that which we are now doing is science, it should be possible to conceive a whole new frontier of techniques with which we can deal rather rigorously with humanistic experience.

30. The Humanities in an Age of Science *

Willis W. Harman
Stanford University

The Nature of the Scientific Inquiry

Let me attempt to state more precisely where I think the main issue with regard to the claims of the humanities and to those of the sciences really lies. First, it will be necessary to examine briefly the nature of the scientific inquiry, because I wish to suggest the possibility that the scientific enterprise as conducted to date may be limited by some self-imposed constraints of whose implications we have failed to be fully aware.

* Abridged from W. W. Harman. The humanities in an age of science. *Main currents in modern thought,* 1962, **18,** 75–83. Reprinted with permission of the author and publisher.

It seems helpful to attempt to define what we might term "the scientific spirit of inquiry" and to distinguish this from "the scientific method" as it is found in any of the present sciences. I think we could agree without difficulty on the essential characteristics. Probably we could order human experience with the aid of hypothetical constructs intuitively arrived at and experimentally tested. It implies a willingness to apply to these hypotheses such tests as are appropriate, and to discard theories which prove by testing to be inadequate. (This includes testing by experiment and observation, drawing upon the experience of others by checking with other authorities, insisting upon logical consistency, and testing intuitively—as for example, when the aesthetic test is applied that the deepest truths appear to be expressible with elegant simplicity.)

One thing more, the scientist constructs theories and models which in some sense represent discernible aspects of the universe, and it sometimes happens that more than one model is available which adequately orders the available evidence. An example would be the geocentric and the heliocentric models of the solar system in Copernicus' day. The choice is made on the basis of several factors—primarily simplicity, elegance and fertility of the model in suggesting new experiments. The principle often known as Occam's razor—that a model should be no more elaborate than necessary to accommodate the relevant data—is one formulation of a basis for selection. (In some of my remarks a little later I shall suggest that Occam's razor is sometimes misused in a way the good friar surely never intended—to justify the discarding or invalidating of subjective experience which does not fit in well with theories based on measurable data.)

Now this description of the scientific spirit has a significance in what it does not say. It does not say that a complete science of man can be constructed on the patterns of the physical sciences. It does not imply that all aspects of reality are accessible, directly or indirectly, to our senses, i.e., if you can't see it, taste it, smell it, hear it, or touch it, it doesn't exist. It implies instead that one employs his senses to examine the physical universe and maintains an openness to the possibility that non-physical aspects of reality may manifest themselves to use by other routes.

Making an inquiry in the scientific spirit does not presuppose (in spite of what might be inferred from Lord Kelvin's famous statement, "When you can measure what you are speaking about, and express it in numbers, you know something about it.") that all qualitative properties are ultimately reducible to quantitative ones (color becoming wavelength, through being reduced to brain waves of measurable intensity, hate and love being the chemical composition of glandular secretions, and so on). It implies instead that we measure what we can, and humbly study the rest with methods appropriate to its nature. A more satisfactory maxim than Kelvin's would be that of St.-Exupéry: "Truth is not that which is demonstrable but that which is ineluctable." In particular, truth is surely not merely that which is quantifiable.

The true scientific spirit does not start from the premise that values are simply products of human cultures, that there is no such thing as an inherent value structure in the universe. Instead, it adopts the approach of observing and partaking of human experience, and basing tentatively held conclusions on that experience. The declaration that "science is nonnormative" is simply a restriction which scientists place upon their activities, and is not equivalent to "the universe is nonnormative."

Thus, the basic spirit of inquiry in science at its best is not, I would contend, antithetical to or different from the basic spirit of inquiry in the humanities. The ordering of subjective experience can be based upon the same essential principles as the constructing of theories in the physical and biological sciences. This is not, however, to say that the methods and prejudices of the natural scientists are to be carried over intact into the explorations of man's subjective nature. To do so may result in a situation reminiscent of Eddington's notorious icthyologist who combed the oceans with a net having a one-inch mesh and finally announced his conclusion that there are no creatures in the sea having a cross-sectional dimension of less than one inch.

There are important differences, to be sure, but also a significant similarity between a statement from the physical sciences such as, "like charges repel; unlike charges attract" and such a principle of life as that expressed in the so-called Great Paradox of Christianity, "he who seeks to save his life shall lose it, but he who loses his life shall find it." The latter, evaluated by the English poet, A. E. Housman, as "the greatest truth ever uttered and the most important discovery ever made," is, like the former, a concise ordering of human experience, verifiable by observation and experiment.

Where, then, lies the central issue over which the line is drawn making the positions of the behavioral scientist and the scientific humanist appear so far from those of the poet, the artist, or the religious philosopher? They are all looking at the same universe, and their inquiries are, or may be, made in the same open-minded spirit.

It seems to me that this basic issue has to do with the physical and the spiritual aspects of reality, or, to use some venerable philosophic terms, the phenomenal and the noumenal worlds. (The physical or phenomenal is that portion of the universe, including such things as electric fields and neutrons, which is observed, in the end, by a flow of physical energy manifesting itself in sense perception. The nonphysical includes those elements of my observed universe, knowledge of which is ultimately extrasensory —personal identity, "my feelings," "my will," the nonreversible movement of time, etc.) In practice the scientist, at least when playing his professional role, tends to operate on the implicit assumption that only the physical has reality, whereas the poet and the mystic live with both realms. The behavioral scientist tends to see values as culturally generated and acquired, the poet as inherent in the structure of things.

But if the issue is really as clearcut as this, why is this not a question to be settled by the usual forms of inquiry? Questions about the nature of reality are not to be decided by disputation among ourselves, but by conducting such experiments as will enable us to discern what that nature really is. The question as to whether there is a basic human nature, such that what constitutes truth, beauty, and goodness is not to be decided by arbitrary individual choice, is surely a valid field for inquiry.

Possible Limitations of the Present Scientific Outlook

I should like to suggest a tentative answer to the question in the preceding paragraph, which will be in part a pointing out of factors possibly inhibiting the approach from the scientific end, and in part a pointing out of deterrents that seem to me to operate in the humanities.

First, let us examine the proposition that in our present view of science there tend to be hidden restrictions and constraints which may possibly result in a distorted picture of reality. Scientists have, by and large, restricted their inquiries to the ordering of knowledge acquired through the senses. (One exception to this is the practically extinct introspectionist school of psychologists.) Thus the attempts of such investigators as C. G. Jung to order man's subjective experiences have been considered by most behaviorally-oriented psychologists—by the charitable ones at least—to be valuable but not really within the realm of science. But it is one thing to state that, because scientists choose to work with sense data and "objective" observations, subjective experience is, by definition, outside the realm of science. It is quite another to make the illogical jump that therefore subjective experience in the realm of meaning and values is illusory and has no validity in itself. We tend today to assume, perhaps far more than we consciously realize, that if scientists don't study it, it doesn't exist or isn't important. Scientists don't ask questions about life's highest values and deepest meanings; ergo, such questions are meaningless or profitless.

There is a very widespread, though not always declared or evident, basic faith held both by contemporary workers in science and by laymen contemplating the results of their work. It might be stated something like this: It is possible to make a clear distinction between objective data and subjective experience. Objective data is that which is available to us through our physical senses (and their technological extensions—the electron microscope, radio telescope, electroencephalograph, etc.), and it is only on the basis of this "public" knowledge that testable and meaningful statements about the nature of objective reality can be made. Thus, by examining this physical data with the methods of science (patterned after the "ideal" science of physics), we will ultimately possess as complete a picture of the nature of things as it is possible to have.

A corollary of this is the faith that there are no causes outside the physical universe. Hence it follows that man's freedom to decide is an illusion, not just in part, but essentially. "The hypothesis that man is not free is essential to the application of scientific method to the study of human behavior. The free inner man who is held responsible for the behavior of the external biological organism is only a pre-scientific substitute for the kinds of causes which are discovered in the course of a scientific analysis. *All* these causes lie *outside* the individual." [1]

Following, too, from the assumption that the universe is exclusively physical is the complete rejection of the teleological viewpoint of the Middle Ages in favor of the assumption that the evolution of the universe and man has come about through purely random, materialistic causes; the insistence that neither in the evolution of the

[1] B. F. Skinner, *Science and Human Behavior*, The Macmillan Company, New York, 1953. Quotation reprinted with permission of the author and publisher.

mind nor in the strivings of the individual is there justification for any concept of universal purpose.

Now it is not a matter of the evidence being preponderantly in favor of these assumptions; on the contrary, there is an impressive amount of scientifically gathered evidence arrayed against them, which we can only hint at here. But the human mind has a notorious ability to filter out data that are at variance with assumptions which are deeply believed.

Models of the Universe and of Man

There is nothing inherently unscientific—(i.e., not in the scientific spirit) about making use of a model of the universe in which there are aspects not perceptible to man through his senses and hence, by definition, not "physical." In fact, there is nothing unscientific about employing two models which appear, at one level of understanding, to be contradictory. Precisely this situation arose in physics when a wave picture of light was found to be most suitable for ordering certain experimental data and the particle picture proved more helpful in understanding other phenomena. It is in atomic and nuclear physics, where perhaps we come closest to inquiring about the ultimate structure of the universe, that mechanical models most clearly display their inadequacy. It is here that we are brought most inexorably to face the probability that our logical minds, working largely with visualizable symbols and concepts, are capable of comprehending reality *only* in terms of inadequate models.

An interesting and instructive principle relating to a somewhat parallel situation appears in physics, the principle of complementarity. If we think in terms of the wave picture of light, one of the significant quantitative measures used to describe a given situation is the wavelength. On the other hand, in terms of the particle picture a significant bit of data is the position of the light particle or photon. We are free to use either model, and to measure either wavelength or position as precisely as we choose. But the two quantities do not appear in the same model, and if we attempt to think in terms of both at the same time we encounter a paradoxical situation. For the principle of complementarity states that the greater our knowledge of the wavelength, the greater is our ignorance regarding the position, and vice versa. That is, what is "real" in one model is elusive, if not illusory, in the other. Yet both models are valid and useful in representing aspects of reality in a form such that our rational minds can deal with them.

With this sort of precedent in the highly respected science of physics we can, perhaps, approach with more courage the possibility of thinking in terms of two models of the universe: one, the practical, physical model in which space, matter, energy, and time are "real," but consciousness is a mere epiphenomenon and values are relative; the other, the spiritual, if you will, in which mind, will, love, truth, beauty and goodness appear "real" and the transcendence of space or time is not precluded. The instrument of perception is in the first, physical realm, the senses; in the second, mental realm, the deep mind. We need not be overly concerned if what is "real" in one realm appears illusory in the other—something like an extended principle of complementarity may here, as in physics, be a reflection of the fact that one model by itself is inadequate. We need not be surprised or dismayed at the appearance of paradox; physicists have learned to live comfortably with paradox. Thus, apparent determinism when the world is looked at through the practical frame of reference need not preclude the freedom to choose which appears in the other. (Something like this seems to be required to remove us from the incongruous position that the "free world" we are attempting to preserve is explicitly denied by the determinism of most contemporary science, with its insistence that freedom is merely behavior for which we have not yet found a cause.)

In the one frame of reference love may seem to be an outgrowth of the sex drive, with the ultimate end of procreation of the race. This need not prevent us from also viewing, in the other reference frame, sex as an elemental form of love, serving as an introduction to love experiences which only became possible high on the evolutionary scale. With this viewpoint the experience of love, like aesthetic experience, may seem to be the result of a fundamental hunger, manifest in the evolution of the race and in the life of the individual, for ever-increasing consciousness and awareness, for knowledge of and alignment with whatever creative forces exist in life, and for psychological and spiritual union with others and with the universe.

The recognition of both a physical and a mental order, if this seems to be necessary to encompass the whole of human experience, is not less in the scientific spirit than dogmatically insisting that there must be the physical universe and nothing else. Indeed, it may be considerably more so.

At present, research on man's subjective experience tends to fall between the chairs. The humanists do not have a tradition of this kind of research, and furthermore, feel squeamish about the possibility of uncovering relationships with clairvoyants, mystics, and drug-takers. The social scientists, on the other hand, are predominantly concerned with that which is measurable in quantitative terms by physical means. They tend to feel uneasy with an area in which the possibility of clear-cut operational definitions of the central concepts seems very remote, at least in time, if not in probability.

But the problem of who is to do it—social scientists or humanists—is by no means the most serious problem in the way of this research development. Probably far more crucial is the fact that a new type of research is needed, research in many ways conceptually different from traditional scientific research. Its language will be more that of the poet than of the mathematician, for the knowledge to be ordered has to do with feelings as well as thoughts, and the symbols to be used are not subject to mathematical manipulation. Its methodology will be different, for the investigator must be willing to become the instrument of investigation.

Some of the patterns for this research are already laid down in the area of depth psychology, in the work of Carl Jung, and others. As this field has begun to outgrow its clinical origins, some of its methods appear to afford valuable means of probing the more remote realms of subjective experience, and some of its concepts show promise of performing a valuable ordering of inner experience. The psychedelics, properly used, possess great promise as an investigational tool. It seems likely that important and exciting new discoveries will follow closely after we free our thinking from the "physicalism" which has become dominant through the remarkable successes of the physical sciences.

Editor's Note

The ancient problem of the one and the many is still much with us today. The idiographic-nomothetic debate in psychology is fundamentally one of reconciling the opposing demands of particular and universal, of concrete and abstract. Much of the tension between humanism and science originates in the same way. Poets and novelists are sensitive observers of human feeling who go no further than to describe the living experience of an individual. Psychological analysis would only destroy its personal significance. Scientists, on the other hand, first press all the nectar of personal meaning from their data to arrive at a conclusion which will apply to everyone. Neither approach to experience tells the whole story: one lacks human warmth, the other universality. Sharing insights would enrich both fields.

31. Science, Humanism, and Man *

Hadley Cantril
Princeton University
and Charles H. Bumstead

The Complementarity of Science and Humanism

"The proper study of mankind is man, says man," says James Thurber. Because of the great technological advances of the past few decades men's lives have become more and more closely involved with each other, and so it seems that the most crucial problems of the second half of the twentieth century will be those of man's relation to man. Solutions to these problems obviously can only advance insofar as we increase our understanding of "human nature."

Without underestimating the progress toward understanding human living which scientists, including psycholo-

* From H. Cantril & C. H. Bumstead. Science, humanism, and man. In *Reflections of the human venture*. New York: New York University Press, 1960. Pp. 1–6. Reprinted with permission of the senior author and publisher.

gists, have made in recent years the present writers feel that the sciences, and especially psychology, can be enormously enriched, and their constructs acquire greater applicability to the problems of living, if they pay closer attention to the insights so frequently provided in the humanities. For the humanists also are basically concerned with the nature of human experience and with the communication of all its nuances. Hence a poem, a painting, or a prayer should be regarded as a psychological datum just as much as the establishment of a sensory threshold in the laboratory or the measurement of an I.Q. It is interesting and relevant here to note the definition *Webster's New International Dictionary* gives of the word "fact": "That which has actual existence, whether subjectively or objectively considered; any event, mental or physical; an occurrence, quality, or relation, the reality of which is manifest in experience or may be inferred with certainty. . . ."

And just as the psychologist should benefit from the humanist, so should science and particularly psychology give humanism new dimensions by magnifying the potential values with which it may deal and by enabling the poet, the musician, the painter, or the prophet to find some inspiration and direction in the "facts" the scientist discovers and the constructs he creates.

The first-order data of human living, whether sought by the poet or the scientist—the nature of naïve on-going experience and behavior—seem unattainable or at least unreportable. As Amiel put it: "To speak is to disperse and scatter. Words isolate and localize life in a single point; they touch only the circumference of being; they analyze, they treat one thing at a time." If it is true that experiencing *as* experiencing, living *as* living, is unreportable and unanalyzable without destroying its "reality," it is perhaps true that humanism gives us the closest approach to the raw, descriptive data we desire. "True poetry is truer than science, because it is synthetic, and seizes at once what the combination of all the sciences is able at most to obtain as a final result."

A most important point, then, to understand clearly at the outset is that experience *as* experience, as it occurs independently of any purpose to describe or analyze it, is almost inaccessible both to the humanist and to the psychologist. Naïve, on-going human experience seems unreportable, ineffable. But it is the men and women we call "humanists" who seem to come closest to capturing and conveying these ineffable, unconceptualizable experiences. Hence we return to them over and over again in trying to get a toe hold on our own awareness, or in trying to lift ourselves up to more satisfying levels of experience. This point is nicely illustrated by a passage from Robert Henri's *The Art Spirit:*

> There are moments in our lives, there are moments in a day, when we seem to see beyond the usual—become clairvoyant. We reach then into reality. Such are the moments of our greatest happiness. Such are the moments of our greatest wisdom.
>
> It is in the nature of all people to have these experiences; but in our time and under the conditions of our lives it is only a rare few who are able to continue in the experience and find expression for it.
>
> At such times there is a song going on within us, a song to which we listen. It fills us with surprise. We marvel at it. We would continue to hear it. But few are capable of holding themselves in the state of listening to their own song. Intellectuality steps in and as the song within us is of the utmost sensitiveness, it retires in the presence of the cold, material intellect. It is aristocratic and will not associate itself with the commonplace—and we fall back and become our ordinary selves. Yet we live in the memory of these songs which in moments of intellectual inadvertence have been possible to us.

They are the pinnacles of our experience and it is the desire to express these intimate sensations, this song from within, which motivates the masters of all art.[1]

Just as the young infant cannot report the nature of his experiential world in verbal terms, so the adult, while doing the work of the world, is not able to describe and report the process of events he is experiencing. There is much evidence to indicate that when an individual's purpose is to describe and report experience then the very structure and flow of experience itself is altered. The process of living seems most satisfactorily conceptualized as a single, undivided, unitary, but extremely complex process which no single symbol is capable of expressing. Description is necessarily analytical and successive. As soon as one starts to speak or to write, something is left out. In short, one is already dealing with fictions, abstractions, or concepts at least one step removed from the first-order data. Furthermore, every person has experiences which he feels are wholly incapable of communication to others.

Vivid descriptions of human experience by nonscientists may therefore supply protocol data with which the scientist may begin his task of cross-examining nature in his attempt to arrive at a set of constructs in terms of which he can summarize, understand, "explain," and better predict the process of human living. For the scientist, who seeks a purely rational conception of our existence, must analyze, classify, and make use of abstractions and concepts—fictions which may be useful and fruitful, but nevertheless still fictions. Whitehead has reminded us that: "Matter-of-fact is an abstraction, arrived at by confining thought to purely formal relations which masquerade as the final reality. This is why science, in its perfection, relapses into the study of differential equations. The con-

[1] From Robert Henri, *The Art Spirit*, J. B. Lippincott, Philadelphia, 1923. Reprinted with permission.

crete world has slipped through the meshes of the scientific net." [2]

The function of concepts and abstractions was noted by Havelock Ellis: ". . . our thinking would itself be fluid if it were not that by fiction we obtain imaginary standpoints and boundaries by which to gain control of the flow of reality. It is the special art and object of thinking to attain existence by quite other methods than that of existence itself. . . . Our conceptions, our conventional signs, have a fictive function to perform; thinking in its lower grades is comparable to paper money, and in its higher forms it is a kind of poetry." [3]

And no matter how fashionable or respectable concepts of *value* and *valuing* are within the domain of science from one decade to another, psychologists must lend an ear to those humanists who have made the study and expression of values their work. For in the pursuit of the ultimate ends of living, what we know as reason, logic, or intelligence may all play a very minor role, leaving out as they do the feeling-tones and values which permeate the totality of human experience. Here are some sample observations of what an orthodox "scientific account" leaves out:

> When you understand all about the sun, and all about the atmosphere, and all about the radiation of the earth, you may still miss the radiance of the sunset. (*Whitehead*)

> When we are told that the leaves of a plant are occupied in decomposing carbonic acid, and preparing oxygen for us, we begin to look upon it with some such indifference as a gasometer. It has become a machine . . . , its emanation of inherent light is no longer pure. (*Ruskin*)

[2] From Alfred North Whitehead, *Modes of Thought*, The Macmillan Company, New York, 1938, p. 25. Reprinted with permission.
[3] From Havelock Ellis, *The Dance of Life*, Houghton Mifflin, Boston 1923, pp. 101–102. Reprinted with permission.

As everyone knows, experience from the first-person point of view—from *your* point of view—is pervaded by feelings and value-overtones that are in a sense unlimited by space and time, even though they are only called into play in the here and now. These feelings and value-overtones must be carefully differentiated from what the psychologist generally calls emotions and, more often than not, refers to as emotions brought about by reflex action. The feelings and value-overtones of experience are what provide man's experience with its peculiarly "human" qualities. And these feelings and value-overtones, as already noted, must be carefully distinguished from our rational thought processes.

The Orchestration of Living

The life of each one of us might be likened to a symphony. Thousands of occurrences are orchestrated into what we call experience—or better, experiencing, since experience is always on-going. Sometimes the flow is smooth and harmonious, sometimes rough and discordant; basic themes repeat themselves periodically in the midst of continued development with varied and new overtones. The span from birth to death has movements with a certain emphasis in each; sometimes the melody is carried by one or a few instruments easily detectable but more often the effect is produced by a variety of instruments with the sound of each lost in the total orchestration.

While the basic themes of each life-symphony may be given in bold outline by our unique heredity, still the final score written is one which we definitely help to compose as we go along. We build a pattern as we progress, a pattern from which it becomes increasingly difficult to deviate. Some sounds and arrangements we filter out since they would spoil our composition. Sometimes our tempo is fast and sprightly, at other times slow and stately. Some of us compose in a style that follows compositions we are familiar with or that are accepted for our day; others of us boldly deviate and become more idiosyncratic and radical. For each of us the symphony that constitutes our living is uniquely ours. And only parts of it are heard from time to time by others as it is heard by ourselves. Much of it we ourselves can hear only when we are with other human beings.

A Beethoven or a Mozart has the genius to communicate to others a whole symphony he hears himself. Similarly, some individuals possess a rare talent to communicate in words the totality of their experiences in such a way that a concrete event has an aura of universality and universals are reflected in concreteness. Such individuals provide "cues," "insights" which the psychologist cannot afford to ignore. And, of course, the reverse of this proposition is equally true if we assume that the humanist also seeks to understand human living. Thus, although the methods of science provide one of our most productive ways of knowing, science, at least as ordinarily conceived and carried on, is limited in the nature of the problems it can attack. For example, science seems unable to answer alone the question of what the goal or goals of human beings *should be*. And the psychologist, particularly, needs to understand much more precisely than he does now the role the ineffable value-aspects of experience play in determining our purposes, both immediate and ultimate, and the role they play in all human behavior not governed by reflexes or simple homeostatic principles. For this reason, if for no other, we should pay attention to what is revealed through other avenues to "truth," to modes of inquiring that differ from those of science. Most human beings carry on their living, their learning, their observing, outside the scope of the scientist's laboratory or constructs. Hence they are relatively unencumbered by the need to be consistent in terms of an established set of abstractions.

It is generally recognized that some poets, artists, novelists, prophets, or other observers possess an unusual sensitivity to the non-rational aspects of living. Although psychology has by no means failed to investigate these abstracted aspects of human experience and although non-scientific writers have by no means confined their attention to them, there does seem to have been a difference in the interest in and appreciation for the role of feelings and values among humanists and scientists, at least in western culture.

There is, of course, no intention here of implying either that man is wholly "rational" or wholly "irrational," or that psychology has dealt exclusively with rational processes and poetry (in the generic sense) exclusively with feelings. Nor do we intend to convey the impression that poets experience "pure" feeling while scientists are devoid of feelings. Both psychology and poetry reveal important truths about the whole of human living, including its intellectual and non-intellectual aspects. But the emphasis has been different. And the recognition of this fact should provide some balance to anyone interested in learning from both.

PART THREE

Psychology and Human Values

CHAPTER 9

Cognitive Maps

Psychologists have always been ambivalent about values. Raising the question of final purpose is almost certain to provoke a clash of opinion. Science, it is often said, deals with facts, not values. "This attitude," Dukes remarks,[1] "was incorporated into psychology by Titchener, who in his zeal to make psychology scientific, imitated the classical physicists and excluded value along with meaning and utility from the new science."

No scientist can disavow an interest in purpose without becoming involved in contradictions. As soon as he turns his attention from isolated part-processes to the study of man, he is forced to make value judgments about human behavior and his own relationship to the people he attempts to help or to study. C. A. Mace observes that,[2] "The educational psychologist behaves as if he knows what is good for the child. The psychotherapist behaves as if he knows what is good for the patient. The occupational psychologist conducts himself as though he knows what is good for the workers. *And so in fact they do.*" It is inconceivable that the experience of being human would not throw some light on what is suitable for mankind in general. Actually, theoretical disagreements in this matter do not ordinarily carry over into practice. What the individual educator or psychotherapist attempts to accomplish in the classroom or clinical

[1] W. F. Dukes. Psychological studies in values. *Psychol. Bull.*, 1955, **52,** 24–50.

[2] C. A. Mace. Homeostasis, need and values. In John Cohen (Ed.) *Readings in psychology*. London: Allen & Unwin, 1964. P. 104.

interview is approximately the same despite differences in philosophical orientation.

Obviously values presuppose an end or goal. As illustrated in learning experiments, objects in themselves are desirable only if they serve a useful purpose. Poker chips acquire "value" for a chimpanzee when they can be used to obtain grapes. He soon loses interest in them when they fail to pay off. In the case of man, purposive striving forms the warp and woof of personality, and consistent trends associated with the things he prizes determine his pattern of behavior. The surest key to knowledge of the person is an understanding of his value system. Although textbooks do not belabor the point, there seems to be considerable agreement in this matter. Hall and Lindzey [3] point out that, "In general, then, most personality theorists seem to conceive of man as a purposive creature but even where this is not taken for granted it does not seem to be a matter of hot dispute."

This should not be taken to mean that the Titchenerian distrust of values has completely disappeared from psychology as one of the readings in this chapter attests. What some psychologists seem to fear is that concern for values will inevitably lead to problems of purpose beyond the scope of empirical investigation. Final answers to such questions as, "What is man for?" are not obtained by observation and measurement but must be sought in other disciplines. To raise issues about the nature of man seems to invite endless debate of a philosophical nature. Would it not be better to ignore the value aspects of psychology as far as possible? First of all, we need not press the quest of value to the breaking point. "What is man for?" has many answers, a large number of which are implicitly contained in the way behavioral scientists design their experiments and apply the principles of psychology in such

[3] C. S. Hall and G. Lindzey. *Theories of personality.* New York: Wiley, 1957. P. 539.

diverse areas as esthetics, counseling, and human engineering. Secondly, psychological laws related to thinking and other human processes are obtained as a behavioral residue after boiling away all individual differences. They are descriptive of mankind in general rather than this or that person. Before they can be used in a meaningful way to study an individual, some of the personal equations lost in the process of generalization must be restored. Not least in importance among these are the cognitive maps which serve to give direction to all his striving.

Editor's Note

Psychologists as a group as well as individuals have final purposes. If any proof were needed of the extent to which the ultimate aims of the profession are at least implicitly recognized, the Ethical standards of psychologists, *published by the American Psychological Association, would suffice. As an exercise, it is suggested that the student list all the implicit and explicit major value judgments appearing in some portion of the book, such as Section 3, "Ethical Standards in Teaching."*

Although it is possible that the hard core of resistance to the acceptance of value mentioned below more frequently centers around problems of methodology than the existence of values in science, any mention of final aims is likely to be freighted with philosophical embarrassment. Nonetheless, an uninhibited discussion of the topic, illustrated in the two following selections, can add considerable depth to our understanding of personal and professional responsibility.

32. Psychology—Becoming and Unbecoming *

G. H. Turner
University of Western Ontario

There are taboos in psychology and one of them seems to be the consideration of ultimate aims or ends. Such delicate matters are normally shunned in the professional literature and in conversation among psychologists, and one does not have to go far to find reasons. The most obvious is the prevailing philosophical climate of logical positivism or scientific empiricism, with its futile disavowal of metaphysics. Its more deliberate devotees undoubtedly eschew final purposes on the high grounds of personal conviction; others seem to do so out of either indifference to,

* Presidential address to the Canadian Psychological Association, Kingston, Ontario, June 3, 1960. Abridged from G. H. Turner. Psychology—becoming and unbecoming. *Canad. J. Psychol.*, 1960, **14,** 153–165. Reprinted with permission of the author and the University of Toronto Press.

or irresolution on, these weighty issues. Still others may know where they stand but regard it as a highly personal matter, or may fail to speak out of respect for the taboos. Whatever the reasons I regard this conspiracy of silence as tragic, and consequently I am going to make the question of ends the first major concern of my talk this evening.

Since ultimate aims or values receive such scant attention, I can hardly be accused of labouring the obvious if I take a moment to argue that we are lost without them in our professional as well as our private lives. How long can an intelligent clinical psychologist function without wondering, in a profound way, what he is trying to do? Is he there to help remove undesirable symptoms, to reduce psychic pain, to improve efficiency, to restore a former level of function, to contribute to growth or independence, or what? Does he see mental health in positive terms and, if so, what is the desirable state at which he is aiming?

The problem of the industrial psychologist is no different. Is his function to assist in the attainment of his client's goals, to increase production and efficiency, to improve the administrative process, to share his own perspectives with the client, to help in achieving community-oriented goals, or what? Division XIV of the American Psychological Association brought this problem into sharp focus for me by suggesting that graduate students in industrial psychology be made aware of the "realities" of business and industrial life. If I interpreted this statement aright, it meant that to be a satisfactory consultant you must know the goals of your client and help him attain them—a proposition that is by no means as innocent as it sounds! The university teacher and administrator faces the same difficulties. Would he revise the programme of studies? To what end? Is the goal to impart the core curriculum, to develop the currently fashionable skills, to turn out scientists, or what?

Let us touch a more sensitive nerve and bring the problem closer to home. How can we order our own lives and maintain health and stability if we have no overriding purposes or values, if we are busily treading the activity cage to nowhere? Without some hierarchy of values life must be chaotic and pointless. Without awareness of our values, how can we accept responsibility for them and avoid being slaves to whatever early cultural influences fell to our lot? If we once grant the desirability of self-awareness, of integrity and synergy of thought, feeling, and action, then professional, scientific, academic, and private problems begin to merge into one, namely: What are our ultimate objectives and how may these best be implemented in our private and professional lives?

But what do we concern ourselves with at present? To avoid becoming involved in disputes over philosophy, or, worse still, religion, we will openly admit the pursuit of only the most banal and patently penultimate or antepenultimate purposes such as increasing production, efficiency, and profit, or, even better, improving employer-employee relations, or effecting better personal adjustment, or facilitating the process of socialization, or, better still, raising standards, in the profession or training better scientists, or, best of all, adding to knowledge or advancing psychology as a science and as a profession. How perfectly respectable, how normal, but how unsatisfactory. They all leave unanswered the question, why bother? To stop short of God, Mammon, the state, the fully actualized man, or some equally final alternative, is to admit that we do not know what we are doing or that if we know, we will not say.

Going the whole distance and specifying our ultimate purpose would, of course, end in nothing but words if we were not simultaneously under the necessity of retracing our steps and establishing the hierarchies of lesser purposes that in effect constitute its definition. It is only from such a hierarchy of aims that any clear implications for behaviour can emerge and by which behaviour may be consistently evaluated. Thus the healthy person who is intellectually alive and growing is cognizant of his goals, ever mindful of the need to revise them and always modifying his behaviour, the better to achieve them.

To expect us to reach agreement about ends is quite unreasonable, although much of our disagreement is, I am sure, semantic rather than real, but to be unwilling to be explicit about them seems indefensible. What greater barrier to effective communication could one devise? What more subtle form of misrepresentation could one practice? One can with honour admit indecision or confusion. But what can be said of those who would deny or ignore the issue?

To accept responsibility for deciding, no matter how tentatively, and for stating, no matter how provisionally, the final grounds on which we base our lives might not seem to constitute a formidable assignment since the answers are already implicit in our behaviour. By our every action we commit ourselves to some purpose or other. But this is surely a taller order than I am making out. What is harder than to discover and make explicit one's assumptions? More than that, the values we assume, the ends implicit in our behaviour, do not enjoy some sort of separate independent existence. On the contrary they are firmly embedded in a view of man, in some conception of the nature of the universe and of man's place in it. What is his nature, what does he need, where is he going, how can we account for him? It is how we answer these questions that determines our hierarchy of purposes.

Only our total concept of man can provide us with the master cognitive map into which all our little maps must fit if we would have a coherent view of life. But how poorly supplied we are with comprehensive models and the bits and pieces that constitute the conventional wisdoms are characterized by unrevealed assumptions, inconsistencies, grave omissions, and questionable validity. If we are so uncertain of man's nature, how can we be so sure we are doing what is best for him as consultants, counsellors, clinicians, and teachers? How can we be so confident we know the best questions to ask of nature in pursuing our study of man? As we are well aware it is hard to find good answers to poor questions.

Do not think that this is none of our business, or that it concerns only the incorrigibly speculative personality theorists. Do we waive all claim to a part in policy setting? Are we content to implement the decisions of others? If this is not our business, then what is?

An objection that seems to appeal to many is that it is not of immediate concern to us as scientists, because psychologists do not at present know enough to provide a coherent picture of man. Their rejoinder is "Give us a hundred years or so and we may have something of significance to offer." The case for ignorance is easy to make out but the argument from it would be much more convincing if it were not for the fact that the self-same psychologist-scientist lives the real life of a real person at home, in the community, and among his professional colleagues, fighting for what he thinks is right and making his way in a real world, on the basis of very real assumptions about the nature of man. (Rigorous experimentalists have, by the way, been known to scorn the less certain findings of their colleagues who study children, while confidently raising their own on principles handed down with the family silver.)

I grant that our knowledge is limited and that our concept of man must be rounded out with borrowed or improvised propositions. But surely we must continually incorporate such knowledge as we have. It would be the height of irony for a psychologist to devote his life to the task of building the empirical foundations of knowledge about man while living his life on postulates that take no account of the knowledge already available in his discipline.

Let us make no mistake about it, our job is to throw light on the nature of man. As practical and realistic men, we must and do, in the interim, commit ourselves completely to those views about man we think are most worth the gamble. As psychologists, we owe it to ourselves, and to others, to say what particular assumptions we are prepared to act upon, in order to clarify our own thinking, to give more consistent direction to our action and, with respect to clients, to let them know what they are paying for.

If we do this we shall find ourselves no longer declaring knowledge to be for its own sake and no longer regarding psychology as an end in itself—a way of thinking that has crept into our textbooks and into articles discussing, for example, the importance to psychology of recruitment and proper selection, or the danger to psychology of early professionalization, and so on. This is only a manner of speaking, but perhaps it is an unfortunate one. Unintentional reification seems to develop easily into unintentional deification. While there is still so much question of psychology's effectiveness as a means, we hardly dare promote it to an end.

Man may need a lot of things but one thing he certainly needs is an adequate view of himself, one that is consistent with and grounded in his fullest knowledge of himself and of his world. This is where psychology fits in. The world does not go round in order to accommodate psychology. The study of psychology derives such significance as it has from its power to contribute to our knowledge of and perspective on man.

It may be well at this point to remind ourselves that psychology is by no means the only source of knowledge about and perspective on man. How easy it is to bow perfunctorily to the natural sciences, to neglect the other social sciences, to ignore philosophy and theology, and to completely overlook the rich resources of literature, history, and the arts. But how unwise and how ungrateful. Other disciplines are not merely "fruitful sources of hypotheses" but the sources of most of our concepts and nearly all of our new ideas. And where do we get the postulates on which we gamble our lives?

The point cries out for greater elaboration than I have the competence or time to give it here. I will content myself with the guess that before long psychology and the humanities will be on much better speaking terms and that even in secular institutions psychologists themselves may be teaching philosophy to their students for the same reasons that they now teach statistics, namely, because there is an important job to do that cannot safely be farmed out to other departments.

In this connection I was interested to discover that mutual practical problems had brought together three theologians, a psychologist (Paul Meehl), and a psychiatrist, to undertake the serious task of comparing their respective views on man and of presenting, in collaboration, the points of similarity and difference in their positions, along with, be it carefully noted, the practical implications for counselling and therapy. The results were published in 1958 as a symposium under the title *What, Then, is Man?* It struck me as a conspicuous success and as an encouraging sign that we may be growing up. If theologians and psychologists can communicate to good effect on such troublesome matters, it should not be too difficult for psychologists to communicate with other psychologists if they really set their minds to it.

It is well to remember, then, that psychology can not claim sole possession of man. Moreover we should be encouraged by the thought that there are other shoulders to the wheel as well as ours. A great deal may depend on us but, fortunately, not everything.

We might also pause to reflect that marvellous as are man's cognitive functions they would be pale pathetic things without other modes of experience, and that we may too readily take for granted that science and knowledge and reason are all that matter in life. Just as we recognize in psychology the pitfalls in fragmenting the individual for purposes of study, we might also recognize the danger of fragmenting life for the purpose of living, as we do when we act as if *knowing* were everything. So when we return to a consideration of psychology, let us remember that it is psychology within science, in the context of human knowledge, within the context of human life. Not only are there other toilers in the vineyard but there are other things to be done besides studying the grapes. Perhaps this dubious metaphor may serve to summarize all I have said so far and also, if stretched to the breaking point, to convey all that I now plan to add.

My next observation, then, is that we do not seem to be sufficiently respectful of man, if one can judge by the theories currently in vogue. Certainly we pay little attention to his finest attributes and greatest achievement. And since personality theory, broadly conceived, provides a framework for living, for the selective organization of experience and for systematic scientific observation, I agree with Bronfenbrenner and others like him who feel that the maturity of psychology as a science is peculiarly dependent upon the work we do in this area over the years ahead.

As far as current theorizing goes, I trace much of my dissatisfaction to certain of the presuppositions on which it seems to rest. To begin with, most of us seem to be epistemological empiricists determined to trace all knowledge to sense perception, as if, in some inevitable fashion, the data of experience combine themselves into coherent principles or understandings or generalizations. Speculation unrelated to and unrestrained by the facts of observation has no place in modern psychology, but we must not let our enthusiasm for objectivity blind us to the fact that it is the active observer who apprehends the sense data and provides the frames of reference without which the facts would be meaningless. The implication I object to is that man brings nothing to a situation that he has not acquired through previous observations. This is just one of the ways in which we sell the psyche short, and also one of the ways in which we dichotomize our thinking and fail to appreciate the possibility of some intermediate position, such as, in this case, a combination of empiricism and rationalism.

To push this idea a little further we might well, for example, stop pretending that scientific insights are arrived at by pursuing a logical path of reasoning following a series of observations. A scientist's theories arise neither spontaneously from data nor from an application of logical modes of thought. His theoretical contributions rest on no such rational accomplishments, accessible to training, but upon the irrational and still mysterious resources of his own psyche. A scientific training in verification procedures (that is, in the testing of hypotheses), is no guarantee of the release or development of scientific creativity.

Combined with a thorough-going empiricism, we generally find a materialist monism, the idea that all psychic events are, in principle, reducible to physical events. For me, this is carrying the law of parsimony too far. It asks us to accept that the very psychic processes by which the world is apprehended are to be reduced to the objects held in apprehension. It is at very least a high-handed way to treat consciousness and is a further instance of the tendency to downgrade the human psyche. Dualism has its problems, but are they any more formidable than those inherent in monism? Dualism may be devilishly inconvenient, but it strikes me as being much more realistic. But more of this in a moment.

Our theories are also, for the most part, mechanistic. And after Ketchum's brilliantly persuasive article in the *Canadian Psychologist* on the virtues of mechanism, properly conceived, it might seem foolish of me to take issue. But he made two mistakes. The first was to refer to my favourites, the teleological self-realization psychologists, as a tribe; and I did not think he intended it as a compliment. From that moment, I knew that mechanism could not be permitted to go unchallenged. Certainly there is mystery enough in mechanism for anyone and certainly mechanism is essential as a methodological assumption, but why as a metaphysical one? The second mistake was, I feel, to assume that a biological vitalism is the only alternative to mechanism. Vitalism may or may not yet be dead, but emergentism and existentialism still have to be conquered and what guarantee there will not be others?

Let us take another illustration, the perennially troublesome opposition of determinism and free will. Christians and all others who like to feel that their sense of freedom and responsibility is not an illusion are upset by the claims of thorough-going scientific determinists; and social scientists, at least when they are functioning as social scientists, seem to panic at the suggestion, implicit in the doctrine of free will, that they have to add to their list of variables one that is belligerently, and in principle, uncontrollable. They are inclined to feel that if this sort of thing is going to be allowed to go on they might just as well pack up and go home—a decision for which they would, curiously enough, be prepared to take full credit, and responsibility. There is obviously some difficulty here that needs to be resolved. But the issue is important for other reasons. One cannot give a very coherent or comprehensive account of man without committing oneself on this matter and, in addition, the view held by the applied psychologist or other practitioner dealing with human problems, influences his attitude, understanding, treatment, or advice.

The scientific determinists would never have been quite so alarmed had they been fully aware of the views of the sophisticated advocates of free will who have never accorded man unlimited psychic freedom under all circumstances, but rather limited, if very important, freedom under certain optimal conditions; and all this within the framework of a very necessary determinism. Thus free will is not squarely opposed to determinism but is superimposed upon it, and the real adversary of determinism is seen to be indeterminacy. These ideas have been elaborated, with much more philosophical and psychological sophistication than I could possibly muster, by Father Mailloux in an article in the *Canadian Journal of Psychology* in 1953 that well repays careful reading. Feigl has taken essentially the same position in the brief reference he makes to the problem in the *American Psychologist* in March, 1959. But the substitution of indeterminacy for free will as the principal adversary has hardly had the effect of quietening the determinist's nerves. For a while he could, if getting the worst of it, threaten to appeal to the higher courts of the natural sciences. Then he made the unsettling discovery that, of all people, the physicists, those paragons of scientific respectability, had admitted to full membership in the family the impudent, rebellious little principle of indeterminacy, not, of course, without some reluctance and only with respect to the behaviour of the minutest of particles, but nonetheless with full privileges. Scientific determinism is then in a double dilemma. It has to make some kind of peace with freedom and with indeterminacy.

Fortunately, psychologists are beginning to recognize this problem and to do something about it. Paul Meehl suggests that we have three choices. The first he calls *methodological* determinism. This is the attitude that you are looking for, and expecting to find, laws in the domain of human behaviour. If you find ones that hold strictly, all well and good. If you have to settle for probabilistic laws, that will be fine, as they will still be very useful. Obviously one can have all this and free will too.

The second type he calls *empirical* determinism. Here we have the somewhat harder view that since the assumption of determinism has paid off so handsomely and so much regularity has already been found in behaviour, apparent exceptions are almost certainly due to incomplete information, and thus the assumption has been empirically vindicated and will, henceforth, be firmly held unless, of course, impressive counterevidence should appear. Such people can at least sit down and talk about free will without becoming emotional.

The third and last category is that of *metaphysical* determinism. This is simply the proposition that all psychological events take place according to universal laws, adhered to as a metaphysical presupposition in no sense dependent upon empirical evidence. Those who hold this view are the people who must, if they are consistent, confess without pride or shame that they may be enjoying life and glad to be part of it but can take no credit or blame for what they do, or do not do, and who should be ready to apologize if, owing to habits of long standing, they speak as if anyone *should* do anything.

Each of us must resolve it in his own way. I should just like to say that since we all talk as if, and act as if, we had some modicum of freedom, and since life would seem to be, for many, a rather bad joke if we did not have a little freedom, I rather wish we would be honest and consistent enough to provide for a little when going beyond our findings and telling our little story about man. It would not change by one iota the level of confidence of a single statistical difference. It might on the other hand bring our words into a little closer harmony with our behaviour and our experience, as well as have a desirable effect on our approach to many practical problems.

Perhaps the most significant point worth making about empiricism, materialist monism, mechanism, determinism and a number of other postulates or presuppositions underlying our theorizing about man is that neither philosophy nor science can demonstrate their necessity. They represent preferences, not some sort of final truth, and if they have the effect of limiting our methods of study and of restricting our theorizing about man we may abandon them or modify them as we wish. The most we will have to contend with will be social pressure since psychologists as well as others put great pressure on one another to conform. So let us abandon the notion that the little we know is the full measure of man and write him up in terms that do some justice to the full range of his intellectual, emotional, and moral virtuosity. The picture should be consistent with our scientific knowledge but not limited to it.

There are three other common dispositions in psychological theory that I deprecate which are not so clearly of methodological significance yet which create both theoretical and practical difficulties and also contribute to the general devaluation of man. One can be traced to Descartes, the others are of much more recent origin.

The first, and oldest, is our inveterate habit of subdividing our subject, man, into a number of separate processes, isolated for more convenient study. As Snygg has reminded us, we leave out, in our study of process, the unifying principle, the person in whom the process resides, and then wonder why we cannot get the processes to fit together into a recognizable picture of a human being. For reference, see any introductory textbook in psychology. For this, and much more besides, read Father Malone's masterpiece in the April number of the *Canadian Psychologist.*

Our tendency to fragment our subject-matter is nowhere better illustrated than in the unfortunate splitting of psychological scientists and theory builders into three camps, the experimental-physiological enthusiasts, the devotees of social psychology, and the followers of personality dynamics. This division has led to a certain amount of misunderstanding, rivalry, and petty bickering. Certainly each has been inclined to look down his nose at the others (with predictable consequences) and so far attempts to resolve differences have not been very successful, possibly because the theoretical basis for union has been conspicuously lacking—at least until our little-known European friends, the existential psychotherapists, came along. They regard the individual as existing simultaneously and inseparably, in the biological, social, and self aspects of his world, and rather than pick any favourites they insist that none of the three be neglected. As all readers of Rollo May's *Existence* will know, their terms are, respectively, Umwelt, Mitwelt, and Eigenwelt and they mean essentially what Nuttin means by psycho-physical, psycho-social, and spiritual. This would seem to be a rather radical suggestion and whether or not the high-flying Umwelters will associate themselves with what are mistakenly perceived to be the lesser breeds remains to be seen. Certainly it is a major part of my thesis that it is imperative that they do so or we may never be able to put Humpty Dumpty together.

Also prominent among the assumptions implicit in much psychological discourse, but of much more recent origin, is that of the relativity of values. This not only embraces the fact that there are obvious differences between societies in the notions of what is right and wrong, but the more fundamental denial that there could be universal values, unless at some distant date a universal culture should emerge. If we are prepared to regard healthy tissue and a strong ego as better than damaged tissue and a weak ego, then the gap between fact and value has been bridged and it becomes obvious that the necessary assumption of universal lawfulness carries with it the assumption of universal values. We know that men in different cultures satisfy needs in vastly different ways. But if they are satisfying the *same fundamental needs*, and if satisfying a need is a value, then such values must be universal. If this were not so, one could make sense neither of psychology nor of humanistic ethics.

This is by no means a trivial point, for a relativity of values as the only alternative to Christian ethics suggests that for the non-believers social disapproval is the only factor to be considered in evaluating one's conduct. We cannot be unmindful of the social effects of the theories we propound and to encourage such a conclusion as this is, in my estimation, both irresponsible and stupid.

In keeping with the conception of values as relative is the acceptance of conscience as essentially Freudian, as an introjection of parental standards. One cannot, of course, deny the reality of Freudian conscience, but one can deny it exclusive rights to the territory, especially as it is by no means the only alternative to a Christian conscience. Rogers hints at, and Maslow boldly postulates, an intrinsic conscience, a hypothetical construct with as much empirical validity as a good many respectable psychological concepts. Philosophically I suppose this represents a preference for ethical intuitionism rather than ethical empiricism, a preference I share for much the same reasons that I accept the universality of basic human values. But this is another question that is being dealt with much more profoundly by the existential psychotherapists with their concept of ontological guilt, a culture-free form of guilt that arises, at least in part, from the forfeiting of one's potentialities. They are now providing powerful secular reinforcement for what has been, in psychology, a rather thinly defended but crucially important position, that of the universality of human values.

My last point has to do with a particularly difficult feature of the life of a psychologist, namely, that he is, in a very real sense, part of his own subject-matter. Consequently, all he learns about man must, if he is to maintain intellectual and emotional integrity, be applied to his own life. In most other disciplines new theories or new understandings may present a substantial intellectual challenge, but that is merely part of the job and affects only a technical segment of the scholar's thoughts and actions. The psychologist must not only be constantly modifying his theoretical viewpoint but simultaneously be making appropriate adjustments in his whole outlook on and style of life. If he commits himself to a non-directive philosophy, he must change some of his behaviour. Likewise if he becomes a Skinnerian. It gives a certain urgency and seriousness to the consideration of new ideas and is undoubtedly wearing, but not to do so is to be either dissociated or fraudulent. All signs point to the necessity of focusing attention on our own personal intentions, convictions, and behaviour. For the psychologist more than anyone else, it is essential that he concentrate on his own growth as the only sound basis for rendering any help to others.

In conclusion, I am very optimistic concerning the future of psychology, not simply on the basis of past achievements but because of the tremendous potential still latent in a scientific approach to the understanding of man and his problems. It is my conviction, however, that psychology's potential, both as a science and as an art, will be more fully realized if we are clearer about the ultimate objectives to which we are prepared to commit ourselves, if we are more problem- rather than method-oriented in our research, and if we are less inclined to base the inferences we draw concerning the nature of man on the presuppositions underlying our research methodologies and on a range of information restricted to our own field. We must, in other words, break out of the methodological and philosophical traps in which we have already become ensnared. As to what some of these traps may be and what we might be doing about them, I have just offered a few suggestions, or more accurately, I have just offered my selection from among the many suggestions that have been made by others. My selection has, of course, been determined by my own orientation which might best be described, at the moment, as that of a Maslowian humanism under the first impact of existentialism. In any event, I have indicated in what direction I am headed and my plea is not that you should come with me, although I would much enjoy the company, but that you should let the rest of us know where you are going. That arrival can never be guaranteed is no excuse for failing to reveal the proposed destination.

33. Toward Scientific and Professional Responsibility *

M. Brewster Smith
University of California

How are responsibility and values related? By *values* I shall mean a person's implicit or explicit standards of choice, insofar as they are invested with obligation or requiredness. Values are closely related to ends or goals, but not all goals are values in this sense; for the American child, the eating of spinach becomes much more value-laden than the eating of ice cream cones. *Responsibility* has to do with the relation of a person's behavior to his values. One could also include the kind of values to which the person subscribes. To simplify my task, however, I will assume that our new code of ethics indicates that we are in fair consensus on a number of generally acceptable values. Our ethical problems, it seems to me, may have more to do with the relation of our values to what we actually do as psychologists than with what our values happen to be.

As I intend to use the term, then, a person acts responsibly to the extent that his behavior meets at least these conditions: First, he is aware of the value context in which he is acting. His goals have been subjected to conscious scrutiny, and his behavior is explicitly related to his values. Second, his choices are made in the light of as adequate an understanding of their probable consequences as he can achieve. The relations that he assumes between means and ends are examined critically, not taken for granted. Third, he is ready to be judged in terms of his choices of both ends and means, and has the flexibility to reconsider both. In a word, he assumes responsibility for his decisions and actions.

* From M. B. Smith. Toward scientific and professional responsibility. *Amer. Psychologist,* 1954, **9,** 513–516. Reprinted with permission of the author and publisher.

If these remarks sound like pious platitudes, perhaps it is an indication that there is indeed consensus on responsibility, so conceived, as itself a value. Yet as we know, personal motives and conflicts between values often stand in the way of responsible action. Some of the other members of the symposium are addressing themselves to sources of irresponsibility in the social situation of psychology. For my part I should like to examine some of its forms. I have eight sins—mortal or venial—for your consideration.

Fixation on Means

One can easily find in the activities of psychologists examples of a kind of "functional autonomy of motives," in which too narrow a focus on means leads to behavior that hardly advances the goal values toward which it is still presumably oriented. Consider, for example, fixation on the trappings of science. Are we really pursuing the advancement of understanding, we may from time to time ask ourselves, or are we being sidetracked by our indiscriminate enthusiasm for a particular fashionable gadget, or research technique, or convention of statistical analysis? Fads in research topics and methods may result, to a larger extent than we like to admit, less from the concerted pursuit that follows a significant "break-through" than from failure to keep our sights set on goals within the larger context that gives significance to our scientific activities. Fixation upon trivia is the easier for us because of the naiveté with which "common sense" and college sophomores pose problems for psychology. From legitimate insistence on formulating our own questions in ways that permit scientific investigation, it is only a step to smugness that sometimes seems to attribute ritual significance to the forms of science.

Means can become ends in the professional as well as the scientific aspect of psychology. Shall the patient be vertical or horizontal; is the tradition of Rorschach interpretation to be preserved intact at all costs; how sacred is the feeding schedule or the permissive attitude? Heat tends to exclude light when means are taken as ends in themselves. Happily, functional autonomy in this setting is incomplete, and the ends of effective therapy, diagnosis, or upbringing, though sometimes latent, are rarely abandoned. A clear view of means *as* means—that is, in relation to goals—is the best safeguard against fixation on them.

Absolutism of Means

The second form of irresponsibility in my list shades into the first without sharp distinction. By "absolutism of means," I mean positing such an invariant, rigid, or foolproof relation that the need for evaluating the appropriateness of means to end is supposedly bypassed. The examples I have in mind here—controversial ones, to be sure—involve conscious commitment to the means rather than blind fixation. But the results may be much the same. Through the insistence that things are conveniently simpler than they are, the psychologist excuses himself from responsible choice.

Consider first the gospel of democratic group process. Impressive data indicate that when a teacher, leader, or "change-agent" thrusts the members of a group on their own resources, the changes that occur in their knowledge, attitudes, and behavior, coming as they do from within, have stability and personal significance that cannot be attained through more didactic or "authoritarian" procedures. This is an important discovery. It does not follow, however, that *authoritative* intervention may not often be indispensable, nor does it mean that the democratic techniques —or reasonably exact facsimiles thereof—may not be employed in the service of questionable objectives. What is irresponsible, because it rules out discriminating choice where choice is needed, is to set such stock on the technique per se that questions of its suitability to the objective, or the desirability of the objective itself, are overlooked. It is misleading to assume, for instance, that democratic group process as employed by management consultants automatically guarantees a democratic result in keeping with the best interests of worker and supervisor alike. Much manipulation is rationalized in the name of democracy.

When it is elevated to dogma, the parallel nondirective technique in psychotherapy may present similar pitfalls. Only to the extent that the therapist is aware of the degree and nature of his intervention can he direct his *own* role in therapy responsibly.

The foolproof technique, the "simple and sovereign" relationship, has appeal as it promises to let us avoid or delegate responsibility for judgment in the face of complexity. Even if our attempts at simple principles turn out to be valid, however, their application to complex real situations will surely continue to require the best and most explicit judgment we can muster.

Absolutism of Ends

Here I turn to another controversial matter. Psychologists and other social scientists have helped to undermine the absolute standing of traditional, theologically supported ends and values. We are perhaps ready enough to detect an abdication of responsibility when persons justify their choices by recourse to a superhuman scheme of things, or to the ways of our own culture writ large as the proper ways of humanity. Yet the search for values to fill the gap left by theology has often remained a quest for other absolutes with some of the old magic. Psychologists have on occasion offered or imposed their own partial values as absolutes blessed in the name of science. I am thinking for example of "adjustment," which as a be-all-and-end-all is already in sufficient disrepute to make my point clear. It is certainly not irresponsible of psychologists to favor adjustment and to seek to promote it; the difficulty comes when we mislead ourselves and others that science lends its authority to an obligation to be adjusted. Science can of course do no such thing, and the pretense that it can closes off prematurely the exploration of alternative standards.

The choice of ends is a personal matter, which can be exercised responsibly or irresponsibly, or abdicated in favor of tradition or mere conformity. As scientists, we have the special competence to consider the bearing of an important realm of facts on the choice of ends—facts about the side consequences, the boomerang effects of our choices. The pitfall for us to avoid, however, is losing sight of the element of personal choice that remains once the facts are in.

Escape into Relativism or "Value Neutrality"

Seeing that science yields no absolutes, psychologists may, conversely, try to make peace with themselves by raising the anthropologists' banner of cultural relativism—values are a chance of nurture to be accepted without fuss as one accepts table etiquette. Or they may flatly deny that the realms of scientific fact and value have anything to do with one another. But the psychologist cannot stop making choices, as scientist, teacher, therapist, or human engineer. The choices may be witting or unwitting, responsible or irresponsible, but they are made, and they entail consequences. Acceptance of the values of one's culture as given and beyond reconsideration implies a conservative choice; it can add the psychologist's voice, in fact, to the crescendo urging total conformity, a trend which in the long run may be not at all conservative of our traditional values. And the claim to a value-free science, when it goes beyond insistence on a disciplined regard for fact whether or not it accords with our wishes, only obscures the value elements in the choice of problem, of research setting, of conceptual framework, in the decision as to when to rest with negative findings, when results are reportable, and so on endlessly. Only if we know what we are choosing, only if the values involved in our choices are explicit, do our decisions become responsible ones.

Isolation of Conflicting Values

Some of the devices we have already listed, as well as still others, may have their appeal because they serve to isolate conflicting values from one another. Insistence on value neutrality may, for instance, serve to contain a conflict between major values for the psychologist who must depend for the support of his work on sources that are not equally disinterested. Isolation—"logic-tight compartments"—may be an essential expedient in the functioning of a less than perfectly integrated society or personality. It excludes, however, the productive interplay in which new means of resolution may be invented and previously held values redefined, and from which can emerge—much as the common law grows from successive judicial decisions—workable consensus on fundamentals and priorities. Conflict, after all, is a serious and difficult matter that is hard to face, harder to tolerate, and hardest to resolve. But the more squarely we are able to confront the alternatives in making our choices, the less frequently we are likely to encounter basic conflicts that exceed our powers.

Token Payments to Conscience

One response that many of us make to value conflicts in science and profession as in personal life could be tagged as "token payments." We have our cake and eat it too, but only because we take a small, not very nourishing, bite. Caught between our obligations to research and to our teaching, professional, or administrative duties, we appease conscience by writing little research papers—not very good or very significant, to be sure, but neither do they detract *very* much from the performance of our other obligations. In a program of applied research to satisfy a client, we work in somehow a methodological study to present at the altar of science. Vacillating between commitment to science and responsibility as citizens, we act as if doing a little study of, say, prejudice would show that we are on the right side.

Good results obviously come from these compromises. But if we were more fully on to ourselves as scientists and professionals and citizens, perhaps we might advance our values more effectively. Much research that is done for the sake of such a token payment to social responsibility might as well not be done. The topic picked as a compromise is often not strategic either for scientific advance or for social action. And the effort that can be committed to the investigation is often insufficient to achieve more than token, "suggestive" results. If the conflict were squarely faced, perhaps one would then be in a position to choose between making a more ambitious effort or none at all; perhaps one would decide to capitalize on the advantages of the ivory tower rather than bemoaning its isolation; or to play scientist and citizen on separate occasions, not in combination. Or one might come back to the same compromise as the most satisfactory resolution. At all events, the decision would be a considered one.

Parochialism

Involved in most of the blind alleys we have explored is, in fact, a kind of blindness—of cognitive inadequacy that precludes explicit and adequate decision. The parochialism of our particular perspectives as psychologists can also limit the range of appropriate choice. The vogue of perception-centered theory in social psychology, for example, may without our intending it leave us preoccupied with social perceptions at the expense of social facts. The facts are outside the competence of our psychological kit bag, while it is easy for us to ascertain what people think the facts are. Important as it is to understand people's perceptions, such a partial description points more obviously to the techniques of the public relations man than to more direct measures for coping with unsatisfactory situations. Psychological warfare and employee relations programs seem, indeed, to be most popular where the juggling of appearances appeals as a painless short cut that does not disturb the *status quo*. Perhaps psychotherapies that center on altering the person's self-perceptions have a similar appeal.

Whenever we seek to apply psychological knowledge to the world of affairs in which the psychological is only one of several relevant aspects, parochialism is a real danger. Psychologists could make a more valid claim to be consulted in councils of high policy if we were less prone to regard the factors that we know most about as the only important ones. Problems of communication and its failure, for example, seem to us inherently psychological; we leave power conflict between organized social structures to the political scientist. But if we then prescribe better communication as a panacea for situations of power conflict, we give poor and irresponsible advice. If "wars are born in the minds of men," individual tensions, frustrations, and misunderstandings take on political significance only as they occur in organized social contexts. Responsible recommendations on policy require of the psychologist an understanding of the place of his distinctive contribution among those of the other social disciplines. Knowledge of our limitations should increase our real power.

Professional Vanity

It is still a new thing for psychologists to find their advice on important practical affairs sought and sometimes heeded. Perhaps it would be well for us to remember the limited aspects of our field that have actually paid our way and won for psychology the ear of practical men: aptitude testing, clinical counseling, and a few others, none of which are very close to what we like to think is the theoretical core of the science. As scientists we are still groping —perhaps as professionals, too. When we are tempted by fantasies of power to try to set the world in order, we need an occasional dose of scientific humility. The hardheaded approach that insists on systematic doubt in the absence of confirmation, and holds even established propositions with tentativeness, remains our special contribution. We can ill afford to neglect our function as scientists in the pursuit of problems that are too big for us to cope with. Our responsibility must be measured against our competence.

My strategy in this paper has been to focus our attention on the implications of responsibility, on the assumption that since it is a value that we already share, explicitness about it should make us more likely to act responsibly as psychologists. Explicitness about the relation of values —including this one—to our behavior would seem to be a necessary if not sufficient condition of rational progress toward valued goals.

CHAPTER 10

Wholesome Personality

Some concepts used in ordinary conversation and apparently understood by everyone are exceedingly difficult to analyze. Few educators fail to bring up the topic of "liberal education" from time to time, but fewer still agree on what they mean by it. "Democracy" is another word that conveys the general notion of freedom, tolerance, and equality, but it is used flexibly enough to be appropriated even by our friends behind the Iron Curtain.

A similar situation exists in the psychology of adjustment. Who does not recognize a mature personality, but, at the same time, who can define "maturity" with precision? Earlier attempts emphasized the notion of conformity. People with emotional problems usually conduct themselves in ways that appear deviant to the observer. Even the terms "normal" and "well-adjusted" suggest conventional behavior. Most psychologists today are opposed to any formulation of the question that would seem to make wholesome personality a function of the environment rather than something inside the individual.

By all odds, psychoanalysis has exerted the greatest influence on personality theory. Freud thought of the individual as being victimized by three sets of irreconcilable forces: instinctual urges, conscience, and the demands of reality. To the extent that a person is able to reduce conflict to a minimum, he achieves maturity. Henry Murray calls attention to a large number of psychological needs emphasizing the individual need-pattern in which they occur, while Sullivan and Horney are more concerned with social influence. Erickson stresses the sense of identity or the individual's answer to the question, "Who am I?" which determines how he relates to the outside world and other people.

Although Allport, and a few other writers have always stressed the role of purposive behavior, the rise of existentialism in recent years has revived interest in the long neglected intentional components of personality. Maslow judges the highest level need to consist in a consuming urge for self-actualization of one's personality potential. In a reading in Chapter 8, Charlotte Buhler lists four basic tendencies she has discovered in the individual's quest for self-fulfillment. Frankl [1] speaks of the necessity for neurotic patients to find some worthwhile meaning in life. "What man actually needs is not homeostasis but what I call *noödynamics,* i.e., that kind of appropriate tension that holds him steadily oriented toward concrete values to be actualized, toward the meaning of his personal existence to be fulfilled. This is also what guarantees and sustains his mental health whereas escaping from any stress situation would even precipitate his falling into the existential vacuum [Doubt that life has any meaning—Ed.]." Mowrer and Szasz see a close relationship between mental health and living up to one's moral and ethical commitments.

Among the frequently listed criteria for a mature personality are: an objective perception of oneself and reality, acceptance of personal limitations, the ability to give and receive affection, creative self-fulfillment, a sense of responsibility, and a unifying philosophy of life. Obviously any comprehensive discussion of wholesome personality cannot fail to raise questions concerning personal values and ethical behavior.

[1] V. E. Frankl. Dynamics, existence and values. *J. existential Psychiat.*, 1961, **2,** 5–16.

Editor's Note

Mental illness has had a long and interesting career. In the course of its checkered history, it has found itself associated with causes as diverse as divine intervention, diabolical possession, physical illness, and unconscious conflict.

Equally elusive is the related concept of normality. Originally derived from the statistical notion of conformity to certain standards of behavior, it has gradually acquired greater depth of meaning. Commenting on the elimination of final causality in classical physics, Royce says, "Since the concept of norm is intimately bound up with the design (purpose, final cause) of a thing, it was easy for it to be supplanted by a purely statistical approach which yields averages. Now averages are very useful, and the fault is not with statistics. But regardless of the excellence of the statistical techniques used, they yield norms only *on the supposition that most people (average) will* function according to the inherent design of nature (*normal*)." [1]

In the same vein Shoben concludes, "One way to meet this challenge is by frankly postulating a basic principle of value. The fundamental contention advanced here is that behavior is 'positive' or 'integrative' to the extent that it reflects the unique attributes of the human animal." The time has long since passed when normal behavior can be conceived in terms of the mere absence of pathology.

[1] J. E. Royce, S.J. *Personality and mental health* (rev. ed.). Milwaukee: Bruce, 1964. P. 49.

34. Toward a Concept of the Normal Personality *

Edward Joseph Shoben, Jr.
Teachers College
Columbia University

Clinical practice and the behavioral sciences alike have typically focused on the pathological in their studies of personality and behavior dynamics. While much of crucial importance remains to be learned, there is an abundant empirical knowledge and an impressive body of theory concerning the deviant and the diseased, the anxious and the neurotic, the disturbed and the maladjusted. In contrast, there is little information and even less conceptual clarity about the nature of psychological normality. Indeed, there are even those who argue that there is no such thing as a normal man; there are only those who manage their interpersonal relationships in such a way that others are strongly motivated to avoid them, even by commiting them to a mental hospital or a prison, as opposed to those who do not incite such degrees of social ostracism.

This argument has two characteristics. First, it disposes of the issue by simply distributing people along a dimension of pathology. All men are a little queer, but some are much more so than others. Second, it has affinities with the two major ideas that have been brought to bear on the question of what constitutes normal or abnormal behavior: the statistical conception of the usual or the average and the notion of cultural relativism. If pathology is conceived

* From E. J. Shoben, Jr. Toward a concept of the normal personality. *Amer. Psychologist,* 1957, **12,** 183–189. Reprinted with permission of the author and publisher.

This paper is revised from versions read on March 26, 1956, at the convention of the American Personnel and Guidance Association in Washington, D. C., and on November 16, 1956, at a conference on mental health research at Catholic University in Washington, D. C., the University of Maryland, and the U. S. Veterans Administration.

as the extent to which one is tolerated by one's fellows, then any individual can thoretically be described in terms of some index number that reflects the degree of acceptability accorded him. The resulting distribution would effectively amount to an ordering of people from the least to the most pathological. Similarly, if the positions on such a continuum are thought of as functions of one's acceptance or avoidance by others, then they can only be defined by reference to some group. The implications here are twofold. First, the conception of pathology is necessarily relativistic, varying from group to group or culture to culture. Second, the degree of pathology is defined as the obverse of the degree of conformity to group norms. The more one's behavior conforms to the standards of the group, the less one is likely to be subject to social avoidance; whereas the more one's behavior deviates from the rules, the greater is the probability of ostracism to the point of institutional commitment.

Statistical and Relativistic Concepts of Normality

Yet it is doubtful that the issues are fully clarified by these statistical and culturally relativistic ideas. Is it most fruitful to regard normality or integrative behavior as merely reflecting a minimal degree of pathology, or may there be a certain merit in considering the asset side of personality, the positive aspects of human development? This question becomes particularly relevant when one is concerned with the socialization process or with the goals and outcomes of psychotherapy or various rehabilitative efforts.

It seems most improbable that the family, the church, and the school, the main agents of socialization, exist for the minimizing of inevitable pathological traits in the developing members of the community. Rather, parents, priests, and educators are likely to insist that their function is that of facilitating some sort of positive growth, the progressive acquisition of those characteristics, including skills, knowledge, and attitudes, which permit more productive, contributory, and satisfying ways of life. Similarly, while psychotherapists may sometimes accept the limited goals of simply trying to inhibit pathological processes, there are certainly those who take the position that therapy is to be judged more in terms of how much it contributes to a patient's ability to achieve adult gratifications rather than its sheer efficiency in reducing symptoms or shoring up pathological defenses.

A general concern for such a point of view seems to be emerging in the field of public mental health. Beginning with an emphasis on treatment, the concept of community mental health swung to a preventive phase with the main interest focused on identifying the antecedents of mental disease and on reducing morbidity rates by attacking their determinants. The vogue of eugenics was one illustrative feature of this stage. More recently, there has been a considerable dissatisfaction with the whole notion of interpreting psychological states in terms of disease analogues. Maladjustive behavior patterns, the neuroses, and —perhaps to a lesser extent—the psychoses may possibly be better understood as disordered, ineffective, and defensive styles of life than as forms of sickness. In consequence, there seems to be a growing tendency to conceive of the public mental health enterprise as emphasizing positive development with the prevention and treatment of pathology regarded as vital but secondary.

But in what does positive development consist? The statistical concept of the average is not very helpful. Tiegs and Katz, for example, reported a study of college students who had been rated for fourteen different evidences of "nervousness." By and large, these traits were normally distributed, suggesting that those subjects rated low must be considered just as "abnormal" (unusual) as those rated high. This conception seems to provide a superficial quantitative model only at the expense of hopeless self-contradiction and violence to the ordinary categories of communication. Even in a case that at first blush seems to cause no difficulty, the problem remains. Criminal behavior, for example, is distributed in a J-shaped fashion with most cases concentrated at the point of zero offenses, ranging to a relatively few instances of many-time offenders. Few would argue that the usual behavior here is not also the most "positive." But one suspects that the sheer frequency of law-abiding behavior has little to do with its acknowledged integrative character. If conformity to social rules is generally considered more desirable than criminality, it is not because of its rate of occurrence but because of its consequences for both society and the individual.

Thus, a statistical emphasis on the usual as the criterion of positive adjustment or normality shades into a socially relativistic concept with an implied criterion of conformity. The terms "usual" or "most frequent" or "average" are meaningless without reference to some group, and this state of affairs poses two problems. First, conformity in itself, as history abundantly demonstrates, is a dubious guide to conduct. Innovation is as necessary to a culture's survival as are tradition and conservation, and conformity has frequently meant acquiescence in conditions undermining the maturity and positive development of human beings rather than their enhancement. On more personal levels, conformity sometimes seems related in some degree to personality processes that can quite properly be called pathological. Second, relativistic conceptions of normality pose serious questions as to the reference group against which any individual is to be assessed. Benedict, for example, has made it quite clear that behavior which is considered abnormal in one culture is quite acceptable in others, that certain forms of abnormalities which occur in some societies are absent in others, and that conduct which is thought completely normal in one group may be regarded as intensely pathological in another. Such observations, while descriptively sound, can lead readily to two troublesome inferences. One is that the storm trooper must be considered as the prototype of integrative adjustment in

Nazi culture, the members of the Politburo as best representing human normality Soviet–style, and the cruelest adolescent in a delinquent gang as its most positively developed member. The other is that any evaluative judgment of cultures and societies must be regarded as inappropriate. Since normality is conceived only in terms of conformity to group standards, the group itself must be beyond appraisal. Thus, the suspicion and mistrust of Dobu, the sense of resigned futility that permeates Alor, and the regimentation that characterizes totalitarian nations can logically only be taken as norms in terms of which individual behavior may be interpreted, not as indications of abnormal tendencies in the cultures themselves.

Wegrocki, in criticizing such relativistic notions, argues that it is not the form of behavior, the actual acts themselves, that defines its normal or pathological character. Rather, it is its function. What he calls the "quintessence of abnormality" lies in reactions which represent an escape from conflicts and problems rather than a facing of them. This formulation, implying that integrative adjustments are those which most directly confront conflicts and problems, seems essentially free of the difficulties inherent in statistical conceptions and the idea of cultural relativism. But it presents troubles of its own. For instance, what does it mean to "face" a problem or conflict? On what ground, other than the most arbitrarily moralistic one, can such confrontations be defended as more positive than escape? Finally, does this facing of one's problems have any relationship to the matter of conformity in the sense of helping to clarify decisions regarding the acceptance or rejection of group standards?

To deal with such questions requires coming to grips with certain problems of value. It is at this point that the behavioral sciences and ethics meet and merge, and it seems unlikely that any conception of normality can be developed apart from some general considerations that are fundamentally moral. Once the purely relativistic ideas of normality are swept away, it becomes difficult to avoid some concern for the issues of happiness and right conduct (*i.e.*, conduct leading to the greatest degree of human satisfaction) that are the traditional province of the literary interpreter of human experience, the theologian, and the moral philosopher. A primary challenge here is that of providing a rational and naturalistic basis for a concept of integrative adjustment that is at once consistent with the stance and contributions of empirical science and in harmony with whatever wisdom mankind has accumulated through its history.

Symbolic and Social Aspects of Human Nature

One way to meet this challenge is by frankly postulating a basic principle of value. The fundamental contention advanced here is that behavior is "positive" or "integrative" to the extent that it reflects the unique attributes of the human animal. There are undoubtedly other ways of approaching a fruitful concept of normality. Nevertheless, this assertion is consistent with the implications of organic evolution, escapes the fallacy of the survival-of-the-fittest doctrine in its various forms, and permits a derivation of more specific criteria of positive adjustment from the distinctive characteristics of man. No discontinuity within the phylogenetic scale need be assumed. It seems clear, however, that man, while certainly an animal, can hardly be described as "nothing but" an animal; and his normality or integration seems much more likely to consist in the fulfillment of his unique potentialities than in the development of those he shares with infrahuman organisms.

Foremost among these uniquely human potentialities, as Cassirer and Langer make clear, is the enormous capacity for symbolization. What is most characteristic of men is their pervasive employment of *propositional* language. While other organisms, especially dogs and the higher apes, react to symbols, their faculty for doing so indicates only an ability to respond to mediate or representative as well as direct stimuli. Man, on the other hand, uses symbols designatively, as a vehicle for recollecting past events, for dealing with things which are not physically present, and for projecting experience into the future. Goldstein makes the same point in his discussion of the "attitude toward the merely possible," the ability to deal with things that are only imagined or which are not part of an immediate, concrete situation. In patients whose speech has been impaired because of brain damage, this attitude toward the possible is disrupted. Thus, aphasics are typically unable to say such things as, "The snow is black" or "The moon shines in the daytime"; similarly, they are incapable of *pretending* to comb their hair or to take a drink of water, although they can actually *perform* these acts. Such patients appear to have lost the uniquely human capacity for thinking *about* things as well as directly "thinking things."

It is his symbolic ability, then, that makes man the only creature who can "look before and after and pine for what is not." Propositional speech makes it possible for him to learn from not only his own personal experience but from that of other men in other times and places, to forecast the consequences of his own behavior, and to have ideals. These three symbol-given attributes—the aptitude for capitalizing on experience, including the experience of others, over time, the capacity for foresight and the self-imposed control of behavior through the anticipation of its outcomes, and the ability to envision worlds closer than the present one to the heart's desire—constitute a basic set of distinctively human potentialities.

A second set of such potentialities seems related to the long period of helpless dependence that characterizes infancy and childhood. Made mandatory by the relative biological incompleteness of the human baby, this phase of development is likely to be lengthened as cultures become more complex. Thus, in such simpler societies as the

Samoan, children can achieve a higher degree of independence at an earlier age than in the civilizations of the West, for example, where the necessity for learning complicated and specialized economic skills extends the period of dependence through adolescence and even into chronological young adulthood. The central point, however, is that unlike the young of any other species, human children in *all* cultural settings must spend a long time during which the gratification of their most basic needs is mediated by somebody else and is dependent on their relationship to somebody else.

This state of affairs exposes youngsters during their earliest and most formative stages of development to two fundamental conditions of human life. The first is that one's survival, contentment, and need fulfillment involve an inevitable element of reliance on other people. The second is that the relative autonomy, authority, and power that characterize the parent figures and others on whom one relies in childhood are always perceived to a greater or lesser extent in association with responsibility and a kind of altruism. That is, the enjoyment of adult privileges and status tends to occur in conjunction with the acceptance, in some degree, of responsibility for mediating, in some way, the need gratifications of others. Mowrer and Kluckhohn seem to be speaking of a similar pattern when they describe the socialization process as progressing from childhood *dependency* through *independence* to adult *dependability.*

Moreover, this reciprocal relationship between reliance and responsibility seems to obtain on adult levels as well as between children and parents, with the degree of reciprocity a partial function of the complexity of the culture. In simpler societies, a relatively small number of persons may assume primary responsibility for virtually all of the needs of the group in excess of its bare subsistence demands. Under civilized conditions, however, the specialization made necessary by technology and the pattern of urban living means that each adult is dependent on some other adult in some way and that, conversely, he is responsible in some fashion for the welfare of some other adult. The difference between the simpler and the more complex cultures, however, is only one of degree. The crucial point is that, throughout human society, men are in one way or another dependent on each other both in the familiar situation of parents and children and in the course of adult living. This pattern of interdependency gives to human life a social character to be found nowhere else in the animal kingdom. Even among the remarkable social insects, the patterns of symbiosis found there seem to be a result of a genetically determined division of labor rather than the fulfillment of a potentiality for the mutual sharing of responsibilities for each other.

It is in this notion of the fulfillment of distinctively human potentialities that a fruitful conception of positive adjustment may have its roots. From the symbolic and peculiarly social character of human life, it may be possible to derive a set of potential attributes the cultivation of which results in something different from the mere absence of pathology and which forms a standard against which to assess the degree of integration in individual persons. To accept this task is to attempt the construction of a normative or ideal model of a normal, positively developed, or integratively adjusted human being.

A Model of Integrative Adjustment

In the first place, it would seem that, as the symbolic capacity that endows man with foresight develops in an individual, there is a concomitant increase in his ability to control his own behavior by anticipating its probable long-range consequences. The normal person is, first of all, one who has learned that in many situations his greatest satisfaction is gained by foregoing the immediate opportunities for comfort and pleasure in the interest of more remote rewards. He lives according to what Paul Elmer More, the Anglican theologian, calls "the law of costingness":

> . . . the simple and tyrannical fact that, whether in the world physical, or in the world intellectual, or in the world spiritual, we can get nothing without paying an exacted price. The fool is he who ignores, and the villain is he who thinks he can outwit, the vigilance of the nemesis guarding this law of costingness . . . all [one's] progress is dependent on surrendering one interest or value for a higher interest or value.[1]

Mowrer and Ullman have made the same point in arguing, from the results of an ingenious experiment, that normality results in large part from the acquired ability to subject impulses to control through the symbolic cues one presents to oneself in the course of estimating the consequences of one's own behavior. Through symbolization, the future outcomes of one's actions are drawn into the psychological present; the strength of more remote rewards or punishments is consequently increased; and a long-range inhibitory or facilitating effect on incipient conduct is thereby exercised.

This increase in self-control means a lessened need for control by external authority, and conformity consequently becomes a relatively unimportant issue. The integratively adjusted person either conforms to the standards of his group because their acceptance leads to the most rewarding long-range consequences for him, or he rebels against authority, whether of persons or of law or customs, on *considered* grounds. This considered form of revolt implies two things. The first is an honest conviction that rules or the ruler are somehow unjust and that the implementation of his own values is likely to lead to a more broadly satisfying state of affairs. Such an attack on authority is very different from revolts that occur out of sheer needs for self-assertion or desires for power or as expressions of displaced hostility. The main dimension of

[1] From P. E. More, *The Catholic Faith*, Princeton University Press, N. J., 1931, p. 158. Quotation reprinted with permission.

difference is that of honesty as opposed to deception. The normal person is relatively well aware of his motives in either conforming or rebelling. The pathological rebel, on the other hand, tends to deceive himself and others about his goals. His reasons for nonconformity amount to rationalizations, and his justifications are typically projections. This kind of self-defeating and socially disruptive deceptiveness is seen daily in clinical practice.

The second characteristic of nonconformity in the normal person is that it is undertaken with an essential acceptance of the possible consequences. Having considered the risks beforehand, he is inclined neither to whine nor to ask that his rebellious conduct be overlooked if he runs afoul of trouble. In keeping with the "law of costingness," he is willing to pay the price for behaving in accordance with his own idiosyncratic values. "We have the right to lead our own lives," John Erskine makes Helen of Troy say to her daughter Hermione, "but that right implies another—to suffer the consequences. . . . Do your best, and if it's a mistake, hide nothing and be glad to suffer for it. That's morality." A psychological paraphrase of this bit of belletristic wisdom is not inappropriate: The assumption of responsibility [2] for one's actions is one of the attributes of personal integration.

But if personal responsibility and self-control through foresight can be derived as aspects of integrative adjustment from man's symbolic capacity, a third characteristic of interpersonal responsibility can be deduced from his social nature. If interdependency is an essential part of

[2] This conception of responsibility is by no means anti-deterministic. As Fingarette points out, one can *understand* his own or another's behavior, in the sense of accounting for it or rationally explaining it, by the retrospective process of examining the past. Responsibility, on the other hand, is neither retrospective in orientation nor explanatory in function. It is future oriented and refers to the *act* of proclaiming oneself as answerable for one's own conduct and its consequences. Thus, "responsibility," in this context, is not a logical term, implying causation, but a behavioral and attitudinal one, descriptive of a class of human actions.

human social life, then the normal person becomes one who can act dependably in relation to others and at the same time acknowledge his need for others. The roots of the former probably lie, as McClelland has pointed out, in the role perceptions which developing children form of parent figures and other agents of the socialization process. By conceiving of such people as at least in some degree the nurturant guides of others and through identification with them, the integratively adjusted individual "wants to be" himself trustworthy and altruistic in the sense of being dependable and acting out of a genuine concern for the welfare of others as he can best conceive it. Altruism in this context, therefore, means nothing sentimental. It certainly includes the making and enforcement of disciplinary rules and the imposition of behavioral limits, but only if these steps are motivated by an interest in helping others and express concern and affection rather than mere personal annoyance or the power conferred by a superior status.

Similarly, the acknowledgment of one's needs for others implies a learned capacity for forming and maintaining intimate interpersonal relationships. Erikson refers to this aspect of the normal personality as the attitude of "basic trust," and it is not far from what can be meaningfully styled in plain language as the ability to love. One suspects that the origins of this ability lies in the long experience during childhood of having need gratifications frequently associated with the presence of another person, typically a parent figure. By this association and the process of generalization, one comes to attach a positive affect to others. But as the youngster develops, he gradually learns that the need-mediating behavior of others is maintained only by his reciprocating, by his entering into a relationship of mutuality with others. If this kind of mutuality is not required of him, he is likely to perpetuate his dependency beyond the period his biological level of development and the complexity of his culture define as appropriate; whereas if he is required to demonstrate this mutuality too soon, he is likely to form the schema that interpersonal relationships are essentially matters of traded favors, and that, instead of basic trust, the proper attitude is one of getting as much as possible while giving no more than necessary. The pursuit in research and thought of such hypotheses as these might shed a good deal of light on the determinants of friendship, marital happiness, and effective parenthood, the relational expressions of effective personal integration.

But there is still another interpersonal attitude relevant to a positive conception of adjustment that is somewhat different from that bound up with relationships of an intimate and personal kind. There is a sense in which each individual, even if he regards himself as unfortunate and unhappy, owes his essential humanity to the group which enabled him to survive his helpless infancy. As studies of feral children have shown, even the humanly distinctive and enormously adaptive trait of propositional speech does not become usable without the stimulation and nurture of other people. A kind of obligation is therefore created for the person to be an asset rather than a burden to society. It is partly to the discharging of this obligation that Adler referred in developing his concept of social interest as a mark of normality. While the notion certainly implies the learning of local loyalties and personal affections, it also transcends the provincial limits of group and era. Because man's symbolic capacity enables him to benefit from the record of human history and to anticipate the future, and because his pattern of social interdependency, especially in civilized societies, reaches across the boundaries of political units and parochial affiliations, it seems reasonable to expect the positively developed person to behave in such a fashion as to contribute, according to his own particular lights, to the general welfare of humanity, to take as his frame of reference mankind at large as best he understands it rather than his own group or clan.

Ideologies are at issue here, but there need be

neither embarrassment nor a lack of room for debate regarding the specifics of policy and values in the hypothesis that democratic attitudes are closely bound up with personality integration. After all, democracy in psychological terms implies only a concern about others, a valuing of persons above things, and a willingness to participate in mutually gratifying relationships with many categories of persons, including those of which one has only vicarious knowledge. Departures from democratic attitudes in this psychological sense mean a restriction on the potentiality for friendship and imply both a fear of others and a valuation of such things as power over people, thus endangering the interpersonal rewards that come from acting on the attitude of basic trust. Democratic social interest, then, means simply the most direct route to the fulfillment of a distinctively human capacity derived from man's symbolic character and the inevitability of his social life.

Finally, man's ability to assume an attitude toward the "merely possible" suggests that the normal person has ideals and standards that he tries to live up to even though they often exceed his grasp. For an integrative adjustment does not consist in the attainment of perfection but in a striving to act in accordance with the best principles of conduct that one can conceive. Operationally, this notion implies that there is an optimum discrepancy between one's self concept and one's ego ideal. Those for whom this discrepancy is too large (in favor, of course, of the ideal) are likely to condemn themselves to the frustration of never approximating their goals and to an almost perpetually low self-esteem. Those whose discrepancies are too low, on the other hand, are probably less than integratively adjusted either because they are failing to fulfill their human capacity to envision themselves as they could be or because they are self-deceptively overestimating themselves.

This model of integrative adjustment as characterized by self-control, personal responsibility, social responsibility, democratic social interest, and ideals must be regarded only in the most tentative fashion. Nevertheless, it does seem to take into account some realistic considerations. It avoids the impossible conception of the normal person as one who is always happy, free from conflict, and without problems. Rather, it suggests that he may often fall short of his ideals; and because of ignorance, the limitations under which an individual lives in a complex world, or the strength of immediate pressures, he may sometimes behave in ways that prove to be shortsighted or self–defeating. Consequently, he knows something of the experience of guilt at times, and because he tries to be fully aware of the risks he takes, he can hardly be entirely free from fear and worry. On the other hand, a person who is congruent to the model is likely to be one who enjoys a relatively consistent and high degree of self-respect and who elicits a predominantly positive and warm reaction from others. Moreover, it is such a person who seems to learn wisdom rather than hostile bitterness or pathologically frightened withdrawal from whatever disappointments or suffering may be his lot. Guilt, for example, becomes a challenge to his honesty, especially with himself but also with others; and it signalizes for him the desirability of modifying his behavior, of greater effort to live up to his ideals, rather than the need to defend himself by such mechanisms as rationalization or projection. Finally, the model permits a wide variation in the actual behaviors in which normal people may engage and even makes allowance for a wide range of disagreements among them. Integrative adjustment does not consist in the individual's fitting a preconceived behavioral mold. It may well consist in the degree to which his efforts fulfill the symbolic and social potentialities that are distinctively human.

Editor's Note

Another aspect of wholesome personality seldom stressed in textbooks is the element of spontaneity—daring to be oneself. Basic to spontaneity is an habitual alertness to what one actually feels. In place of vague uneasiness in the presence of keen emotion, as if it were somehow inappropriate, strong feelings are accorded full status as an integral part of normal psychological functioning.

In the unusual selection that follows, the author delicately draws aside the veil to reveal the zestful inner life of an authentic person who feels completely at ease with himself.

35. The Sense of Self *

Clark Moustakas
Merrill Palmer Institute of Human Development and Family Life
Detroit, Michigan

Once, as I sat with a child, I met him with a concentrated and watchful hovering, absorbing as fully as I could every word and motion, trying with deliberate effort to comprehend the exact meaning of his expression. I used my powers and resources to understand, to see through and beyond his fumbling ways, his distortions of reality and into his basic intentions and feelings. My efforts were directed at helping him to release inner tensions, to achieve a sense of inner harmony and to restore a whole being with integrity. To understand, to clarify, to say just the right words which would bring him to a higher level of comfort or comprehension—these were directions for which I could exert myself. If only I could help him see how, in giving up his own wishes and interests and ways, he had denied his own unique heritage and destiny. If only I could help him realize that he was a worthy self; and, even if every-

* Abridged from C. Moustakas. The sense of self. *J. humanistic Psychol.,* 1961, **1**(1), 20–34. Reprinted with permission of the author and publisher.

thing else were lost, he still existed as a self and this existence could never be taken away. To realize, to understand, to see, with greater clarity and deeper meaning and insight, to bring the pieces together into a comprehensible whole and to value what I saw—these were among the personality changes which distinguished my work as successful psychotherapy or failure.

But what was being clarified? What was being understood? And what did the uncovering of missing links and the patterning of broken pieces provide? What did examination of the relation render? Only a self in pursuit of understanding itself? Only a series of responses and interactions and influences? Only an unbroken chain of associations and events? Only an organization of discrete items? Only a clarification of what one says and does, of habits and attitudes, of projections and defenses? Is this a living human being engaged in encounters with other human beings? Is this a life being lived fully in the human sense? Is this a self growing as a self in touch with inner resources and in correspondence with nature and other selves?

There is no doubt that the unique human gifts of logic and reasoning are of great value in clarifying ideas, understanding basic causes and motivations, solving problems, uncovering hidden meanings, meeting challenges and making decisions. But reasoning and logic are only pieces of man engaged in certain kinds of intercourse with the universe. What about the experience of pain and suffering and love and beauty and the sun and the stars and the mountains and the seas? What about faith and God? And the food I share with my brother, or the walk I take in a silent moonlit night, or the games I play with my children? What about the tears I shed and the ecstacy I share with those I love? And my loneliness and sense of being apart even when part of group life? Are there not many, many human experiences beyond logic and beyond reason, in which it takes courage to live the meaning, to embrace the other, to share a journey, long before there is any understanding or insight or clarification, long before there is any separated knowledge and comprehension? The individual engaged in the human situation, exploring life, where the self is involved and committed, those isolated hours of quiet self-reflection, of lonely self experience, those moments when I truly meet my neighbor with whom I am bound by intrinsic interests and organic ties, those times when I feel related to a falling leaf, to an isolated flower on a frosty day, to thunder and wind and rain, when my senses bring me a whole universe of harmony and color and form, when all is related to all and belongs to all and remains as it is. William Wordsworth [1] conveys such a sense of self in this poem:

> I have felt
> A presence that disturbs me with the joy
> Of elevated thought; a sense sublime
> Of something far more deeply interfused,
> Whose dwelling is the light of setting suns,
> And the round ocean and the living air,
> And the blue sky, and in the mind of man—
> A motion and a spirit, that impels
> All thinking things, all objects of all thought,
> And rolls through all things.

Are experiences like these not important in the creation of the self? Yet where is the understanding and the comprehension? What concept or definition or reasoned discourse, what thoughtful essay could ever communicate the wonder and awe of holistic experience where man is man, and a tree is a tree, and the dawn is the dawn, yet each merges into the other, and each gives meaning to the other, and in unity they create something entirely new, a poetry of living form?

Two years ago, the winter in Michigan exceeded

[1] William Wordsworth, *Poetical Works,* Vol. II, Hurd and Houghton, Boston, 1877.

records for frigid temperatures, ice formations and accumulations of snow. On an especially cold, blustering day, the noisy violence of a raging wind kept me indoors. After almost two days of internment, I began to feel dull and insensible to the children's play and the other events going on around me. Everything seemed colorless and toneless. I was on the edge of despair, in the shadows of life, and felt trapped by the violent storm outside. The wind came swaggering through the walls and lashed against the windows, echoing throughout the house. The screaming, fluttering sounds came through the weather stripping of the doors. Yet these auditory vibrations barely entered my awareness. I had been taught that the safest place in a blizzard was the warm comfort of home. And this had been my retreat for almost two days, not out of choice, but from tradition and fear. I was annoyed that a wild and fitful wind had forced me into an asylum and that I had conformed in the ordinary, intelligent way. But something was wrong. The household scenes were gloomy. I saw only the coverings and felt the lethargy and boredom of a static life. The more I thought about my situation, the more restless I became. A growing inner feeling surged within me. I decided to face the wind. I had never been in a blizzard before—by choice—but in that moment I decided to enter the turbulent outside.

Immediately I experienced an exhilarating and exciting feeling. The cold, turbulent flow of wind was inciting retreat and withdrawal in every direction. Momentarily I was stung and pushed back. I hesitated, uncertain whether I could move forward. Holding my ground, I stood in the way of the wind. We met head-on. I knew for the first time the full meaning of a severe wind. I felt it in every pore of my body. I stood firm; and gradually, slowly, I began to move forward in spite of the violent, shattering gusts which emerged repeatedly to block my path. Tears fell down my face. It was a painful experience but at the same time peculiarly, wonderfully refreshing and joyous. It was cold, yet I was warmed by a tremendous surge of emotion. I felt radiant and alive as I continued my journey. As the wind met me and moved me, I became aware of the whole atmosphere. It was like a powerful dynamo, electrified with clear, ringing sounds which extolled the universal virtues of nature. My senses became totally immersed in them. Crackling, crunching, clanging noises were everywhere; yet each sound had its own unique quality and was so pure that in spite of the rushing, swaying, churning turbulence, I could perceive each single tone as a distinctive unity. I listened and experienced an inner peacefulness and joy in the wild crushing that filled the atmosphere. I felt completely unafraid and strangely elated as I walked forward in a world charged with electric fury. It was a moment of inspiration and an inner victory over superstition and fear. For the first time in my life I truly understood the meaning of a blizzard from my own direct experience. All about me were shining elements and sharp, penetrating sounds which I could see, and hear, and feel without effort. It was an awesome feeling, witnessing the wild turbulence. Everything was charged with life and beauty. The magnitude and intensity of the blizzard entered my system. The meeting with the wind revived me and restored me to my own resourcefulness. I felt an expansive and limitless energy. I returned home. Everything took on a shining light and a spark of beauty. I played ecstatically with my children, with a burst of boundless enthusiasm and excitement. I seemed to be inexhaustible. I made repairs, painted, helped with the evening meal, assisted with the children's baths and bedtime, and spent a joyous evening reading and conversing with my wife. Out of the tumultuous experience, I found new joy in life, new energy, uniqueness and beauty. I conquered my lethargy and discovered a lively affinity with everything I touched. Everything which had been dull and commonplace took on a living splendor. I realized how out of the wild, confused, turbulent experience came a sense of inner exaltation, peace, and symmetry and, along with it, a recognition of the vital manifestations of life, how out of the initial conflict came a sense of individual aliveness and a feeling of harmony and relatedness to a raging wind.

It is this dimension—call it spiritual or mystic or aesthetic, or creative, or simply man being man. I am speaking about unknown forces in man merging with unknown forces in the universe and letting happen what will happen, permitting the truth and reality which exists to merge in its fullest sense and letting the unpredictable in oneself encounter the unpredictable in the other. Then a breakthrough of self occurs in which man does the unexpected and unanticipated, in which man emerges newly born and perceives and senses and experiences in a totally different way.

How can the individual develop latent resources and hidden talents, how can he meet the other in a meaningful sense when he is urged to conform, to compete, to achieve, to evaluate, to establish goals? How can the uniqueness of the person take form in a living situation, when he is pressured to communicate in precise ways, to copy or model himself along the usual norms and standards, to complete certain developmental tasks?

We live in an age of reasoning where the self is a self system, a series of rationalities and concepts which describe and define, where skills are used to exploit and manipulate, where the abstractions are more relevant than the realities abstracted, and where the symbol has become more real than the person or thing symbolized. We live in an age of comfort, ready to receive and consume, where it is better to keep quiet and look away when there is a vibrant cry for justice and truth, when it is better to stay on the edges of a real relationship, because a genuine meeting often brings pain and suffering and grief as well as joy and happiness. We live at a time when a calm, deliberate, reasonable voice is the way to be and when spontaneous excitement and joy, when enthusiasm, emotional fervor and pitch, when indignant cries for justice and appeals to individual truths are interpreted calmly by the wiseacres as signs of immaturity, hostility, selfish goals, projections of oral needs or sexual deprivations.

We live in a time of machines and technological advances and techniques and procedures, where one can get a list of approved ways to speak and act, and of inappropriate behaviors for almost any situation.

We live in an age of adjustment where, if the individual does not adapt by consent, he is forced into group modes and preferences, either by authority or popular vote. Unanimity is simply not practical or expedient. Inevitably, individual differences create a split within the individual, a breach between himself and others. Then either the group or the individual is sick, but both must suffer. Neither the group nor the individual can grow and develop fully without the other. There is no way to realize the full possibilities in group life as long as one person is rejected, minimized, ignored or treated as inferior or as an outcast. To the extent that there is malice toward one, the ill will and ill feeling spread; and every person in the group is inflicted and unable to bring the resources available to creative expression and realization. One cannot carry evil thoughts and feeling and intentions in his heart without at the same time deterring and restraining himself in his own purposes or directions. One must live through and work out one's state of rejecting or being rejected before group life can contain a depth of spirit and devotion and authentic communality. The personal issues and disputes, the challenge of the individual confronting the group must first be met. Otherwise, the split in the group prevents each man from deriving a sense of integrity and a sense of being whole. Only by learning to live with the deviant one, by recognizing his right to be, and respecting the issues he raises or the problems he creates, can a high level of group living be realized. The personal matters must be settled first; social or group life follows.

We are dissatisfied with the meaningless motions and habits and goals of modern day life and the estrangement which results from being part of a mechanical, absurd existence or from devoting one's energies to impersonal study and attempts to understand, rather than living imminently in terms of the requirements or challenges of each situation.

CHAPTER 11

Value Orientation in Counseling

The basic freedom in a democracy is that of self-determination. Each individual has, at least in theory, an inalienable right to develop his potentialities as he wishes so long as he does not interfere with the same right of other people. In a pluralistic society, there is little agreement about ultimate goals toward which the individual and the group as a whole should strive. Instead, each person is confronted with a broad range of value systems from which he must select the one that seems to him most valid.

Respect for the prerogative of every individual to control his own destiny creates a difficult situation for the guidance worker. How can he be true to himself and remain authentic if he dissembles his own value system in the counseling interview, and, on the other hand, how can he guard against imposing a philosophy of life on the defenseless client if he does not? One solution that appeals because of its simplicity and its association with earlier notions of scientific methodology is to deny that the counselor's values enter in any way into the relationship. As a trained scientist, he merely applies tested objective techniques to the solution of personal problems without influencing the client's purposes and goals.

For many years this widely held opinion was scarcely challenged, but more recently it has become obvious that no one can avoid communicating his primary commitments at least at the nonverbal level. Value judgments, Williamson points out, are implied even in structuring the counseling situation and the selection of techniques. The counselor's choice in these matters will be guided by what he believes the outcome of counseling should be. More central to the problem is Gardner Murphy's[1] reflection that, ". . . if he who offers guidance is a whole person, with real roots in human culture, he cannot help conveying directly or indirectly to every client what he himself sees and feels, and the perspective in which his own life is lived." The personal commitments around which a person organizes his living are held with an intensity that suggests the presence of nonrational components. Any challenge of their validity even by indirection is likely to evoke a defensive attitude. The counselor, by virtue of his professional training, is presumably in full control of his conscious feelings, but it is too much to expect that he avoid every unconscious betrayal of his reactions.

The course of action the counselor should take presents an even greater challenge as the surface difficulties mentioned in the initial interview gradually lead to problems of life orientation involving ethical and moral issues. Unless the counselor has clarified his own value system to the extent of explicitly understanding his key motives, he cannot guard against imposing them on others in many covert ways. He must likewise be alert to the value context of the interview and assess where the reactions he sets going in the client may eventually lead.

In these selections, it appears that not every mention of value judgments, even the counselor's own, necessarily encroaches upon the individual's inviolable right to make his own decisions. Nor is a frank discussion of the possible range of values from which an adolescent may choose always contraindicated. What is important is that the counselor remember that even when he speaks of values as relatively established as those of Western culture, he views them in the framework of his own personal commitments.

[1] G. Murphy. The cultural context of counseling. *Personnel Guid. J.*, 1955, **34,** 4–9.

Editor's Note

Williamson discriminates between the roles of the school counselor and the psychotherapist. In place of deep-seated conflicts requiring traditional psychotherapy, the problems of adolescents more frequently center around the choice of values to serve as guiding motives. In many cases where some outside help is required before the adolescents are able to resolve conflicting issues clear-headedly, a modified and simplified relationship-therapy will suffice.

The student may wish to answer to his own satisfaction some of the questions raised in this selection. How is the task of the school counselor related to the general aims of education? In what sense, if any, is the counselor a teacher? In what ways can a counselor impose his values on the student without being aware he is doing so? Must the counselor be neutral to whatever the student decides? Is it ever legitimate for the school counselor to teach values? If so, what kind and under what circumstances?

36. Value Orientation in Counseling *

Edmund G. Williamson
University of Minnesota

Some counselors appear to believe that, as counselors, they should have no value orientation; that in interviewing clients they should maintain a role which resembles a posture of neutrality. These same counselors may assert that the value orientation of the counselee should be the sole determinant of the direction, the pace, and the goal of the counseling process. Now, there are two puzzling aspects in such an advocacy of neutrality. Counselors of such persuasion seem to contend that the individual possesses all the resources needed in achieving his fullest possible growth. And while I yield to no one in confidence in the great potentiality of individuals for furthering their own

* From E. G. Williamson. Value orientation in counseling. *Personnel Guid. J.*, 1958, **36,** 520–529. Reprinted with permission of the author and publisher.

growth, yet I do not believe in autonomous individualism. I believe, rather, and there is rich historic support in Western culture, that the individual, often desperately, needs other individuals to help him achieve optimum development. In fact, the history of human societies points to the interpretation that a civilized state of mutual interdependence is more productive of optimum human development than is the so-called naturalistic state of social and psychological self-dependency.

I am perplexed by another aspect of what I interpret to be an advocacy of autonomous individualism, and that is the role of the counselor himself in such a counseling process. If he literally follows such a concept, then he must seek self-effacement and a condition of at least marginal influence in counseling. Now, I can understand a concept of approximation to such a position or posture, but I cannot conceive that effacement is ever achieved by a structured personality, since individuality is an inherent part of personality. Therefore, it seems evident that at least some dimensions of the value orientation and commitment of the counselor would be perceived by the counselee and, thereby, would be functionally of some influence in the counseling relationship. It may be operationally true that a counselor can act in a self-effacing way and yet, in other circumstances, maintain his own individuality. I presume that this is what is meant by such a contention, although few such outer limits of neutrality are identified by advocates of the principle of self-effacement.

Counseling Model

Whatever may be valid in these two puzzling aspects of the advocacy of neutrality, there are additional bases for abandoning such a position in favor of an open and explicit value orientation in counseling. Before detailing further my argument, let me sketch my concept of counseling so as to make explicit the premises from which my argument proceeds. I shall sketch a model of the counseling process which has been greatly influenced by the writings of others and by my own counseling experiences. Then I shall explore some of the ways in which the counselor's value orientation influences that process. My concept is, of course, determined by the context of my experience, counseling that takes place in college with adolescents. For me, counseling is not identical with psychotherapy and its content is not psychopathology. Other types of counseling may be clinical and therapeutic but I wish to explore and evaluate a different concept, one that embraces and integrates vocational and educational guidance with personality dynamics and interpersonal relationships.

Counseling is a peculiar type of relatively short-term human relationship between a "mentor" with some considerable experience in problems of human development and in ways of facilitating that development, on the one hand, and a learner, on the other hand, who faces certain clearly or dimly perceived difficulties in his efforts to achieve self-controlled and self-manipulated forward-moving development. These difficulties range in content from the choice of a career goal and training to strained relationships with parents, friends, and fiancé. There are several dimensions of human relationship taking place in the personal interview between counselor and counselee which seem to be relevant to our discussion.

Most importantly, the climate of human relationship in counseling is of a peculiar sort. These relationships are highly personal and in that respect are subjective rather than objective, business-like, or official in tone and feeling. The counselor really "cares" for the counselee in a personal way—to be sure, not as intimately and deeply as a parent cares for the personal development of a child, but nevertheless far more personally than we usually experience in the casual or day-to-day relationships of life. Such a climate of relationship is a most necessary ecological condition for the solving or resolving of the developmental problems encountered, felt, and perceived by the counselee. We assume that, without such a climate, the counselee would not be so effectively encouraged to seek a solution of his problems, to understand himself and his difficulties, or to appraise the available ways out of his current difficulty. One may generalize from experience that the relationship in counseling does not need to be as pervasive and involved as one would experience in psychoanalysis or any other type of deep therapeutic relationship. Nevertheless, the affect climate must be perceptibly present if counseling is to achieve effectiveness.

A second dimension of this personal relationship stems from the fact that many of the developmental problems of the counselee arise out of his disturbances or conflicts among value options he has open to him for adoption as his dominant guiding motivations. Some of these disturbances may be very profound and pathological and, therefore, may require some form of deep and prolonged psychotherapy rather than counseling. But even in the simpler kinds of disturbances, these conflicting feelings may thwart or restrict the individual's motivation to take confident and aggressive control of his own development. In such cases, within the friendly climate of the counseling interview, the individual may need modified and simplified relationship therapy before he can face his problems clear-headedly.

The Counselor Teacher

All of these and others are necessary dimensions of counseling relationships. Man is, we now believe, a feeling individual, and his affect is a most necessary and normal dimension of his individuality. And helping clients "feel good" is a basic goal of counseling. But for me, a most essential and distinctive feature of counseling is its problem-solving dimension with respect to objective difficulties in the external world and also with regard to associated, subjective, affect disturbances. In our culture, man not only is trying to "feel good" but he also seeks to become and to maintain himself as a rational, problem-solving being. True, his affect usually interferes with his attempts to be rational, and he may become so highly irrational that his rationality needs to be clarified and restructured before he can regain his rational posture and process. And, moreover, his affect, especially when it is of the "right" kind, is constantly a most necessary source of motivation in his behavior as a rational problem-solving individual. Thus, affect is never disassociated from rationality and the two are intimately interrelated, sometimes in a negative way, but usually in a positive, harnessed-tandem-way, so that one reinforces the other or there is a reciprocating relationship of some sort.

In counseling, the counselor as a teacher helps the individual learn how to use problem-solving approaches and techniques in approximating control of his own development. In schoolmen's terminology, the "curriculum" of counseling, as I choose to call it, is the individual himself and his own style of living, his mistakes and his "correct" responses in relationships with others. In counseling, he is turning upon himself his own intelligence or rationality in trying to use certain canons of logic and certain psychological insights so that he approximates, but seldom fully achieves, rationality in controlling his own life. Thus he seeks to approximate his "right" and his opportunity to achieve freedom to become his real self through liberation from the handicap of ignorance of self and through freedom from other obstacles to his full development.

The role of the counselor is clear then—to teach or help the individual learn to understand and accept himself in terms of capabilities, aptitudes and interests; to identify his own motivations and techniques of living; to appraise them in terms of their implications or consequences; and, when appropriate, to substitute more adequate behavior to achieve desired life satisfactions that the individual has set as his personal goal. The role of the counselee is to use himself as a curriculum of learning how to understand himself and his complex motivations and complex techniques of living, the consequences of his behavior, and to correct those techniques which produce the responses he does not wish to achieve. He also seeks to learn substitute responses which bring the kind of results and consequences in his life that he desires and which add further to his own richness of liberating relationships with other individuals.

Of course, he is not entirely or absolutely self contained or self sufficient in his own life objectives and life style, because he needs perforce to modify his inner impulses by virtue of his membership in groups and societies and his interrelationships with other individuals in school, home, and community. And it is this interaction with other individuals (and within himself) which he learns to analyze and comprehend, correct, and modify in the counseling interview—a sort of microcosm set apart and structured in a way that he can see and feel himself in a friendly way and without threat to his own security. Through mastery of the techniques of understanding and controlling the interview microcosm, he is preparing for the real task of transferring those skills and confidences to the outside world of interpersonal relationships which perforce require adjustment to and incorporation of external standards and guiding principles of behavior.

The interactions of the counselee and counselor are, therefore, those of teacher and learner, and it is a highly personalized teaching and learning process in which, sometimes, the communication is not only oral but contextual and situational as well. On some occasions, the relationship may be characterized as direct teaching through explicit explanations, suggestions of possible hypotheses, assistance in searching for relevant facts (aptitudes, interests, motives, etc.) that illuminate the counselee's problems, and so on. On other occasions, the teaching method may be one of friendly, encouraging listening. And, not infrequently, the counselee takes the posture of teacher of himself. That is, the counselee may use the carefully structured universe of the interview to "practice-teach" himself how to understand such a one as he is and how to attain maturity with such a repertoire of capabilities and motivations as he, the counselee, now is able to perceive himself to have. Such practice sessions permit him to stand off and look at himself in an objective manner—a perspective often difficult to produce except in the warm and rational ecology of interpersonal relationships with the counselor. After *N* number of such practice sessions, he may feel confident and ready to "go it alone," thus unifying and integrating within himself the counselor-counselee roles. That is, he then becomes his own teacher to an extent determined by his own potentialities and other controlling circumstances. And he thus approximates a working integration sufficient for further development and satisfying in the consequent behavior results.

Values and Goals in Counseling

Now, with such a rough model before us, let me explore the role of value orientation in counseling. A most complex and often confusing question now arises when we seek to assess or even to identify the goals or objectives sought through counseling. Sometimes we pose our question: are any goals of students' development properly predetermined; or do they arise, *sui generis,* in the counseling process itself; and, are goals set solely by the counselee himself? Let us examine our model of counseling in terms of this question of goals—a most crucial question in understanding value counseling. And immediately we face these subordinate questions: To what purposes and outcomes do we lend our services as counselors? Are they outcomes of a type that we can justify and accept? Are they socially useful for the "common good," and are they "good" for the individual?

In phrasing such questions, we remind ourselves that in counseling we have long accepted as tribal dogma the generalization that counselors should not express negative value orientation or disapproval, that is, condemnation of anything the counselee says or does, has done, or will do. This dictum reflects the common observation that we counselors greatly weaken our effectiveness, especially in dealing with clients who are in conflict with others, if we scold, admonish, order, preach, or otherwise intrude upon the counselee's search for understanding and resolution of his problems.

Now, while we all may agree that such expressions of condemnation or exhortation have no place in a counselor's office, it does not necessarily follow that we need approve a counselor's maintenance of value neutrality in relation to the client's self-concept, ideals, behavior, and interpersonal relationships. Yet, such a doctrine of value neutrality sometimes may be extended to the total developmental pattern of the counselee, perhaps on the supposition that the desirable goal, ". . . the development of each person in all ways to his fullest possible extent," can best be reached if we minimize disruptive external interference.

Such a goal in human development, given recent restatement by Lloyd-Jones and Smith, who explicitly advocate value orientation, is one that most educators and counselors would be happy to see achieved. And it has been highly productive of concepts, motivations and programs of action in counseling. But a re-examination of some of its implicit assumptions has been made by these same authors. I follow their lead in re-examining the contention that counselors need be neutral with respect to outcomes of the counseling process. For example, if we should accept the above statement of objectives unqualifiedly, we seem to be embracing the doctrine that all growth is acceptable if it meets only two conditions, "in all ways," and the "fullest possible extent." Such a doctrine would smack of the contention that any and all forms of growth contain within themselves their own, and sufficient, justification. But some doubting questions would then arise concerning acceptance of such a universal doctrine: Have we come to view optimum development as justified without regard to standards and forms that bend it toward a "good" goal rather than toward a "bad" end? Do we counselors believe that in counseling "anything goes" or that any kind of development behavior is as good as any other? Do we believe that the fullest growth of one individual inevitably enhances the fullest growth of all other individuals? Are there no relevant and valid standards of growth in individuality? Must any individual choose between the bipolar opposites of absolute autonomy of an individual and object and supine conformity of the individual to someone's (or society's) imposed standards of development—are there no other options to choose in developing one's life?

And do we conclude, then, that the illumination and acceptance of standards and limits as guiding principles of development is irrelevant, if not inhibiting, in counseling? Could it be that such an open-ended objective has shackled us with the impediment of "perpetual rotation" around the limited starting point of absolutistic and autonomous self-direction, long since identified and found deficient by Bode with respect to an education that is unattached to a philosophy, or at least not to an explicit one?

These questions may motivate us to consider important implications for both the techniques and the goals we choose in counseling: what part should expression of society's and the counselor's value orientation play in the counseling situation? Acceptance of the extended doctrine of neutrality would lead many to answer, "None!" Yet I question whether counselors, at least those who work in schools and colleges, can meet their professional obligations if they remain, to paraphrase Carmichael, merely spectators or neutral observers in viewing education and its role in society.

The Need for Values

In my exploration of the place of value orientation in counseling, I am not wise enough to have found a single, final answer, but I have reached a point of view regarding the necessity of commitment to the moral and social purposes of counseling. And I am comforted in my long study of this neglected dimension of counseling by Paul Meehl's conclusion: "A rigorous, sophisticated consideration of the ethics of therapeutic 'guidance'—by workers competent in axiology and casuistry is long overdue. Current thinking on this topic is almost wholly confined to clichés." [1]

In my present search for a formulation of value orientation concerning the outcomes of counseling, I shall first consider whether it is necessary, or desirable, for the counselor to eliminate value judgments from the counseling interview in order to give to clients necessary freedom to investigate and solve their problems responsibly.

We might begin by asking whether we can in fact ever detach our behavior from our own and society's values in any situation. According to Taylor's definition of a value as ". . . an idea on which people act, or a principle on which they judge how to act," [2] we cannot, since every choice and action must be based upon explicit or implicit acceptance of a value. Even the most rigorously disciplined scientist, who supposedly must divorce his values from his work in order to maintain objectivity, cannot function independently of his values. Smith has said:

> . . . the claim to a value-free science when it goes beyond insistence on a disciplined regard for fact whether or not it accords with our wishes, only obscures the value elements in the choice of problem of research setting, of conceptual framework, in the decision as to when to rest with negative findings, when results are reportable, and so on endlessly.[3]

[1] From Paul E. Meehl, *Annual Review of Psychology*, Annual Reviews, Inc., Stanford, California, 1955. Vol. 6, p. 373. Quotation reprinted with permission.

[2] From Harold Taylor, *On Education and Freedom*, Abelard-Schuman Ltd., New York, London, Toronto, 1954, pp. 208. Quotation reprinted with permission.

[3] From M. Brewster Smith, "Toward Scientific and Professional Responsibility," *American Psychologist*, **9**, 515, 1954. Quotation reprinted with permission of the author and publisher.

Conant, too, suggests that we do not act without revealing, implicitly or explicitly, subjectively chosen values which are based upon "personal experience and its prolongation by history." He goes on to say:

> . . . I doubt the ability of most people to escape from some elements of a conceptual scheme which is keyed to human conduct, to moral principles or ethical rules, and to value judgments.[4]

Values Are Inevitable

If we agree that value judgments are implicit in every action we take, we should also agree that counselors cannot fully escape introducing their own value systems into the counseling interview. While the counselor's moral and ethical standards may not be made clear to clients, or even to the counselor himself, they are influential in his reactions to the client's story, his emphases, his choice of objectives and counseling method, and in the techniques he uses to carry out the chosen method of interviewing.

Further thinking reveals that while the techniques used by a counselor depend partly upon his own assumptions concerning desirable outcomes of counseling, yet these assumptions are not the only set of values helping to determine his methods and objectives. Indeed, for the school counselor, the prevailing beliefs within the college or school system concerning the nature of human nature, the aims of education, and the place and purpose of counseling will determine in some measure the objectives toward which the counselor is expected to direct his efforts, and the techniques which he is expected to employ. While the private practitioner in counseling would, at first glance, seem to be freed of such guide lines in his relationships with clients, I believe that further examination will identify some "outer" limits of his freedom from responsibility for influencing the

[4] From James B. Conant, *Modern Science and Modern Man*, Doubleday & Co., 1953, p. 181. Reprinted with permission of the author and Columbia University Press (copyright holder).

client to choose one behavior standard rather than another. But that is another story.

It seems clear to me that we cannot and indeed should not attempt to eliminate some consideration of values from the counseling situation. It is also clear, so it seems to me, that the standards and attitudes of society and those prevailing in the counselor's educational institution, as well as those of the counselor himself, will be reflected in the counselor's behavior throughout each interview. And such a reflection need not be, but can sometimes be under some circumstances, an undue or inhibiting influence upon the client's efforts to assume control of his own development.

It is not enough, however, to recognize that one's value orientation determines behavior. Action is irresponsibly taken in spite of this recognition, according to Smith, unless the values, assumptions, and goals underlying the action are investigated and as clearly as possible understood. Smith makes the point in these words:

> . . . a person acts responsibly to the extent that his behavior meets at least these conditions: First, he is aware of the value context in which he is acting. His goals have been subjected to conscious scrutiny, and his behavior is explicitly related to his values. Second, his choices are made in the light of as adequate an understanding of their probable consequences as he can achieve. The relations that he assumes between means and ends are examined critically, not taken for granted. Third, he is ready to be judged in terms of his choices of both ends and means, and has the flexibility to reconsider both. In a word, he assumes responsibility for his decisions and actions.[5]

This definition of responsibility as applied to counselors has several implications in relation to our present subject. It implies, among other things, that counselors

[5] *Op cit.*, p. 513.

need to understand explicitly their objectives and to examine the technology with which they have been preoccupied in terms of its relevance to these objectives. It implies, too, that clients—who, like counselors, act in terms of recognized or unrecognized values—need to learn to identify and understand the implications of their moral and ethical codes and other value orientations in order to act responsibly. And these two implications suggest the second question I want to consider here: Is it a proper function of counseling to help students learn to identify and accept commitment to their value orientation and to accept responsibility for behavior derived from that orientation?

With respect to counseling that takes place in an educational setting or institution, my analysis of the identification of desirable end-goals is based on the assumption that counseling is a central, not a peripheral, part of democratic education. In my opinion, the objectives of counseling in educational institutions are bound up with those of education in general, especially with respect to the societal responsibility of education to influence the pattern of development being achieved by students. Then the question arises whether education in general should be concerned with students' development of and commitment to values. It seems to me that it must be, if it is to help students prepare for adulthood which will be satisfying and useful to them and to their associates in home and community. As Feigl contends: ". . . The aims of education presuppose some ideals of human nature and . . . such ideals are supported by value judgments." [6]

Variety of Values

Much of present day counseling takes place in an educational context and is directed toward the goal of

[6] From Herbert Feigl, *Fifty Fourth Yearbook of the National Society for the Study of Education:* Part 1, *Modern Philosophies and Education.* Chicago, 1955, pp. 324, 336. Quotation reprinted with permission of the author and publisher.

facilitating the development of maturity in student clients. And I contend that counselors, as educators, should modify our current open-ended concept of autonomously self-determined development by incorporating in our concept of desirable objectives of counseling a variety of "loose-fitting" (*i.e.*, neither rigid nor prescribed) dimensions which diverse experiences indicate may be desirable in our type of pluralistic democratic society. The client's search for a variety of optional and desirable models would give new richness, it seems to me, to our teaching usefulness as counselors. And because of our cultural and value pluralism, we are, I believe, in little danger of constructing a rigid and universal orthodoxy to which each counselee will need to commit himself.

In using the phrase, variety of "loose-fitting" (*i.e.*, not rigid or prescribed) goals, I have in mind, among others, such value standards as those suggested by Taylor and Feigl in their discussion of the necessity of infusing education with explicit moral values.

> There are moral values to be found in the student's experience which he cannot avoid accepting—the value of reason, of honorable conduct, of cooperation. If he refuses to accept them, he cannot remain a student. There are other moral values—courage, independence, charity, generosity, sensitivity—which he may not find in his experience as a student, but which he should find there if he is to be truly educated.[7]

Feigl suggests other dimensions of the individual that education should develop:

> In addition to these ideas of rational thought and conduct, education should foster the development of constructive and benevolent attitudes. It should help

[7] Harold Taylor, *op. cit.*, p. 35.

every individual in maintaining a sufficiently high level of aspiration for self-perfection.[8]

I repeat, we need not restrict ourselves to the outcomes advocated by these two observers of education. Nor need we advocate that counselors should persuade student clients to commit themselves to these or any other particular values. Indeed, I quote them only as authority for the general contention that each student in education should be aided to explicate his own self-developing guide lines for his motivated behavior and to choose those that will further his optimum development and that of his associates and community. On the latter obligation, Dewey had this to say: "But if democracy has moral and ideal meaning, it is that a social return be demanded from all. . . ."[9]

It appears that to think of counseling as non-value-bound is contradictory so long as counselors function in facilitating an individual's development within the limits imposed by his social situation. We are, rather, in the business of helping each client to choose (his own choice) to become one kind of person rather than another and to approximate an integrated concept of his universe which will correlate and give meaning to his life and that of others, and which will provide guiding principles or values to influence his daily behavior.

Self Determination of Values

And now that we agree, perhaps, that providing orientation and education in values is an important function of counseling, there remains the question of how the counselor deals with values in the counseling interview. In this paper I shall merely make a few points; in another paper I hope to explore and examine techniques more critically. In the first place, the counselor, of course, conducts himself in the interview in a way in which his behavior itself exemplifies and illuminates his own commitments to

[8] M. Brewster Smith, *op. cit.*, p. 336.
[9] J. Dewey, *Democracy and Education*, Macmillan, New York, 1916.

certain personal and professional values—for example, respect for integrity of the student, clarity of perception in self-evaluation, the individual's freedom of choice of value orientation, and many others. Thus behavior manifestations are of course a technique of "teaching" (influencing) students to give consideration to "choosing" to adopt for themselves such value orientation.

Secondly, a central guide line for counselors in schools and colleges in their search for effective roles in value orientation is the fact that others who work with adolescents may have achieved greater competence and acceptance in this area of human development and relationships than we have yet or may ever achieve. Thus, we counselors need to avoid disruptive and forced intrusion into the privacy and primacy of the relationships of students with home and church. In particular, we need to explore in cordial, not competitive, consultation with pastors, religious workers, and others long active in this dimension of human development the ways through which we counselors may forge our own unique roles with maximum teamwork relationships in our common task.

In the third place, counselors need to safeguard their role in value orientation with respect to the sensitivity of adherents of some religious beliefs to external review by "outsiders" and the penchant of some counselors to become critical of those value systems which are related to beliefs and values personally not held or advocated by the counselor in his private life. With regard to these and other aspects, the counselor needs to respect the client's right of self determination of his value orientation, as is the case with vocational orientation and other choices of a free individual in Western culture.

Turning to the positive aspects of the counselor's interviewing role, there appear to be a number of approaches, some effective and others ineffective, in which the counselor, as educator, may handle values in his relationships with his client in the voluntarily sought and maintained counseling interview. He may, for example, use the propaganda method in arguing for a predetermined set of values in order to impose these values upon the individual. He may also use persuasion to influence the client in the "right" direction. But it is well established in the experiences of counselors that these are the very antithesis of the proper techniques to be used. Indeed, counseling in educational institutions, in many of its aspects, arose as a protest against impositional methods of forcing the individual to adopt a given value orientation. While imposition may be necessary in some institutional situations, yet it is by no means the preferred counseling method with respect to value orientation in the usual counseling relationship.

On the other hand, sometimes counselors may be tempted to argue logically for the "right" value orientation. Now, while argument may have the virtue of making rationally clear to the student the basis for a value system so that he can, if he likes, accept it at least intellectually with some degree of independence, this method is still unlikely to provide the student with a deeply meaningful learning experience which will have lasting effect.

Evaluating Values

In contrast, the most effective and acceptable counseling method aids students in applying to the problem of values those techniques, analysis, clarification, and understanding which we hope they will habitually apply to the solution of other developmental problems. That is, the counselor helps the individual to use his intellect and his emotions to analyze his developmental situation and to identify the pivotal point of the issue—in this case, values as sources of behavior motivation and determination. Then the counselor, as teacher, helps the counselee to identify and to evaluate alternative value systems and to examine the consequences of alternative answers to moral and ethical questions. The counselor's role as teacher is thus emphasized, as is the student's role as one who explores issues, chooses, and acts upon values, and subsequently experiences the consequences of his choices. In many respects the counselors' techniques are similar to those used in counseling students about vocational, educational, and other developmental problems.

I add at this point my own opinion that a counselor may, as a teacher sometimes does, illustrate the range of possible value choices by explaining as objectively as possible his own, or others, value approach to life's questions. True, this procedure is not always appropriate, since the counselor's experience may not be relevant to the problems faced by a given student, or the student may not be interested in the counselor's point of view. But when it is appropriate, it seems to me that the counselor need not hesitate to make clear his own position, so long as he avoids persuading or influencing the student to imitate him.

One point needs further emphasis in the use of each technique of counseling about value options, a point stressed by Taylor in these words:

> Freedom defined in a personal sense consists in an attitude, to oneself and to authority. It rests on the conviction that each person has the right to make up his own mind about the truth of an idea on the basis of the best evidence he can find, and that he must retain the right to choose his own course of action within the limits of an accepted social framework.[10]

That is, in counseling about values, as in the case of vocational and educational counseling, we limit ourselves to helping a student understand the options open to him, one with his capabilities and responsibilities, and their implications for him. At that point, within the framework of institutional and societal responsibilities and limitations, the student is free to make his own choice from these or other options. The choice is his and his alone (as is also the responsibility for the consequences of that choice), and this is itself a moral principle we hold precious in our

[10] *Op. cit.*, pp. 118–119.

pluralistic democracy. I have always thought it unnecessary (because of obvious validity) to argue for the student's right to make his own decision about any problem. But I have long held that the exercising of such a right does not preclude "direct" assistance from counselors, or anyone else, prior to and after choices have been made.

Summary

I have argued that counseling cannot be independent of values, whether or not we would like to make it free. Rather is counseling, especially in an educational institution, value-oriented and not open-ended both regarding the goals sought through aspirations and strivings of both counselor and student within their counseling relationship. And I have further argued for making explicit our own value orientations as individual counselors, not in order that we may adopt a counselor's orthodox creed, but rather that we may responsibly give societal and moral direction to our individual work in terms of the explicitly desired goals chosen by our student clients. I have suggested that we accept the "teaching" of values as a function of counselors, but that we remain aware of the risk of imposing a set of values upon a student and of thus depriving him of his right to and responsibility for self-determination. Rather should we aid him in using rational and emotional clarity in facing his problems, so that he may choose from among a variety of guides to action those which seem promising to him in leading to forward development in him and in his relationships with others. For one individual, this may mean adherence to or new adoption of a code of values, formal, religious or otherwise. For another client, it may mean the choice of a less formally structured and comprehensive value system. In any case, the counselor will have helped teach the counselee how to understand more clearly his own value orientation and how to guide his behavior more rationally and constructively in terms of the standards he has chosen.

Editor's Note

Introducing the topic of religion may further embarrass the counselor already concerned about differences in value systems. A more basic philosophy of life can scarcely be imagined than one giving meaning and purpose to existence. Psychology and religion are not inimical: they play supporting roles in the development of the mature person. The counselor should no more ignore religion than any other personality potential which can be used constructively. His task is to help the client integrate into his pattern of living whatever positive convictions he possesses.

37. Psychology, Religion, and Values for the Counselor *

C. Gilbert Wrenn
University of Minnesota

The postulate of this paper is that religion and psychology complement each other. Psychology contributes to an understanding of the *nature* of self and of one's relationships with others, religion to an understanding of meaning and purpose in life, and the *significance* of these same relationships. Both may contribute to more effective living. Their purposes are parallel and supporting, not antagonistic. The psychologist conceives of emotional maturity as including an awareness of others, as a development beyond infantile Narcissism toward social perceptivity. The religious counselor speaks of one's concern for others as an extension of the love of God for us. One is concerned in a pragmatic sense with social development which contributes to personality integration, the other with purposeful concern for those who are brothers in the family of man. The personality goal for the client of each has much in common with the other.

*** From C. G. Wrenn. Psychology, religion, and values for the counselor. (Symposium: The counselor and his religion, Part III.) *Personnel & Guid. J.*, 1958, 36, 331–334. Reprinted with permission of the author and publisher.**

Psychology (in its therapeutic sense) can be more effective if it considers the place of religious values and relationships in a client since these attitudes and values are as real as are aptitudes and skills. They cannot be disregarded. Beyond this, to be sure, psychology can meet some human needs that cannot be met by religion. An understanding of *self* involves, perhaps, a different discipline than an understanding of *life*. A counselor [1] uses his particular psychological knowledges and skills to help a person understand himself better, his life realities, his daily behavior, his personality potentials. Upon occasion, and if he deems himself competent, he deals with repressed feelings and experiences and attempts to secure better self-acceptance on the part of the client, some resolution of inner conflicts and anxieties. This *is* psychology's domain, the application of what is known about behavior to client needs, the use of relationship and communication procedures in a manner that is a normal outgrowth of the counselor's unique personality style. He may or may not (and this decision is important) go beyond this and assist the client in an understanding of life's purposes and meanings, and the alternate ways in which one may relate oneself to the Infinite.

The Counselor and Religion

Most counselors would accept what I have just written about the psychological functions of the counselor. But does he have any religious functions? This question brings

[1] A counseling psychologist is a psychologist who has had special emphasis on counseling in his professional education and in his practice. The counseling psychologist, as distinct from other psychologists, is concerned primarily with developmental counseling, with appraisal of potentials and assets, with the client's understanding of and integration with social reality, with the various roles played by the client in different areas of life, with client awareness of his own dynamics and of the nature of his psychological defenses. And the counselor, in the sense used in this paper, is a person with at least modest psychological knowledge and sophistication. Some recent statements on counselor and counseling psychologists are found in Wrenn, Perry, and Committee on Definition.

out the goose pimples on any counselor—including the writer! I do not know just what these functions are but I am sure that counselors can no longer act as though religion —the client's and the counselor's—does not exist. We are fearful of admitting religion into our professional thinking for a variety of reasons—the emotional imbalance involved in some religions, the seeming artificiality in others, the exclusive attention that has been given in the professional education of the counselor to the empirical and the intellectual with a consequent neglect of the spiritual and the aesthetic, the counselor's own religious insecurity or his failure to convert creed (belief) and cult (ritual) into conduct. These threats to the counselor's peace of mind still do not deny the reality of religious problems among clients, or keep him from a further fear that he is neglecting a resource that might be tapped in the interests of his client.

Mowrer clearly points up the danger in neglecting religion as a resource because we have been so much under the influence (and properly so) of objective and analytic psychology in the development of psychology as a field of study. Both objective psychologists and analysts, writes Mowrer, have erred in making the mind a product of or a servant of the body in assuming that mind (or spirit) has no independent and autonomous function and existence. All is not well with behaviorists and psychoanalysts who cling to this barren rock. Rather than to be objective and to study *about* religion or to reduce it to a form of psychopathology, religion might well be considered as something having *psychological survival value*. It is now being studied as a resource and as having survived because it has developed in response to man's unique personality needs.

It is hard for the counselor to brush aside the significance of this resource when he hears deeply serious and influential psychiatrists of the National Academy of Religion and Mental Health [2] making such statements as

[2] *About the National Academy of Religion and Mental Health.* The National Academy, New York, Academy of Medicine Bld., 2 E. 103rd St., N. Y. 29, 1956. Reprinted with permission.

these: "What a man believes is a factor in his emotional health. The problems of mental illness include the disorganization of an individual's philosophy of life. It concerns the sufferer's attitude toward the world and other people. . . . Religion has always, in many times and many places, played its part in healing. The ultimate values of mankind are spiritual."

Or these: "The Academy does not advocate psychiatric treatment by the ministry, or religious instruction by psychiatrists. It seeks to discover and make known, for the benefit of the people and the professions, the psychiatric and religious resources now available and usable in developing healthy emotional attitudes, in preventing mental illness, and in healing."

The counselor does not need to know the concern of the psychiatrist about religion or to have authority invoked, however, to be convinced. All that he needs is a little reflection on the place of religion in the thoughts and feelings of people, its incalculable potential for societal welfare, the need among young people for an enduring and integrated value structure, a memory recall of clients and students who have been troubled about their place in life, their significance as human beings. All he needs to do is to reflect upon his own uneasiness when confronted by his client with problems of religion. This is an uneasiness that may spring from his own religious immaturity or from his uncertainty about the appropriateness of communicating what are to him personal certainties.

Many of us do not know how to manage *ourselves* in counseling when the client appears to have a religious need. Can we continue to be accepting or should we propound our faith? Can we be empathic and nonjudgmental and still keep faith *with* our faith? Arbuckle [3] deals sympathetically with this problem in his discussion of those who consider "client-centered" counseling as antagonistic to re-

[3] Dugald Arbuckle, *Student Personnel Services in Higher Education*, McGraw-Hill Book Company, Inc., New York, 1953, pp. 170–177. Reprinted with permission of the author and publisher.

ligious counseling which should be "God-centered." He writes that "client-centered" is not "self-centered" and that whether one is troubled about religious counseling in this sense depends upon both one's concept of God and one's concept of the process of counseling.

What may a counselor do about religion—his own and others? These things at least:

1. Study the significance of religion, positive and negative, in personality development.
2. Be prepared, by thought in advance, to deal with religious problems as permissively and thoughtfully as he would any other emotion-laden experience of the client—marriage relations, parental relations, sexual experiences and fears, repressed guilt, shyly expressed hopes and dreams.
3. Clarify his own religious experience so that immaturity and confusion here will not act as an interference in the counseling relationship.

Values, Ethics, and Religion

As "life in these United States" becomes more complex and our relation to the other parts of the world more intimate, the need for meanings and purposes becomes more urgent, the possession of a carefully considered value system becomes a requirement. A clinical psychologist's discussion of the relation of values to mental health, involving the phenomenon of "value lag," is found in a recent article by Korner. He is concerned with the reluctance with which the social scientist in the past has dealt with values, speaks of the matrix of values within which the adjustment mechanisms function to protect the ego from value conflict and value lag, touches on the difference between short-term values and stable values. The discussion is well worth reading (his "arteriosclerotic" and "super ego deadwood" values must be read to be appreciated) but I am here concerned with Korner's stable, "relatively immutable," values and their relation to religion.

Several years ago I attempted to point up the central ethical conflict with which counselors are often confronted, loyalty to the integrity of the counselor-counselee relationship versus loyalty to society and to the institution of society for which one may work—the integrity of the individual or the integrity of the state? Do I keep faith with the confidence of my client, or tell my boss what he is demanding to know? The adopted code of ethics of the American Psychological Association from which I made my adaptation to the ethics of the counselor is based upon the value system of our American culture.

But such a code of ethics merely defines the problem, it does not solve it. When a person is faced with a conflict of loyalties he is thrown back upon his own personal values, those convictions and beliefs of what is "most right," which are in part, at least, the product of his religious experience. "Each man has his own pattern of values —(but) back of these personal values, which are sometimes pitted against those of his society, is another set of values. These are part of our great human heritage, great principles of truth and mercy and justice that are as yet, and perhaps always will be, only dimly understood." Systematic and dedicated religious thinking is the source of much of our mature values system and a thoughtful religious faith appears to the writer to be the best of backlog resources for a counselor when problems of ethics arise.

In conclusion, allow me to comment upon what appears to me to be the psychological pertinence of many value statements. Values are the tested outcome of experience and have proved their pragmatic worth. They would necessarily be reflections of behavior. But so frequently do psychologists eschew value considerations, that it seems desirable to point out that *values do not necessarily exist in a non-psychological world.* Some years ago I heard Dr. Kenneth Brown, Director of the Danforth Foundation, speak on a hierarchy of values that made much psychological sense. There are no notes of this address available to me but three points are recalled as at the apex of a hierarchy of values in our culture: (1) Man is distinguished from all other creatures by his endless quest for the ultimate, his never-ceasing search for the absolute in truth and beauty; (2) Each human being is to be respected for [his] own personal worth; (3) Living is giving, life is a service, growth is through giving of self not through withholding. These are value statements to be sure, but they have a pragmatic psychological integrity as well.

More recently I have tried to state concisely some principles of human relations that I have used in both educational and industrial consulting work, principles that can be justified psychologically. As one reads these, they also appear to be value statements. In either sense they may be useful to the counselor as he deals with colleagues and family as well as with clients. Behavior objectives such as these are a stiff test of one's psychological sophistication as well as of one's religious maturity. (1) I shall strive to see the positive in the other person and praise it at least as often as I notice that which is to be corrected; (2) If I am to correct or criticize someone's action I must be sure that this is seen by the other as a criticism of a specific behavior and not as a criticism of himself as a person; (3) I will assume that each person can see some reasonableness in his behavior, that there is meaning in it for him if not for me; (4) When I contribute to another person's self-respect I increase his positive feelings toward me and his respect for me; (5) To at least one person, perhaps many, I am a person of significance, and he is affected vitally by my recognition of him and my good will toward him.

CHAPTER 12

Future Man

How does man fit into the pattern of an orderly universe? Is he the crowning achievement of a continuing creative process or an unruly offshoot bent upon frustrating his own existence? Considering the history of human failure and "man's inhumanity to man," what lies in store for him in future millenniums? At first glance it might seem more appropriate to address these questions to someone claiming preternatural knowledge of future events or the coming of doomsday. Should science be concerned at all with such tenuous problems?

Although it is impossible to predict with certainty the course of human progress in the scores of centuries that lie ahead, extrapolating evolutionary and behavioral trends into the future might prove instructive. Nor is this a matter of idle curiosity. Intelligent planning of any kind bears some resemblance to gazing into the crystal ball. Man has reached a stage of development where he may be able to assume an active role in his future evolution. The use of tools has already made unnecessary any further specialization of his hands or limbs and cooked food has resulted in a recession of the lower jaw. Modern communications and such organizations as the UN may be harbingers of an era of man's intensive cultivation of his social nature with consequent changes that will be reflected in his intellectual interests and interpersonal relationships.

Short-range predictions may prove to be of greater utility. Enough is known of the dynamics of society to offer hope for a world culture better suited to the tastes and needs of humanity current at any given time. Painful cultural lags are no more inevitable than the prospect of moral decay. John W. Gardner[1] reflects that, "We understand better than ever before how and why an aging society loses its adaptiveness and stifles creativity in its members. And we are beginning to comprehend the conditions under which a society may renew itself."

Transformation of the individual person is likely to proceed at a quicker pace. A great volume of scientific data on the precedents of behavior, not available to earlier generations, is daily accumulating. Important questions are being answered about the climate of child training that nurtures spontaneity and creative talent, the kind of self-images compatible with self-confidence and a sense of responsibility, the exhilarating as well as the stultifying effects of competition, the use of authority to foster inner growth rather than repression, and similar aspects of personality development. In one of the readings in this chapter Rogers points out the desirability of using our knowledge of psychology to help ". . . individuals become more self-responsible, make progress in self-actualization, become more flexible, more unique and varied, more creatively adaptive."

Where will evolution of the individual eventually lead? If we trace the history of human culture from the earliest glimmerings of civilization to the present, it should not be too difficult to project the curve of man's development some thousands of years into the future. Beyond that, we can only ponder with Teilhard de Chardin,[2] "Our *modern*[3] world was created in less than 10,000 years and in the past 200 years it has changed more than in all the preceding millennia. Have we ever thought of what our planet may be like, psychologically, in a million years time?"

[1] J. W. Gardner. *Self-renewal: The individual and the innovative society*. New York: Harper & Row, 1964. P. xiv.

[2] P. Teilhard de Chardin. *The future of man*. New York: Harper & Row, 1964. P. 71.

[3] Italics added by the editor.

Editor's Note

If the lowest common denominator of human motivation could be extracted, it would probably be a function of influencing people. Few things we do beyond surviving are understandable in the absence of such a motive. Nor is there much doubt about the human urge for power. Lacking examples from political history, we could always fall back on our own experience of suffering under the authority of minor officials.

Little wonder, then, that recent experiments promising almost unlimited control over people have aroused so much uneasiness. Drugs, stimulation of brain areas, and conditioning suggest the possibility of making people do approximately what one wishes while they remain content with a condition of servitude. The fanciful power of fairy godmothers and witches, harmless enough in children's story books, now threatens to become a reality How will it be used once nature's secrets are unlocked Presuming we choose the role of the kindly spirit, what course of action should we take? One that manipulates the individual from birth to make him happy according to some predetermined plan? Or one dedicated to raising the individual to new heights of freedom and dignity?

There is some reassurance in the suggestion of Carl Rogers that a cold, impersonal "Science" cannot make such a decision. Only people can.

38. The Place of the Person in the New World of the Behavioral Sciences *

Carl R. Rogers
Western Behavioral Sciences Institute
La Jolla, California
formerly University of Wisconsin

The science of psychology, in spite of its immaturities and its brashness, has advanced mightily in recent decades. From a concern with observation and measure-

* From C. R. Rogers. The place of the person in the new world of the behavioral sciences. *Personnel Guid. J.*, **34,** 442–451. Reprinted with permission of the author and publisher.

ment it has increasingly moved toward becoming an "if-then" science. By this I mean it has become more concerned with the discernment and discovery of lawful relationships such that *if* certain conditions exist, *then* certain behaviors will predictably follow. It is rapidly increasing the number of areas or situations in which it may be said that if certain describable, measurable conditions are present or are established, then predictable, definable behaviors are learned or produced.

Now in one sense every educated person is aware of this. But it seems to me that few are aware of the breadth, depth, and extent of these advances in psychology and the behavioral sciences. And still fewer seem to be aware of the profound social, political, ethical, and philosophical problems posed by these advances. I would like to focus on some of the implications of these advances.

Let me venture first to review a few selected examples of what I mean by the increased ability of psychology to understand and predict or control behavior. I have chosen them to illustrate the wide range of behaviors involved. I shall summarize and greatly simplify each of the illustrations, with only a suggestion of the evidence which exists. As a general statement I may say that each illustration I will give is supported by reasonably rigorous and adequate research, though like all scientific findings, each is open to modification or correction through more exact or imaginative future studies.

What then, are some of the behaviors or learnings for which we now know how to supply the antecedent conditions? I would stress that we know how to produce these effects in the same way, though not with the same exactitude, that the physicist knows how to set up the conditions under which given substances will go through a process of atomic fission or fusion. They are instances of what we know how to achieve or accomplish.

We know how to set up the conditions under which many individuals will report as true, judgments which are contrary to the evidence of their senses. They will, for example report that Figure A covers a larger area than Figure B, when the evidence of their senses *plainly* indicates that the reverse is true. Experiments by Asch later refined and improved by Crutchfield show that when a person is led to believe that everyone else in the group sees A as larger than B, then he has a strong tendency to go along with this judgment and in many instances does so with a real belief in his false report.

Not only can we predict that a certain percentage of individuals will thus yield and disbelieve their own senses, but Crutchfield has determined the personality attributes of those who will do so and by selection procedures would be able to choose a group who would almost uniformly give in to these pressures for conformity.

We know how to change the opinions of an individual in a selected direction, without his ever becoming aware of the stimuli which changed his opinion. A static, expressionless portrait of a man was flashed on a screen by Spence and Klein. They requested their subjects to note how the expression of the picture changed. Then they intermittently flashed the word "angry" on the screen, at exposures so brief that the subjects were consciously completely unaware of having seen the word. They tended, however, to see the face as becoming more angry. When the word "happy" was flashed on the screen in similar fashion, the viewers tended to see the face as becoming more happy. Thus they were clearly influenced by stimuli which registered at a subliminal level, stimuli of which the individual was not, and could not be, aware.

We can predict, from the way individuals perceive the movement of a spot of light in a dark room, whether they tend to be prejudiced or unprejudiced. There has been much study of ethnocentrism, the tendency toward a pervasive and rigid distinction between ingroups and outgroups, with hostility toward outgroups, and a submissive attitude toward, and belief in the rightness of, ingroups.

One of the theories which has developed is that the more ethnocentric person is unable to tolerate ambiguity or uncertainty in a situation. Operating on this theory Block and Block had subjects report on the degree of movement they perceived in a dim spot of light in a completely dark room. (Actually no movement occurs, but almost all individuals perceive movement in this situation.) They also gave these same subjects a test of ethnocentrism. It was found, as predicted, that those who, in successive trials, quickly established a norm for the amount of movement they perceived, tended to be more ethnocentric than those whose estimates of movement continued to show variety.

This study was repeated, with slight variation, in Australia, and the findings were confirmed and enlarged. It was found that the more ethnocentric individuals were less able to tolerate ambiguity, and saw less movement than the unprejudiced. They also were more dependent on others and when making their estimates in the company of another person, tended to conform to the judgment of that person.

Hence it is not too much to say that by studying the way the individual perceives the movement of a dim light in a dark room, we can tell a good deal about the degree to which he is a rigid, prejudiced, ethnocentric person.

We know the attitudes which, if provided by a counselor or a therapist, will be predictably followed by certain constructive personality and behavior changes in the client. Studies we have completed in recent years in the field of psychotherapy justify this statement. The findings from these studies may be very briefly summarized in the following way.

If the therapist provides a relationship in which he is (a) genuine, internally consistent; (b) acceptant, prizing the client as a person of worth; (c) empathically understanding of the client's private world of feelings and attitudes; then certain changes occur in the client. Some of these changes are: the client becomes (a) more realistic in his self-perceptions; (b) more confident and self-directing;

(c) more positively valued by himself; (d) less likely to repress elements of his experience; (e) more mature, socialized and adaptive in his behavior; (f) less upset by stress and quicker to recover from it; (g) more like the healthy, integrated, well-functioning person in his personality structure. These changes do not occur in a control group and appear to be definitely associated with the client's being in a relationship with these qualities.

We know how to provide animals with a most satisfying experience consisting entirely of electrical stimulation. Olds has found that he can implant tiny electrodes in the septal area of the brain of laboratory rats. When one of these animals presses a bar in his cage, it causes a minute current to pass through these electrodes. This appears to be such a rewarding experience that that animal goes into an orgy of bar pressing, often until he is exhausted. Whatever the subjective nature of the experience it seems to be so satisfying that the animal prefers it to any other activity. I will not speculate as to whether this procedure might be applied to human beings, nor what, in this case, its consequence would be.

We know how to provide psychological conditions which will produce vivid hallucinations and other abnormal reactions in the thoroughly normal individual in the waking state. This knowledge came about as the unexpected byproduct of research at McGill University. It was discovered that if all channels of sensory stimulation are cut off or muffled, abnormal reactions follow. If healthy subjects lie motionless to reduce kinaesthetic stimuli, with eyes shielded by translucent goggles which do not permit perception, with hearing largely stifled by foam rubber pillows as well as by being in a quiet cubicle, and with tactile sensations reduced by cuffs over the hands, then hallucinations and bizarre ideation bearing some resemblance to that of the psychotic occur within a relatively short time in most subjects. What the results would be if the sensory stifling were continued longer is not known because the experience seemed so potentially dangerous that the investigators were reluctant to continue it.

I hope that these few illustrations will have given some concrete meaning to the statement that the behavioral sciences are making strides in the understanding, prediction, and control of behavior. In important ways we know how to select individuals who will exhibit certain behaviors; to establish conditions in groups which will lead to various predictable group behaviors; to establish conditions which, in an individual, will lead to specified behavioral results; and in animals our ability to understand, predict, and control goes even further, possibly foreshadowing future steps in relation to man.

If your reaction is the same as mine then you will have found that this picture I have given has its frightening as well as its strongly positive aspects. With all the immaturity of this young science, and its vast ignorance, even its present state of knowledge contains awesome possibilities. Perhaps it makes clear the reason why Robert Oppenheimer, one of the most gifted of our natural scientists, looks out from his own domain of physics, and out of the experiences in that field voices a warning. He says that there are some similarities between physics and psychology, and one of these similarities "is the extent to which our progress will create profound problems of decision in the public domain. The physicists have been quite noisy about their contributions in the last decade. The time may well come—as psychology acquires a sound objective corpus of knowledge about human behavior and feeling—when the powers of control thus available will pose far graver problems than any the physicists have posed." [1]

Among behavioral scientists it seems to be largely taken for granted that the finding of such science will be used in the prediction and control of human behavior. Yet

[1] Robert Oppenheimer, "Analogy in Science," *American Psychologist*, **II,** 127–135, 1956. Quotation reprinted with permission of the author and publisher.

most psychologists and other such scientists have given little thought to what this would mean.

I should like to try to present, as well as I can, a simplified picture of the cultural pattern which emerges if we endeavor to shape human life in terms of the behavioral sciences. This is one of two possible directions I wish to consider.

There is first of all the recognition, almost the assumption, that scientific knowledge is the power to manipulate. Dr. B. F. Skinner of Harvard says: "We must accept the fact that some kind of control of human affairs is inevitable. We cannot use good sense in human affairs unless someone engages in the design and construction of environmental conditions which affect the behavior of men." [2]

Let us look at some of the elements which are involved in the concept of the control of human behavior as mediated by the behavioral sciences. What would be the steps in the process by which a society might organize itself so as to formulate human life in terms of the science of man?

First would come the selection of goals. In a recent paper [Freedom and the control of men] Dr. Skinner suggests that one possible goal to be assigned to the behavior technology is this: "Let man be happy, informed, skillful, well-behaved, and productive." In his book, *Walden Two,* where he can use the guise of fiction to express his views, he becomes more expansive. His hero says, "Well, what do you say to the design of personalities? Would that interest you? The control of temperament? Give me the specifications, and I'll give you the man! What do you say to the control of motivation, building the interests which will make men most productive and most successful? Does that seem to you fantastic? Yet some of the techniques are available, and more can be worked out experimentally.

[2] B. F. Skinner, "Freedom and the Control of Men," *American Scholar,* **25,** 47–65, 1955–1956. Reprinted with permission of the author and copyright holder.

Think of the possibilities . . . Let us control the lives of our children and see what we can make of them." [3]

What Skinner is essentially saying here is that the current knowledge in the behavioral sciences, plus that which the future will bring, will enable us to specify, to a degree which today would seem incredible, the kind of behavioral and personality results which we wish to achieve.

The second element in this process would be one which is familiar to every scientist who has worked in the field of applied science. Given the purpose, the goal, we proceed by the method of science—by controlled experimentation—to discover the means to these ends. The method of science is self-correcting in thus arriving at increasingly effective ways of achieving the purpose we have selected.

The third element in the control of human behavior through the behavioral sciences involves the question of power. As the conditions or methods are discovered by which to achieve our goal, some person or group obtains the power to establish those conditions or use those methods. There has been too little recognition of the problem involved in this. To hope that the power which is being made available by the behavioral sciences will be exercised by the scientists, or by a benevolent group, seems to me a hope little supported by either recent or distant history.

It seems far more likely that behavioral scientists, holding their present attitudes, will be in the position of the German rocket scientists specializing in guided missiles. First they worked devotedly for Hitler to destroy Russia and the United States. Now, depending on who captured them, they work devotedly for Russia in the interest of destroying the United States, or devotedly for the United States in the interest of destroying Russia. If behavioral scientists are concerned solely with advancing their science, it seems most probable that they will serve the purposes of whatever individual or group has the power.

[3] B F. Skinner, *Walden Two*, The Macmillan Company, New York, 1948.

But this is, in a sense, a digression. The main point of this view is that some person or group will have and use the power to put into effect the methods which have been discovered for achieving the desired goal.

The fourth step in this process whereby a society might formulate its life in terms of the behavioral sciences is the exposure of individuals to the methods and conditions mentioned. As individuals are exposed to the prescribed conditions this leads, with a high degree of probability, to the behavior which has been desired. Men then become productive, if that has been the goal, or submissive, or whatever it has been decided to make them.

To give something of the flavor of this aspect of the process as seen by one of its advocates, let me again quote the hero of *Walden Two*. "Now that we *know* how positive reinforcement works, and why negative doesn't" he says, commenting on the method he is advocating, "we can be more deliberate and hence more successful, in our cultural design. We can achieve a sort of control under which the controlled, though they are following a code much more scrupulously than was ever the case under the old system, nevertheless *feel free*. They are doing what they want to do, not what they are forced to do. That's the source of the tremendous power of positive reinforcement—there's no restraint and no revolt. By a careful cultural design, we control not the final behavior, but the *inclination* to behave —the motives, the desires, the wishes. The curious thing is that in that case *the question of freedom never arises*." [4]

The Picture and Its Implications

Let me see if I can sum up very briefly the picture of the impact of the behavioral sciences upon the individual and upon society, as this impact is explicitly seen by Dr. Skinner and implied in the attitudes and work of many, perhaps most, behavioral scientists. Behavioral science is

[4] B. F. Skinner, *Walden Two*, The Macmillan Company, New York, 1948, p. 218. Quotation reprinted with permission of the author and publisher.

clearly moving forward; the increasing power for control which it gives will be held by some one or some group; such an individual or group will surely choose the purposes or goals to be achieved; and most of us will then be increasingly controlled by means so subtle we will not even be aware of them as controls. Thus whether a council of wise psychologists (if this is not a contradiction in terms) or a Stalin or a Big Brother has the power, and whether the goal is happiness, or productivity, or resolution of the Oedipus complex, or submission, or love of Big Brother, we will inevitably find ourselves moving toward the chosen goal, and probably thinking that we ourselves desire it. Thus if this line of reasoning is correct, it appears that some form of completely controlled society—a Walden Two or a 1984—is coming. The fact that it would surely arrive piecemeal rather than all at once, does not greatly change the fundamental issues. Man and his behavior would become a planned product of a scientific society.

You may well ask, "But what about individual freedom? What about the democratic concepts of the rights of the individual?" Here too Dr. Skinner is quite specific. He says quite bluntly, "The hypothesis that man is not free is essential to the application of scientific method to the study of human behavior. The free inner man who is held responsible for his behavior . . . is only a prescientific substitute for the kinds of causes which are discovered in the course of scientific analysis. All these alternative causes lie *outside* the individual." [5]

I have endeavored, up to this point, to give an objective picture of some of the developments in the behavioral sciences and an objective picture of the kind of society which might emerge out of those developments. I do however have strong personal reactions to the kind of world I have been describing, a world which Skinner explicitly

[5] B. F. Skinner, *Science and Human Behavior,* The Macmillan Company, New York, 1953, p. 447. Quotation reprinted with permission of the author and publisher.

(and many another scientist implicitly) expects and hopes for in the future. To me this kind of world would destroy the human person as I have come to know him in the deepest moments of psychotherapy. In such moments I am in relationship with a person who is spontaneous, who is responsibly free, that is, aware of his freedom to choose whom he will be and aware also of the consequences of his choice. To believe, as Skinner holds, that all this is an illusion and that spontaneity, freedom, responsibility, and choice have no real existence would be impossible for me.

I feel that to the limit of my ability I have played my part in advancing the behavioral sciences, but if the result of my efforts and those of others is that man becomes a robot, created and controlled by a science of his own making, then I am very unhappy indeed. If the good life of the future consists in so conditioning individuals through the control of their environment and through the control of the rewards they receive, that they will be inexorably productive, well behaved, happy or whatever, then I want none of it. To me this is a pseudo-form of the good life which includes everything save that which makes it good.

And so I ask myself, is there any flaw in the logic of this development? Is there any alternative view as to what the behavioral sciences might mean to the individual and to society? It seems to me that I perceive such a flaw and that I can conceive of an alternative view. These I would like to set before you.

Ends and Values in Relation to Science

It seems to me that the view I have presented rests upon a faulty perception of goals and values in their relationship to science. The significance of the *purpose* of a scientific undertaking is, I believe, grossly underestimated. I would like to state a two-pronged thesis which in my estimation deserves consideration. Then I will elaborate the meaning of these two points.

1. In any scientific endeavor—whether "pure" or

applied science—there is a prior personal subjective choice of the purpose or value which that scientific work is perceived as serving.

2. This subjective value choice which brings the scientific endeavor into being must always lie outside of that endeavor and can never become a part of the science involved in that endeavor.

Let me illustrate the first point from Dr. Skinner's writings. When he suggests that the taks for the behavioral sciences is to make man "productive," "well-behaved," etc., it is obvious that he is making a choice. He might have chosen to make men submissive, dependent, and gregarious, for example. Yet by his own statement in another context man's "capacity to choose," his freedom to select his course and to initiate action—these powers do not exist in the scientific picture of man. Here is, I believe, the deep-seated contradiction or paradox. Let me spell it out as clearly as I can.

Science, to be sure, rests on the assumption that behavior is caused—that a specified event is followed by a consequent event. Hence all is determined, nothing is free, choice is impossible. But we must recall that science itself and each specific scientific endeavor, each change of course in a scientific research, each interpretation of the meaning of a scientific finding, and each decision as to how the finding shall be applied rests upon a personal, subjective choice. Thus science in general exists in the same paradoxical situation as does Dr. Skinner. A personal, subjective choice made by man sets in motion the operations of science, which in time proclaims that there can be no such thing as a personal, subjective choice. I shall make some comments about this continuing paradox at a later point.

I stressed the fact that each of these choices, initiating or furthering the scientific venture, is a value choice. The scientist investigates this rather than that, because he feels the first investigation has more value for him. He chooses one method for his study rather than another because he values it more highly. He interprets his findings in one way rather than another because he believes the first way is closer to the truth, or more valid—in other words that it is closer to a criterion which he values. Now these value choices are never a part of the scientific venture itself. The value choices connected with a particular scientific enterprise always and necessarily lie outside of that enterprise.

I wish to make it clear that I am not saying that values cannot be included as a subject of science. It is not true that science deals only with certain classes of "facts" and that these classes do not include values. It is a bit more complex than that, as a simple illustration or two may make clear.

If I value knowledge of the "three R's" as a goal of education, the methods of science can give me increasingly accurate information as to how this goal may be achieved. If I value problem-solving ability as a goal of education, the scientific method can give me the same kind of help.

Now if I wish to determine whether problem-solving ability is "better" than knowledge of the three R's, then scientific method can also study those two values, but *only* —and this is very important—only in terms of some other value which I have subjectively chosen. I may value college success. Then I can determine whether problem-solving ability or knowledge of the three R's is more closely associated with that criterion. I may value personal integration or vocational success or responsible citizenship. I can determine whether problem-solving ability or knowledge of the three R's is "better" for achieving any one of these values. But the value or purpose which gives meaning to a particular scientific endeavor must always lie outside of that endeavor.

Though our concern here is largely with applied science what I have been saying seems equally true of so-called pure science. In pure science the usual prior subjective value choice is the discovery of truth. But this is a subjective choice, and science can never say whether it is the best choice, save in the light of some other value. Geneticists in Russia, for example, had to make a subjective choice of whether it was better to pursue truth, or to discover facts which upheld a governmental dogma. Which choice is "better"? We could make a scientific investigation of those alternatives, but only in the light of some other subjectively chosen value. If, for example, we value the survival of a culture then we could begin to investigate with the methods of science the question as to whether pursuit of truth or support of governmental dogma is most closely associated with cultural survival.

My point then is that any scientific endeavor, pure or applied, is carried on in the pursuit of a purpose or value which is subjectively chosen by persons. It is important that this choice be made explicit, since the particular value which is being sought can never be tested or evaluated, confirmed or denied, by the scientific endeavor to which it gives birth and meaning. The initial purpose or value always and necessarily lies outside the scope of the scientific effort which it sets in motion.

Perhaps, however, the thought is that a continuing scientific endeavor will evolve its own goals; the initial findings will alter the directions, and subsequent findings will alter them still further and that the science somehow develops its own purpose. This seems to be a view implicitly held by many scientists. It is surely a reasonable description, but it overlooks one element in this continuing development, which is that subjective, personal choice enters in at every point at which the direction changes. The findings of a science, the results of an experiment, do not and never can tell us what next scientific purpose to pursue. Even in the purest of science, the scientist must decide what the findings mean and must subjectively choose what next step will be most profitable in the pursuit of his purpose. And if we are speaking of the application of scientific knowledge, then it is distressingly clear that the increasing scientific knowledge of the structure of the atom carries with it no necessary choice as to the purpose to which this knowledge will be put. This is a subjective personal choice which must be made by many individuals.

Thus I return to the proposition with which I began this section of my remarks—and which I now repeat in different words. Science has its meaning as the objective pursuit of a purpose which has been subjectively chosen by a person or persons. This purpose or value can never be investigated by the particular scientific experiment or investigation to which it has given birth and meaning. Consequently, any discussion of the control of human beings by the behavioral sciences must first and most deeply concern itself with the subjectively chosen purposes which such an application of science is intended to implement.

An Alternative Set of Values

If the line of reasoning I have been presenting is valid, then it opens new doors to us. If we frankly face the fact that science takes off from a subjectively chosen set of values, then we are free to select the values we wish to pursue. We are not limited to such stultifying goals as producing a controlled state of happiness, productivity, and the like. I would like to suggest a radically different alternative.

Suppose we start with a set of ends, values, purposes, quite different from the type of goals we have been considering. Suppose we do this quite openly, setting them forth as a possible value choice to be accepted or rejected. Suppose we select a set of values which focuses on fluid elements of process, rather than static attributes. We might then value:

Man as a process of becoming; as a process of achieving worth and dignity through the development of his potentialities;

The individual human being as a self-actualizing process, moving on to more challenging and enriching experiences;

The process by which the individual creatively adapts to an ever new and changing world;

The process by which knowledge transcends itself, as for example the theory of relativity transcended Newtonian physics, itself to be transcended in some future day by a new perception.

If we select values such as these, we turn to our science and technology of behavior with a very different set of questions. We will want to know such things as these.

Can science aid us in the discovery of new modes of richly rewarding living? More meaningful and satisfying modes of interpersonal relationships?

Can science inform us as to how the human race can become a more intelligent participant in its own evolution—its physical, psychological and social evolution?

Can science inform us as to ways of releasing the creative capacity of individuals, which seem so necessary if we are to survive in this fantastically expanding atomic age? Dr. Oppenheimer has pointed out that knowledge, which used to double in millennia or centuries, now doubles in a generation or a decade. It appears that we will need to discover the utmost in release of creativity if we are to be able to adapt effectively.

In short, can science discover the methods by which man can most readily become a continually developing and self-transcending process, in his behavior, his thinking, his knowledge? Can science predict and release an essentially "unpredictable" freedom?

It is one of the virtues of science as a method that it is as able to advance and implement goals and purpose of this sort as it is to serve static values such as states of being well-informed, happy, obedient. Indeed we have some evidence of this.

A Small Example

I will perhaps be forgiven if I document some of the possibilities along this line by turning to psychotherapy, the field I know best.

Psychotherapy as Meerloo and others have pointed out can be one of the most subtle tools for the control of one person by another. The therapist can subtly mold individuals in imitation of himself. He can cause an individual to become a submissive and conforming being. When certain therapeutic principles are used in extreme fashion, we call it brainwashing, an instance of the distintegration of the personality and a reformulation of the person along lines desired by the controlling individual. So the principles of therapy can be used as a most effective means of external control of human personality and behavior. Can psychotherapy be anything else?

Here I find the developments going on in client-centered psychotherapy an exciting hint of what a behavioral science can do in achieving the kinds of values I have stated. Quite aside from being a somewhat new orientation in psychotherapy, this development has important implications regarding the relation of a behavioral science to the control of human behavior. Let me describe our experience as it relates to the issues of today's discussion.

In client-centered therapy, we are deeply engaged in the prediction and influencing of behavior. As therapists we institute certain attitudinal conditions, and the client has relatively little voice in the establishment of these conditions. Very briefly, as I indicated earlier, we have found that the therapist is most effective if he is: (a) genuine, integrated, transparently real in the relationship; (b) acceptant of the client as a separate, different, person, and acceptant of each fluctuating aspect of the client as it comes to expression; and (c) sensitively empathic in his understanding, seeing the world through the client's eyes. Our research permits us to predict that if these attitudinal conditions are instituted or established, certain behavioral consequences will ensue. Putting it this way sounds as if we are again back in the familiar groove of being able to predict behavior, and hence able to control it. But precisely here exists a sharp difference.

The conditions we have chosen to establish predict such behavioral consequences as these: that the client will become more self-directing, less rigid, more open to the evidence of his senses, better organized and integrated, more similar to the ideal which he has chosen for himself. In other words we have established by external control conditions which we predict will be followed by internal control by the individual, in pursuit of internally chosen goals. We have set the conditions which predict various classes of behaviors—self-directing behaviors, sensitivity to realities within and without, flexible adaptiveness—which are by their very nature *unpredictable* in their specifics. The conditions we have established predict behavior which is essentially "free." Our recent research indicates that our predictions are to a significant degree corroborated, and our commitment to the scientific method causes us to believe that more effective means of achieving these goals may be realized.

Research exists in other fields—industry, education, group dynamics—which seems to support our own findings. I believe it may be conservatively stated that scientific progress has been made in identifying those conditions in an interpersonal relationship which, if they exist in B, are followed in A by greater maturity in behavior, less dependence upon others, an increase in expressiveness as a person, an increase in variability, flexibility, and effectiveness of adaptation, an increase in self-responsibility and self-direction.

Thus we find ourselves in fundamental agreement with John Dewey's statement: "Science has made its way by releasing, not by suppressing, the elements of variation, of invention and innovation, of novel creation in individuals." [6] We have come to believe that progress in personal life and in group living is made in the same way, by releasing variation, freedom, creativity.

A Possible Concept of the Control of Human Behavior

It is quite clear that the point of view I am expressing is in sharp contrast to the usual conception of the relationship of the behavioral sciences to the control of human behavior, previously mentioned. In order to make this contrast even more blunt, I will state this possibility in a form parallel to the steps which I described before.

1. It is possible for us to choose to value man as a self-actualizing process of becoming; to value creativity, and the process by which knowledge becomes self-transcending.
2. We can proceed, by the methods of science, to discover the conditions which necessarily precede these processes, and through continuing experimentation, to discover better means of achieving these purposes.
3. It is possible for individuals or groups to set these conditions, with a minimum of power or control. According to present knowledge, the only authority necessary is the authority to establish certain qualities of interpersonal relationship.
4. Exposed to these conditions, present knowledge suggests that individuals become more self-responsible, make progress in self-actualization, become more flexible, more unique and varied, more creatively adaptive.
5. Thus such an initial choice would inaugurate the beginnings of a social system or subsystem in which values, knowledge, adaptive skills, and even the concept of science would be continually changing and self-transcending. The emphasis would be upon man as a process of becoming.

[6] J. Ratner (Ed.), Intelligence in the Modern World: John Dewey's Philosophy, Modern Library, New York, 1939.

I believe it is clear that such a view as I have been describing does not lead to any definable Utopia. It would be impossible to predict its final outcome. It involves a step by step development, based upon a continuing subjective choice of purposes, which are implemented by the behavioral sciences. It is in the direction of the "open society," as that term has been defined by Popper, where individuals carry responsibility for personal decisions. It is at the opposite pole from his concept of the closed society, of which *Walden Two* would be an example.

I trust it is also evident that the whole emphasis is upon process, not upon end states of being. I am suggesting that it is by choosing to value certain qualitative elements of the process of becoming, that we can find a pathway toward the open society.

The Choice

It is my hope that I have helped to clarify the range of choice which will lie before us and our children in regard to the behavioral sciences. We can choose to use our growing knowledge to enslave people in ways never dreamed of before, depersonalizing them, controlling them by means so carefully selected that they will perhaps never be aware of their loss of personhood. We can choose to utilize our scientific knowledge to make men necessarily happy, well-behaved, and productive, as Dr. Skinner suggests. We can, if we wish, choose to make men submissive, conforming, docile. Or at the other end of the spectrum of choice we can choose to use the behavioral sciences in ways which will free, not control; which will bring about constructive variability, not conformity; which will develop creativity, not contentment; which will facilitate each person in his self-directed process of becoming; which will aid individuals, groups, and even the concept of science to become self-transcending in freshly adaptive ways of meeting life and its problems.

If we choose to utilize our scientific knowledge to

free men, then it will demand that we live openly and frankly with the great paradox of the behavioral sciences. We will recognize that behavior, when examined scientifically, is surely best understood as determined by prior causation. This is the great fact of science. But responsible personal choice, which is the most essential element in being a person, which is the core experience in psychotherapy, which exists prior to any scientific endeavor, is an equally prominent fact in our lives. That these two important elements of our experience appear to be in contradiction has perhaps the same significance as the contradiction between the wave theory and the corpuscular theory of light, both of which can be shown to be true, even though incompatible. We cannot profitably deny the freedom which exists in our subjective life, any more than we can deny the determinism which is evident in the objective description of that life. We will have to live with that paradox.

Editor's Note

Nowhere is the optimism of Pierre Teilhard de Chardin more apparent than when he speaks of the future of mankind. The story begins with the formation of the universe. He thinks of every particle of matter as being caught up in a process of becoming—an irreversible evolution, concentrating more on consciousness than on body structure, leading ever in the direction of higher levels. Man at the vertex of the pyramid of life is the key to understanding all that has gone on in past geological ages and the key to predicting the direction of future progress. Man is at the top, the bottom, and uniquely at the center of the earth's story. Nor does Teilhard de Chardin think that the process is completed: ". . . between our modern earth and the ultimate earth, there stretches an immense period, characterised not by a slowing-down but a speeding-up and by the definitive florescence of the forces of evolution along the line of the human shoot."

Some of the questions on which he ventures an opinion in the selection below are: Why does the human species appear to be still in its infancy? How has the course of evolution changed since man appeared on earth? What evolutionary developments in man can be expected in future ages? How will they alter the sense of unity of the human race? What will be the repercussions on science? As the work of analysis tapers off, and as science concentrates more intently on synthesis, what more will be needed to achieve a comprehensive view of the universe?

39. The Ultimate Earth *

Pierre Teilhard de Chardin

The Approaches

Without going beyond the limits of scientific probability, we can say that life still has before it long periods of geological time in which to develop. Moreover, in its thinking form, it still shows every sign of an energy in full

* Abridged from P. Teilhard de Chardin, *The Phenomenon of Man*, Harper & Row, Publishers, Inc., New York, 1959, pp. 276–285. Reprinted with permission of Mlle Jeanne Mortier, Paris, and Harper & Row, New York.

expansion. On the one hand, compared with the zoological layers which preceded it whose average duration is at least in the order of eighty million years, mankind is so young that it could almost be called new-born. On the other hand, to judge from the rapid developments of thought in the short period of a few dozen centuries, this youth bears within it the indications and the promises of an entirely new biological cycle. Thus in all probability, between our modern earth and the ultimate earth, there stretches an immense period, characterised not by a slowing-down but a speeding-up and by the definitive florescence of the forces of evolution along the line of the human shoot.

Assuming success—which is the only acceptable assumption—under what form and along what lines can we imagine progress developing during this period?

In the first place, *in a collective and spiritual form.* We have noticed that, since man's advent, there has been a certain slowing down of the passive and somatic transformations of the organism in favour of the conscious and active metamorphoses of the individual absorbed in society. We find the artificial carrying on the work of the natural; and the transmission of an oral or written culture being superimposed on genetic forms of heredity (chromosomes). Without denying the possibility or even probability of a certain prolongation in our limbs, and still more in our nervous system, of the orthogenetic processes of the past, I am inclined to think that their influence, hardly appreciable since the emergence of *Homo sapiens,* is destined to dwindle still further. As though regulated by a sort of quantum law, the energies of life seem unable to spread in one region or take on a new form except at the expense of a lowering elsewhere. Since man's arrival, the evolutionary pressure seems to have dropped in all the non-human branches of the tree of life. And now that man has become an adult and has opened up for himself the field of mental and social transformations, bodies no longer change appreciably; they no longer need to in the human branch; or if they still change, it will only be under our industrious control. It may well be that in its individual capacities and penetrations our brain has reached its organic limits. But the movement does not stop there. From west to east, evolution is henceforth occupied elsewhere, in a richer and more complex domain, constructing, with all minds joined together, *mind*. Beyond all nations and races, the inevitable taking-as-a-whole of mankind has already begun.

With that said, we have now to ask: *along what lines* of advance, among others—judging from the present condition of the noosphere—are we destined to proceed from the planetary level of psychic totalisation and evolutionary upsurge we are now approaching?

I can distinguish three principal ones in which we see again the predictions to which we were already led by our analysis of the ideas of science and humanity. They are: the organisation of research, the concentration of research upon the subject of man, and the conjunction of science and religion. These are three natural terms of one and the same progression.

A. The Organisation of Research

We are given to boasting of our age being an age of science. And if we are thinking merely of the dawn compared to the darkness that went before, up to a point we are justified. Something enormous has been born in the universe with our discoveries and our methods of research. Something has been started which, I am convinced, will now never stop. Yet though we may exalt research and derive enormous benefit from it, with what pettiness of spirit, poverty of means and general haphazardness do we pursue truth in the world today! Have we ever given serious thought to the predicament we are in?

Like art—indeed we might almost say like thought itself—science was born with every sign of superfluity and fantasy. It was born of the exuberance of an internal activity that had outstripped the material needs of life; it was born of the curiosity of dreamers and idlers. Gradually it became important; its effectiveness gave it the freedom of the city. Living in a world which it can justly be said to have revolutionised, it has acquired a social status; sometimes it is even worshipped. Yet we still leave it to grow as best it can, hardly tending it, like those wild plants whose fruits are plucked by primitive peoples in their forests. Everything is subordinated to the increase in industrial production, and to armaments. The scientist and the laboratories which multiply our powers still receive nothing, or next to nothing. We behave as though we expected discoveries to fall ready-made from the sky, like rain or sunshine, while men concentrate on the serious business of killing each other and eating. Let us stop to think for a moment of the proportion of human energy devoted, here and now, to the pursuit of truth. Or, in still more concrete terms, let us glance at the percentage of a nation's revenue allotted in its budget for the investigation of clearly-defined problems whose solution would be of vital consequence for the world. If we did we should be staggered. Less is provided annually for all the pure research all over the world than for one capital ship. Surely our great-grandsons will not be wrong if they think of us as barbarians?

The truth is that, as children of a transition period, we are neither fully conscious of, nor in full control of, the new powers that have been unleashed. Clinging to outworn habit, we still see in science only a new means of providing more easily the same old things. We put Pegasus between the traces. And Pegasus languishes—unless he bolts with the band-waggon! But the moment will come—it is bound to—when man will be forced by the disparity of the equipage to admit that science is not an accessory occupation for him but an essential activity, a natural derivative of the overspill of energy constantly liberated by mechanisation.

We can envisage a world whose constantly increasing 'leisure' and heightened interest would find their vital issue in fathoming everything, trying everything, extending everything; a world in which giant telescopes and atom smashers would absorb more money and excite more spontaneous admiration than all the bombs and cannons put together; a world in which, not only for the restricted band of paid research-workers, but also for the man in the street, the day's ideal would be the wresting of another secret or another force from corpuscles, stars, or organised matter; a world in which, as happens already, one gives one's life to be and to know, rather than to possess. That, on an estimate of the forces engaged, is what is being relentlessly prepared around us.

In some of the lower organisms the retina is, as it were, spread over the whole surface of the body. In somewhat the same way human vision is still diffuse in its operation, mixed up with industrial activity and war. Biologically it needs to individualise itself independently, with its own distinct organs. It will not be long now before the noosphere finds its eyes.

B. The Discovery of the Human Object

When mankind has once realised that its first function is to penetrate, intellectually unify, and harness the energies which surround it, in order still further to understand and master them, there will no longer be any danger of running into an upper limit of its florescence. A commercial market can reach saturation point. One day, though substitutes may be found, we shall have exhausted our mines and oil-wells. But to all appearances nothing on earth will ever saturate our desire for knowledge or exhaust our power for invention. For each may be said: *crescit eundo.*

That does not mean that science should propagate itself indifferently in any and every direction at the same time like a ripple in an isotropic medium. The more one looks, the more one sees. And the more one sees, the better one knows where to look. If life has been able to advance, it is because, by ceaseless groping, it has successively found the points of least resistance at which reality yielded to its thrust. Similarly, if research is to progress tomorrow, it will be largely by localising the central zones, the sensitive zones which are 'alive,' whose conquest will afford us an easy mastery of all the rest.

From this point of view, if we are going towards a human era of science, it will be eminently an era of human science. Man, the knowing subject, will perceive at last that man, 'the object of knowledge,' is the key to the whole science of nature.

Carrel referred to man as 'the unknown.' But man, we should add, is the solution of everything that we can know.

Up to the present, whether from prejudice or fear, science has been reluctant to look man in the face but has constantly circled round the human object without daring to tackle it. Materially our bodies seem insignificant, accidental, transitory and fragile; why bother about them? Psychologically, our souls are incredibly subtle and complex: how can one fit them into a world of laws and formulas?

Yet the more persistently we try to avoid man in our theories, the more tightly drawn become the circles we describe around him, as though we were caught up in his vortex. As I said in my Preface, at the end of its analyses, physics is no longer sure whether what is left in its hands is pure energy or, on the contrary, thought. At the end of its constructions, biology, if it takes its discoveries to their logical conclusion, finds itself forced to acknowledge the assemblage of thinking beings as the present terminal form of evolution. We find man at the bottom, man at the top, and, still more, man at the centre—man who lives and struggles desperately in us and around us. We shall have to come to grips with him sooner or later.

Man is, if I have not gone astray in these pages, an object of study of unique value to science for two reasons. (i.) He represents, individually and socially, the most synthesised state under which the stuff of the universe is available to us. (ii.) Correlatively, he is at present the most mobile point of the stuff in the course of transformation.

By this two-fold right, to decipher man is essentially to try to find out how the world was made and how it ought to go on making itself. The science of man is the practical and theoretical science of hominisation. It means profound study of the past and of origins. But still more, it means constructive experiment pursued on a continually renewed object. The programme is immense and its only end or aim is that of the future.

We need and are irresistibly being led to create, by means of and beyond all physics, all biology and all psychology, *a science of human energetics.*

It is in the course of that creation, already obscurely begun, that science, by being led to concentrate on man, will find itself increasingly face to face with religion.

C. The Conjunction of Science and Religion

To outward appearance, the modern world was born of an anti-religious movement: man becoming self-sufficient and reason supplanting belief. Our generation and the two that preceded it have heard little but talk of the conflict between science and faith; indeed it seemed at one moment a foregone conclusion that the former was destined to take the place of the latter.

But, inasmuch as the tension is prolonged, the conflict visibly seems to need to be resolved in terms of an entirely different form of equilibrium—not in elimination, nor duality, but in synthesis. After close on two centuries of passionate struggles, neither science nor faith has succeeded in discrediting its adversary. On the contrary, it becomes obvious that neither can develop normally without the other. And the reason is simple: the same life animates both. Neither in its impetus nor its achievements can science go to its limits without becoming tinged with mysticism and charged with faith.

Firstly *in its impetus.* We touched on this point

when dealing with the problem of action. Man will only continue to work and to research so long as he is prompted by a passionate interest. Now this interest is entirely dependent on the conviction, strictly undemonstrable to science, that the universe has a direction and that it could —indeed, if we are faithful, it *should*—result in some sort of irreversible perfection. Hence comes belief in progress.

Secondly *in its construction.* Scientifically we can envisage an almost indefinite improvement in the human organism and human society. But as soon as we try to put our dreams into practice, we realise that the problem remains indeterminate or even insoluble unless, with some partially super-rational intuition, we admit the convergent properties of the world we belong to. Hence belief in unity.

Furthermore, if we decide, under the pressure of facts, in favour of an optimism of unification, we run into the technical necessity of discovering—in addition to the impetus required to push us forward and in addition to the particular objective which should determine our route—the special binder or cement which will associate our lives together, vitally, without diminishing or distorting them. Hence, belief in a supremely attractive centre which has personality.

In short, as soon as science outgrows the analytic investigations which constitute its lower and preliminary stages, and passes on to synthesis—synthesis which naturally culminates in the realisation of some superior state of humanity—it is at once led to foresee and place its stakes on the *future* and on the *all.* And with that it out-distances itself and emerges in terms of *option* and *adoration.*

Thus Renan and the nineteenth century were not wrong to speak of a Religion of Science. Their mistake was not to see that their cult of humanity implied the re-integration, in a renewed form, of those very spiritual forces they claimed to be getting rid of.

When, in the universe in movement to which we have just awakened, we look at the temporal and spatial series diverging and amplifying themselves around and behind us like the laminae of a cone, we are perhaps engaging in pure science. But when we turn towards the summit, towards the *totality* and the *future*, we cannot help engaging in religion.

Religion and science are the two conjugated faces or phases of one and the same act of complete knowledge—the only one which can embrace the past and future of evolution so as to contemplate, measure and fulfil them.

In the mutual reinforcement of these two still opposed powers, in the conjunction of reason and mysticism, the human spirit is destined, by the very nature of its development, to find the uttermost degree of its penetration with the maximum of its vital force. Always pushing forward in the three directions we have just indicated, and taking advantage of the immense duration it has still to live, mankind has enormous possibilities before it.

Suggested Readings

Chapter 1

Cantril, H. Toward a humanistic psychology. *Etc.* 1955, **12,** 278–298.

Chein, I. The image of man. *J. soc. Issues,* 1962, **13** (4), 1–35.

Harlow, H. F. Mice, monkeys, men, and motives. *Psychol. Rev.,* 1953, **60,** 23–32.

Chapter 2

Boring, E. G. When is human behavior predetermined? *Sci. Monthly,* 1957, **84,** 189–196.

May, R. Will, decision and responsibility: Summary remarks. *Rev. existent. Psychol. Psychiat.,* 1961, **1,** 249–259.

Muller, H. J. *Issues of freedom,* (*World perspectives series.* Vol. 23.) New York: Harper & Row, 1960. Part I.

Zavalloni, R. *Self-determination: the psychology of personal freedom.* Chicago: Forum Books, 1962.

Chapter 3

Allport, G. W. The psychologist's frame of reference. *Psychol. Bull.,* 1940, **37,** 1–28.

Katz, D. *Animals and men: Studies in comparative psychology.* London: Longmans, 1937.

Kellogg, W. N. & Kellogg, L. A. *The ape and the child.* New York: McGraw-Hill, 1933.

Matson, F. W. *The broken image: Man, science, and society.* New York: Braziller, 1964. Pp. 53–81.

Moore, T. V. Human and animal intelligence. In H. S. Jennings *et al., Scientific aspects of the race problem.* London: Longmans, 1941. Pp. 93–158.

Chapter 4

Burt, C. The structure of the mind: A reply. *Brit. J. statist. Psychol.*, 1961,**14,** 145–170.

Buytendijk, F. The body in existential psychology. *Rev. existent. Psychol. Psychiat.*, 1961, **1,** 149–172.

Feigl, H. The "mental" and the "physical." In H. Feigl *et al.* (Eds.), *Minnesota studies in the philosophy of science.* Vol. 2. *Concepts, theories, and the mind-body problem.* Minneapolis: University of Minnesota Press, 1958. Pp. 370–497.

Luijpen, W. A. *Duquesne studies, philosophical series.* Vol. 12. *Existential phenomenology.* Pittsburgh: Duquesne University Press, 1960, Pp.181–192.

Olds, J. Pleasure centers in the brain. *Scient. American.* October, 1956, **195,** 105–116.

Penfield, W. The physiological basis of the mind. In S. M. Farber & R. H. L. Wilson (Eds.), *Control of the mind: Man and civilization.* New York: McGraw-Hill, 1961.

Sinnott, E. W. Matter, mind, and man: The contribution of biology toward a solution of mind-body relationships. *Main Curr. mod. Thought,* 1957, **13,** 75–80.

Von Holst, E. & U. von Saint Paul. Electrically controlled behavior. *Scient. American.* March, 1962, **206,** 50–59.

Chapter 5

Murray, H. A., *et al.* Cultural evolution reviewed by psychologists. *Daedalus,* 1961, **90,** 570–586.

Oppenheimer, R. *Some reflections on science and culture.* Chapel Hill, N. C.: University of North Carolina Press, 1960.

Rogers, C. R. Toward a science of the person. *J. humanist. Psychol.*, 1963, **3** (2), 72–92.

Toulin, S. *Foresight and understanding: An inquiry into*

the aims of science. London: Hutchison, 1961. Pp. 99–115.

Waters, R. H. Behavior: Datum or abstraction? *Amer. Psychologist,* 1958, **13,** 278–282.

Chapter 6

Burt, C. Logical positivism and the concept of consciousness. *Brit. J. statist. Psychol.*, 1960, **13,** 55–70.

Caldin, E. F. *The power and limits of science*. London: Chapman & Hall, 1949.

Heisenberg, W. & E. Schrodinger, *et al. On modern physics*. New York: Collier, 1961. Pp. 1–66.

Matson, F. W. *The broken image*. New York: Braziller, 1964. Pp. 31–45.

Tamm, T. W. (Ed.) *Behaviorism and phenomenology: Contrasting bases for modern psychology*. Chicago: University of Chicago Press, 1964.

Weaver, W. Scientific explanation. *Science,* 1964, **143** (3612), 1297–1300.

Chapter 7

Ginsberg, A. Operational definitions and theories. *J. gen. Psychol.*, 1955, **52,** 223–245.

Northrop, F. S. C. *The logic of the sciences and the humanities*. New York: Macmillan, 1947. Pp. 124–131.

Scheerer, M. On the relationship between experimental and non-experimental methods in psychology. *Psychol. Rec.*, 1958, **8,** 109–116.

Valois, A. J. *A study of operationism and its implications for educational psychology.* Washington, D. C.: Catholic University Press, 1960.

Chapter 8

Holt, R. R. Imagery: The return of the ostracized. *Amer. Psychologist,* 1964, **19,** 254–264.

Johnson, E. P. On readmitting the mind. *Amer. Psychologist,* 1956, **11,** 712–714.

Koch, S. Psychological science versus the science-humanism antinomy: Intimations of a significant science of man. *Amer. Psychologist,* 1961, **16,** 629–639.

Kuenzli, A. E. (Ed.) *The phenomenological problem.* New York: Harper & Row, 1959. Chaps. 1, 2, 5, 12.

Morris, C. *Varieties of human values.* Chicago: University of Chicago Press, 1956.

Chapter 9

Dukes, W. F. Psychological studies in values. *Psychol. Bull.,* 1955, **52,** 24–50.

Maslow, A. H. Fusion of facts and values. *Amer. J. Psychoanal.,* 1963, **23,** 117–131.

Watson, G. Moral issues in psychotherapy. *Amer. Psychologist,* 1958, **13,** 574–576.

Chapter 10

Allport, G. W. *Pattern and growth in personality.* New York: Holt, 1961. Pp. 275–307.

Frankl, V. E. Existential dynamics and neurotic escapism. *Universitas,* 1962, **5,** 273–286.

Kimball, W. L. Mental health and selective detachment from culture. *J. humanist. Psychol.,* 1962, **2**(1), 80–88.

Szasz, T. S. The myth of mental illness. *Amer. Psychologist,* 1960, **15,** 113–118.

Chapter 11

Allport, G. W. Models for guidance. *Harv. educ. Rev.,* 1962, **32,** 373–381.

Curran, C. A. Counseling, psychotherapy, and the unified person. *J. Relig. Hlth,* 1963, **2,** 95–111.

Frankl, V. E. Dynamics, existence and values. *J. existent. Psychiat.,* 1961, **2,** 5–16.

Mowrer, O. H. Science, sex, and values. *Personnel Guid. J.* 1964, **42,** 746–753.

Murphy, G. The cultural content of counseling. *Personnel Guid. J.*, 1955, **34,** 4–9.

Rychlak, J. F. Control and prediction and the clinician. *Amer. Psychologist,* 1964, **19,** 186–190.

Schneiders, A. A. Religion and psychological health—A new approach. *J. existent. Psychiat.*, 1961, **5,** 93–104.

Williamson, E. G. Value commitment and counseling. *Teachers Coll. Rec.*, 1961, **62,** 602–608.

Chapter 12

Gardner, J. W. *Self-renewal: The individual and the innovative society.* New York: Harper & Row, 1963.

Huxley, A. *Brave new world.* New York: Harper & Row, 1932, 1946.

Luijpen, W. A. *Duquesne studies, philosophical series.* Vol. 12. Pittsburgh: Duquesne University Press, 1960. Pp. 260–355.

Maslow, A. H. Existential psychology—What's in it for us? In Rollo May (Ed.), *Existential psychology.* New York: Random House, 1961. Pp. 52–60.

Teilhard de Chardin, P. *The future of man.* New York, Harper & Row, 1964.

INDEX